Homosexualities
and French Literature

Homosexualities
and French Literature :

Cultural Contexts / Critical Texts

Edited with an Introduction by
GEORGE STAMBOLIAN
and
ELAINE MARKS

Preface by
RICHARD HOWARD

CORNELL UNIVERSITY PRESS
Ithaca and London

1979

PQ
145.1
.H66
H6
1979

First published 1979 by Cornell University Press.
Published in the United Kingdom by Cornell University Press Ltd.,
2-4 Brook Street, London W1Y 1AA.

International Standard Book Number 0-8014-1186-6
Library of Congress Catalog Card Number 78-25659
Printed in the United States of America
*Librarians: Library of Congress cataloging information appears on the last page
of the book.*

Acknowledgments

We are grateful to Michael Hampton, Richard Howard, and Yvonne Ozzello for their advice and support, and to our contributors and translators for their patience and encouragement.

All the texts, with the exception of the essay by Serge Doubrovsky, were written expressly for this collection. All the interviews have been edited and abridged. A shorter version of the interview with Eric Bentley appeared in *Christopher Street* (December 1977). Serge Doubrovsky's essay has been published under the title "The Nine of Hearts: Fragment of a Psychoreading of *La Nausée*," in a translation by Carol Bové, in *Boundary 2* (Winter 1977) and in *Psychoanalysis, Creativity, and Literature: A Franco-American Inquiry,* ed. Alan Roland (Columbia University Press, 1978).

GEORGE STAMBOLIAN

ELAINE MARKS

Neuilly, France
Wellesley, Massachusetts
Madison, Wisconsin

5

Contents

7

Critical Texts

Preface

Considerations of a Transfuge

Richard Howard

"We cannot assist another's Night," Emily Dickinson once wrote to her sister-in-law (next door), and by the capitalized noun she meant what contemporary discourse, in its terse and sparkling way, calls the hypostatization of a methodological category: she meant what Michel Foucault, who uses the same capitalized noun (to his translator's despair), also means by *déraison,* that cluster of opacities which for each of us surrounds the body's relations with itself and with others. We are reminded that children, unprepared for the look of intercourse, generally believe the participants to be fighting, not lovers but contestants. Very well, we cannot assist, but we can see that such a Night as this *is* another's without obscuring its stars and meteors by our own darkness. That is why I would call my remarks *considerations,* a word which first meant seeing the stars together as significant constellations, in relation to one another. The last twenty-five years have afforded us some remarkable scrutinies, sweeps of the telescope across the black heavens of sexuality (the dark fields of Venus, as the venerealists, just so, have afforded us the phrase). And of course one's own biography, coinciding with this quarter of a century, cannot be left out of the reckoning. Perhaps the best way to avoid such an omission is by the commis-

sion of a mild indiscretion. Here are four encounters with the
great French homosexual literary men of my time, of that time,
which generate if they do not too much disconcert the context of
my reflections; our remembered experience, like filings in a
magnetic field, impedes the figure from emerging by the very
means it must employ to be seen, and it is a distinctly "modern"
notion that the very medium which enables the existence of
form is also the obstacle to form. The contention is apparent, of
course, in these appearances—of Gide, Cocteau, Genet,
Jouhandeau—but I hope something like a contour makes it way
past my glimpses.

In 1950, as editors of the *Columbia Review,* Robert Gottlieb and
I wrote a letter to André Gide: would he like to speak, in his
trenchant magisterial way, to our situation from his; would the
man who had written "I believe that what is called 'experience' is
often but an unavowed fatigue, resignation, blighted hope" care
to address himself to a group of attentive students who had in
common, chiefly and precisely, their inexperience? And, of
course, their fervor for his achievement, which so paradoxically
seemed to be the encoding of his . . . experience? Gide answered,
not trenchantly or magisterially, but with a seemly generosity,
just one month before he died; his letter (Lord, what did I expect!) sounds the voice of the prepared (the overprepared?)
Counselor of Youth, useful on almost any occasion, rather what
we hear—the resonance of the frowning public man—in the
replies of the old Goethe to like solicitations, for in the history of
literary effrontery there are always "like solicitations":

22 January 1951

That I am touched by the homage of certain young people of
your university, expressed in your most courteous letter, goes
without saying. But I should like to be sure there is no misunderstanding, and that their attention is indeed such as my writings
deserve. It is essential not to make a mistake about this. I never
laid claim to providing the world with a new doctrine. And indeed
I have often deserved the reproach of not stating quite clearly
what I wanted and of not defining in detail rules of conduct which
might have given hope of saying what we feel to be in danger

today: a culture slowly and painfully acquired throughout centuries, which belongs to a common heritage and seems to have ceased to be of value today. New values have replaced those which formerly allowed us to commune together, which provided us with a reason for living and for sacrificing ourselves for them. I believe that if we let ourselves be stripped of that past, we shall experience a forever irreparable loss, all the more tragic since the new generations will not even be aware of their impoverishment.

But to tell the truth, surrounded by blasted hopes, I am getting to the point of no longer really knowing to what to apply my ardor and my allegiance. On the other hand, I know ever more clearly what I do not want, what I cannot accept, and against what my whole being revolts: falsehood. Whether it comes from the right or from the left, whether it be political or religious, falsehood tends to suppress human personality by depriving it of the right to free enquiry. It is the stifling of the individual with the hope of an illusory advantage to the herd. Each of us is asked to abdicate his critical spirit in order to make it easier to strangle himself. This is what we must not accept. How readily I subscribe to Jean-Jacques Rousseau's admirable statement: "He who prefers truth to fame may hope to prefer it to life."

I have no doubt of being in complete agreement, on this point, with you, young representatives of a country which has done more than any other to teach and to protect that "self-reliance" of which your Emerson speaks so eloquently and without which we are at the mercy of those who would exploit us. Refusal to tolerate falsehood, either in others or in oneself, is the watchword around which I think we can and must rally.

With every sympathy and, despite everything, hopefully, your most attentive

André Gide

(Translated by Justin O'Brien)

I do not think the letter needs—or indeed can sustain—much analysis; it was the making of our "Gide issue," as I am sure the old man knew it would be, for he wrote it out by hand, and characteristically *ondoyant* in its evasion of real platitudes, real plunges into the depths. As the years have gone by, plunges seem less and less appropriate, and the steadfast refusal to lie (Gide leaves out the "social" as a likely source of untruth, perhaps because he had so much exposed "society" in his own fictions) glows quite steadily enough to constitute a first beacon, an initial light cast on a much-vexed darkness—not the darkness I wanted, not the darkness I needed to plunge into, of course, but an outer darkness, the kind that usually gains so ruinously upon the inner one. Enough that the letter—and for this I give it here—constituted a first contact with that world (and it seemed a world, was that not the point?) of French literature in its mastery of what the London *Times* in its obituary of Gide termed "heterodoxy" (homosexuality?). Or if not mastery, then acknowledged mystery—at least, acknowledgment.

Take three years, as the child in the game tells you to take three giant steps. Mine were Lilliputian enough, but they had brought me to Paris, the capital—was it not?—of my propensity, as the masters of its literature had persuaded me, perhaps of malice prepense. It was Gide, with his splendidly personal sense of Vicissitude, of diverging, opposing, and ultimately complementary . . . ultimates ("extremes meet . . . *me*"), who so finely characterized that literature (which he could not escape any better than could Genet or Sade, the world's freest minds in the world's most imprisoned bodies) as one immense and endless conversation. And if to eavesdroppers like myself, in 1953, it sounded more like an argument than a *causerie*, that was merely because I had not been listening long enough. For the dialogue, like the dance, continues, the unappeasable do-it-yourself dialectic proceeds, asking questions not to be answered for five hundred years, answering others the season before they are asked—a system of provocation and response without a temporal variable:

> Hydre absolue, ivre de ta chair bleue,
> Qui te remords l'étincelante queue
> Dans un tumulte au silence pareil.

> Absolute hydra, drunk on your blue flesh,
> Who swallows your own sparkling tail
> In an uproar equal to silence.

> [Paul Valéry, "Le cimetière marin"]

At any given point of entry, the reader of this literature as the alien resident of this city has the encircling, often constricting awareness—has the *conviction*—that he is inside a completed structure, has the suspicion, crossing even the broadest steppes the city affords—the Place de la Concorde under a stormy sky, the vitrines of the Librairie de la Hune after the *rentrée*—that all of Paris is really *inside,* somehow preposterously enclosed and housed in one enormous chamber, and a *salon* at that! just as all of its literature is really collected in one giant Edition de la Pléiade. . . .

The pride of it all, and the horror, as I left it in Paris in the early fifties, was that it keeps going on, apparently able to assimilate whatever is proposed, even whatever is opposed (as Gide opposed to it the Bible, Shakespeare, Dostoevsky, even Dashiell Hammett), a myth of our human happening. Endless this sense of stylization; the only unpunished French vice and certainly the only unpublicized one, such accommodation may operate either upward or downward, as F. W. Dupee, my old adviser on the *Columbia Review,* had once pointed out—we may get something like *Steinbeck-ou-les-nobles-sauvages,* or we may get *Hamlet-ou-le-distrait.* The point is we do not get Steinbeck or Hamlet, we get a French stylization; French literature, like Sainte-Beuve, is "inclined to accumulate incompatibles"—whereat such creatures are found to lie down together, like Villon and Genet, like Bossuet and Péguy. Recuperative, burrowing, exorbitantly metropolitan, in its voice—which I was hearing in Paris now, was I not, to the extinction of any accents of my own—abided the resonance of an entire human survival, the interminable, unnamable gossip in which, that season, Mr. Beckett had the last word, the last adjective. . . .

That season: perhaps even so brief a spell was too wide a net. My sense, my mythology of French literature twenty-five years ago (and it is what has *not* changed since) is that of the remark made by a friend, a woman of immense intellect and charm who held, who gave, what was perhaps one of the last salons in Paris (in the Proustian sense of *salon,* if not that of Mme du Deffand); the chronology was fixed forever when this astonishing woman said to me, speaking of Michel Foucault upon his entry into the

Collège de France, "But you see, Richard, he's the only real genius of the moment!" To be interested, we are reminded by no less an authority than Martin Heidegger, means to be among and in the midst of things, to be at the center of a thing and to stay with it, though the "interest" of French literature as I am reporting it today accepts as valid only what is *interesting*—the sort of thing that can readily be regarded as indifferent *the next moment* and be replaced by another thing. The conflict between these attitudes, the contradiction between these acceptations of a word—the psychomachia, really, between the ecstatic moment-out-of-time and the movement *of* time (resolved only if we remember that the moment *is* the movement, the smallest unit of movement being a *momentum*)—this confrontation supplied the torque, the twist of impulse which, during my first apprehension of the world of letters in Paris, reached a pitch of excruciation so supersonic that I sought an answer in the most unlikely, some will feel, of quarters. I had met Jean Cocteau in those days—surely a genius of some moment or other, and at the end of what I might, or what I must, call in the full sense of the word an *audience*, the poet gave me some advice which it turns out he gave to a great many others as well—perhaps because it was such sage counsel in his own case. Dryly, wryly, as he spread his famous hands between us, Cocteau said: "What other people reproach you for, cultivate—it is yourself." As so many Prix Goncourt winners have so drastically demonstrated, there is only one thing worse than to be reproachable as a writer—it is to be irreproachable. In literature, if not in the salon, the posture Cocteau advocated is precisely the posture to which I aspire, for it suggests the means whereby all the problems—for instance, the problem of homosexuality—once raised, or at least tilted upward, become rather guides and familiars in the enterprise.

It was Freud who first taught us that a perversion is the opposite of a neurosis, that homosexuality, for instance, is not a problem but the solution to a problem. We are learning more—we are learning, quite as sensationally, that madness itself (what we call, nowadays, schizophrenia) is a *language*, an attempt to communicate rather than a refusal to do so. We have begun learning the language of the mad, to enter into a dialogue with them. And it was in Paris, following upon Cocteau's deposit of a grain of sand in the timid oyster of my mind, that I began secreting the (cultured) pearl of the one generalization I should care to hazard as to how we *should* respond to literature: when we are troubled—bored, provoked, offended—by characteristic features of a writer's work (and might one not say, by characteristic behavior of a person's sexuality?), it is precisely those features (and that behavior) which, if we yield to them, if we treat them as significance rather than as defect, will turn out to be that writer's (and that person's) *solution* to what we mistakenly regarded as *problems* of composition and utterance (and character and consciousness).

The "problems" of character bring me, of course, to those encounters with Jean Genet—not nearly so evangelical on the master's part, not nearly so conspicuous in the transmission of that Word which had been sought, if not taken, from Gide and from Cocteau. Though Genet had dismissed Gide ("I do not like judges who bend amorously over their victims") and patronized Cocteau ("We deny Jean Cocteau the stupid title of enchanter: we declare him *enchanted*"), he was clearly elsewhere: on the other side of that invisible barrier Sartre had so astonishingly described, the barrier of transcendence where all values were reversed, where abjection became sanctity, and self-hatred a kind of divinity. Sartre's book came out in the spring of 1952, and I had read it, copied out hundreds of passages, by the time I had the first meeting with its subject, whose own books had so transformed my notions (Shaker Heights! Columbia University! The Sorbonne!) of what sexuality could do with your life, not to mention other people's. There, in the Galerie Paul Morihien, in the Palais Royal, stood the great fabulist—he had come to pick up his mail, and though by 1952 Jean Genet was no longer a criminal, no longer proscribed, he was not yet sterilized by world celebrity (it is always the theater which disinfects, in our culture), and it was with some trepidation I advanced to be introduced by my friend who ran the gallery. It was not to receive the word that one went up to Genet—he *was,* as his friend Cocteau liked to say, the word—but to have seen the master plain: as if there were some sort of lineage conferred by no more than presence, and by no less. Between us then, beyond the introduction, passed but one exchange, symbolic enough, and perhaps with a little morality of its own. After trying to tell the author how much I loved his books, and how deeply they had affected me, I found I could do no more than thank him for my pleasure. "Very well. You are homosexual? Very well. It's all pornography." This was not what I wanted to hear, nor do I believe it to this day, but it had its tonic, its abstergent note to sound, as did the close: I asked Genet what he liked to read. "Myself, I never read." Sartre had already defused that rocket, but the insistence on the attitude was its own lesson, was it not?—particularly to an excessively bookish Sorbonnard of twenty-three. It took eighteen years, it took till 1970, when I translated Genet's May Day Speech given at Yale and his introduction to the prison letters of George Jackson, for the lesson to take hold. In the next room sat the pink-and-silver Genet, surrounded by Black Panthers, while I typed version after version, asking questions when the vile political rhetoric seemed to defeat even Genet's gifts of narrative persistence. Unfailingly courteous, unfailingly curious about linguistic properties as I might wield them in his behalf, the writer "who never read" was indeed before me, though he had of course ceased to be a writer: the political activist was among us, and he was indeed someone who never read. The lying panache had become a particular white feather, worn with the pride of a moralist, and as Cocteau had prophesied of him in 1949: "Genet is a moralist in the sense that he possesses a moral philosophy and never strays from it by an inch. The result, sometimes, is a kind of sermon."

The fourth encounter, with Marcel Jouhandeau, is clouded for me by the sense that I had overprepared myself. When I first met him, Jouhandeau's seventy-sixth book had just appeared. So much ink had created a city, Chaminadour (actually Guéret), and a man, Monsieur Godeau (Jouhandeau himself, lacerated and loved by his wife Elise), a whole literature plummeting deep into the self and at the same time spreading into a wide, reflecting pond. All with a wickedness that rouses headlines in Catholic literary weeklies: *Is Marcel Jouhandeau the Devil?* Knowing, then, that the same writer, the very man I was about to visit, was a

moralist of the most glittering, aphoristic species, a village
chronicler à la Balzac, a religious mystic, a Satanist, a zoologist, a
hagiographer, a naturalist of the self, not to mention a
homosexual pornographer, I think I must have expected to find
M. Jouhandeau staggering beneath the burden of his own diversity. At seventy-odd (this was 1958), however, he was as steely
and springy as . . . as Madame Jouhandeau, for instance. Like
Gide, of whom he regards himself as the spiritual heir, Jouhandeau has made his greatest contribution, perhaps, to morality in
aerating and enlarging our sense of the Family by feigning to
destroy it. His style makes it possible to have read at least thirty-
five of his books and not know, as Sartre says of him in that book
on Genet, what he has in store. Clearer to me than my house call
is the contour of an afternoon in the Arènes de Lutèce, where
Jouhandeau and Jean Paulhan went on Sundays to play *boules*
with Jérôme Lindon and Claude Simon. Jouhandeau stood a
little apart from the others—it was a cold Sunday in January,
and his coat collar was turned up to his harelip. He questioned
me, I remember, about what I was doing there, as well he might.
I told him I felt, for the first time, *inside the egg*, using the French
expression which suggested one had approached, at last, the
good things of life. "And now, the difficulty will be to get out."
That was the author constrained, as Sartre had said, to accept a
religious asceticism of damnation, and he was giving me, I think,
the clue that might lead me out of this complacent labyrinth of
commérages; but of that in a moment; here I have yet to record
my sense of acquittal, my release which came, over the years, as a
translator of these men (however minimally in Genet's case—it
was all I had the chance to do, and I did it); to translate *L'immoraliste,* and a whole volume of selected writings by Cocteau,
and to be preparing a similar volume of such writings by
Jouhandeau, is the one gesture of gratitude (and revenge?)
which I can make to these exemplary disasters of my youth,
taking that word (disaster, not youth) in its astrological sense of a
baleful, necessary star. That they have helped or hurt us is not
the fault of the great writers, and it is not why they are great
writers. When they are homosexual writers—not writers who are
homosexuals, but *homosexual writers*—the help and the hurt may

be great in proportion to the greatness of the figures, but the fault is still not theirs, nor the responsibility. That is, fortunately, our own.

There had been, though I had not the wit to hear it, a particular note sounded in these encounters—an admonitory note, the sigh from the prison-house, from the captive, each, of his own singularity. For the French genius, or call it the French demon of stylization, which moves so tentacularly toward the accommodation of outliers and eccentrics into a vast social institutionalization, a homogeneity made up of perpetual *frottements scolaires*, exacts a terrible price from the gifted nature which would resist its blandishments or even its sledgehammer blows. If you are not to sink into the warp-and-woof, the very weaving of the endless *causerie*, you must resolve upon a freakishness so extreme that its . . . extremities will be the silence or the spasm. You must be Genet or else you are in danger of being caught up in that very rhythm of adaptations you had set out to correct, to call into question. Now in the case of Gide and even more coquettishly in that of Cocteau, there is a certain dither of complicity about being swallowed up by the dragon, fostered always by the illusion that one can fight just as well against it from inside the stomach walls (Cocteau to the Académie Française), but I think I detect, now, in Jouhandeau's bitter observation about the difficulty of getting *out of* the egg, the consciousness of how much has been exacted, in France, from her heterodox geniuses in literature as the price of remaining so, in however tempered a fashion.

The change, then, in my lifetime, or in the twenty-five conscious years of it which have been engaged in a troubled dedication to precisely this omnivorous literature, is the change I can see—I began to see it around 1968, with the help of my friend Roland Barthes and his writing—in the status of the homosexual writer. Perhaps, too, of the homosexual *tout court*, for the change is the charge that there is no *tout court*, that the homosexual—the homosexual writer—is not, or need not be, a sacred monster, perpetrating those vast destructions upon others and chiefly upon himself which enable him to survive "not like the others," as the child Gide put it to his nurse in *Si le grain ne meurt*. The astonishing appearance in France in just these years of a discur-

sive literature, a literature of criticism (as it is often, and critically, labeled), a clustered body of texts (whether by Barthes,
Foucault, Deleuze, or Dumézil) has surely made us aware of a
transformation from the old pattern. Of course we still—the
French still—refer literature to an author, with all the sacra-
ments and superstitions which hang about that venerable spook.
Our culture tyrannically centers on the artist as scapegoat:
Tchaikovsky's music is the product—and the counterbalance—
of his "vice," though perhaps even in this realm . . . I believe one
no longer hears it said of Proust that his homosexuality is the
ransom of his heroic quest. But as a consequence of the splendid
inquiries of the last quarter of a century, I believe we have, in
France, the sense that the author is no longer regnant (hence too
a certain murmur that the imagination is dead in France). When
we believe in a writer, he is always conceived as the past of his
book, Barthes tells us—the book and the author take their places
on the same line, cast as a BEFORE and an AFTER. The writer
is supposed to feed his book, he pre-exists it, thinks, suffers, and
lives for it—he maintains with his work the same relation of
antecedence which a father maintains with his child.

Whereas the homosexual writer, specifically, in France today,
is born simultaneously with his text: it is his text which brings
him into being. He does not exist as a glorious or scandalous
progenitor, he is in no way supplied with a being which precedes
or transcends his writing, his écriture. If there is a certain invisibility about the homosexual writer in France today, it is because there is a way to escape being no more than a monstre sacré
(and a monstre most likely to be tamed into the famished texture
of literary history, not to mention social history, even Society).
When the homosexual is no longer the subject of which his book
is the predicate, then he eludes the scandal and parade of before
and after: there is the time of the writing which is also the time
of our reading, and the problem (is it not what my four fathers
were trying to tell their problem child?) becomes the solution. Of
course solutions raise other problems, but that is no more than
the dialectics of life itself; one betrays one's father, in our Oedipal tradition of parricide and piety, and I turn with a certain
relief—or a relieved certainty—from my great ancestral voices,
or do I turn perhaps, for the first time, to their voices them-

selves, and no longer to the lying echoes of what a scandalized culture provoked them to become? Perhaps I am not a traitor after all, not a transfuge—perhaps I am merely no more than a translator.

Introduction

George Stambolian
Elaine Marks

Villon, Montaigne, Brantôme, Rousseau, Voltaire, Diderot, Sade, Balzac, Baudelaire, Gautier, Rimbaud, Verlaine, Mallarmé, Zola, Maupassant, Louÿs, Vivien, Proust, Gide, Colette, Cocteau, Jouhandeau, Green, Sartre, Genet, Beauvoir, Beckett, Yourcenar, Peyrefitte, Leduc, Barthes, Rochefort, Mallet-Joris, Wittig, Duvert, Irigaray.
All the writers on this incomplete list have written in French about homosexuality. But there similarities end. Many of them were (or are) homosexual, others heterosexual or bisexual, and the precise sexual facts concerning a few are unknown. Most were men writing primarily about men, others were women writing about women; but some men wrote almost exclusively about women, and at least one woman wrote only about men. Some wrote extensively on homosexuality, others treated it sparingly. In the works of some the presence of homosexuality is easily identified, while in the works of others it is far more cryptic. They wrote in different styles and genres, had different conceptions of the purpose of art and the functions of language. They lived in different times and were affected by different private and public circumstances. Some were married, others not, and all had different attitudes toward love, sex, friendship, and homosexuality itself. It is unlikely that any of them would accept

23

the label "homosexual writer" or the category "homosexual literature."

These obvious if often neglected facts demonstrate the reality of "homosexualities." They also illustrate the difficulties confronting critical analysis, difficulties that are intensified by the equally significant fact that the works of many writers who never wrote about homosexuality nevertheless contain fantasies, patterns of imagery, or structures of language that some critics have begun tentatively to identify as "homosexual."

When faced with such pluralism and diversity, critics have generally restricted themselves to discussing the effects of homosexuality within the limits of the work or life of avowedly homosexual writers. This approach is not only justified, it is indispensable. But there is also a need to determine whether or not there are configurations that both inform and transcend individual works and writers: a homosexual typology related to the sources, historical and textual, of homosexual personae and concerned with the growth and decline of different stereotypes; a homosexual topography of enclosed spaces—rooms, prisons, convents, schools; a homosexual intertextuality, particularly important in an area where the difficulty of writing and the relative paucity of texts results in a more pronounced absorption and transformation of literary models; a homosexual literary tradition establishing the major texts from antiquity to the present and devoting particular attention to the interaction and literary manifestations of both classical and popular myths; a homosexual discourse, defined either as a specifically homosexual relation to language or (a distinctly different meaning) as a way of writing about homosexuality in a given time and place.

A complete study of any of these topics would necessarily involve the consideration of non-French writers, and we have attempted in this book to acknowledge, albeit in a limited manner, the importance of this broader context. But as the preceding list of names attests, France has not only produced a great number of writers who discuss homosexuality, she has produced a remarkable number of great writers whose works have encouraged, and at times forced, readers, critics, and above all, successive generations of younger writers to devote attention

to it. The French possess a strong tradition of writing on homosexuality which since the late eighteenth century has nurtured
its own growth. In the perspective of history one can now say
that the proliferation of critical and biographical studies on
Gide and Proust, the emergence of Genet, the rediscovery of
Sade, and the rise of Sartrean existentialism mark a moment in
the middle of the twentieth century when this accumulated tradition attained a "critical mass" in France and became an inescapable presence to a degree not reached in other countries.

It is a more difficult task to determine the distinctive features
of this tradition. For many readers the creation of imposing
homosexual characters best defines the French achievement.
Diderot's Mother Superior, Balzac's Vautrin, Gide's Michel,
Ménalque, and Edouard, Proust's Charlus and Albertine, Colette's Ladies of Llangollen, Genet's Divine and Querelle, Sartre's
Daniel Sereno and Inès Serrano, Yourcenar's Hadrian, Wittig's
J/e are indeed complex and richly ambiguous members of a
changing homosexual typology. Because many are frequently
seen as avatars, within an ideal fictionalized autobiography, of
the authors themselves, they are immediately and contagiously
fascinating.

Other readers would insist not on ambiguity but on lucidity—on
the fact that French writers have repeatedly elaborated, through
explicit narrative and critical commentary, on the various aspects
of homosexual experience. Sade's numerous treatises, Gide's
Corydon, the overture of Proust's *Sodome et Gomorrhe,* Colette's
Le pur et l'impur, Cocteau's *Le livre blanc,* Genet's *Journal du voleur,*
Sartre's *Saint-Genet,* despite the divergence of their positions and
modes of discourse, are among a small number of primary texts
that have shaped and at times radically disrupted the Western
world's moral and intellectual vision of homosexuality. Many of
these texts were directly generated by those that preceded them,
and they offer perhaps the most convincing examples we have
of a definite homosexual intertextuality in France. Although
they have been praised and condemned by homosexuals and
heterosexuals alike, most are also courageous texts that have
established their authors, in word and deed, as teachers, less of
homosexuality than of human possibilities.

We would propose, however, that the finest achievement of

the French writers derives from their profound understanding of the value of homosexuality as a transgression. Homosexuality tends to move through definitions and across lines of conceptual demarcation. Because it perpetually questions the social order and is always in question itself, homosexuality is other. The French have perceived in this otherness a privileged instrument for analysis, a question to raise questions. Their works can therefore be seen as so many demonstrations of the uses of homosexuality—to discover the laws of love and jealousy, to explore sexual differences, to test morality and metaphysics, to examine the validity of psychological concepts, to expose social and political myths, to reinterpret literary conventions, to pose the problems of authenticity and sincerity, to chart the secret channels of desire.

This value of homosexuality as an instrument for analyzing a cultural and linguistic context extending in all directions largely accounts for the interest shown in it by recent writers. It also underlies one of the purposes of this book, which is to reformulate many of the concepts, established and new, of literary criticism. The very juxtaposition of the words "homosexuality" and "literature" obliges us to confront the definitions of what is and is not literary proposed by a distinguished line of formalist critics. It also obliges us to determine the locus of sexuality within the text and its relevance as an object of critical analysis. Some of these issues have been addressed before, and this book owes much to the insights provided by earlier studies. Our intention is to continue a tradition of questioning, and to do so in the only way a tradition can be continued—by turning it on itself, by questioning the questioners. That is one reason why the material presented in the first section of the book is in the form of essays by and particularly interviews with leading psychoanalysts, feminists, writers, and thinkers in France and in the United States. It is their ideas that shape the cultural contexts so essential to an analysis of our topic.

Since the 1950's, Parisian intellectuals have elaborated and publicized theories on the reading and writing of texts and on the constitution of the reading and writing subject which have reordered our thinking about language and its intricate relationship to sexuality and society. The void left by the absence of God and the absence of Man has been filled by the presence of Language. In what ways has this intellectual reorientation affected writing about homosexuality? The prevalence of the word "discourse" in many contemporary texts, including the interviews in this book, reveals an awareness of the distance between words and that to which they refer. What is most often under consideration is a language about homosexuality, not homosexuality itself. The relentless attacks against the humanist concept of Man have altered the discourse on homosexuality by shifting the emphasis from nature to culture and from identity to difference. The attempts to retrieve what was repressed in the name of "nature" or "natural" bring homosexuality out of its confinement in literary, religious, medical, and legal texts into the broader inquiry on sexuality and politics.

The events of May 1968 may be interpreted as an eruption of repressed elements within French society, a merging of theoretical considerations with a concrete economic and social situation. This has been evident in the directions taken by some members of the French women's liberation movement, particularly in the passionate discussions on what they consider the exploitation of women within a male society that refuses to acknowledge its profound homosexuality and from which women's difference has been systematically excluded. It has also been evident in the proclamations of homosexual groups denouncing the oppressive conformity imposed by bourgeois values and insisting on the inseparable connection between sexual liberation and social revolution. In the United States the discourse on homosexuality has been strongly influenced by the visibility of the black and student movements of the mid-1960's, by the women's movement in which lesbian-feminists represent the avant-garde, and by gay liberation. There is a tendency in all politicized minority groups to reject stereotypical categories and affirm the right to exalt difference.

Questions are now being raised in both countries that either were not asked before or were not asked with the same intensity. What is the relationship between desire in its various manifestations and writing? What differences are there between masculine and feminine discourses, and how are they related to male and female homosexuality? Is there a distinctly homosexual im-

agination or relationship to creativity? How has the recently
heightened consciousness of femininists and gay liberationists
influenced the general context of literary discussion? Are all
forms of writing conditioned by sexual politics? What are the
effects of the dominant sexual ideology on literary criticism?
What are the value and limits of psychoanalysis when applied to
the study of language and to literary texts? These are some of
the questions raised by the interviewers and by the writers themselves. Most will remain without conclusive answers.

The interviews and essays in the first section of the book demonstrate that in matters sexual and literary a period of relative
consensus has ended, a period of intense contestation has begun.
Contestation can be exciting when it offers new ideas and
methods of analysis, but it may also be irritating to some when it
is uncompromising. It can promise more inclusive systems of
thought, but it may also reveal contradictions and not a little
confusion. "We are swimming in molasses," concludes Serge
Leclaire after discussing the present state of psychoanalysis, and
his remark is at once an indication of the work that remains to be
accomplished in all fields and a warning to those who might
accept as definitive one or another of the theories being advanced.

An evident conclusion to be drawn from these interviews and
essays is that the position one advocates largely depends on the
conventions one is questioning or rejecting. While many of the
writers reveal an exacerbated awareness of the dangers that ac-
company definition, they are nevertheless engaged in an extensive redefinition of the concepts related to sexuality and language, for it is only by such a process that one can hope to escape
the parameters of the old discourse. Insofar as definitions inevitably imply exclusions, each contributor participates, no matter how reluctantly, in a politically charged dialogue. Through
these dialogues one can discern the emergence of new discourses. And precisely because they are new, they must themselves be read critically, for within each discourse what is unknown is as important as what is known, what is attacked as
significant as what is defended, what is denied as revealing as
what is affirmed.

While some of the questions raised within this cultural context find answers in the second section of the book, the new French critical discourses displayed by several among our first group of contributors inform relatively few of these essays. There is also in the second section less overt insistence on the political and ideological dimensions of our topic. The majority of the essays have been produced in accordance with modes of thematic criticism that many readers will find more accessible and perhaps more immediately relevant to our observations concerning the homosexual literary tradition in France and the achievements of French writers. By focusing on the works of individual writers from the eighteenth century to the present, these essays reveal how the poets and novelists themselves struggled with language, how they employed and transformed the literary conventions and psychological theories of their time. In other words, we are here again concerned with attempts at redefinition.

Whether they are asked explicitly by the contributors or implied through their judgments and analyses, other questions are suggested by these essays. How significant is the role of homosexuality in the work of an individual writer? What weight should be given to biographical information? For what reasons have the Romantic stereotypes of the homosexual figure undergone such radical transformations? How does homosexuality affect the language, style, and structure of a writer's work? Is there a connection between a writer's sexuality and his or her literary practices? How do the dominant sexual myths and erotic fantasies of a period shape a work or determine a writer's reputation? In what ways does a text produce semiotic connections that can be read as homosexual? How does a work reflect, consciously or unconsciously, the prevailing discourse on homosexuality? In what ways does all writing on homosexuality struggle with the polarities male/female, homosexual/heterosexual?

Viewed as an analysis of homosexualities and their relation to French literature, this book cannot aspire to be complete. Our topic is expanding too rapidly, opinions are too diverse. But because it seeks to capture a complex moment of history, the book can and should be judged for the perspectives it offers on current thinking and research. Twenty years ago our title, had the volume been possible, would have been "Homosexuality and French Literature," and the introduction would have been much easier to write. Both homosexuality and literature would have been conceived of as fixed categories of human behavior and creation. We would probably have started with a chronological survey of those works of fiction in which homosexuality plays a role, a well-defined, generally accepted corpus of literary texts. We would have adhered strictly to traditional French period divisions, and we would have shown character transformations corresponding to these divisions: romantic, symbolist, decadent, surrealist, existentialist.

It used to be difficult to write about homosexuality and literature for moral or religious reasons. Today, it is difficult for linguistic and psychoanalytic reasons. The break-up of fixed categories and the microanalyses of signs must now be considered alongside thematic and evolutionary considerations. We are witnessing not only projects for the creation of a new discourse, but a competition among discourses and modes of criticism. There are no universally applicable conventions about how discussion of our topic is to be conducted, no unquestioned standards and values, no established distance from which to make judgments. It is for these reasons that we have designed a book that itself transgresses boundaries and presents a variety of discourses from the theoretical and scholarly to the personal and polemical.

Although each interview and essay may be read for its own merits, each is also a source of material for future exchanges—between the French, who tend to become involved in theorizing about the Text and Discourse, and Americans, who tend to conceive of literature as the expression of an individual mind; between psychoanalysts and critics, feminists and gay liberationists, formalists and nonformalists. The emphasis throughout is on difference, or rather on the multiple differences that exist among theories and texts, between men and women, within time and space. By revealing the limits of "homosexuality" and the categories and oppositions it supports and by exposing what the singular has dissimulated or suppressed, "homosexualities" invites us to rethink differences, as well as to think in terms of difference. Within this play of various and changing relations no centrally imposed meaning can be justified, no ultimate meaning can exist. Roland Barthes has suggested that this process of differentiation and pluralization may someday make it pointless to speak about homosexualities at all. Until that day, however, the movement toward the abolition of meaning can serve as a tool for the production of new meanings. If our book celebrates anything, it is this expansion of a topic whose possibilities for meaning are only beginning to receive adequate attention. And these new possibilities influence everything one writes, including the titles of books.

Cultural Contexts

The opposition of the sexes must not be a law of Nature; therefore the confrontations and paradigms must be dissolved, both the meanings and the sexes be pluralized; meaning will tend toward its multiplication, its dispersion (in the theory of the Text), and sex will be caught in no typology (there will be, for example, only *homosexualities,* whose plural will baffle any constituted, centered discourse, to the point where it seems . . . virtually pointless to talk about it).

In what we write we each protect our sexuality.
—Roland Barthes

Homosexual desire is specific; there are homosexual utterances. But homosexuality is nothing; it's only a word. So let's take the word seriously, let's go with it and make it yield all the possibilities it contains.
—Gilles Deleuze

For, concerning the specificity of the desire between women, nothing has been revealed, nothing has been enunciated.
—Luce Irigaray

We must define the functions and the raisons d'être of the triumvirate power-knowledge-pleasure that in our culture sustains the discourse on human sexuality.

—Michel Foucault

Our interpretive worldly-wisdom has been applied, in a sense, to everything except ourselves; we are brilliant at deconstructing the mystifications of a text, at elucidating the blindness of a critical method, but we have seemed unable to apply these techniques to the very life of texts in the world, their materiality, their capacity for the production of misery or liberation, their monumentality as Foucault has spoken of it. As a result we are mesmerized by the text, and convinced that a text is only a text, without realizing how saying that is not only naive, it is worldly-blind. . . . The critic of texts ought to be investigating the system of discourse by which the "world" is divided, administered, plundered, by which humanity is thrust into pigeonholes, by which "we" are "human" and "they" are not.

—Edward W. Said

Robert Champigny

Sexual and Literary

Have types of homosexuality, or heterosexuality, anything to do with literariness, by which I mean the ludic[1] and aesthetic aspect of texts? The question isolates an aspect, not a collection, of linguistic items. All the aspects of a text that happens to be mentioned in histories of "literature" are not literary in this sense; and a study of such a text is not necessarily an example of literary (that is, meta-literary) criticism. The question has no relation to propagandistic issues: how effective the diffusion of a text was in bringing about practical changes, whether these changes are judged to be good or bad, and whatever the author's intentions may have been. Nor is it related to the historical component: what a text states, or expresses, regarding a psychosocial state of affairs.

In an essay or a work of fiction, homosexuality may be an overt theme. As far as characters are concerned, the spectrum

1. "Ludic" is the adjective that corresponds to "play," or "game," as opposed to "cognitive and utilitarian activities or perspectives." As far as literature is concerned, "aesthetic" characterizes the experience, not only of playing with the text, but of identifying with it (not with what the text signifies). "Playful" does not cover the whole semantic range of "ludic." "Lusion," as opposed to "illusion," is equivalent to "play."

extends from conscious homosexuals like Charlus, in Proust, to
less definite examples like Orgon in Molière's *Tartuffe*. In a
homologically polysemic text, a topic may function as one
semantic zone: as one "code" (Lévi-Strauss), or "isotopy"
(Greimas). By "homological polysemy," I mean a systematic
superimposition, limited by punning possibilities, of various
meanings, each of which could stand on its own. Pierre Guiraud
has interpreted in this Mallarmean way some cryptic poems by
Villon, extracting three isotopies, one of which happens to be
homosexual.

This type of composition may be said to be poetic. Each
isotopy developed independently would supply a prosaic meaning. Their fusion is poetic. This strategy should be distinguished
from explicit metaphors: for instance, in mystically oriented
texts, a presentation of relations between human and divine in
sexual terms. It should also be distinguished from practical
ciphers which hide a target meaning under an obvious meaning.
Homological polysemy is averse to asymmetries between apparent and concealed, superficial and deep, mask and face. The
various meanings are on the same footing; they mask one
another, determine one another. If one is interested in this
kind of game *per se*, it hardly matters which semantic zones are
brought into play; it hardly matters, for instance, whether one of
the isotopies is sexual or not.

But one may also consider as an aesthetic factor a certain
amount of originality in the treatment of a given topic, either as
an overt theme or as a scrambled isotopy: variations in its inner
development and in its connections with other topics; changes in
valuation (relative importance, positive and negative value
signs). These modifications are particularly striking if they invert relations that a reader has been accustomed to consider
normal on the basis of a socially embedded ideology or of some
rhetorical tradition or fashion. For instance, the treatment of
heterosexual love in Troubadour poetry can be looked at in
relation to the theory of love in Plato's *Phaedrus*, which takes
male homosexuality as a springboard, and, on the other hand, to
set metaphors that echo male and female roles existing within a
culture.

If, however, it is exemplified by a number of authors in

spatio-temporal proximity, a certain treatment of a topic is apt to
be viewed as a cultural, or countercultural, phenomenon, as a
symptom or tool of a conservative or militant ideology. In this
perspective, it is a historical, and perhaps a propagandistic, aspect that will be of interest. In a meta-aesthetic perspective, variation in the treatment of topics is to be considered as an intellectual and imaginative exercise to be enjoyed in itself. Beyond the appreciation of variations for their own sake, the preferences of different readers for various selections and treatments should also be taken into account. Authors, or particular
texts, and readers might be grouped according to affinities, instead of some sociohistorical decoupage: two readers with the
same upbringing, cultural background, and social position, may
react quite differently to a given text, contemporary or not. A
distinction between cultural molds and socioreligious ideologies
on the one hand, and ludic and aesthetic tastes on the other, is
thus possible. But, if a theme is definitely sexual, if it can be
recognized as homosexual, heterosexual, bestial, or what have
you, how is a voyeuristic, or a mythical, appeal to be distinguished from a ludic and aesthetic aspect?

With luck, sexual activities may be lived playfully; and, in this
respect, their conversion into imaginative themes will not be as
mystifying as a verbal aestheticization of work or pain. But literary enjoyment consists either in treating the text as ludic team-
mate and opponent, or in reaching the status of signifying act
through an identification, a partial one to be sure, with the text.
It does not consist in having what is signified presented as a
game; and it does not consist in identifying with a character.
Success stories are not successful stories.

One way to avoid a possible interference of the nature of the
content with an appreciation of the text is to develop the content
(sexual, for instance) as a ludic failure. Another strategy consists
in making the content somehow congruous with the literary
game itself, in supplying the latter with a fictional echo. The
most simple means of avoiding the interference is to add quotation marks. Traditionally, characters in love are characters who
talk love. A verbal transposition thus occurs within the fictional
content itself.

With or without quotation marks, love talk, in novel, drama, or poetry, has been remarkably partial to metaphors. Masking the human animal, clothing the featherless biped with metaphors may be ascribed to social propriety, often topped with suggestive coquettishness; should personal modesty be added? It would rather tend to eliminate the theme altogether. A metaphorical treatment may also be viewed as a mythical inflation of sexuality, as an attempt to make an aspect of human finitude pass for a cosmic principle. But it may also be considered as a first step toward the scrambling of isotopies I mentioned, as a way to disintegrate the topic, thus preventing it from assuming precedence over the text itself: words of love, or about love, would prime a love of words, if not of Platonic "ideas." Meta-mythical and meta-aesthetic interpretations could both be based on the assumption that human desire in general has cosmic aspirations and that, while they may satisfy some limited need, sexual activities of any type cannot fulfill this desire, though they may be connected with it. Unlike an aesthetic awareness, the mythical ambition, in this domain as well as others, would be to conceal the discrepancy, to try to forget that, if the transcendent gap is spanned, it is spanned with words, and that words can be ontologically real to the extent that what they signify is not.

Would some of the metaphors in which Proust indulges be aesthetically better, or worse, if "Albert" were substituted for "Albertine"? I doubt that it would make any difference to me. What I do happen to think is that the limitation of the homosexual theme to third-person characters is one of the factors (others are more important) that make the narrated ego an unsatisfactory character, his positioning on the fictional map awkward, and the relation between narrated ego and narrating ego a basic weakness if *A la recherche du temps perdu* is regarded as a narrative.

It might be said that, within the official French cultural tradition, the part played by homosexuality in some of Genet's texts is a factor of originality and that the rhetorical inflation to which it is subjected acts as an ironical pastiche of the conventional mythicization of heterosexual love, thus showing what is aesthetically unauthentic about it. But it might also be said that it is not by turning myth into countermyth, white mass into black mass,

that one is going to extricate "lusion" (play) from illusion, fiction
from legend, the aesthetic from the religious.

Philosophically, I am inclined to define religious intentionality
as a confusion between cognitive (true or false) and fictional
(neither true nor false), practical and ludic, moral and aesthetic.
One of the relations between aesthetic and moral emergences is
that, theoretically at least, extrication on one side should allow
extrication on the other. The treatments of homosexuality in
Proust and Genet, as well as in other authors, cannot supply
clear examples regarding the possibilities of a properly aesthetic
transposition since, in different ways, they are determined by
socioreligious conventions bearing on the topic.

(Perhaps I should add that aesthetic judgments should not be
confused with the ranking of authors and texts as great or not,
major and minor. This kind of evaluation is a socioreligious
phenomenon, according to tradition, fashion, sometimes definite political dictates, and its agreement with the aesthetic tastes
of various readers, living or dead, is purely coincidental.)

It might be alleged that, as a theme, homosexuality is more
consonant with the aesthetic intention of a text than heterosexuality would be, since homosexual relations are sterile, while
heterosexual relations may not be. Whether a rhetorical exaltation of heterosexual love conceals or stresses its possible link with
reproduction, it does not discuss the moral issue that it should
raise: whether it is good or bad to help the human species to
survive a little longer.

By itself, however, this argument is not a literary recom-
mendation in favor of homosexuality rather than, say, onanism
or necrophilia. Besides, socioreligious connotations, which confuse practical-moral and ludic-aesthetic values, are bound to affect the literary treatment of sexuality, to the extent that, unlike
a philosophical essay on morals, a piece of fiction will not be able
clearly to present a certain kind of behavior as morally good,
bad, or indifferent, a clarification that would dispel the mythical
confusion.

Rather incoherently, Christian ideology blesses both chastity
and reproduction. In any case, it condemns homosexuality. In
order to be stamped Christians, mystics had to picture relations
with the divine in heterosexual terms, the divine being on the

male side. To the extent that he links homosexuality with beauty instead of ugliness, someone like Genet attacks the Christian conglomerate in an amusing (or silly?) way. But he does not, perhaps cannot, make clear the relation between homosexuality and moral value or anti-value: whether the sterility it implies is morally good or bad. According to Sartre's interpretation of Genet's mentality, the term opposed to beauty would be goodness, rather than ugliness: hence an identification of beauty with evil. If so, we would not be dealing with a distinction and articulation between aesthetic and moral values. The link between homosexuality, ugliness, and evil would be partially modified, but the structural superimposition would be blindly maintained.

To eliminate a confusion between aesthetic tastes and spellbound reactions, conformist or counterconformist, to cultural states of affairs, an attempt to determine possible relations between varieties of sexual leanings and varieties of ludic and aesthetic aspirations and tastes had better consider texts only to the extent that they do not exploit sexuality as a conspicuous topic or even as a scrambled isotopy. Freudian psychoanalysis can be oriented in this direction. But, despite its derivation from a branch of Romantic philosophy (Schopenhauer, Eduard von Hartmann), it has not adopted a clear and distinct notion of the aesthetic; it has not developed a basic axiology in the domains of epistemology, ethics, aesthetics. This neglect may be attributed to scientific ambitions: the business of a science is to supply cognitive and practical tools; it does not have to bother with philosophical understanding, not even with a theory of knowledge, except in times of crisis. But in the case of psychoanalysis the accumulation of data has not been accompanied by the development of a scientific language. A move similar to the transformation of alchemy into chemistry, to the mutation of analogy and contrast between cause and effect into strict causal laws and mathematical probability, has not occurred. It is also to be noted that psychoanalytic interpretations of texts have concentrated on content (definitely sexual or not) rather than on semiotic type, genre, and style. Fairly recent attempts to wed psychoanalysis and linguistics allow a change of orientation. But, except, perhaps, for phonetics, linguistics, like psychoanalysis, has so far failed to reach a scientific status, while providing some writers with excuses for philosophical irresponsibility. Bridges between psychoanalysis and linguistics put me in mind of, say, conjunctions between alchemy and astrology, rather than of equations relating branches of physics and chemistry.

If various ludic and aesthetic aspirations and tastes are to be granted some specificity, some authenticity, they should be considered as manifesting themselves despite the cultural conventions and fashions, dams and sponges, through which they have to steal their way; and their diversity, which does not correspond to the diversity of these conventions and fashions, and which, by the way, involves games and arts other than linguistic, should be seen as being grounded in a diversity of temperaments. But how could this philosophical postulate, derived from intuition and personal experience, become a scientific hypothesis, with regard, for instance, to possible connections between sexual orientations and stylistic tastes? Even if relevant, reliable, and sufficiently extensive biographical information could be obtained concerning authors and readers, it would still not allow a distinction between innate propensities and haphazard channeling through circumstances. One would have to turn to genetics, the science of the brain, biochemistry; and, at present, the analysis of genetic codes cannot tell us, so far as I know, whether such a dichotomy as that between homosexuality and heterosexuality makes temperamental sense and, if it does, whether it should be construed as a primary division or as a subdivision, some other principle of classification being privileged in the latter case. In the absence of such data, relations between various types of sexual dispositions on the one hand and ludic and aesthetic tastes on the other, will remain, as far as I can see, a matter of blind dogma or of speculative fancy.

Serge Leclaire

Sexuality: A Fact of Discourse

An Interview by Hélène Klibbe

HÉLÈNE KLIBBE: Today in the United States the question of homosexuality is being explored with greater freedom, especially in literature. Could you elaborate on the meaning of homosexuality from the standpoint of psychoanalysis?

SERGE LECLAIRE: No, because to talk about homosexuality today, one must talk about sexuality, and I don't believe that there has been much progress on the sexual question in psychoanalysis. We are working with relatively recent *idées reçues*—of the last fifty years or so—which do not enlighten us on homosexuality because they have not enlightened us much on sexuality.

H. K.: Has the Oedipal myth undergone any modifications of structure? Are the heterosexual and homosexual structures the same?

S. L.: They are certainly the same as far as the Oedipal structure is concerned; but I don't think that the Oedipal point of view is the most comprehensive approach to this problem. At present, it is difficult to undertake an analysis referring solely to the history of the family—the bourgeois family—in which you can find the Oedipus structure or the Oedipus myth. Social structure, the history of ideologies, and history in general play

as important a role. For that matter, the *Anti-Oedipe* by Gilles
Deleuze and Félix Guattari (not that I agree with it or approve
of it) is symptomatic of something that points up the limited
character of the Oedipal reference, what it has become and
the way it is being apprehended today. This is merely to give
you an example; it is not an answer.

H. K.: What interests me is whether you believe homosexuality
plays a determining role in literature and art?

S. L.: Certainly. But how? I don't have ready-made answers on
the subject. What does impress me is the fact that many
women writers are homosexual. I can't say that they all are; I
have no idea. Nevertheless, those who "truly" write seem to be.
For the moment, however, let us set aside the elucidation of
what it means to be homosexual. I don't believe there are any
definitions of homosexuality. What are the criteria of normal
sexuality for man and for woman? Do you know?

H. K.: No. I know, however, that you were impressed by the
quality of woman's language at the Cerisy colloquium.[1] What
do you mean by woman's language and how is it different
from man's?

S. L.: Here I can give you a precise answer. At Cerisy, I was
struck by the fact that women were speaking, for the first time
so consistently, without taking the "masculine position"—that is, they did not adhere to a discourse that was
conceptual, philosophical, or academic. Apart from some exceptions (there are always exceptions) they were more direct,
they were not defensive about their work or what they created.
Here I am thinking of Hélène Cixous. The way she spoke
was quite exceptional—I would even say independently of content.

H. K.: Didn't she use man's language, in that she made many
references to Freud?

S. L.: Certainly. But it was not "constructed." In the diversity of
discourses evoked at Cerisy (psychoanalytic, scientific,

1. Dr. Leclaire initiated and directed a ten-day colloquium on the
psychoanalytical, scientific, literary, political, and religious discourses at the International Cultural Center of Cerisy (France), July 1974.

philosophical, religious)—I am referring to the Lacanian implication of the term "discourse"—the fact that man's discourse is fundamentally different from woman's speech (*parole*) was never taken into account, and *in psychoanalysis this difference is perfectly evident.*

H. K.: What exactly is this difference? Is it a difference of structure?

S. L.: Yes. *Man's discourse* is typically the *discourse of repression.* At the risk of entering into technical considerations, what I mean is that man's position in relation to castration is different from woman's, and a different position in relation to castration results in a different discourse.

H. K.: What happens when a woman speaks like a man and vice versa? Isn't their relation to castration put in question?

S. L.: Of course, and this is fortunate. The only interest and "truth" of a discourse lie in the fact that this very relation to castration is what is being implicitly put in question.

H. K.: Have you noticed differences between the discourses of a heterosexual and a homosexual in your psychoanalytical practice?

S. L.: Certainly there are differences. It is very rare to encounter "pure" woman's speech—one that is not affected by man's discourse. Inversely, the same is true of man's. *Bisexuality is a fundamental fact,* fundamental in terms of what sex is, in the psychoanalytic sense of the term. Sex is a fact of discourse which takes into account anatomical determinations. The sexual situation is a subjective one—one which is not, from the psychoanalytic standpoint, purely biological or anatomical, even if anatomy does partly determine those sexual situations in relation to castration.

H. K.: It seems to me that the terms "woman's speech" and "man's discourse," instead of clarifying the problem, lead to confusion. Wouldn't it be better to invent a new terminology?

S. L.: Absolutely. I prefer the terms "discourse of repression" and "signifying Word" (*parole signifiante*). In the latter the words retain their value as signifiers. This is clearly the privileged discourse.

H. K.: I would like to come back to Cerisy. Don't you think that the speech of the women writers you heard was essentially a protest and a revolt against man's discourse and the society that ostracizes them because of their homosexuality?

S. L.: Yes, if you like. But if you insist on thinking in terms of these categories, I would reverse the problem. Today, when a woman wishes to speak in public, she is compelled in a certain way to take refuge in a so-called homosexual position. Only at that price can a woman speak. But man, too, faces this problem. If he wants to free himself from the prevailing ideological discourse, from a power discourse in which he necessarily participates, he, too, is compelled to call upon *something of the woman in him.* At present, a man who truly wants to say something, to speak, to create, must somehow rediscover this repressed part in him. Is that what one calls a homosexual position? For me, the term homosexual remains quite enigmatic.

H. K.: You have made many references to castration. Is your concept of castration different from Freud's?

S. L.: Fundamentally, castration is linked with language. Access to language implies something of castration—a renouncing of a primal narcissistic image or, better yet, a renouncing of the first words which support the representation that parents have of us. Castration—sexual determination—is a way of access to language, to speech.

H. K.: Are you implying that access to language is also access to creativity?

S. L.: Yes and no. When a child learns in school how to write and speak, there is little chance that his language will remain creative. He is taught to respect the language of the prevailing system; that is the institutionalization of language.

H. K.: You have mentioned that the relation to castration is different for man and woman. What is the difference?

S. L.: Castration is the relation to the phallus. The phallus is not the penis, although the ordinary representative of it is. Early on, everything related to the phallus revolves around the penis.

H. K.: If the phallus is not the penis, then to what extent is the relation to the phallus different for woman?

S. L.: Let me try to explain it simply. Let us call the phallus "God." It is an old tradition. You don't see "God," properly speaking, you have no image of him. "God" (the phallus) is invisible; therefore, the relation to the phallus is marked by a nonformalizable relation, a relation of exclusion. At the same time, everything is in relation to the phallus; everything is in relation to "God." Let's suppose that there is a child, Jesus, the son of God, who serves as mediator. Now, let's replace the "child Jesus" with the penis, which happens to be the most convenient representative of the phallus. Because man has in his body a relation with his *penis as the representative of the phallus*, schematically, his natural inclination leads him to forget the fact that the phallus ("God") is invisible, unseizable, unnamable. But woman does not have this representative in her body; therefore, her relation to the phallus is less veiled. She is less tempted to forget the fact that the phallus is always absent. Consequently, man's and woman's relations to castration are profoundly different. I am referring to castration as the relation to the phallus, to the Invisible, to an unnamable term. In Lacanian language I would say it is both signifier and object. Anatomy is destiny, says Freud, that is why the relation to this Invisible is different for man and woman. Of course, very quickly for woman, there is a series of substitutes for the penis, the representative of the phallus; her own body or parts of it become phallic substitutes. Moreover, woman represents, in her entirety, something of a phallic substitute for man. But this does not change the fact that access to language is different for man and woman. In the whole evolution and history of woman, nothing has ever come as a screen between the invisible "God," phallus, and the way she speaks. For man, the possession of the penis, which is highly cathected, serves as a screen denying the fundamental character of castration. Man comes to believe that he has not been castrated. Even psychoanalysts don't recognize the phallus as absent. They think that castration is a fact for woman and that man only fears castration. Psychoanalytically, this is simply false. The important thing is that two types of relation to the phallus determine two types of discourse which are, of course, always blending. No man has a purely masculine discourse of absolute negation of castration; and no woman constantly has a discourse of the unconscious or primary type. In fact, most intellectual women have adopted the universal discourse, the conceptual discourse, the systematic discourse, which *is always a discourse of repression*—a discourse that denies castration. This is why I was impressed at Cerisy when women did not feel compelled to take such a position.

H. K.: Do you mean that women expressed emotions and ideas reflecting their unconscious?

S. L.: I would not use the terms "emotions" and "ideas." A woman's speech is one of *jouissance,*[2] of desire. She speaks of something much closer to what Freud called primal organization. Her words, instead of being agents of repression (ideas or words to fill the gaps and make coherent systems), keep their original value of signifier, in the Lacanian sense of unconscious representatives, that is, if she is not too defensive. With a man this is much rarer. Again, this way of separating the two is artificial in the sense that all our education and culture are the same. What I mean is that each one maintains a speech of repression and a speech that goes against repression. Otherwise no man would undergo psychoanalysis.

H. K.: Don't you think repression in woman is more intense because of the taboos and education imposed upon her by society? Her attempts to express herself freely with regard to her sexuality are relatively recent.

S. L.: What you are describing is her oppression. Repression in the Freudian sense, primal repression, is the first recognition that the phallus is lost. In order to speak one must resign oneself, at a given moment, to renoucing the words or representations of others. To start speaking is indeed to create one's words by giving up, at least once, the words of others. Primal

---

2. As Anthony Wilden states in a footnote to his translation of Lacan in *The Language of the Self* (Baltimore: Johns Hopkins Press, 1968), "*Jouissance* has no simple English equivalent. In a less significant context, it might be translated "enjoyment," "possession," "appropriation," "right," "pleasure." Since in Lacan's view the enjoyment of possession of an object is dependent for its pleasure on others, the ambiguity of the French *jouissance* nicely serves his purpose" (p. 101, n. 29).

repression consists in the loss of the first unconscious representations, the first signifiers: this is the access to language.

H. K.: Isn't it the same for both man and woman?

S. L.: Yes. The difference comes later on. The primal repression is forgotten and then proper repression, as Freud describes it, takes place. The secondary repression involves everything that is in formal relation, signifying relation with the first repressed signifiers. As an example, let us imagine that something like a golden eye (the reflection in a golden eye) has been repressed. If one day, at Easter time—I am constructing at random—a two-year-old child sees a yellow egg, there is every reason to believe that this golden egg, this representation or signifier, will be repressed because of the first repressed signifier, in this case, the golden eye. The yellow egg will then constitute the unconscious which is the product of secondary repression. It is at this point that the difference occurs. The secondary repression is not of the same order in man and woman. The representation—yellow egg—will not be repressed in the same way. The golden egg will remind the child of the golden eye—of castration. The little boy, who has already cathected his penis, does not want to be reminded of this first castration, that is, his true access to language. Therefore, this golden egg will be repressed rapidly and solidly. It is urgent to repress what reminds him of the primal signifiers because he feels that, if he does not, he will lose his penis. With a woman, too, there will undoubtedly be repression, but not quite in the same way. She is less threatened in her secondary narcissism, in the sense that while the golden egg reminds her of a first castration, it also reminds her of her natural castration, if I may so phrase it. In short, everything related to sex, to *jouissance*, tends to be repressed, but differently in boys and girls. This is why we have different discourses.

H. K.: Let us consider Proust's discourse, a literary discourse where metaphors and images are often a reflection of the narrator's desires, dreams, and fantasies. Could you compare his writing to the speech of certain women writers of today?

S. L.: Why is he writing? In search of past time. He is entirely devoted to this search. What woman could write in search of past time? For her, it is the present that matters.

H. K.: When Hélène Cixous wrote *Portrait du soleil,* don't you think she was in search of her past—using a different style, of course?

S. L.: No. It is not the same thing. It is an extemporaneous production which cannot be distinguished from the living (*le vécu*) in the primary process. Hélène Cixous writes about her dreams, and she dreams in order to write.

H. K.: You previously said that the male homosexual was trying to speak woman's language by bringing to the surface the repressed part in him. From that basis, could you elaborate on the relationship of a homosexual, male or female, to language, discourse, and creativity?

S. L.: Yes, but what word is to be examined? "Creativity" is a man's fantasy, a sociologist's fantasy. The word "creativity" gets on my nerves. Seminars on creativity! What does that mean? Let us start with the word "procreation" and all those fundamental fantasies which are equally problematic for woman. The fact that she really gives birth does not mean that she is not in the same type of impasse as man. He has a penis but she has, if I may put it thus, something in reality which gives her the illusion of creativity. In fact, she reaches the same impasse with her "famous" maternity as man does with his penis. It is of the same fantasy order and quite obstructing in relation to the "truth." When there is something new, what does it consist of? I would call it a nascent language. There are many gimmicks to create new forms, new gadgets. All the pseudocreative people make different use of the same gimmicks. The truly creative people are those who are faithful to their original fantasms, who never cease repeating them and working on them. They may be called great neurotics, if you like, but they are faithful to some unconscious representations, to the first lost things; they speak only about them. They don't "create" anything, since they keep repeating the same thing. I think that virtually all pseudocreation is part of a game: a gimmick is found and exploited; the sentence is constructed differently; the painting is composed differently— that is, exactly in *the same way.* It is very rare to find something new. What I would call new is when someone speaks of what is true in him without mediation; when he gives us, for once, a

sort of direct look at his castration, his *jouissance,* his relation to
"God," something that is totally his and therefore universal. I
prefer the term "new" to creation, although it is a creation in a
certain way when someone says something "true."

H. K.: Would you say that something true could be found in
certain poets like René Char or Yves Bonnefoy, who express
themselves in unusual structures and images that may come
from unconscious representations?

S. L.: Yes, certainly. But I think there is also a difficulty. The
poet handles words; therefore his relation to language and his
truth is directly caught up in a specific register. He works with
words; he is in a different and privileged position. The poet
must relive something or say something of the *origin of the
Word*—the access to his own language.

H. K.: When you refer to "truth" and "words," do you mean
"words" that express an intense and authentic emotion?

S. L.: I can't tell you. For me these are *right* words. On the one
hand, you have all the padding words and, on the other, the
right words.

H. K.: How can the *right* words be determined?

S.L.: By the construction itself. I think that *A la recherche du temps
perdu* is right from beginning to end. In spite of appearances,
it contains no padding. It is such a working of words, such a
rigorous search in the way it covers all fields, leaving nothing
unelucidated, nothing to chance. Everything is accounted for
in a slow, progressive search comparable to a scientific investigation of words. And words don't have a ready-made meaning, but are always anchored in what truly lives: the unconscious discourse.

H. K.: I would like to go back to the beginning of our conversation. During the last few years, there have been all sorts of
liberation movements in the United States: movements of
blacks, women, homosexuals. All have expressed a desire to
assert themselves in a struggle against oppression. What is
your point of view on this subject as a psychoanalyst?

S. L.: Now I am going to be very brutal. What is your own
interest in asking me this? You will probably say, "I don't
know." I think it has become a very good alibi to be interested

in blacks, women, homosexuals, children, etc. It puts one on the wrong scent. One acknowledges one's interest in sexuality with all its implications, but at the same time it is a marvelous way to avoid questioning oneself about one's own sexuality. It is a way to avoid speaking "truly" by speaking about others, because one feels a little bit homosexual. It is also a way of avoiding the question of one's own work as a writer, as a critic, or as a teacher, inasmuch as sexuality is concerned. These undertakings seem to deal with something interesting and relevant, but in the final analysis they are peripheral.

H. K.: What do you think of today's criticism which applies psychoanalysis to literary interpretation? Do you think that from the point of view of fantasies there is a relationship between this literary analysis and the psychoanalysis of a subject on the couch?

S. L.: Absolutely none. I am not saying that such work is not possible. One can always analyze a text through its fantasies, its structure, its images, its punctuation, and its content. But that is a textual analysis. In my opinion, it would be quite pernicious to think that there is a relationship. The only relationship that could be found is in the *metaphors,* which are those of *unconscious inscriptions.* But what is the relationship between this unconscious "text" and a literary text written on a piece of paper? It *is* an entirely metaphorical relationship, but you can write fifty articles on that relationship and not hit upon the "truth."

H. K.: Do you think there is a homosexual discourse?

S. L.: No.

H. K.: Therefore, there is no homosexual literature. There are just homosexual writers.

S. L.: In order to specify something homosexual, we ought to know a little more about sexuality, about the difference between sexes, the relationship of the sexes and, above all, the relationship of sexuality to speech. Any way of answering questions whose true content is yet unknown seems to me a way of closing the question before it is open.

H. K.: When Freud writes about the different stages of sexual development, he states that the boy, when the father is absent

or weak, is fixated on the love of the mother and that that
fixation accounts for his homosexuality. The boy directs his
sexual desire toward men because he does not want to "betray" his mother. Is your position different from Freud's?

S. L.: No. In the enunciation of this description, in this theory
and type of reference, something fundamental was said for
the first time. It has a logic in which a certain number of terms
are brought in. We were given the first elements to allow us to
think in terms other than the endocrinological, de-
monological, or religious. But while this was so, the problem
was not exhausted; it was not settled. The problem was
opened up; it entered a *new stage*. With regard to the true life
of desire, in the way it happens, this theory is inadequate
today. It is not an explanation, it is but a first landmark.

H. K.: How would you formulate it today?

S. L.: Today, it is better formulated by marking out the duality
of discourses—of woman, of man—as relating specifically to
sexuality. Sexuality is a fact of discourse. This is Freudian,
even if Freud did not say so directly. To be able to say it in
those terms permits us to formulate things differently.
Perhaps it is only a question of words. But, if you replace the
Freudian formulas "the mother," the "father," etc. with
mother's speech and father's discourse, things become a little
more precise. How does a mother speak? What does she speak
about? She speaks of sexuality from her position as a woman,
whether she wills so or not. This is necessarily not the father's
position. A woman's speech in its relationship to castration is
not a negation of castration; it says something positive about
desire, about the possibility of *jouissance* or the possibility of
love. A man's discourse is somehow a systematic, an ideological discourse—a so-called masculine position and, ultimately, a
power position.

H. K.: When you say that woman's desire is positive, don't you
think that man's desire is as powerful—even more powerful?

S. L.: Man's desire to dominate, yes. I am reminded here of a
pre-Freudian proverb: what woman wills, God wills.

H. K.: Isn't that proverb actually a reference to women's power
of seduction? Men traditionally have been allowed to be free

in their expression of desire while women have felt free
enough to speak about their desire, their *jouissance,* only recently.

S. L.: With regard to *jouissance,* I am not so sure that it works as
well with men. What you take for gospel truth on the good
sexual functioning of a man is the evidence of his erection and
ejaculation. But, if he claims to be satisfied with this good
sexual functioning, it is simply because he is less demanding.
It does not prove anything concerning *jouissance.* I don't believe that erection and ejaculation are criteria of appreciation
which correspond to the truth. But I also think that the demands made by women are both legitimate and paradoxical.
On the one hand, a woman wishes to free herself; she wants to
live, to express herself, etc. Yet she attempts to appropriate,
on an equal footing, man's discourse, to the extent of seeking
an orgasm rather than *jouissance.* There is something very
contradictory in the feminist movement. Women fall into the
same trap that they denounce; and in doing so they produce a
man's super-discourse.

H. K.: Are you referring to political discourse?

S. L.: That is just one example. This appropriation of the male
discourse leads to a desexualization, a kind of refusal to acknowledge woman's own individuality. There are exceptions,
of course, but, all in all, it is quite paradoxical and contradictory. What do women want? Do they want a discourse of
power? Such a discourse has nothing to do with woman's
speech. Indeed, it is a political question.

H. K.: Don't you think that women have to adopt this male
discourse, the discourse of power, in order to assert themselves as women and be treated equally?

S. L.: That's just another tactic, and the essential thing is lost.

H. K.: What do you mean by the essential thing?

S. L.: The essential thing is that societies live sexually and not
homosexually. Only a woman can assert sexuality. When a
man says, "*I* am a man!" what does that mean? It is, at the very
least, suspect!

To conclude: as far as method is concerned, at present it is
quite useless to extrapolate and to claim to have assimilated

something which has not yet been understood—for example, psychoanalytical concepts like phallus, lack, and castration. The people who use these terms often are incapable of providing an account of their true content; they completely bypass their meaning. Most of the time they give lip service to these concepts though in effect they fail to understand them. Everything that has been said here cannot be purely and simply transposed into a literary discipline. This would require a series of considerations, reservations, and analyses of what writing is in relation to the unconscious. What is the relationship of the analysis of a literary inscription to the unconscious inscription? They are two different things. In order to illustrate the legitimacy of this reservation of methodology, let us take an example—the term "phallus." People continue to refer to the term as specifically masculine—that is false, psychoanalytically speaking. The phallus is an unconscious reference to be constructed, to be worked out and understood. The term has no masculine implication. That is the reason why I referred, in a rather ambiguous way, to "God" in place of the phallus. I don't like this reference, I must say immediately, because it leads us into a theological discourse, which is more a regression than a progression. I only meant to emphasize the invisible, unseizable, and nonrepresentable character of the phallus concept.

Today, the terms "castration" and "phallus" are used in a mythical and magical way. They are used in the particular ideology or counterideology that is being upheld. Considered from an emotional point of view, this is an interesting process. For scientific work it has no value. Reference to a phallocentric or phallocratic society is a contradiction in terms. The discourse of repression is precisely a discourse that represses what is related to the phallus, to castration. Therefore to call something phallocratic or phallocentric which specifically excludes the problem of castration is a contradiction in terms. Such a discourse is the discourse of repression, a discourse that does not want to know anything. It is a complete contradiction unless phallus is given another meaning like "possessor of penis." That would be fine, but, in that case, what progress would have been made? We would then remain at the level of preanalytical ideologies that have nothing to do with psychoanalysis.

H. K.: It seems to me there is a frightful confusion in the theories of psychoanalysts, sociologists, women, and men!

S. L.: As was said in a seminar at the University of Paris (Vincennes), we are swimming in molasses!

Translated by Hélène Klibbe

Félix Guattari

A Liberation of Desire

An Interview by George Stambolian

GEORGE STAMBOLIAN: In 1970 the authorities forbade the sale to minors of Pierre Guyotat's novel, *Eden, Eden, Eden*. More recently they outlawed and seized the special issue of the review *Recherches* ("Encyclopédie des homosexualités") to which you had made important contributions. You were even taken to court on the matter. How would you explain these reactions by the French government?

FÉLIX GUATTARI: They were rather old-fashioned reactions. I do not think that the present government would behave the same way because there is, on the surface at least, a certain nonchalance regarding the literary and cinematographic expression of sexuality. But I don't have to tell you that this is an even more subtle, cunning, and repressive policy. During the trial the judges were completely ill at ease with what they were being asked to do.

G. S.: Wasn't it because this issue of *Recherches* treated homosexuality, and not just sexuality?

F. G.: I'm not sure, because among the things that most shocked the judges was one of the most original parts of this work—a discussion of masturbation. I think that a work devoted to homosexuality in a more or less traditional manner would have had no difficulty. What shocked perhaps was the expression of sexuality going in all directions. And then there were the illustrations—they were what set it off.

G. S.: In your opinion, what is the best way to arrive at a true sexual liberation, and what dangers confront this liberation?

F. G.: The problem as I see it is not a sexual liberation but a liberation of desire. Once desire is specified as sexuality, it enters into forms of particularized power, into the stratification of castes, of styles, of sexual classes. The sexual liberation—for example, of homosexuals, or tranvestites, or sadomasochists—belongs to a series of other liberation problems among which there is an a priori and evident solidarity, the need to participate in a necessary fight. But I don't consider that to be a liberation as such of desire, since in each of these groups and movements one finds repressive systems.

G. S.: What do you mean by "desire"?

F. G.: For Gilles Deleuze and me desire is everything that exists *before* the opposition between subject and object, *before* representation and production. It's everything whereby the world and affects constitute us outside of ourselves, in spite of ourselves. It's everything that overflows from us. That's why we define it as flow (*flux*). Within this context we were led to forge a new notion in order to specify in what way this kind of desire is not some sort of undifferentiated magma, and thereby dangerous, suspicious, or incestuous. So we speak of machines, of "desiring machines," in order to indicate that there is as yet no question here of "structure," that is, of any subjective position, objective redundancy, or coordinates of reference. Machines arrange and connect flows. They do not recognize distinctions between persons, organs, material flows, and semiotic flows.

G. S.: Your remarks on sexuality reveal a similar rejection of established distinctions. You have said, for example, that all forms of sexual activity are minority forms and reveal themselves as being irreducible to homo-hetero oppositions. You have also said that these forms are nevertheless closer to homosexuality and to what you call "a feminine becoming" (*un devenir féminin*). Would you develop this idea, in particular by defining what you mean by "feminine"?

F. G.: Yes, that was a very ambiguous formulation. What I mean
is that the relation to the body, what I call the semiotics of the
body, is something specifically repressed by the capitalist-
socialist-bureaucratic system. So I would say that each time the
body is emphasized in a situation—by dancers, by homosexuals, etc.—something breaks with the dominant semiotics that
crush these semiotics of the body. In heterosexual relations as
well, when a man becomes body, he becomes feminine. In a
certain way, a successful heterosexual relation becomes
homosexual and feminine. This does not at all mean that I am
speaking of women as such; that's where the ambiguity lies,
because the feminine relation itself can lose the semiotics of
the body and become phallocentric. So it is only by provocation that I say feminine, because I would say first that there is
only one sexuality, it is homosexual; there is only one sexuality, it is feminine. But I would add finally: there is only one
sexuality, it is neither masculine, nor feminine, nor infantile; it
is something that is ultimately flow, body. It seems to me that
in true love there is always a moment when the man is no
longer a man. This does not mean that he becomes a woman.
But because of her alienation woman is relatively closer to the
situation of desire. And in a sense, perhaps from the point of
view of representation, to accede to desire implies for a man
first a position of homosexuality as such, and second a
feminine becoming. But I would add as well a becoming as
animal, or a becoming as plant, a becoming as cosmos, etc.
That's why this formulation is very tentative and ambiguous.

G. S.: Isn't your formulation based in part on the fact that our
civilization has associated body and woman?

F. G.: No, it's because woman has preserved the surfaces of the
body, a bodily *jouissance* and pleasure much greater than that
of man. He has concentrated his libido on—one can't even say
his penis—on domination, on the rupture of ejaculation: "I
possessed you," "I had you." Look at all the expressions like
these used by men: "I screwed you," "I made her." It's no
longer the totality of the body's surface that counts, it's just
this sign of power: "I dominated you," "I marked you." This
obsession with power is such that man ultimately denies him-

self all sexuality. On the other hand, in order to exist as body he is obliged to beg his sexual partners to transform him a bit into a woman or a homosexual. I don't know if homosexuals can easily accept what I'm saying, because I don't mean to say that homosexuals are women. That would be a misunderstanding. But I think that in a certain way there is a kind of interaction between the situation of male homosexuals, of transvestites, and of women. There is a kind of common struggle in their relation to the body.

G. S.: "Interaction," "transformation," "becoming," "flow"—these words suggest a recognition of our sexual or psychic multiplicity and fluidity which, as I understand it, is an essential aspect of what you call schizo-analysis. What then is the basic difference between schizo-analysis and psychoanalysis which, I believe, you have completely abandoned?

F. G.: I was Lacan's student, I was analyzed by Lacan, and I practiced psychoanalysis for twelve years; and now I've broken with that practice. Psychoanalysis transforms and deforms the unconscious by forcing it to pass through the grid of its system of inscription and representation. For psychoanalysis the unconscious is always *already there*, genetically programmed, structured, and finalized on objectives of conformity to social norms. For schizo-analysis it's a question of *constructing* an unconscious, not only with phrases but with all possible semiotic means, and not only with individuals or relations between individuals, but also with groups, with physiological and perceptual systems, with machines, struggles, and arrangements of every nature. There's no question here of transfer, interpretation, or delegation of power to a specialist.

G. S.: Do you believe that psychoanalysis has deformed not only the unconscious but the interpretation of life in general and perhaps of literature as well?

F. G.: Yes, but even beyond what one imagines, in the sense that it's not simply a question of psychoanalysts or even of psychoanalytical ideas as they are propagated in the commercial press or in the universities, but of interpretative and representational attitudes toward desire that one finds in persons who don't know psychoanalysis, but who put themselves in the position of interpreters, of gurus, and who generalize the technique of transfer.

G. S.: With Gilles Deleuze, you have just finished a schizoanalysis of Kafka's work. Why *this* method to analyze and to comprehend literature?

F. G.: It's not a question of method or of doctrine. It's simply that I've been living with Kafka for a very long time. I therefore tried, together with Deleuze, to put into our work the part of me that was, in a way, a becoming as Kafka. In a sense the book is a schizo-analysis of our relation to Kafka's work, but also of the period of Vienna in 1920 and of a certain bureaucratic eros which crystallized in that period, and which fascinated Kafka.

G. S.: In a long note you speak of Kafka's joy, and you suggest that psychoanalysis has found only Kafka's sadness or his tragic aspect.

F. G.: In his *Diaries* Kafka gives us a glimpse of the diabolic pleasure he found in his writing. He says that it was a kind of demonic world he entered at night to work. I think that everything that produces the violence, richness, and incredible humor of Kafka's work belongs to this world of his.

G. S.: Aren't you really proposing that creation is something joyful, and that this joy can't be reduced to a psychosis?

F. G.: Absolutely—or to a lack.

G. S.: In the same book on Kafka you say that a "minor literature," which is produced by a minority in a major language, always "deterritorializes" that language, connects the individual to politics, and gives everything a collective value. These are for you, in fact, the revolutionary qualities of any literature within the established one. Does homosexuality necessarily produce a literature having these three qualities?

F. G.: Unfortunately, no. There are certainly homosexual writers who conduct their writing in the form of an Oedipal homosexuality. Even very great writers—I think of Gide. Apart from a few works, Gide always transcribed his homosexuality and in a sense betrayed it.

G. S.: Despite the fact that he tried to prove the value of homosexuality in works such as *Corydon?*

F. G.: Yes, but I wonder if he did it in just one part of his work, and if the rest of his writing isn't different.

G. S.: In the *Anti-Oedipe* you and Deleuze note that Proust described two types of homosexuality—one that is Oedipal and therefore exclusive, global, and neurotic, and one that is a-Oedipal or inclusive, partial, and localized. In fact, the latter is for you an expression of what you call "transsexuality." So if there are two Gides, aren't there also two Prousts, or at least the possibility of two different readings of his work?

F. G.: I can't answer for Proust the man, but it seems to me that his work does present the two aspects, and one can justify the two readings because both things in effect exist.

G. S.: You spoke of the demonic in Kafka. Well, Gide, Proust, and Genet have been accused of being fascinated by the demonic aspect of homosexuality. Would you agree?

F. G.: To a point. I wonder sometimes, not specifically concerning the three names you mention, if it isn't a matter of persons who were more fascinated by the demonic than by homosexuality. Isn't homosexuality a means of access to the demonic? That is, they are the heirs of Goethe in a certain way, and what Goethe called the demonic was in itself a dimension of mystery.

G. S.: But the fact remains that in our civilization homosexuality is often associated with the demonic.

F. G.: Yes, but so is crime. There's a whole genre of crime literature that contains a similar demonic aspect. The demonic or the mysterious is really a residue of desire in the social world. There are so few places for mystery that one looks for it everywhere, in anything that escapes or becomes marginal. For example, there's something demonic in the life of a movie star. That's why it's used by the sensationalist press.

G. S.: Doesn't that tell us that we are hungry for the demonic; that we are hungry for things that aren't "natural"; that we have exploited movie stars and homosexuals to satisfy our need for the demonic?

F. G.: I'm not against that because I'm not at all for nature. Therefore artifice, the artificially demonic, is something that rather charms me. Only it is one thing to live it in a relationship of immediate desire, and another thing to transform it into a repressive machine.

G. S.: Let's go back to the homosexual writers. I'd like to quote here a remark of yours that struck me. It's the last paragraph of your interview published in the August 1975 issue of *La quinzaine littéraire*. You say: "Everything that breaks something, everything that breaks with the established order, has something to do with homosexuality, or with a becoming as animal, a becoming as woman, etc. Any break in semiotization implies a break in sexuality. It is therefore not necessary, in my opinion, to raise the question of homosexual writers, but rather to look for what is homosexual, in any case, in a great writer, even if he is in other respects heterosexual." Doesn't this idea contain a new way to approach or perhaps to go beyond a question that has so obsessed certain Freudian critics and psychoanalysts—namely, the connection between homosexuality, or all sexuality, and creativity?

F. G.: Yes, of course. For me, a literary machine starts itself, or can start itself, when writing connects with other machines of desire. I'd like to talk about Virginia Woolf in her relation to a becoming as man which is itself a becoming as woman, because the paradox is complete. I'm thinking about a book I like very much, *Orlando*. You have this character who follows the course of the story as a man, and in the second part of the novel he becomes a woman. Well, Virginia Woolf herself was a woman, but one sees that in order to become a woman writer, she had to follow a certain trajectory of a becoming as woman, and for that she had to begin by being a man. One could certainly find in George Sand things perhaps more remarkable than this. So my question is whether writing as such, the signifier as such, relates to nothing, only to itself, or to power. Writing begins to function in something else, as for example for the Beat Generation in the relation with drugs; for Kerouac in the relation with travel, or with mountains, with yoga. Then something begins to vibrate, begins to function.

Rhythms appear, a need, a desire to speak. Where is it possible for a writer to start this literary machine if it isn't precisely outside of writing and of the field of literature. A break in sexuality—therefore homosexuality, a becoming as woman, as addict, as missionary, who knows? It's a factory, the means of transmitting energy to a writing machine.

G. S.: Can a break in semiotization precede a break in sexuality?

F. G.: It's not a break in semiotization, but a semiotic connection. I'll give you a more familiar example. Take what are called mad people from a poor background from the point of view of intellectual formation—peasants who have never read anything, who have gone only to grade school. Well, when they have an attack of dissociation, a psychotic attack, it happens sometimes that they begin to write, to paint, to express extraordinary things, extraordinarily beautiful and poetic! And then when they are "cured," they return to the fields, to the sugar-beets and asparagus, and they don't write any more at all. You have something of a psychotic attack like that in Rimbaud. When he became normal, he went into commerce; all that stopped. It's always a question of a connection. Something that was a little scholastic writing machine, really without any quality, connects with fabulously perceptive semiotics that start in psychosis, or in drugs, or in war, and that can animate this little writing machine and produce extraordinary things. You have a group of disconnected machines, and at a given moment there is a transmission among them, and everything begins not only to function but to produce an acceleration of operations. So you see, I'm not talking about sexuality. Sexuality is already specified as sex, caste, forms of sexual practice, sexual ritual. But creativity and desire are for me the same thing, the same formula.

G. S.: I'd still like to ask you the following question. Could you begin the search for what is homosexual in a heterosexual writer with a great writer like, for example, Beckett, whose work offers us a "homosexuality" which seems at times to be the product of extraordinary semiotic connections, and which, in any case, confounds all previous representations and goes beyond them?

F. G.: I think of those characters who travel by twos and who have no sexual practice because they live completely outside of sexuality, but who nevertheless represent a kind of collective set-up of enunciation, a collective way of perceiving everything that happens. And so many things are happening that it's necessary to select, to narrow down, in order to receive and distill each element, as if one were using a microscope to capture each of the intensities. Indeed, there is perhaps in Beckett a movement outside of the sexes, but then there is the absolutely fabulous relation to objects, a sexual relation to objects. I'm thinking of the sucking stones in *Molloy*.

G. S.: Then how does one explain the elements of homosexuality, of sadomasochism, in his work?

F. G.: But that's theater, because if there's a constant in Beckett's work, it's that even when he writes novels, he creates theater, in the sense of a *mise en scène*, a *mise en acte*, of giving something to be seen. So then inevitably, he gathers up representations, but he articulates them to create literature. What's more, Beckett is someone, I think, who was very interested in the insane, in psychopathology, and therefore he picked up a lot of representations. The use he makes of them is essentially literary, of course, but what he uses them for is not a translation, it's a collage, it's like a dance. He plays with these representations, or rather, he makes them play.

G. S.: You said in your article on the cinema (*Communications*, no. 23 [1975]) that any representation expresses a certain position with respect to power. But I wonder if Beckett hasn't succeeded in writing a politically "innocent" text.

F. G. : I no more believe in innocence than I do in nature. One thing should be made clear—if one finds innocence, there's reason to worry, there's reason to look not for guilt, of course, because that's the same thing as innocence, it's symmetry, but for what is politically in germination, for a politics *en pointillé*. Take Kafka again. Although his text isn't innocent, the supremely innocent character is K., and yet he is neither innocent nor guilty. He's waiting to enter a political scene. That's not fiction; it's not Borges, because he did enter a political scene in Prague, where one of the biggest political dramas was played around Kafka's work. So, innocence is always the anticipation of a political problem.

G. S.: Everything that's written is therefore linked in one way or another to a political position?

F. G.: Yes, with two fundamental axes: everything that's written in refusing the connection with the referent, with reality, implies a politics of individuation of the subject and of the object, of a turning of writing on itself, and by that puts itself in the service of all hierarchies, of all centralized systems of power, and of what Gilles Deleuze and I call all "arborescences," the regime of unifiable multiplicities. The second axis, in opposition to arborescence, is that of the "rhizome," the regime of pure multiplicities. It's what even innocent texts, even gratuitous games like those of the Dadaists, even collages, cut-ups, perhaps especially these things, will make possible one day to reveal—the pattern of similar breaks in reality, in the social field, and in the field of economic, cosmic, and other flows.

G. S.: So sexual liberation is not going to rid us of political connections.

F. G.: Sexual liberation is a mystification. I believe in, and will fight for, the taking of power by other castes and sexual systems, but I believe that liberation will occur when sexuality becomes desire, and that desire is the freedom to be sexual, that is, to be something else at the same time.

G. S.: How does one escape from this dilemma in which one caste replaces another?

F. G.: What these liberation movements will reveal by their failures and difficulties is that there really aren't any castes. There's the possibility that society will reform itself through other types of subjective arrangements that are not based on individuals in constellation or on relations of power that communication institutes between speaker and listener. There will be arrangements, I don't know what, based neither on families, nor on communes, nor on groups, where the goals of life, politics, and work will always be conjugated with the analysis of unconscious relations, of relations of micro-power, of micro-fascism. On the day when these movements fix as their goals not only the liberation of homosexuals, women, and children, but also the struggle against themselves in their constant power relations, in their relations of alienation, of repression against their bodies, their thoughts, their ways of speaking, then indeed, we will see another kind of struggle appear, another kind of possibility. The micro-fascist elements in all our relations with others must be found, because when we fight on the molecular level, we'll have a much better chance of preventing a truly fascist, a macro-fascist formation on the molar level.

G. S.: You and Deleuze often speak of Artaud, who wanted to rid us of masterpieces and perhaps even of written texts. Can one say that the written text already contains a form of micro-fascism?

F. G.: No, because a written text can be lengthened. Graffiti in the street can be erased or added to. A written text can be contradictory, can be made into a palimpsest. It can be something extremely alive. What is much less alive is a work, *une oeuvre* (and Artaud himself did not write a work) or a book. But then, one never writes a book. One picks up on books that have been written; one places oneself in a phylum. To write a book that wants to be an eternal and universal manual, yes, you're right; but to write after one thing and before another, that means participating in a chain, in a chain of love as well.

G. S.: I'd like to return for a moment to what you said about desire and the problems of liberation. I think of people who might profit from that kind of formulation in order to circumvent the question of homosexuality and the specificity of this struggle, by saying that all that is just sexuality and that sexuality alone matters.

F. G.: I'm very sympathetic to what you say. It's a bit like what they say to us regarding the struggle of the working class. I understand that, but I'd still like to give the same answer: it's up to the homosexuals. I'm not a worker or a homosexual. I'm a homosexual in my own way, but I'm not a homosexual in the world of reality or of the group.

G. S.: Yes, but the theories one proposes on homosexuality are always important, and they are never innocent. Before writing

Corydon, Gide read theories. Before writing *La recherche,* Proust was totally aware of the psychological thought of his time. Even Genet was influenced after the fact by the theories of Sartre. Obviously, it's often writers themselves who are the first to see things that others transform into theories. I'm thinking of Dostoevsky, Proust, and of course, Kafka. You've already begun to use your own theories to study the literature of the past, and they are related perhaps to what may someday be called a "literature of desire." Writers, critics, and homosexuals have the choice of accepting or rejecting these theories, or of playing with them. But they can neither forget them nor ignore the words of moralists, psychoanalysts, and philosophers, certainly not today and certainly not in France.

F. G.: Right, I completely agree. It's truly a pollution. But in any case, what do you think of the few theoretical propositions I've advanced here? It's my turn to question you.

G. S.: Judging your position by what you've said here and by what you've written, I think that you and Deleuze have seriously questioned Freud's system. You have turned our attention away from the individual and toward the group, and you have shown to what extent the whole Oedipal structure reflects our society's paranoia and has become an instrument for interiorizing social and political oppression. Also, I'd like to quote the following passage from the *Anti-Oedipe*: "We are heterosexuals statistically or in molar terms, but homosexuals personally, whether we know it or not, and finally transsexuals elementarily, molecularly." I can't claim to understand fully this or other aspects of your theory, but you do show that the time has come to address ourselves to the question of sexuality in another way, and that's a kind of liberation.

F. G.: Well, I want to say to those people who say "all that is sexuality" that they must go farther and try to see what in fact is the sexuality not only of the homosexual, but also of the sadomasochist, the transvestite, the prostitute, even the murderer, anyone for that matter, in order not to go in the direction of reassurance. They must see what a terrible world of repression they will enter.

G. S.: Despite the passage from your work I just quoted, when you speak you often cite groups that are always outside the dominant field of heterosexuality.

F. G.: For me desire is always "outside"; it always belongs to a minority. For me there is no heterosexual sexuality. Once there's heterosexuality, in fact, once there's marriage, there's no more desire, no more sexuality. In all my twenty-five years of work in this field I've never seen a heterosexual married couple that functioned along a line of desire. Never. They don't exist. So don't say that I'm marginalizing sexuality with homosexuals, etc., because for me there is no heterosexuality possible.

G. S.: Following the same logic there is no homosexuality possible.

F. G.: In a sense yes, because in a sense homosexuality is counterdependent on heterosexuality. Part of the problem is the reduction of the body. It's the impossibility of becoming a totally sexed body. The sexed body is something that includes all perceptions, everything that occurs in the mind. The problem is how to sexualize the body, how to make bodies desire, vibrate—all aspects of the body.

G. S.: There are still the fantasies each of us brings. That's often what's interesting in some homosexual writing—this expression of fantasies that are very specialized, very specific.

F. G.: I don't think it's in terms of fantasies that things are played but in terms of representations. There are fantasies of representations. In desire what functions are semiotic flows of a totally different nature, including verbal flows. It's not fantasies; it's something that functions, words that function, speech, rhythms, poetry. A fantasmal representation in poetry is never the essential thing, no more than is the content. Fantasy is always related to content. What counts is expression, the way expression connects with the body. For example, poetry is a rhythm that transmits itself to the body, to perception. A fantasy when it operates does not do so as a fantasy that represents a content, but as something that puts into play, that brings out something that carries us away, that draws us, that locks us onto something.

G. S.: Aren't there fantasies of form as well?

F. S.: Fantasies of form, fantasies of expression, become in effect micro-fascistic crystallizations. This implies, for example, in scenes of power of a sadomasochistic character: "Put yourself in exactly this position. Follow this scenario so that it will produce in me such an effect." That becomes a kind of fantasy of form, but what counts there is not the application of the fantasy, it's the relation to the other person, it's complicity! Desire escapes from formal redundancies, escapes from power formations. Desire is not informed, informing; it's not information or content. Desire is not something that deforms, but that disconnects, changes, modifies, organizes other forms, and then abandons them.

G. S.: So, a literary text escapes all categorization as well as any sexuality that can be called one thing or another?

F. G.: Take any literary work you love very much. Well, you will see that you love it because it is for you a particular form of sexuality or desire, I leave the term to you. The first time I made love with Joyce while reading *Ulysses* was absolutely unforgettable! It was extraordinary! I made love with Kafka, and I think one can say that, truly.

G. S.: Proust said it: "To love Balzac; to love Baudelaire." And he was speaking of a love that could not be reduced to any one definition.

F. G.: Absolutely. And one doesn't make love in the same way with Joyce as with Kafka. If one began to make love in the same way, there would be reason to worry—one might be becoming a professor of literature!

G. S.: Perhaps! Then literature can be a liberation of desire, and the text is a way of multiplying the sexes.

F. G.: Certain texts, texts that function. Nothing can be done about those that don't function. But those that do function multiply our functioning. They turn us into madmen; they make us vibrate.

Translated by George Stambolian

Hélène Cixous

Rethinking Differences

An Interview

Since Hélène Cixous granted this interview in 1976, her beliefs about women have undergone great changes, and she now hears the opinions expressed in these pages as emanating from a voice that belongs completely to the past. Both political and biographical distances separate this text from her more recent writings. We respect Hélène Cixous's altered position, although our interest in the document that follows has not wavered.—*Eds.*

INTERVIEWER: You have pointed out that masculine sexuality gravitates around the penis, engendering a centralized body. How could one, by contrast, define the feminine libido?

HÉLÈNE CIXOUS: Sexuality and libido are not synonymous. We're always finding ourselves in a delicate area where culture and whatever escapes it are obviously interwoven, and everything we talk about is trapped in this kind of overly inscribed, knotted, and complex sphere. I think feminine sexuality is organized quite differently from masculine sexuality, and when I say organized, here again one must consider the enormous cultural element. But there is also the libidinal element, that is, whatever is untamed and feeds into the cultural, and can be described by all sorts of metaphors. Personally, I would conceive of it, I would describe it, by means of metaphors of effusion, overflowing (*épanchement*). I think feminine sexuality is distributed throughout the body. It does not need to organize itself centrally and at the same time make itself erect, as is the case for a man, whose body must yield to the command of the ruling phallus and whose pleasure (*jouissance*) is "phallocentralized."

Q.: Is that the difference between diffusion and erection?

H. C.: One should consider the two bodies: they are oriented toward very different things. For a woman, I think in terms of overflow, in terms of an energy which spills over, the flow of which cannot be controlled. It's related to effusion, which, to continue with metaphors, is a source, a source of anguish, woman's anguish as well as man's, because culture, on the contrary, demands that we calculate, plan, that we reach an objective (*une fin*), because in the cultural sphere one always works with an end in mind, from which a well-regulated little circuit is planned.

Q.: To establish itself, the feminine discourse has at its disposal nothing but categories, metaphors, rhetorical modes that have been borrowed from the masculine discourse, which has always existed in these forms. Is it possible, then, to effect a dephallocentralization while still using this traditional discourse?

H. C.: I think, first of all, that what organize, imprison, censure, are models, the fact that there are modes of thought, models, ready-made structures into which one pours all that is still fermenting in order to congeal it. But metaphor breaks free; all that belongs to the realm of fantasmatic production (*la production fantasmatique*), all that belongs to the imaginary and smashes language from all sides represents a force that cannot be controlled. Metaphors are what drive language mad. This process can be very rigid, it can be very tightly organized, there can be a rhetoric of metaphor, and you'll find there's a kind of poetry organized in just such a way, but it is first of all through figures that language is dislocated. In other words, I think that one must work on the metaphor; but one must work on it by trying to pull it, as far as possible, away from the *strict meaning* to which it always refers, to which it always alludes; it must be drawn toward the figure and away from the strict meaning.

Q.: You have pointed out that our entire system of thought is established on the basis of oppositional pairs, of binary oppositions. If the oppositional pair is what establishes all ideology, how can we escape this eroticizing of inequality.

H. C.: That is *the* question I am always asked. The people who have decided that the world is unalterable usually say to me: it is the cultural element which speaks, isn't it? We are formed by what is cultural so we do not really see what could change. Because they unconsciously establish the cultural element as the basis of all things, they in effect see it as natural! From the very moment that anything connected to desire begins to speak up, and begins to speak against the established forms, against what closes, what codifies, from the moment an anticode arises, it necessarily indicates that there is an open channel. It's a narrow channel, to be sure; it is perhaps, for the time being, only a crack, perhaps hardly a fissure. Nonetheless, it has always existed, otherwise the woman's movement would not exist, nothing would have ever come about to say whether *something else* existed. The very question of a *something else* indicates that there is always otherness. It is from this point that we must work.

Q.: Does the work of people like Gilles Deleuze and Félix Guattari—for example, the *Anti-Oedipe*—seem to you to be of some use in bringing about the advent of the feminine discourse?

H. C.: I don't know if what Deleuze proposes directly concerns the feminine discourse. What he does belongs to the general strategy of deconstruction which is being carried out in France by contemporary philosophy, and it is of course a very important thing. But for me it remains a part of the settling of accounts between philosophies; it remains in the game. This does successfully, even though it always runs the risk of being trapped in and related to the philosophical discourse, and cannot avoid the curse of the philosopher, which involves the constant production of concepts, even those he labels anticoncepts. I think that Deleuze is inevitable, necessary, but what does his work bring to women? Every blow dealt to the establishment has a positive countereffect, of course, as far as the woman's movement is concerned, but it doesn't contribute directly to femininity.[1] Anyway, that's not at all his objective. And nowadays, only works produced by women can contribute something to the reflections on femininity.

Q.: So then, one could say that the feminine discourse is something which refuses all conceptualization?

H. C.: It is a discourse which refuses the trap of concepts, that is to say, which is not trapped by a concept that comes to preestablish what the place of this discourse will be or to teach it its own rules. That's what it is first of all; on the other hand, it is a discourse which does not completely refuse to conceptualize, but does refuse to define the concept as absolute. The master's discourse (*discours de maîtrise*), the philosophical discourse, is a way of speaking and thinking which tends to appropriate an external reality (*un dehors*), to circumscribe it, to label and conceptualize it, with all that the word "concept" implies in terms of capture (concept: etymologically, means something that seizes. Violent grip, rape, abduction. A concept has something of the seducer about it). It is a discourse that seizes, congeals. One must recognize to what extent the master's discourse is a fragile, completely ephemeral and transitory one—an instance of thought motivated by calculation and wariness. I think that women can speak of what is related to the real without having to produce a discourse which imposes itself as definitive, as impossible to exceed or surmount, and that they can do this without adopting merely an opposing position. Women "unthink" without restraint (*Elles* [*dé-*] *pensent*).

1. The word *féminité*, which is translated here by its direct equivalent of "femininity," is used by Cixous in the strict meaning of "what pertains to women." It has nothing to do with the common social usage of the word which has become grafted upon its essential meaning, and which implies effeminacy, coyness, and all other characteristics that have been distributed on only one side of the arbitrary social polarization, and erroneously attributed to "nature." The same, of course, goes for Cixous's use of the words "masculine" and "masculinity."

Q.: You have said that the feminine libido is cosmic and that its unconscious is global: "Ultimately the inexhaustible imaginary capacity of the feminine will unfold." What do you mean by that?

H. C.: This also belongs to the realm of metaphors, but a metaphor, once again, refers back to something beyond the strict meaning it represents and beyond the figure itself. This is how I see it: contrary to what characterizes masculine structures, that is, a tendency to edification, to centralization (which inserts itself within a political reality under the guise of state, of leader, of nation), which goes back to the father, back to the mind, back to government, the feminine libido is a spreading-overflowing. It spills out, it is limitless, it has nothing to do with limits, and I am sure that woman's body cannot not be fantasized about (*fantasmé*) if one considers it as an expanse of land, as a territory, as regions, as precisely what spills out beyond the state, expanding, globalizing itself easily. It's related also to woman's constant openness toward others.

Q.: Genet has written that when a man fucks another man, what results is a double male. Here in the United States there are large numbers of feminist lesbians who claim that the lesbian milieu is the most conducive to the growth of a feminist discourse because the male's presence is totally excluded. Do you see in this lesbian doubling a kind of superfemininity that furthers such growth?

H. C.: That's a complicated question. First of all I can't speak about the situation in the United States, since I don't know it well. When I find myself with American women, I am aware mostly of the differences. Therefore I can speak only for France. As far as what I see in France, terms aren't used in the same way that they are here. For example, when one speaks of "lesbians" in France, in the milieus related to the woman's movement—because among the general public you find total confusion—definitions are assigned in rather precise ways. Those who are called "lesbians" are women for whom the world is, in fact, analogous to the world as it is, but displaced, inverted, and reappropriated by them. Lesbianism gives way to the latent "man-within," a man who is reproduced, who reappears in a power situation. Phallocracy still exists, the phallus is still present in lesbianism. What it reveals is a woman who "makes like" (*fait*), "counterfeits" (*contrefait*) a man. On the other hand, there is a homosexual side of feminism. It is a dream of femininity, a sort of fiction that resembles the philosophical fictions of olden times. It is a sort of projection of another world, removed from the world as it is now, and implies that it is not worth staying here if you are always being cast in the victim's role. And this dream which tears out radically, which uproots, establishes a new system of human relations which is, in effect, absolutely uncontainable, incompatible with the present world: the dream of an exclusively feminine world, yet one which involves *another dream,* a dream of things to come, the dream of a man to come, one who may appear but hasn't as of now. He is not excluded from these fantasies. Except that the homosexual women I know do not believe they will know this man of the future. However, they do not exclude the possibility of change, change mediated by departures, by break-outs as violent as theirs. They do not exclude the possibility of a transformation whose results would be felt only in the long run. So there is a homosexuality which is entirely feminine and has nothing to do with heterosexuality, and which leaves no room for man such as he is. It's as if one had embarked on a vessel. It has lifted anchor and has completely entered into the feminine. Everything is lived and enjoyed between women, and among them circulates a sort of composite affection, a maternal, sisterly, filial diffusion, or some such combination. And it all functions particularly on the level of nonpower. "Lesbianism" is what maintains power, a power situation, whereas with the entirely feminine homosexuality, that power relationship is disassembled.

Q.: Can one say that there are three types of discourse at the present time: a masculine discourse, a feminine discourse, and a neutral discourse?

H. C.: What would a neutral discourse be?

Q.: Perhaps an objective discourse, or a pseudoobjective one.

H. C.: Then it is necessarily a masculine one. The kind of discourse that does not state its sex, that does not give its name, is coopted by the masculine. Anyway, the masculine does not say: I am masculine. The masculine *is* masculine. There is no realization of the masculine by the masculine. It is characteristic of the masculine to repress the existence of any problem, of any *difference,* never to think of differences. I think that there is a repressed masculine, the results of repression and a repressive force itself, that there is also a somewhat weak feminine which is still searching for its identity, which is beginning to define itself; and that there also exists a "masculine-feminine," that is (but in very rare, very sporadic cases), a masculine which allows femininity.

Q.: Would this be, for example, the male homosexual discourse? For example, Genet?

H. C.: Genet, yes, but for me he is an exception because here again everything must refer back to the real. In general the masculine homosexual discourse appears to exclude woman completely, being a discourse completely limited to the masculine, which omits the feminine totally; this is obviously not the case for Genet. Besides, Genet's work contains not only a feminine element, but also a very pronounced maternal element; it's very much grafted upon a *primal* figure. In this respect, it shows itself as stemming from a masculine source: attachment of the son to the mother.

Q.: But if one takes the queen (*la folle*)—for example, Genet's character, Divine—whose homosexual personality parodies women, who imitates a lady, can this character give us certain insights into the situation of women? Can we say that when the homosexual acts like a queen he reveals to us in a privileged way, and by way of parody, the situation which has been imposed on women, and that in this respect he possesses a critical advantage?

H. C.: I think it reveals this to men. In some ways, I think a man necessarily feels solicited, whether in an agreeable or a disagreeable manner, necessarily is put in question by this type of transformation, or what *appears* as a transformation on the part of the transvestite. But all I can say is that for women this does not matter at all, not in the least. This disturbance within masculinity can't bring anything to a woman. It is a resistance to the crushing by masculinity of the femininity of masculinity, but it is really only the preoccupation of men. It may be the femininity of the masculine which appears and shows off, but it is very obviously a femininity which is fantasized about. A woman cannot recognize anything of herself in a queen.

Q.: She cannot even recognize the queen under the guise of parody?

H. C.: No. I think that transvestites are of no concern to women. I am struck by the fact that in France, they call the guy who acts like a girl *la folle*, because in my opinion it is exactly that, femininity going crazy (*l'affolement*) within man. In any case, it is something which is always pushed to the second degree of reality. The queen is in a state of imitation, of mimicry. It's the famous "mascarade." However, woman's most important problem is to stop being forced into this kind of mascarade, which is imposed on her as "truth"; that is to say, woman seen by man, but supposedly as pure mascarade, a mascarade without substance, a display without substance, an ornament. This display is still related to the phallus: showing what one doesn't have, what one is afraid of not having.

Q.: What would be the difference between this combination of masculine and feminine in the perverse form of the queen and true bisexuality?

H. C.: That seems obvious to me. I think that the queen—you know, it really bothers me to talk about this precisely because I'm not a man, so I must speak with caution. It seems to me that the queen makes a choice, that is, she decides, she "recognizes" herself in femininity; she does not recognize herself in masculinity. In other words, something is excluded. Bisexuality is obviously not the same thing. First of all, we can see that bisexuality functions in the realm of the *imaginary,* that it is a potential for movement, for alteration if you will, of the individual along the line of differentiation. But this bisexuality, inscribed in the imaginary, does not involve adults, in my opinion, as it does children. Bisexuality is in fact primal (*originaire*), and a child does not define itself immediately as male or female. There is still confusion, still an effect of polymorphism. During adulthood, however, bisexuality can be kept in play only by interacting with another, with a true other. Bisexuality does not consist in being heterosexual and homosexual at the same time, that is, in leading a double life, acting now like a man, now like a woman; rather it consists in being with another, a woman with a man, in a state of dynamic exchange which is so intense, an oscillation of this exchange which is so rapid, in desires which are so strong, that the very process of crossing toward and through the other is made possible, and that something happens that allows woman to go as far as possible into the masculinity of the other, not into her own "masculinity." Of course it also has a reverse effect so that if she has a particularly strong streak of masculinity, it is reactivated. I see bisexuality being played out between two people; in no way do I confuse it with "androgyny."

Q.: The homosexual discourse reveals very clearly the prick at the center of everything, the phallus, the penis, whatever you want to call it at its various levels. There is also the figure of the male as prick and as killer, and I think this takes its sharpest form with Genet. But on the other hand, there is a tradition which represents death in the form of female beings, and I wonder why a system that is centered on the male, bearer of the penis and murderer, on the male killer, ends up assigning the death figure to woman. It's total hypocrisy.

H. C.: It's simple: it's like a mirror effect. But to return to the killer in Genet, it is not so much the killer as the assassin *caught,* because he is always and instantly imprisoned by opposites. The god for Genet is the assassin *condemned to death*; the executioner's child (the executioner being a tender and monstrous mother, the mother-Law).

Q.: The assassin condemned to death or else, as he says, the synthesis of opposites which takes place in the German police, when crime becomes law and decks itself with legality. There's a moment when he says that ultimately the great figure for him is the French Gestapo.

H. C.: That's the figure of the supreme queen, it's the very sublimation of the queen. The passage where he writes this is in *Pompes funèbres.* It's an act, it's also Genet's primal scene. He's always on stage. However, what he's done here is to insert a figure of death, with the morbidity that it represents. I mean it's like going toward death, giving death and going toward death. And you said that it is strange that afterward it is the woman who represents death—well, that's because by definition she is the dead one. It is she who is the *killed one,* and therefore she who points to death. It is definitely she who embodies the death figure.

Q.: Could you explain the situation in which woman's head is cut off?

H. C.: Yes, I think this is essential. Obviously, if women have remained in this state of acceptance, of passive complicity with the bad trick that has been played on them since the beginning of time, if they have allowed themselves to be subjugated, raped, killed, always forced back to the bed-coffin, it's because things have been planned in such a way that they cannot escape this state; and this is accomplished by cutting off their heads, where thought resides, by taking away from them the means of raising their consciousness. One can say that culture has always managed to reserve sublimation for men, to reserve thought for men, and to give women a stupefying antieducation. Education, for women, has always aimed at teaching them inferiority, incapacity, inadequacy, and teaching them to blame it on nature. They have been denied the positive utilization of the "symbolic" (I use, here, the term "symbolic" in the Lacanian sense, that is, as access to language, and to law). And I say that instead of castration, woman suffers decapitation. It's massive, it's absolutely frightening. However, it is exactly the same for all structures of oppression: when dealing with slaves, first and foremost you cut their heads off. That's why if a revolution is to take place, there must first be a fundamental process of education; as long as the oppressed aren't given the opportunity to *think actively* about their oppression, well, they'll remain oppressed.

Q.: We always hear it said that one of the main characteristics of French literature and culture is the fact that for a very long time they have included the voice of women, of women writers, the influence of women, and that in France, perhaps more so than elsewhere, the beginnings of feminine expression came about very early on. Is this a myth?

H. C.: I think it's a myth. In any case you can't lose in saying that sort of thing about any culture; but this kind of statement generally indicates a reactionary position: it's really because you're trying to salvage the past. Obviously, you'll find that everywhere some individuals have managed to escape the massacre. History has always functioned that way. Moreover, France can usually give this impression in that perhaps women have had at their disposal a more elaborate language than the one you find in the States. But that doesn't concern women only—it goes for men, too. It's a general link with the culture which necessarily extends to all who are subjected to it, and it is what accounts for the fact that in France even feminine language can appear more elaborate than elsewhere. It's a completely normal phenomenon. You must not forget that a trick of the phallocentric war is to fabricate codes that concede a certain place to women.

Q.: For example, courtly love, the courtly movement, which in general is described as the continuation of a feminine discourse, and as men's initiation into a type of discourse which they had ignored until then.

H. C.: That point is always made, of course, so we are going to have to do away with this example some day. But one should always carefully analyze the entire situation, studying, for example, what it all meant at the time—in other words, in whose hands the power rested then, who held it, what it implied politically, whom it benefited, whom it served, and whether it wasn't the perpetration of a system of escape valves. I think that one has to go back to Michelet's *La sorcière*. It should always be made clear that what took place, with respect to the feminine *body*, was a sort of resistance which little by little receded, that this resistance went through a phase of sublimation linked in particular to language, and that it was extinguished. And, once more, what this represented in terms of symbolic gains for men should be noted. What did it give them, what did it bring them? Didn't it rectify, in an absolutely necessary way, a matrimonial regime which was unbearable and which made adultery inevitable, so that adultery had to be regulated according to, among other things, poetic codes?

Q.: Do you consider that Michelet's texts on the witch, on woman, are valid texts?

H. C.: Oh yes, I find it all very beautiful. He's truly an extraordinary person.

Q.: Where did Michelet get his vision, his intuition, his style—which stemmed, after all, from a totally masculine discourse?

H. C.: But he's an exceptional being. There have always been exceptions. I think that he truly loved woman, that he understood what was alive, untamed, tragic in the feminine. Who is the man, anyway, who had the fabulous idea of doing research on the witch?

Q.: Could we think of other men who might have an equally salvageable discourse, or who can still bring us something today?

H. C.: Yes, the ones I mention in *La jeune née*. Having gone through literary texts innumerable times, I would put Kleist in first place because every single one of his texts is a true text of freedom. Next, there are passages in certain texts, in Shakespeare, for example. All the texts that concern *passionate love,* as they call it, are texts through which a certain current of femininity flows. But when I say "all the texts" that concern passionate love, well, if you attempted to gather them together, you'd realize that there are extremely few. Maybe someone should do research on the disappearance, in literature, of the text about passionate love. It didn't happen by mere chance. Love necessarily means opening up to another. As society has installed itself increasingly within phallocentrism and found ways to make a profit from an economy based on the repression of women, fewer and fewer texts about love have been written.

Q.: The natural tendency in the homosexual movements and in the feminist movement, at least in the United States, is to go out immediately and find archives, works that were written in the past. Yet in *La jeune née* you mention Kleist, Shakespeare, but you give no examples of women.

H. C.: Yes. I was writing about France, although I did mention Kleist, etc., and as far as France is concerned there are none. Personally, I have never found a woman's text which affirms woman's strength with such ardor.

Q.: How about Colette?

H. C.: Colette, of course. We should include Colette; I'm sure I'm wrong there. I don't know her work very well.

Q.: In *Le pur et l'impur,* for example?

H. C.: *Le pur et l'impur* is indeed very beautiful. At the same time, I'm not sure why, it doesn't seem to me to be a great text. What I'm saying here is very superficial; of course I would need to examine this text more closely, at the level of the signifier. However, I have never been caught up in it. I pick it up and it leaves me again. Generally, Colette doesn't have a grasp on me. As far as I'm concerned, she's not that great. It's a terrible thing to say, isn't it? Yet it's also true that she's someone very, very important. Her text communicates the body as few texts do.

Q.: There's Duras too. What fascinates me about her is her intelligence.

H. C.: Here, it's a question of writing (*écriture*). I mean that when there's nothing "writable," I can't respond; and confronting a classical style doesn't interest me. I totally disagree with Marguerite Duras ideologically, but not at the level of writing. There's something very powerful in her works, like a mathematics of style, a signifying artfulness, which seems to me prodigiously controlled and yet which carries her *farther,* fascinated, overtaken by her own movement, by her own unconscious, and I find this very important. Perhaps what bothers me in Colette is precisely that there are so few things that carry her beyond herself. It's all so perfectly controlled, so well substantiated. It's not mad, it's not excessive. Duras is excessive.

Q.: What you say is disconcerting, because if one thinks about the idea that the existing discourse is the kind which focuses on man and on death, as Michelet realized, then I see Colette as a discourse of life, perhaps not a perfect one, but at least a beginning.

H. C.: That's true. . . . I suppose that I must stop here, first of all because I do not know her well, and then because her texts, at least the ones I have read, are definitely integrated within a certain social milieu, and one in which I feel ill at ease. It's a little like Proust, except that with Proust I willingly go beyond my social reticence, because it is all so immense that it carries me away, despite everything. I worked for a year on Virginia Woolf with my students. Her writing is very powerful, her text registers a feminine unconscious, but it is an unconscious in pain. It involves such loss, such destruction, such fascination with death, it is so much a way of circling around death until being plunged to the core of it, it is so much a way to call for death ceaselessly and to claim oneself dead that it also represents for me the "woman dead," the "woman killed." Therefore it doesn't speak to me because what I feel like working on is the woman alive and to come. But Virginia Woolf can't stop watching herself die, without ever being able to see herself dead, not even managing to economize on death. It's poignant, frightening. I'm not comfortable with it, although I recognize the greatness of the writing. You say that over here one seeks out models from the past; I think this is done precisely because of that fear of facing the void. When you begin to speak of a text in the feminine you wonder: where am I if not in eclipse or in absence? I truly regret that we react with the facile gesture of protection, which leads us to turn to antecedents, if we can call them such, when really everything has yet to be done. The text in the feminine is, fortunately, almost without precedent.

Q.: What do you think of the idea beginning to arise, that critical thought is concentrating too much on sexual matters, and that a phase of obnubilation has succeeded one of repression?

H. C.: I don't know. It's not a dominant phenomenon in France. I would tend to think that it is more widespread over here. What I see being published in the United States are discussions of sexuality as it is practiced, not at all on the level of the unconscious. This kind of discourse, with its commonplace effects, cannot avoid being repressive in certain ways.

Q.: It is rather practical and very pragmatic.

H. C.: Exactly. It is perfectly repressive because it eventually separates sexuality from what produces it, namely the total human being. It separates it from the origin of desire, from everything which belongs to the fantasmatic. It separates it from the unconscious, and so you are left with a body-machine, how to arrive at such and such results with it. That's truly unbelievable. It seems to me that under the guise of removing censorship, this approach is really a complete misreading of sexuality.

Q.: In contemporary France, can you see a collaboration between the feminist discourse and the homosexual discourse?

H. C.: No. I don't have much to say on that subject precisely because they keep away from each other. The political stakes for each are very different, their struggles do not cover similar grounds, and there is no dialogue between the two problems. The woman's movement sees *feminine* homosexuality as a necessary moment, both in a woman's life and in a historical feminist practice. But this refers to feminine homosexuality, not to the other homosexuality, which does not intersect at all with the feminist path.

Q.: In the United States they still think their political interests are almost the same, and therefore that a collaboration must take place.

H. C.: There is none of that in France. For example, there is no struggle for homosexual liberation, as there is here. Women in the movement do not fight as homosexuals; they fight as women. Homosexuality is integrated without anyone's questioning it. Whether you are homosexual or not is not what matters, you're not required either to be a homosexual or not to be one. Obviously, of course, latent homosexuality is present. In the woman's movement today, there is a current of thought which focuses on the results of the destruction of women by fascist states, fascist forms, and which studies what contemporary fascism still represents for women. At the same time, women are giving attention to the subject of rape as a direct result of patriarchy. Both analyses expose symptoms of the oppression exerted by the world of men-fathers. How can the problem of male homosexuality then, since this is what we are discussing, be assumed by the feminist discourse? Male homosexuals, those who are called pederasts, are men who do not like women except as mothers, which is why there is no possibility for alliance between women homosexuals and male homosexuality as it presents itself. Female homosexuality in

France is in fact oriented toward femininity and toward the woman's movement, and not toward homosexuality per se. Anyway, most of these women have been heterosexual and they're not fighting for homosexuality (which they practice openly) but rather for the liberation of women, all women, whereas male homosexuals fight for homosexuality. These are completely different struggles. There's no antagonism, but then there's no dialogue either.

Q.: There's another question I want to ask you. What do you think of the idealization of woman in surrealism?

H. C.: You know, woman is an object for most of the surrealists. They were really a group of pederasts.

Q.: Despite Breton's great declarations?

H. C.: Yes. I've never seen anything as atrocious as *Nadja*. It is so obvious that woman doesn't exist, that she's only a pretext, a body upon which to graft some little dream. Except for the great saga of Aragon and Elsa.

Q.: Aragon and Elsa—does that seem to you to constitute a legitimate discourse?

H. C.: Yes, I think so. I think that they related as different but equal beings.

Q.: Because she also spoke up?

H. C.: Not only that, but because she was certainly someone who imposed herself totally vis-à-vis another.

Q.: You said a strange thing, that pederasts don't like women.

H. C.: What I call pederasts are men who don't like the woman in woman, who don't like the being who desires, who is total, but rather the mother-womb (*la mère matricielle*). I should add that many of the men who appear heterosexual and macho are obviously pederasts. What they love in an other is only their own narcissistic triumph.

Q.: But when you use the word pederast, don't you basically mean homosexuals?

H. C.: No, because what about the queen? You can't call such a person a pederast. I am using the word in the Greek meaning of pederasty, which erected man as absolute good and woman as absence or threat. It's a world of men.

Q.: That goes contrary to an accepted cliché which says that the only Greeks who related to women, who understood them, because they never treated women as objects, were homosexuals.

H. C.: But that's not true for us, it's not true at all. I would say that masculine homosexuals who have good relationships with women are feminine homosexuals. But *pederasts* hate women. I think there's nothing worse than a pederast. For example, the patriarch, that typical pederast.

Translated by Isabelle de Courtivron

Alain Robbe-Grillet

What Interests Me Is Eroticism

An Interview by Germaine Brée

GERMAINE BRÉE: From the beginning—at least since *Le voyeur*—your books and your films have been highly charged with eroticism, thereby attesting to an erotic imagination which is peculiarly yours, and which differs from that of people like Georges Bataille or Pauline Réage, the pseudonymous author of *Histoire d'O.* Could you explain how you understand the link between eroticism and literary creation?

ALAIN ROBBE-GRILLET: No, I can't. I don't think a writer can ever explain that sort of thing. It's partly to try to understand such things that he writes. In the final analysis, the explanations are to be found in the books themselves. It would be very, very difficult, I think, for me to separate my books from explanations of how they work.

I'm struck by the fact that people readily acknowledge that certain of my works are strongly colored by eroticism, but think that others aren't: *Le voyeur* is strongly colored; *La jalousie* a bit less; *Le labyrinthe* not at all; *La maison de rendez-vous,* extremely colored, and so on. This is even clearer for the films, since there are commercial standards: films which no one under 18 may see; films which aren't X rated. Obviously

it's clear to the audience, but whether it's the result of some
sort of chance or coincidence, or, to the contrary, of a causal
relationship, I don't know. Now it happens that those of my
movies which were successful were also X rated, and were thus
those considered to be highly charged with eroticism. Members of the audience often ask me at the end of a film, "But
why do all your films have erotic scenes?" I say, "Which ones
have you seen?" "I've seen *Trans-Europ Express, L'Eden et après,
Glissements progressifs du plaisir, Le jeu avec le feu.*" I say, "Ah yes,
is that all?" "Yes, that's all." "But that's the whole point," I say.
"You haven't seen the others. What's interesting is that you
ought to be asking yourself why you've gone to see those films
and not the others."

I think that works in general, my works, particularly narratives, particularly film narratives, are in any event erotic activities, that is to say, produced by Eros and addressed to the Eros
of others. The classification "erotic work/nonerotic work"
seems utterly absurd to me. Back when *Les gommes* came out,
people talked only about the mania for description in my
novels. I had found a sentence in Kafka's *Diaries* where Kafka
says that the act of description is an erotic act, in the way the
sentence espouses the form of the object. The thing that made
an enormous impression on me was precisely the fact that
there is something typically erotic in this manipulation of
words with such care, such precision, such insistence. And
maybe those works which are the most openly erotic turn out
to be the least erotic, since ultimately there must be some sort
of release caused by the disclosure. As a result, to take an
extreme example, *Dans le labyrinthe* would be a more erotic
work than *La maison de rendez-vous.*

G. B.: But for the reader? You've talked about what it's like for
you, for the person who is writing. But how about for the
reader?

A. R.-G.: Well, reading and writing are sort of the same thing,
particularly in the case of modern works; and I think it's like
that for the reader too. He is a little taken in by the erotic
themes, and he doesn't see that there is also eroticism at work
in the structures, the forms, the movement of literature, etc.
This is even more apparent in the case of film: all films are

erotic films, ever since the famous film by Lumière, where all you see is a train coming into the station at La Ciotat, near Nice—a typically erotic image. And all the railway images and things like that which occur in numerous films—by Hitchcock and others—all the images of horseback riding, of revolvers, which occur in movies are erotic images, and it is as such that they work upon the spectator, even if he doesn't know it.

G. B.: How would you explain the great importance of eroticism, not its expression, but rather the interest that people have in it today, that the public has in everything which is explicitly erotic?

A. R.-G.: Everything which has openly erotic content, openly displayed . . . I don't know. That seems so normal to me. It's rather the time when that wasn't the case which astonishes me. It seems *obvious* to me that that should interest them. I only regret that they limit it not merely to so-called "erotic" works, but often, even in those same works, to the worst parts, that is, to the realistic depiction of sexual acts, and the like.

There has been for a very long time in our society a kind of Judeo-Christian puritanism which has played a very important role.

G. B.: Which has mystified the problem.

A. R.-G.: Yes, yes, which has mystified the problem, and all of a sudden there came a movement that changed things. Only twenty or thirty years ago people used to say, "Erotic books and erotic films are boring. They are boring because they're repetitive"—as if you were to say it's boring to make love because it's always the same! Or they said that they are written for frustrated people, for people who don't have the opportunity for normal activity. And for a very long time people held onto this handy idea. Now they are forced to see that that isn't true, that the people who go to erotic movies, hundreds of thousands of them, are really normal people: lower middle-class couples, or workers—a cross-section of the most normal elements of society.

G. B.: Yes, they go to see *Histoire d'O,* for example.

A. R.-G.: Of course, *Histoire d'O.* Now whether the images are literary images, in sentences, or film images . . . I'm obliged to confuse the two to a certain extent, you see, because if you start talking about the specificity of one or the other, it's going to complicate the problem a bit. But erotic representations, whether photographs, or drawings, or descriptions in books, play a role which is not at all that of the sexual act. They fill a need which is typically human. People used to say, "Eroticism reduces man to the level of an animal." That is absolutely astonishing! It's just the opposite, isn't it? Eroticism is what differentiates man from beast, precisely because it comes about through the imagination: it is the sexual act, but only to the extent that it is picked up by the imagination, which enhances the sexual act, which starts a sort of exchange all over again. It's typically man's; it's his greatest glory: man is an animal with imagination.

G. B.: Would the imaginary dimension of eroticism differ if it were filtered through a feminine imagination or a masculine imagination, or, for example, would you see a difference with a homosexual imagination?

A. R.-G.: Oh, I think that everyone has his own type of imagination. You can classify the main types of imagination, but to say that on one hand there's men's, and on the other, women's, would be very, very precipitous. But in any case, as far as man and beasts are concerned, a thought has just occurred to me: the experiments which were conducted where a male was shown a photo of the sex organs of a female. It didn't work at all on any of the lower animals (called "lower" in the sense of biological classifications, that is, progressive complexity). It began to work on the higher monkeys, on anthropoids: they showed interest in the photograph of the female's sex organs. You can show a cow's sex organs to a bull, but it does absolutely nothing for him; he doesn't understand what you're trying to tell him—it isn't real for him. So that clearly demonstrates that it's something that's a sign of evolution, and that insofar as man is an animal superior to other animals, he is indeed obliged to claim eroticism as one of his greatest glories, is he not?

Then you say: "yes . . . man . . . woman. . . . " For example, they said about *Histoire d'O* that it was interesting for once to see what the fantasies of a woman were. I don't think you can say that, insofar as it's a book written by a woman for a man, and probably a book written with a kind of man-woman complicity, where each projects back to the other. Because fantasizing, contrary to what has always been said, is not necessarily a solitary activity. It's also a means of exchange. And what would a woman write? Perhaps the fantasies of the same author, written for herself, to give herself pleasure, wouldn't be at all the same as those she would have written—she said so, didn't she?—to please the man she loved. Dominique Aury says so in *O m'a dit,* an interview conducted by Régine Deforges, published by Editions Pauvert.

G. B.: So Dominique Aury supposedly wrote *Histoire d'O* for Jean Paulhan.

A. R.-G.: She wrote it for Paulhan. Or perhaps they wrote it together; I don't know, I'm not familiar enough with it. Perhaps they really did both write it; no one has any idea how it was done. From the start, she's been the one who has collected the royalties, but what was Paulhan's role? It's a couple's fantasy, it's not necessarily someone's solitary fantasy. And what is interesting, when you see these individual personal fantasies, is that very often they belong to the opposite sex. For example, Catherine [Robbe-Grillet] will tell you that you find many more—I don't know anything about it, because I'm *certainly* not a homosexual, and I don't go with men, but she'll tell you that the number of men who like to be beaten is considerable, probably greater than the number of women. Theoretically, masochism is a feminine trait, isn't it? Man likes to beat woman, and woman likes to be beaten, according to society's stereotype. And it seems that an individual's real fantasies are often the opposite of his sexual group's. For example, the man who needs a dominating woman is very common, and it would be interesting to do statistics on it. We're not at that point yet, but perhaps we'll get there one day.

So as far as that goes, I absolutely refuse to put feminine fantasies in one group and masculine fantasies in another. All the more so because I'm a biologist by training, and I know that biologists have entirely given up considering women to belong to one category and men to another. There are characteristics which are called "female" and characteristics which are called "male," and which are both present to varying degrees in each individual. Hair, for example. If you inject a bald, bearded man with a strong dose of folliculin, he loses his beard and grows hair. Baldness is considered to be a sign of virility, and in fact, an abundance of hair is linked to a high folliculin level. On the other hand, a bushy beard is linked to a normal level. That's biology.

Of course, people like Simone de Beauvoir will tell you that biology doesn't exist. You know all her overstatements—about height, in particular. When I say that men aren't in one group and women in another, I'm not saying at all that everyone is equal. I only want to say that each individual is representative of his own personal make-up. But in biology there are always what are called "statistical truths," that is, statistically a certain trait may be considered to belong to one group and also to be linked to the presence of hormones. When Simone de Beauvoir says that girls are smaller than boys because they've been trained since childhood to be smaller (you know the line—they're told not to climb trees . . . all those ridiculous tales of Simone de Beauvoir's!), she forgets completely that if you inject a little girl with male hormones, she'll grow. After all, there is something that is connected to *Nature*. Well, modernists are horrified by the idea of Nature. There isn't any Nature at all, is there? Everything is existential and due to environment and to the ideology which society. . . . Yes, but it isn't true. It's very important to determine what is natural and what is ideological, because you have to admit that there are things which are natural.

G. B.: And eroticism, fantasies; for you they vary according to biological type?

A. R.-G.: Yes. For fantasies as for all elements of personal make-up there must be statistical types, that is, traits whose frequency of distribution is such that one can consider there to be a relationship among them. Each individual's fantasies are connected to a large number of things, but these things belong to two categories: natural influences and existential influences, these natural traits being the characteristics of either sex (because there are also things in our genetic heritage which can occur in one sex or in the other). Hence natural influences which include an individual's sex and also his heredity; and then, characteristics acquired either by the individual or by his group, which are thus ideological, and personal too, insofar as each individual's personal experiences can play a role in his own formation.

G. B.: Certain of your women readers say that your own fantasies are one hundred percent masculine.

A. R.-G.: They are very poor readers, I think.

G. B.: Do explain that to us.

A. R.-G.: Not because they are, once again, readers who have been unduly traumatized by the thematic content of the book, but by a thematic content which is present as a stereotype. All my books are organized around a kind of panoply of stereotypes that are carved out of the language society provides me. I live in society, I am part of that society, I am myself inside its ideology, and not exterior to it. But I see a system for maintaining my freedom within this ideological prison. The system is born of the New Novel and of all modern art—of pop art in American painting, and of modern music, too. It consists of detaching fragments from society's discourse and using them as raw materials to construct something else. In society's discourse, these are concepts, but I detach them from their context, take them as building blocks, I push them back to the status of signifiers in order to build another language, which is my own. But society's ideology is so strong that the reader, coming upon these detached concepts, reestablishes their ideological context, and as a result, falls victim, not to *my* ideology, but to *his own*. That's what has to be understood.

G. B.: Could you give us an example of how that works in *Glissements progressifs du plaisir*? I found it extraordinary.

A. R.-G.: You saw the film?

G. B.: No, I read the book.

A. R.-G.: Well, *Glissements* is a book which has been accused of phallocracy. Now I think that is truly hard to believe, and I'm going to tell you why. There are extraordinarily few directors who use a woman as a narrative center. Yes, there are in Marguerite Duras's films, of course, but in men's films, films called "men's"—films by Melville, for example—there are practically no women. In westerns: what is the role of women in westerns? Completely secondary. The narrative heart is one or two men: manly friendship, etc. A woman is not a narrating object, she's a narrated object, right? There are French examples of the same astonishing characteristics, and all French actresses know that there are very few directors—and I am one of them—who choose to embody a film in a girl: Annie Salvina in *Glissements* or Catherine Jourdan in *L'Eden et après*. So there's something, already, that ought to tip you off. Moreover, the film is an acknowledged adaptation of Michelet's *La sorcière*, that is, of a book written by a man but which is anything but phallocratic, since for Michelet, *La sorcière* was precisely the revolutionary principle, the principle of liberty in the midst of the ordered world represented by men. And that, in the most general fashion is how I see my novels as a whole, and my films as a whole.

Each narrative has an ordering principle and subversive elements. The ordering principle is always the voice of a white male narrator. The subversive principles are, to the contrary, always colored people, children, and women. And it seems to me that the best example of this one can give is *La jalousie*, in which there is someone in the middle of the narrative who tries to maintain order. But what is that order? It's middle-class order, it's an order which I can't be suspected of liking, given the fact that all my little efforts are, on the contrary, designed to subvert it. But this narrator is there, he places himself on the side of the house where the banana trees are all neatly ordered. He doesn't willingly go to the other side; he prefers the neatly ordered side because it is also under an overhang. So he counts, he classifies, he really tries to keep order. And then there is what disturbs him, his wife and the blacks. And his wife is suspected of understanding what the blacks say, and of going to bed with them. So there is, then, this order, which represents middle-class order of the most puritan and repressive sort, and, on the other hand, all the principles of, let's say, liberty or revolution, or poetry, or whatever you like, which are there, undermining and invading it. There is African nature, the banana trees, which start to grow wildly, and which are in disorder on the other side. There is his wife, whose movements are enigmatic, who is suspected of understanding the natives' language, who thinks the chauffeur sings well, etc., etc., and the blacks themselves, whose world is perfectly disorderly from the point of view of white organization.

In *La jalousie* it's not the heroine who's the narrative center, it's the hero, who wants to maintain order. But in *Glissements,* to the contrary, the heroine herself is the narrative center. She is there, and she's up against white adult males who are all derisory. They're representatives of the established order, such as you find in Michelet's *La sorcière*: the policeman, the priest—and they're *ridiculous.* They try at all costs to make her tell a coherent story, a proper story, but she absolutely insists upon throwing everything out of order. She destroys the order of the narrative, she destroys the system of causality, and she destroys propriety because she walks about naked and so on, and she does everything necessary to bring them, little by little, to a kind of death: the priest, who sinks into just the kind of madness described by Michelet, and the magistrate, who tries to grasp hold of words. It's very clear when one sees the film, because there's a very important scene in which the magistrate is surrounded by books, which are tables of laws of the society, dictionaries. He's lying on a bed in a scene that's a bit reminiscent of shots in Orson Welles's *The Trial,* where Orson Welles is on the bed, and the magistrate says some words and the girl throws other words back at him, words which he desperately looks for in his books, whose sense he doesn't understand, and which he pronounces in all different ways in an attempt to try to integrate them into a system of meaning. How can anyone say that this film portrays a phallocratic imagination! That seems *aberrant* to me, and at the same time it seems to me very clear, since people never see anything but their own fantasies, do they? They also used to say that Michelet liked to humiliate women, they said it because there are things about women's blood and their periods which seemed very disturbing.

G. B.: We've talked about the cycle of exchange with the audience. How do you explain the fact that people today seem to assign the greatest erotic value, in movies and in photographs, to a woman, by herself, who is in the act of satisfying herself?

A. R.-G.: The greatest? I don't know. Because I regularly look at all the erotic magazines and see all the erotic movies, I have the impression that it is indeed one of the most frequently recurring images, but not *the* most frequently recurring. I have the impression that here again there are different categories. It's very interesting; in pornographic bookstores in New York, the books are arranged by specialty. There are those who like this, there are those who like this, there are those who like that, and so on. And apparently quite often the imaginative elements are addressed to an audience different from the one which creates them; for example, two women together belongs to a masculine imagination, it's one of the great themes of masculine imagination. Two women together, and the woman caressing herself, it's true, is depicted very, very often, but much less often than other elements—fellatio, for example. That is the theme which is everywhere, absolutely *everywhere*.

G. B.: Could you distinguish homosexual sensibility in a text? Does there exist a distinctly lesbian homosexual sensibility which reveals itself in a text? Obviously, there's Monique Wittig, for example; it's so obvious because the content is. . . .

A. R.-G.: Monique Wittig is yet another category; she's militant. You've got to understand that the militant category is already falsified by its militancy. I don't know what Monique Wittig's fantasies are, since she no longer has anything to do with men, does she? She's even gotten to the point of refusing to let a man write an article on one of her books! There is in the whole feminist movement something unspeakably absurd because, as normal as it is to demand equality between the sexes in—how shall I say?—real life, that is, professional life, everything which pertains to nonimaginative life, when, on the other hand, you're dealing with relations between individuals, it is absolutely necessary to demand a freedom which includes even slavery if that's what someone enjoys, you understand? It's all right to say that it's necessary to demand equal pay for equal work, and so on, and that woman be equal to man before the law. But from the moment that imagination takes command, that is, in the life of the couple, equality is nonsense!

G. B.: And it doesn't matter what couple?

A. R.-G.: No, it doesn't matter: two men, two women, a man and a woman. From the moment that there is an exchange between two individuals, they ought to demand the freedom to play it as they wish.

G. B.: At the moment, some criticism in the United States is preoccupied by the question of homosexuality in literature. It's appearing all over. Would you be aware, if someone gave you an erotic text—let's leave militant texts to one side; it's thrust upon you, it's too evident—would you be aware of an imagination that was different from your own?

A. R.-G.: But of course not, because there again, you see, I don't believe that homosexuals are necessarily a separate category. I know *lots* of men and *lots* of girls who are both. I know lots of men who sleep with girls or with boys with just as much pleasure. As for me, it just so happens that I'm on the whole heterosexual—I'd even say very definitely heterosexual—but I'm something of an exception among my friends. The really determining factor is disgust, isn't it? There are all the intermediate stages between the man who's disgusted by women and the man who's disgusted by men, and the same goes for women. There are a great many girls who indulge in homosexual activities to please a man, when that really doesn't interest them. But, as for what truly interests them, I know a great many girls who are also disgusted by girls. And then there are girls who're disgusted by men, like Monique Wittig.

G. B.: In that case, it wouldn't necessarily be revealed in a literary text, it wouldn't come across in the writing?

A. R.-G.: No, no, except in the thematic content, if you like, when in Jean Genet's texts, or Tony Duvert's, there is sud-

denly a description, but which is often a provocation; when
you read Tony Duvert's adjectives, which are put there as
signs—about a little boy's penis: "A darling, pretty little
prick"—or God knows what. That's never, not even in those
cases, a literary parameter; it's a thematic parameter which
belongs to something else. But for me, Tony Duvert's novels
(and he's typically homosexual, isn't he?) are not, literarily
speaking, any different from other New New Novels.

Yes, I believe it's a question of themes, and I think that at
the present time there's much too great a tendency to set up
classifications like that. In short, that's the great danger.
What's necessary is that people try to figure out what they like,
because there's no longer any reason for them to do things
they don't feel like doing. Why should Monique Wittig sleep
with a man if that disgusts her? There's no reason, is there?
But from the moment people manage to figure out how to be
on good terms with their fantasies, and to live for them, too—
live with them, live for them. . . . If you've seen the stuff that's
been written about *Histoire d'O!* They're getting to the point of
saying that it would be immoral for a girl to have herself
beaten if she felt like it! But why shouldn't she? In the name of
what moral, I ask you? Why should there be a Ministry of
Women's Affairs with Françoise Giroud or somebody else in
charge, to say: "Forbidden! That's forbidden by the law!" It's
puritanism, it's puritanism, and I think it's gotten so excessive
now that we're going to have to come around to something
else.

G. B.: I have a question here that comes back again to the question of homosexuality. I don't think that's a topic which really
interests you very much, is it?

A. R.-G.: Not particularly.

G. B.: Exactly what do you think of a subject like "Homosexuality and Literature"? Do you think it's a valid topic?

A. R.-G.: Not in a course on literature. It would be a valid topic
in sociology, it would be a very valid topic for sexology.

G. B.: A topic for sexology. But for you it's not. . . .

A. R.-G.: Oh, you know, thematic criticism isn't very interesting
in any case. It wouldn't be any more interesting to me than

"Africa and Literature" or "Agronomy and Literature". You've got to admit that this extravagant desire to bring everything back to the same thing is present in the demands of certain minorities nowadays, isn't it? If you're a homosexual, you assert homosexuality, and if somebody asks you about literature: "Yes indeed, I have a subject: 'Literature and the Homosexual.'"

You know the famous Jewish joke about the conference on elephants? There was a big international conference on elephants. So each country sent a specialist: the Frenchman's specialty was feeding elephants, the German's was elephant sexuality, the American's was elephants' family life, and there was an Israeli who came with his paper on "Elephants and the Jewish Question." For homosexuals, it's something like that, and for blacks, too. At the end of a showing of *Marienbad*, a black confronted me to ask "Why aren't there any Negroes in that hotel?" It's *incredible!* He said to me, "But why? You must tell us. Do you think that it's because they're not good actors, and you wouldn't want to use them, or maybe you think that blacks couldn't stay in a hotel of that caliber?" It was insane, absolutely *insane*.

Themes don't interest me very much. In my own books there are a series of themes, for example, the theme of masculine sadism. It's a *major* theme, and very, very prominent, but in the final analysis, I can't say that it interests me. In any event, what interests me is eroticism, that is, sexuality to the extent to which it is filtered through the imagination; that is, to which it is an activity not of the sexual organs, but of the brain.

G. B.: I've not asked you all my questions because many of them pertain to homosexuality and I don't think you . . .

A. R.-G.: This book . . . why are there so many questions on homosexuality? Is the book being done by homosexuals? Or is it simply because it's fashionable?

G. B.: I think it's because the question of homosexuality has become so engrossing for some Americans that there is an attempt to try to untangle these themes a little. That's why the editors wanted so much to have interviews with people who aren't necessarily homosexuals, as well as others. Since it's clear that no one could consider you to be a homosexual, that's why it's interesting, because I don't think anyone would ever say, "Alain Robbe-Grillet is a homosexual."

A. R.-G.: I am not suspect!

G. B.: And that raises the question of imagination and the special imagination and the special fantasies of homosexuals.

A. R.-G.: But what really gets me is precisely the fact that now that we've discovered this freedom to be what we want, there are classifications once again. There is the women's movement, yes, the women's movement. Lots of feminist groups seem to want to establish categories again. Here in New York there are girls' nightclubs where they won't let men in! Things like that.

G. B.: Yes, I agree, but do you think that that is really going to affect their freedom of expression—literary or artistic or whatever?

A. R.-G.: I don't know. In any event, they've gotten pretty far now, since they claimed that the entire world was shaped by men and that they were excluded from it; that even *language* was masculine, and that as a result . . . myself, I don't really know what it's all about. Are they going to start speaking a different language from men, for example, because language belongs to men?

G. B.: That is a little bit what Monique Wittig does.

A. R.-G.: What she'd *like* to do! As far as I'm concerned, that's not how things should be done. That would be just the opposite of liberty, wouldn't it? Nowadays, of course, they tell men who say what I'm saying, "It's all well and good for you to talk about freedom because you're in power, you're part of the ruling class, etc."

G. B.: And the others—women, homosexuals—are oppressed.

A. R.-G.: Oppressed, yes, so they can't react in the same way, of course. But I can't take it upon myself to meet demands which aim to destroy me.

Translated by Anne L. Martin

Christiane Rochefort

The Privilege of Consciousness

An Interview by Cécile Arsène

CÉCILE ARSÈNE: The theme of this interview is homosexuality and literature, and I'll begin with a very theoretical question: What are your views concerning the relationships between sexuality, eroticism, and literature?

CHRISTIANE ROCHEFORT: I've never understood the meaning of eroticism. I have the impression that it's a purely intellectual aspect of sexuality, that it doesn't really have anything to do with sex, but is one of those devices that is supposed to stimulate sexuality. It seems to me that the idea of the erotic is primarily male even though women might make use of it. It wouldn't be the first time women have used something that belongs to men. But I see it primarily in reference to someone like Georges Bataille or Pieyre de Mandiargues—a sort of private preserve where they have to invent their own personal discourse on sexuality, an arousing discourse.

The relationship between sexuality and literature is very close, intimate. Writing stimulates sexuality. I have sexual feelings while writing that I have to quickly put down on paper. Afterward, when I reread what I've written, I have to cut out three quarters of it because it's too immediate.

C. A.: What role to you think sexuality should play in the relations between the reader and the text?

C. R.: There must be a certain intimacy on that level. I think it is one of the links between reader and author. But I also think oppression is a link. When I wrote *Les stances à Sophie*, for instance, the book did two things. It alienated me from most men. All the male critics, and many writers too, have hated me since I wrote it. It was a clarification, a sudden one. I had many battles. As for men, it was all-out war. They hated me and still do. They haven't forgiven me.

C. A.: The bourgeois must not have. . . .

C. R.: The bourgeois are used to it. They live off of that, swim in it. The bourgeois don't give a damn about criticism, they are indifferent. As for the women, they spoke of oppression. I got piles of letters from women who said, "So I'm not crazy after all, that happened to me, too." Nothing like "My husband's a bastard, he beats me." Nothing like that, but rather, "So I'm not paranoid; that book did me a lot of good." And then I've been named in a few divorce suits.

C. A.: What a triumph!

C. R.: Yes. On the level of intimacy in oppression, it's a triumph of communication. So for me, there is an intimate and necessary relationship between reader and author, because one completely fantasizes the voice that speaks. But if I could also show, touch, everything—a physical relationship with the reader. I have an intimate relationship with the guy who writes something for me. He writes to me. But I don't seek it out, because I wouldn't know how. I agree with Antonin Artaud. If it is a true creation, it is intended to communicate. If not, you might as well stay home; don't publish. Write if you want to—there is, after all, a purely intellectual, formalist literature.

C. A.: As for that literature, is there an erotic link between reader and author?

C. R.: Writers of formalist literature don't want anything to do with that link, except to consider it as an exercise leading to. . . .

C. A.: A kind of snobbery, a form of dandyism?

C. R.: Yes, you could put it that way. There is also a terrorist dimension. I can conceive of it as a communication with the reader in order to take power over him. For psychological reasons. One needs that to compensate for something, one needs power. I have often seen that kind of literature connected to people in power. It seeks to establish a power it doesn't admit. I think it is an erotic relationship in the sense of dominant/dominated.

C. A.: It's a sadistic relationship.

C. R.: Eroticism—finding sexual excitement in a dominant/dominated relationship. Maybe that is eroticism. It's also possible that it is one part of the definition. Maybe that's why I want nothing to do with it.

C. A.: Do you think there is a connection between a writer's sexuality and the creation of a literary text?

C. R.: Yes. I can say that lots of my fantasies appear in my books. The fantasy of relations between a little girl and a grown man who talks to her in *Les petits enfants du siècle,* for example. The kind of sexuality that doesn't go any further, doesn't go as far as what we usually call "making love," but is expressed in caresses, caresses that are not mutual, where the man is on his knees. That is a fantasy: that particular caress and a little girl, outside, in the woods. There I would say there is a direct connection. I would say there is the least connection in *Le repos du guerrier.*

C. A.: How strange, because one could get the impression. . . .

C. R.: One could get the impression that that book is linked to my sexuality. It isn't. In fact it's a sort of commentary on the alienation of woman. There is one thing missing in *Le repos du guerrier* and that's sex. Sex is *absent.* Sex, that is the desire, longing, feelings, and emotions that are really connected with sexual energy, with the body itself in its purely sexual manifestation. Sex is an organ of communication. But when you take a look at what actually happens, that's not at all what you see. The end result, what with the frantic socialization of that particular mechanism, what with oppression, alienation, exploitation, sublimation, recuperation, that's not at all what it's about. And then all those social obligations: the family and all that

nonsense. Sexual energy is worn down, it's been diverted almost one hundred percent. That's the basis of my own ideology on the subject, or of my vision, to be more precise. It's
clear in *Archaos*. That's where I express my ideas on sexuality.
It's not, strictly speaking, homosexuality, but polysexuality. It
often goes through a homosexual phase, a necessary phase.
For women it's a necessary and normal phase, I would say. For
men it's necessary but shattering. It shatters them. The exclusion of homosexuality prohibits moving on to communication
through sex and so prohibits real sexuality. To limit oneself to
heterosexuality is to not really comprehend, not be able to
comprehend.

C. A.: Comprehend?

C. R.: Yes. To comprehend in fact, in the sense. . . .

C. A.: In the original meaning of the term. Yes, that's it. And so
you have Julia and Céline say in *Les stances à Sophie* that
homosexuality is a luxury.

C. R.: Yes. What happens to Julia and Céline? They are two
women like ourselves. It takes place in 1961, *Les stances à
Sophie*, or '62, during a period of so-called sexual liberation,
when people thought they were liberated, women considered
themselves liberated. But there was no consciousness of oppression, then. Well, there was an individual consciousness of
something.

C. A.: But there was no collective phenomenon, at least not in
France.

C. R.: Right. So try to put yourself back in that period, the early
sixties and you take two married women who are deadened by
marriage, completely repressed, and who meet each other. It's
a meeting of the oppressed and a sudden consciousness of
their condition. It's the first socialization. They socialize as
much as they can and they end up in a loving relationship. It's
love based on sisterhood, a "sisterhood is powerful" where
sexuality is an extension of communication, as it has often
been in my relationships; and in my books, when it's really
authentic, it's like that. So there they are, the two of them, and
they have a loving relationship. They're afraid because
everywhere they go they run headlong into the label "lesbian,"

thanks to men. They're not used to it, they're heteros. Until
then they were naïvely hetero although if you examined their
past closely you could find little goings-on in the dorm, at
school, as for everyone else, all women. But one forgets.
Those things would have been written off as romantic schoolgirl crushes, a "phase," you know. They don't ever think about
it, and it was probably never acted on anyway. So there they
are, the two of them in a homosexual relationship. Scared
shitless of the label, *those women.* Seeing it as a label for others,
not *me.* When one of them looks at this prostitute in the street:
"God, am I becoming a lesbian?" Now that's where I come in.
Not with the fear, but with the word "becoming" a lesbian.
Passing from one category to another. Personally I'm not afraid of being a lesbian, of being considered a lesbian, and all
my life I've been considered a lesbian. I've always been what
they now call bisexual. That is, I've always been innocent in
that way. I know it seems false to say stupid, naïve. But it's a
fact I can't do anything about. I've lucked out sexually, and
I've taken advantage of it. I've loved people, and sometimes
it's been women, sometimes men, that's all there is to it. And I
haven't changed even though the women's movement has
given me a hard time about it. To stick labels like lesbian,
hetero on someone—I hate that. That plays a part in my work.
In any case, they are afraid to be condemned, singled out.

C. A.: "Condemned women," yes. . . .

C. R.: Lesbian, what a horror! I went through that when I was
18 or 19, at the beginning of my heterosexual life, that is,
when I started to sleep with boys, and it didn't do a thing for
me whereas sleeping with women did. And I said to myself,
Christ, I'm a lesbian, condemned. After things evolved a bit I
was no longer condemned. But the horror of being stigmatized for sexual morals, or other things for that matter, the
horror of someone labeling and imprisoning you is very real
to me and plays a role.

Julia and Céline tell themselves they're not lesbians. They're
married women. They wouldn't think of leaving their hus-
bands; they remain normal. They find it difficult to change
their tastes. That's the way they are; they prefer men, they're
not lesbians. It's a defensible position. They've reached the

brink but don't want to fall in, but they can allow themselves a luxury. Actually, I just wrote "luxury" like that. It came up in conversation between the characters. They consider themselves privileged. They were fortunate to have had a love affair with a woman, whereas others haven't. I should have put "privilege" rather than "luxury," though. But in any case, I would say that now Céline would have a stronger tendency to love women than before. She will not exactly become a lesbian, but will have a much lower threshold of tolerance for men than before. She'll have an anti-male reflex, maybe even a hatred. It's exactly like what happened to me. *Les stances à Sophie* is the only autobiographical book I've written. I became more and more intolerant, I put up with less and less from men. That's Céline afterward. That is, she will not be intolerant toward women who are not her oppressors, and she will be intolerant toward men. She can tend toward more openness to women and more intolerance to men. Then she can love only women. Because of this tendency, not because she has become a lesbian. In fact, that has been the case with many women who are called lesbians. It's just that one can no longer tolerate oppression. Céline certainly went in that direction. Even though she wasn't a born lesbian, as they say.

C. A.: Do you think that exists?

C. R.: No, I don't. But I do think there are women who have never tolerated men, who have never been able to, or whose first experiences were so catastrophic that they can love only women. That does exist, and I believe in their experience; it's the experience of a "born lesbian."

C. A.: Do you think there is any connection between the homosexuality of many twentieth-century writers and certain literary and aesthetic trends?

C. R.: Among men or women?

C. A.: Both.

C. R.: That's a very hard question. I don't think it's the same process for men and women. What I have observed personally, and it's widely recognized, even banal, is that most creative women have not accepted that their "anatomy is destiny." That is, they are people who would be "corrected" by

Freudianism in such a way that they would cease being creative. There are many ways of refusing that; for example, identifying as a male. An identification with male values. To be one of the boys. How can one be equal? One can't as long as one is a woman. So you have to be a sort of man in a woman's body: a body rejected and hated. No one loves women less than lesbians who hate the woman inside themselves.

C. A.: You think so?

C. R.: Well, it is strange for me to say something like that, but there is such a thing as self-hatred, the hatred of one's own female body, the hatred of one's femininity. It comes from a confusion between the social image and the reality that is in fact there. She hates the social image of femininity, of course. I certainly do. If I spoke rather bluntly just now, it's because I'm one of them. There is something in the rejection of one's own body that leads to male and female homosexuality. There is a masculine form of female homosexuality, and a feminine form of male homosexuality. In any case it does occur among people who reject their woman's body in the social sense. Not necessarily their woman's body in the physical sense. If one were to look for a synthesis, it would be Monique Wittig. That's really her *zone*. I have fantastic things in common with Monique Wittig, and fantastic differences, too. We have an extraordinary relationship. She's not easy, Monique Wittig, she's subtle, complex, and goes right to the heart of the problem, or problems. And then she feels them, lives it; but they've given her a lot of grief. The women's movement has. It's not easy to go through this movement, not easy for anyone. It's still an ordeal for women.

C. A.: So to get back to the question: you think there may be a connection between homosexuality and certain literary trends.

C. R.: I think there is a connection between the refusal of one's role as a woman and writing. There has to be. It's the same for men, but the process is probably completely different. I don't know to what degree we can know for sure, but when you see how many homosexual men there are among artists and how good they are, it seems there must be a female element in their creation. They admit it themselves, many of them. And even if they're not actively homosexual they recognize a female element in their work. It would seem that one must be double-sexed to be a creator. The person who isn't misses part of the world completely, and his stupidity is glaring as soon as you look at all seriously. To get back to literature—how does homosexuality influence the very forms of literature? I don't know.

But because we don't want men to look at what we do, I cut the intimate scenes between Julia and Céline. That's a direct relationship between sexuality and writing. I don't do it on purpose: it just happens. But there is a difference between what I'd call the style of the oppressed and the style of the oppressor. The oppressed sometimes imitate the style of the oppressor, but the oppressed have the privilege of consciousness. The oppressed know it, the oppressors don't. And the oppressed are weak. They must overcome fantastic obstacles. To speak from personal experience, I had to overcome two obstacles: the obstacle of class—I wasn't exactly born with Livy and Suetonius in my arms, good thing in one sense—and then the obstacle of sex. Others have to get rid of bourgeois clichés, and it's even harder to extricate yourself from those. But I had to get rid of the clichés of public elementary education, and then of my acquired bourgeois clichés after that. At least they were less deeply embedded in my head. I had choices, flexibility. One finds that on the side of the oppressed: flexibility, subtleties. It is likely that the writing of the oppressed is less cliché-ridden. When they succeed, that is; most of them don't. But once they succeed they are naturally more complete.

I think there always has been a relationship between certain literary trends and homosexuality. I can't sort it out very well. There may be a difference, but I would say it was a difference between the literature of the dominant and that of the dominated, rather than between homosexuality and heterosexuality. There is all of black literature, the poets of Latin America, Africa, Madagascar, the whole of the third world culture which is a literature of the dominated, and growing. I would include all of that. Included, too, is women's literature. You can choose whatever term you want: homosexual, women's, oppressed, third world, colonial. I consider women's literature as a specific category not because of biology, but because it is, in a sense, a literature of the colonized. We as women, one might say as homosexual women, are obligated to use the language of the oppressor, so what are we to do? It is difficult not to distort one's thinking in using the language of the oppressor. One must almost write as if twice removed, frame everything in irony and derision, or find other forms, another syntax, break down the whole thing. All of which would ultimately create a literature that would be more interesting, winning over the oppressed, in the end. But I would like to exhaust the social aspect before talking about biology, because if you don't deal with the social first you're going to get all messed up in the anatomy-destiny thing. I'm not sure one writes with one's person.

C. A.: Physiological person.

C. R.: Yes, or at least one's sexual person. The kind of difference that might exist between a lesbian—where there is one sort of acquaintance with women's bodies, one sort of approach, to be more precise—and women who are not exclusively lesbian: clearly there is a difference, in the sense that the latter field is larger. Monique Wittig, for example, is a very specific case. She is completely turned on to women's bodies. Consequently she uses words relating to women's bodies in great abundance: words like "clitoris," "vulva."

C. A.: In *Le corps lesbien,* for instance.

C. R.: In other books, too, such as *Les guérillères.* She likes those words. Now that's what you could call lesbian literature. Monique has a fixation, as do others, too, about sexuality, the body. The body is her subject. Obviously. But I think it's more specifically true of Monique than of lesbianism in general; she embodies lesbianism, exults in it. As for myself, I see no relationship between a specific physiology and what I write. Except a relationship of knowledge. I know the woman's body better than the man's. But imagination does everything. The proof is that in *Printemps au parking* I described two men making love. Nobody has yet criticized it from the point of view of what they do. On the contrary, everyone said, "How do you know about that?" I was quite pleased, I must say. I didn't

make any gross errors. How do you know about that? Imagination, what else. One can put oneself in the place of anything
at all: a cactus, a sea anemone. I'm for the fullest experience
possible. Because of my own comprehension, what they call
bisexuality (I hate that word), I'm for expansion and com-
pleteness, whatever. Not at all—as little as possible—for restrictions. And it has to come from personal experience.

C. A.: What do you think of the theory that all great writers and
artists are androgynous?

C. R.: Monique is a true lesbian. She loves women's bodies.
That's her primary concern; she's also reacting to the absence
of it in the world. She fills the whole space; she wants to take
that place that hasn't been filled. And she's right. For her it's
militant and emotional. You can easily understand why she
does it. That place has never been filled, but it has a right to
be. So she goes at it and takes that place; she can fill it, however, because what she writes is rather strong, I think. Even so,
she is androgynous. Ineradicably and paradoxically, inside of
herself she's androgynous. I thought there might be an exception, I said to myself, "There is Monique, after all." But no.

C. A.: She has both forms of sensitivity?

C. R.: She's a woman-man, man-woman, she's gone through a
long ordeal with herself and hasn't finished yet. No one has
finished, though . . . a love-hate ordeal with her sex.

C. A.: And it's clearly very ambivalent. But at the same time
very rich.

C. R.: That's androgyny. She spent a long time not knowing she
was a woman, or at least in a state of total ambiguity. So even
she is no exception because androgyny is a matter of roles, not
physiology. It's obvious that she represents a sort of bi-role, if
you can say that, but with such a mixed image that Monique
Wittig is not what you'd call dominant. She refuses the dominant role. That could lead you to believe that she has primarily
the image of a woman, and represents a bi-role, but without
the dominant role, which is also, somewhat, my own situation.
Bi-role, yes, but not dominant. That is to say, if I have a
fantasy concerning the male part of me, it's as an adolescent,
as a young boy. Before the traumas start to happen. And

Monique, too, I think. Monique is also a young boy in that sense.

C. A.: Listening to you, I wonder if maybe the male homosexual, who is very oppressed in French bourgeois society, is also in a position to express himself fully.

C. R.: Yes. As we were saying, there are the oppressed, that is, male homosexuals and women who are creative and potentially homosexual. They have to be, since they have transcended their sex, or in any case, transcended their role. It is very difficult to distinguish in the writing of women those who are homosexual, those who could be, and those who believe they aren't; they all are.

C. A.: For instance, Simone de Beauvoir broaches the theme of homosexuality.

C. R.: She didn't start out as a creative writer, you have to take that into account. She was already extremely blocked, inhibited on the creative level, when she wrote her books. She only started to open up creatively late, and with difficulty. It was painful. After that they gave her a lot of grief, which is hardly encouraging. All because she's a woman. It's a complex case, that one. Between where she is now and becoming homosexual, there is still quite a way to go. I don't know if it will happen. But it's really a question of time, it's a question of the rhythm of the whole procedure for Simone de Beauvoir, given the block at the start, the university foolishness. If she had started earlier, one could have put her on the right track. But she's somewhat tardy for a precursor. Her feminism came a bit late. Only now can she really begin to talk to women.

C. A.: We haven't really discussed *Printemps au parking*.

C. R.: We can't allow ourselves not to discuss *Printemps au parking* because it is, after all, the love story of two men, written by a woman. It is strictly homosexual in the sense that most people use the term.

C. A.: Is it made up of your fantasies?

C. R.: Yes. It is related to my fantasies. I certainly fantasized while writing it! I first wrote it in '65–'66. Then I rewrote it in '69. It's about an ordinary male student, not too misogynist, more or less aware, slightly opportunistic, but hetero, who meets an adolescent who is perfectly hetero. An adolescent from the suburbs, not the delinquent type. A little guy who doesn't do well in school, who feels a little rejected and runs away from home on a whim and ... they meet and start to talk. And it leads to passion. Neither of them wants it, God knows; but they end up by really giving in to it. And the scene that is described, the sexual scene, I don't think it could be categorized as erotic, or pornographic.

C. A.: But it is sexual. It's a form of sexual life.

C. R.: It's a physical passion—emotional, intellectual—and they have to admit it and then, what's more, realize it. I couldn't do otherwise with such a story. And yet I didn't expect it and I had written a first version in which it was the story of a friendship, just that. And then the boy returned home after having understood quite a few things. Pygmalion, something like that; it didn't satisfy me in the least. Then I took it up again, writing better this time. I realized, "What is this story anyway, they love each other, for Pete's sake." Then imagination did the rest. Pure imagination. I came to grips with a homosexual story at the heart of a book, but it was two guys.

C. A.: On reflexion, could you explain why?

C. R.: I couldn't explain why because it came in the writing, through the writing. I had given certain symptoms which didn't take hold of me in the first version, but did in the second. I can really say that it was a pleasure, that I was at home with it. I asked myself why I was so much at home and I answered, it's because there was no oppression. Even though I had two characters belonging to the dominant class. Apparently I eliminated all the factors of oppression. Ideally, the oppression of the oppressor, too, but not completely; in any case, I had two persons who were entirely free. After that I realized that I had male homosexual fantasies, too. I didn't have them "consciously," but it was something in me nonetheless.

C. A.: From another planet.

C. R.: But something that, all things considered, I would have liked. Had I been a man I would have been homosexual, too.

Both. Another triumph. Be all four sexes. All four. Yes. Finally, I must say that there is little literature I can conceive of that can do without homosexual relations.

C. A.: So that you think the topic of homosexuality and literature is a valid one?

C. R.: That it is valid is totally obvious, considering that all we've had up until now is heterosexuality and literature. So we should even things up a bit, right? It's a little one-sided. I think it's a valid topic. As for myself, I'd look at it from the point of view of oppression and literature. Oppression is my source of inspiration.

Translated by Marilyn Schuster

Monique Wittig

Paradigm

Desire

In the official discourse of sexuality which psychoanalysis has become today, desire is the "instinct" that makes a person, any person, desire heterosexual intercourse as the only sexual fulfillment and the only manifestation of one's subjectivity. The imaginary, dreams, desire, will, any concept related to subjectivity passes through this sieve and does not survive it. Heterosexualized, these concepts serve as vehicles of oppression.

As lesbians we can well ask heterosexual society: what have you done with our desire? with desire itself? A desire for the penis? A desire for children? A caricature. Something that is the opposite of pleasure—total boredom. What do you want to do with our desire? Make it fit in? Lobotomies, forced therapy. Force it to practice heterosexuality. Obligatory intercourse. Obligatory reproduction. If desire could liberate itself, it would have nothing to do with the preliminary marking by sexes.

Homosexuality is the desire for one's own sex. But it is also the desire for something else that is not connoted. This desire is resistance to the norm.

114

Difference

The fundamental difference, any fundamental difference (including sexual difference) between categories of individuals, any difference constituting concepts of opposition, is a difference belonging to a political, economic, ideological order. All categories that conceal and dissimulate this political, economic, ideological order issue from idealist thought that accepts in nature, or by divine will, differences that are given a priori, that are already there before any sociality. The difference between men and women is dependent on this thought. The difference established between heterosexuality and homosexuality is also dependent on it, even if this difference does not present itself in the same way. The idealist argument makes heterosexuality a "natural" sexuality and homosexuality a sexuality in opposition to "nature" (cf. the misguided efforts of certain homosexuals who seek in "nature" justifications for their sexuality—Gide). And in this sense the difference is indeed given a priori and as a constitutive, ontological difference. On the one hand, this difference also conceals social oppositions: political, economic, ideological. On the other hand, and from the point of view of homosexuality, one can only note that heterosexuality is not "natural," nor is it the only, the universal sexuality. Heterosexuality is a cultural construct designed to justify the whole system of social domination based on the obligatory reproductive function of women and the appropriation of that reproduction.

Heterosexuality

The concept of heterosexuality was created in the French language in 1911. It corresponds to an effort at normalizing the dominant sexuality undertaken particularly by psychoanalysis, despite its pretensions to being a revolutionary science. This concept is a rationalization which consists in presenting as a biological, physical, instinctual fact, inherent to human nature, the seizure by men of women's reproduction and of their physical persons (the exchange of women and goods). Heterosexuality makes the difference of the sexes not a cultural difference but a natural difference. Heterosexuality admits as normal only that sexuality which has a reproductive purpose. Everything else is perversion (see in Freud's *Three Essays on the Theory of Sexuality* at what moment a kiss becomes a perversion—when it strays from and no longer fulfills its function as a preliminary to intercourse. See in the same book all the argument concerning the "stages" of woman's sexuality through which Freud intends to make women pass by force so that they may fulfill their reproductive "destiny." See particularly the myth of the vaginal orgasm denounced a few years ago by Ann Koedt.).

Lesbianism

The most formal manifestation of lesbian culture took place in the sixth century B.C. in Lesbos, whence its name. It is difficult to know if this manifestation was created in resistance to the patriarchy, or if it always existed as such. What remains of Sappho's texts and the titles of lost texts by other poetesses of Lesbos give no evidence that this culture developed *against* the other, but rather outside of it, coexisting with it. To the extent that its origin is to be found outside the patriarchy, one could call it an a-patriarchal, a-heterosexual culture. I know that it is extremely foolhardy to play with hypotheses concerning so distant an epoch. Nevertheless, if one analyzes the art of Crete of the same period, there is every reason to believe that the patriarchy in these regions was not necessarily universal (cf. the frescoes of Knossos showing acrobats playing with bulls). What is certain is that the amazons fought the nascent patriarchy. Was it in homage to them that Damophyla, poetess of Lesbos, wrote her *Hymn to Artemis*? We will never know, since this epic was burned in Alexandria at the same time as the poems of Sappho. But there can be no doubt that war was waged against lesbianism. The systematic destruction of texts born from that culture, the clandestinity into which it has since been plunged bear witness to this fact. One has to recognize that lesbianism must have represented a grave menace to justify such a persecution, indeed a total obliteration, the most spectacular that has been carried out in history, together with that of the amazons. As early as the period of the Roman Empire, Ovid brought Sappho into line by making her the heroine of a heterosexual romance. There has been no worse betrayal than to assimilate, to adapt Sapphism to what was totally alien to it. What was the real menace represented by the Lesbians? They were a living proof that women are not born as the natural servants of men. What's more, they demonstrated that nonheterosexual societies are conceivable, that there is no norm for the constitution of a society. It is only logical that homosexual women look to Lesbos as the unique model of a culture of undominated women, a culture outside the heterosexual social field, where individuals practiced a subjectivity in no way marked by women's supposedly distinctive reproductive function. Pleasure for pleasure's sake, as Baudelaire, the lesbian poet, noted, characterizes this subjectivity/sexuality. Lesbianism is much more than homosexuality (the concept homologous to heterosexuality). Lesbianism is much more than sexuality. Lesbianism opens onto another dimension of the human (insofar as its definition is not based on the "difference" of the sexes). Today lesbians are discovering this dimension outside what is masculine and feminine.

Lesbians

As lesbians we are the product of a clandestine culture that has always existed in history. Until the last century Sappho was the only writer of our literature who was not clandestine. Today lesbian culture is still partially clandestine, partially open, in any case "marginal" and completely unknown to *the* culture. It is, nevertheless, an international culture with its own literature, its own painting, music, codes of language, codes of social relations, codes of dress, its own mode of work. Just as they are unlimited by national frontiers (the lesbian nation is everywhere), so lesbians come from all social categories. Outside the context of the feminist struggle, they already constitute "a 'criminal' subgroup or class. These individuals insist on living outside the 'law' of their class system," as Ti-Grace Atkinson wrote in *Amazon Odyssey*. Within the context of the feminist movement they have developed their international connections. They are there, present in the social field during the "fallow" periods of the feminist movement, because the development of their culture and the very fact of their physical existence are irreversible. Politically,

feminism, as a theoretical and practical phenomenon, encom-
passes lesbianism and at the same time is surpassed by it. Without feminism, lesbianism as a political phenomenon would not
have existed. Lesbian culture and lesbian society would still be as
secret as they have always been. On the level of theory lesbianism
and feminism articulate their positions in such a way that one
always questions the other. Feminism reminds lesbianism that it
must reckon with its inclusion in the class of women. Lesbianism
warns feminism against its tendency to treat as immutable and
determining essences what are simple physical categories. Let's
stop there in order to avoid overly broad generalizations, and
let's content ourselves with this minimal basis: Lesbianism is the
culture through which we can politically question heterosexual
society on its sexual categories, on the meaning of its institutions
of domination in general, and in particular on the meaning of
that institution of personal dependence, marriage, imposed on
women.

Sexuality

The emergence of women's movements and homosexual movements and their struggles have brought sexuality into the
political field. Just like women's movements, homosexual
movements demand the right to dispose freely of the body (of
the physical person appropriated by the political institutions of
heterosexual societies: you will be a mother, you will be a father).
This explains why the men of the Front homosexuel d'action
révolutionnaire shouted in the streets together with the women
of the Mouvement de libération des femmes, "we all had abor-
tions." The homosexuals who fight consider themselves to be
resisting the norm. For us sexuality has only a distant relation
with heterosexuality, since the latter is dominated by its final
cause, reproduction, and since the obligatory exercise of
heterosexuality, far from having as its goal the sexual expansion
of individuals, assures an absolute control of their physical persons. Homosexuals have in common with women the fact of
being only "sex." Homosexuals and women have been dismissed
from humanity.
Nevertheless, if the exercise of sexuality means for society

heterosexual intercourse, we are far from sexuality. We are equally far from understanding that famous idea of sexual difference on which our oppression is founded. For us there are, it seems, not one or two sexes but many (cf. Guattari/Deleuze), as many sexes as there are individuals. Even though they have enclosed us in a sexual ghetto, we do not accord to sexuality the same importance as heterosexuals. Sexuality is for us an inevitable battleground insofar as we want to get outside of genitality and of the sexual economy imposed on us by the dominant heterosexuality. Since sexuality has for us no finality apart from its own exercise, it must be above all an exercise of subjectivity that involves the search for pleasure and the creation of a unique being, irreplaceable, self-sufficient, whom no heterosexual reduction would be able to account for. All reflection on sexuality is new and in its historical context marked through and through by class oppositions (men/women). Such reflection develops these oppositions only to normalize them, to transform them into universals, thus producing a reduction of the entire field of knowledge. The official discourse on sexuality is today only the discourse of psychoanalysis that builds on the a priori and idealist concept of sexual difference, a concept that historically participates in the general discourse of domination.

Snobbery

Not so long ago any form of sexuality not belonging to the norm was called decadent, and consequently all forces of resistance to heterosexual society were supposed to prove the decadence of the system (weakening of "virility," that is, of the domination of women by heterosexual men). In the late Roman Empire the rise of feminist movements and the coming-out of lesbianism were supposed to have precipitated the fall of the empire by weakening the resistance (virile) to the barbarian invasions. That's the language of open reaction. There is another and more perfidious form of reaction to lesbianism, the one which consists in denigrating it and treating it as snobbery. It's in to be a lesbian, it seems; it's fashionable, it's snobbish. Colette already said it. One finds this same method of denigration in a May 1977 article in the *San Francisco Chronicle*. There would seem to be among feminists a "fashion" that consists in having at least one lesbian "experience" in order to be "liberated." And the author of the article calls that snobbery. Obviously, no one would think of saying that a male homosexual is a homosexual out of snobbery. On the contrary, the homosexuality of men is quite often considered with the greatest respect. Eternal and powerful Sodom, said Colette. That's because the fascination that masters exercise on masters is justified and even logical, for how a master can be fascinated by, and desire a slave is not very clear. And, in fact, if one judges by the expressions of "desire" that men use toward women (rape, pornography, murder, violence, and systematic humiliation), there is no desire there but rather an exercise in domination. So, if there is nothing less evident from the point of view of desire than the desire of a man for a woman, the desire of a man for another man needs no justification. On the contrary, from the heterosexual point of view it is completely incomprehensible that one woman (dominated creature) should desire another woman (dominated creature). Also, if in spite of the minimal interest that is offered to one woman by the companionship, desire, and attraction of another woman (how could she do without masters, the only ones capable of giving her a being?), if in spite of everything that woman is a lesbian, it's because she's trying to make herself interesting, to shock, to scandalize even. But certainly not because she wants to give herself pleasure. She's a snob, that's all. The best weapons of heterosexuality: denial of the phenomenon, recuperation (it's erotic for men to see two women together—harem lesbianism), ridicule.

Woman

Woman, female, are terms that indicate semantically that half the human population has been dismissed from humanity. Woman/slave, woman/dominated creature, woman/reproducer by obligation (woman/mother), "woman" like "slave" is a word, an irretrievable concept. The reality "woman" must disappear just as the reality "slave" after the abolition of slavery, just as the reality "proletarian" after the abolition of classes and of forced labor.

Insofar as the virtuality "woman" becomes reality for an individual only in relation to an individual of the opposing class—men—and particularly through marriage, lesbians, because they do not enter this category, are not "women." Besides, it is not as "women" that lesbians are oppressed, but rather in that they are not "women." (They are, of course, not "men" either.) And it is not "women" (victims of heterosexuality) that lesbians love and desire but lesbians (individuals who are not the females of men). And it is a fantastic "misunderstanding," (related to political dishonesty) that consists in reproaching them for "refusing their femininity"—just as one reproaches feminists who, as everyone knows, think only of taking the place of men.

The designation "woman" will disappear no doubt just as the designation "man" with the oppression/exploitation of women as a class by men as a class. Humankind must find another name for itself and another system of grammar that will do away with genders, the linguistic indicator of political oppositions.

Translated by George Stambolian

Eric Bentley

We Are in History

An Interview by George Stambolian

GEORGE STAMBOLIAN: Is there a distinctly homosexual imagination? A distinctly homosexual sensibility?

ERIC BENTLEY: There is no single and constant form of the imagination or sensibility that is well defined by the word "homosexual," but, on the other hand, it does seem possible to apply the word with some degree of cogency to a certain type of imagination and sensibility within a certain period and within a certain geographical limit—"this is how homosexuals at a time X and a place Y do characteristically imagine and feel." What other word would come to the mind of any reader of Ronald Firbank? Only homosexuals—in his time, using the English language—did camp it up that way. Of course, one must avoid using this argument in reverse: not all British homosexuals of the early twentieth century adopted that "lifestyle," were "camp" followers. It was an option the time and place afforded. To pick it was to declare oneself gay. If a heterosexual picked it, that would be a freak case, the exception to prove the rule.

G. S.: Can a homosexual have a nonhomosexual imagination?

E. B.: That is a tricky question. It postulates what I have already declined to postulate: that there is something knowable and definable as *the* homosexual pattern in matters of the mind. On *my* premise, what you call "nonhomosexual" wouldn't have to be so described. I might, for example, just be non-camp, non-Firbank.

G. S.: And as such perfectly indistinguishable from heterosexual? Which is another point I'd like to raise. The polarity between homosexual and heterosexual: should it be transcended or promoted?

E. B.: What should be promoted is complete indifference to this matter. One shouldn't care if one is *the same as* or *different from.* Firbank was not doing wrong in putting himself at a distance from the heterosexual of his day. Another man wouldn't be doing wrong if he omitted to put himself at such a distance.

G. S.: I can think of some dubious instances.

E. B.: Somerset Maugham?

G. S.: For one.

E. B.: I'm not familar enough with his writings, but what I've read about his life suggests he was a hypocrite, and I hadn't intended to champion hypocrisy. In *Don Fernando*—I did read that one—he even puts gay people down; little would the reader guess he was gay himself. I like to think that we writers try to reduce pretense to a minimum. Maugham's macho pose is more like a *sin,* if we are to believe what is told of Maugham in Beverly Nichols's book *A Case of Human Bondage.*

G. S.: Does an artist's homosexuality come through in ways other than a definitely homosexual style or matter?

E. B.: I now want to utter the name "Nikolai Gogol." My friend Simon Karlinsky has persuaded me that Gogol is to be understood as a homosexual, that much in his writing is to be understood as coming from his situation as a homosexual in Russia's of course strictly heterosexual society. Certainly, Gogol's situation did affect his fantasy, his humor, even at times his sanity. So he did have, in a limited sense, a specifically homosexual sensibility—a sense limited, as I suggested before, by time and place. He had the kind of sensibility that certain heterosexual pressures would tend to foster in a homosexual. That is by no means a *definition* of his sensibility. Otherwise every Russian homosexual of that time would have been a Gogol. But sensi-

bility is affected by circumstances, and I have cited circumstances that could not fail to affect the impressionable, hyper-
sensitive Gogol enormously.

G. S.: What—of a comparable nature—are heterosexual writers
affected by?

E. B.: The answer to that question is either very obvious or totally
obscure. It also raises the further question whether anyone is
wholly heterosexual. Let's postulate a wholly heterosexual
writer. What is traditional society doing to him? Passing a
vote of thanks for his heterosexuality? Asking him to perform the sycophantic service to it for which his nature has
so well equipped him? There *is* a body of love poetry in Western literature which is as boring as one would expect of such
an overdetermined situation—it is all written by heterosexual
males saying how much they adore their presumably
heterosexual females on condition that the latter stay in the
niches the former have constructed for them. Take another
postulate: a writer who is wholly heterosexual but for whom
the hetero ideology functions as a protection against the homo
temptation. In art any tension not completely unbearable can
be productive, so why not this? But I wonder if the term
"heterosexual sensibility" is a good description of the result. I
should add that even the Compleat Heterosexual Male, if he
exists, still has a problem: guilt feelings. He cannot escape the
guilt of having oppressed women and male homosexuals. He
cannot escape this guilt any more than the white race can
escape its guilt for having oppressed the red, black, and
brown. So I would expect the heterosexual imagination (if *it*
exists) to be characterized by the bad conscience of the con-
queror. Especially in an age when the conquests—the
empires—are tottering and when, as D. H. Lawrence put it,
"the women are in eruption."

G. S.: Some have argued that the "liberal" tendency toward acceptance of homosexuality has not only been disastrous for
the development of a homosexual consciousness, but has also
led to a critical irresponsibility which, in seeking to equate all
types of experience, has denied the different sexual and social
situations of homosexual and heterosexual writers.

E. B.: Postulated here is precisely what I have contested already—namely, that there is such an entity as *the* homosexual consciousness (imagination, sensibility) which was there in such and such a form at the beginning of time and should be preserved till time's end. If there really were such a "Platonic idea" of homosexuality, one would wonder if it could be shaken by acceptance or anything else. The facts are different. What has been called "homosexual" is to a large extent the creation of that heterosexual audience which today may be accepting and tolerant, but which yesterday was rejecting and intolerant. Do I understand that gay people are now saying they want that rejecting and intolerant audience back? Has self-hatred no limits? What self-respecting Jew would wish to preserve Jewish complexes that are the creation of anti-Semitism? To take another racial analogy, it is true that the quarrels created by racism bring it about that many blacks today want to be separate, not integrated; even so, the march of integration is inexorable. For one thing, now that there is no effective taboo on intermarriage, there will be more and more people of mixed race. So with gays. For a time, liberated (i.e., semi-liberated) homosexuals may choose to draw apart. In the long run just the opposite will occur. As fewer people insist on their heterosexuality, fewer will insist on their homosexuality. Our natural bisexuality—if that's the word—will win out. Gay writers will be less interested in affirming a gay consciousness; ergo, there will be less gay consciousness to be affirmed.

G. S.: Are you saying, in Pirandellian fashion, that gay consciousness exists if you think it does, and doesn't if you think it doesn't?

E. B.: Well, *something* exists. One may want to call it gay consciousness or one may not. People who very much *want* to affirm gay consciousness today won't want that by early tomorrow morning. At which point the notion will evaporate. Pirandello, yes: if you don't want it to be real, it isn't. As with the sexual characterizations of the past: to be a "real man," you had to have qualities a, b, and c. But as soon as people no longer think this, you don't have to have qualities a, b, and c;

you have to have qualities d, e, and f. Or we admit we don't know what qualities you have to have—maybe because there really aren't any such "qualities."

G. S.: We all know critics who, whenever they are confronted with homoerotic elements in a writer's work, go to great lengths to deny that he is homosexual, particularly when the relevant biographical information is lacking. Apart from the homophobic prejudice that influences many of these critics, doesn't such criticism also reflect, perhaps in its most acute form, a problem of critical vocabulary we all share?

E. B.: The problem that leaps to *my* mind is not one of vocabulary; I wish it were. It is the problem of the critics themselves—the ones who "go to great lengths to deny that a writer is homosexual." Why are those lengths so great?

G. S.: Could you answer that yourself?

E. B.: Because homosexual writers are a threat. They rock the boat. Think of that cabin on the boat which is an Ivy League college. A great writer homosexual? Lots of minor writers homosexual? Then—hold your breath now—a little fucking would be OK in the men's dorm. Perish the thought! Death is better than dishonor! And what would one tell the parents? All we are prepared to tell them is that the instructor who read Gaveston's lines in class with such enthusiasm—was he winking at the quarterback in the second row?—has been fired. Don't we have to be clear in our views and firm in our values? The man who wrote *Captain my Captain* cannot be a fag, because, for one thing, the faggery might rub off on Abraham Lincoln, and from there it is but a step to saying Washington did lie, he lied about having jacked off George III on a secret mission to London: George's cherry was the one the cherry-tree story originally referred to. . . . Fill in the blanks for yourself. The hand that rocks the *cradle* rules the world, not the hand that rocks the boat, let alone the hand that gets its rocks off.

G. S.: You didn't pick up my point that some criticism is homophobic.

E. B.: Is any criticism homo*philic* other than the kind that shouts: "Hurrah, gay is good, and Christopher Marlowe's on our team"? Some professors (of English and French and . . .) who hate homosexuals are homosexuals themselves. Maybe they hate themselves. As for the others, some hate us with a hatred as baleful and implacable as they and/or their friends have for women, blacks, Jews, or whomever, but the big haters are not the big problem, since they do not constitute the solid body of prejudice that actually dominates people and runs institutions. Those who do are not the hot haters, but the cool excluders, ostracizers, deciders of who's in, who's out, whom we can use, whom we cannot, who is desirable, who undesirable, the supercilious ones who know what is done and what is not done, who know who can be included in the term *we*, and who is definitely *they*. One of my chairmen at Columbia indicated that in his view, Lionel Trilling had been able to do well on the Columbia faculty because *nobody could tell* he was Jewish even though *everyone knew* he was. In similar manner, everyone could know you were gay, provided no one could tell! So never mind the neo-Nazis: the most effective enemies of civilization are its self-appointed upholders. The effective enemies of homosexuals are not the professional faggot-baiters, but various bland ladies and gentlemen who, never bringing up the topic themselves, are very concerned that it never be brought up. Back to the racial analogy: black people shouldn't talk about race; they should paint themselves white. (Many have.) Gay people are all right, if they don't look gay, don't talk gay, don't dress gay, don't have gay fun. They are all right because no one is forced to know they exist. And in the past, as soon as it was known that a gay person existed, he had to cease to exist. He could avoid being shot only by committing suicide. Which he usually did, literally or—the more painful process—figuratively.

G. S.: If we say, as you have, that the safest definition of homosexual literature is "literature by known homosexuals," aren't we exposing criticism once again to the supposed dangers of the "biographical fallacy"? Wouldn't it be more meaningful (and, granted, perhaps even "safer" for some) to speak of homosexual texts and writing than of homosexual writers?

E. B.: But a text isn't either male or female. If you want to avoid speaking of homosexual writers, all you can do is say, let's speak of (a) writing on homosexual subject matter (which could be by heterosexual writers) or (b) writing perceptibly imbued with homosexual attitudes. (b) will get you right back into what you cite as the biographical fallacy, since to find the attitude is to find the man. I should add, perhaps, that I don't want my interest in an author's life to be set down as fallacious. What is interesting is interesting, and even if biographical study did not enhance my understanding of a writer's writing, I would still study biography. There is such a thing, too, as indirect enhancement. Certain facts may have no *direct* bearing on a work of art, but, since everything is connected with everything, they may have a very interesting *indirect* bearing on it. An author's life may not *explain* his work, but knowledge of his life does place his work in a larger context, brings it in touch with a larger field of action, and, in the end, biographical study may well enrich one's experience of art, even if certain people don't wish it to. And this has its special importance in the case of homosexual writers. For since homosexuality can easily be misunderstood, a special effort to understand the homosexual writer may well pay off: misunderstandings can be eliminated or diminished. The perennial discussion of homosexual elements in Shakespeare's sonnets is not enriched, certainly, by ignorance of what homosexuality is actually like—an ignorance characteristic of some scholars.

G. S.: Many critics believe that while homosexuality or heterosexuality in literature may be interesting from a psychological, historical, or polemical point of view, they are fundamentally extra-aesthetic elements, that is, they have nothing to do with the purely aesthetic value or aspect of a text. What do you think of this position? I am thinking in part of your remark on Forster's *Maurice*: "I am interested in propaganda and regard it as valid in art."

E. B.: What I have just said about biography applies to history generally. History is not part of art, art is part of history. This is really saying no more than that humanity is not part of our art, art is part of our humanity. Certainly there are aesthetic values. But it is not possible to isolate the nonaesthetic or aesthetic elements. To arrive at a sound aesthetic judgment, we need to know all manner of nonaesthetic facts. The work itself presupposes we do know such facts.

G. S.: What about propaganda?

E. B.: Propaganda—deservedly, I admit—has got itself a bad name, but there was nothing wrong with the original idea: propagating truth, propagating a faith in that truth. All art *is* propaganda for truth as each artist sees it, and most art does seek to affirm something that can well be called faith in such truth. Antipropagandist art is propaganda for anti-propaganda. Propaganda against faith is propaganda for faith in nonfaith. I am not playing with words. *Waiting for Godot* does not merely express nonfaith, it also expresses *faith* in nonfaith, in other words, nonfaith as a point of honor, if not quite an oriflamme. Similarly, all those confident asseverations that the artist must *not*, repeat, *not* propagandize constitute vehement propaganda for the idea of autonomous art. When Oscar Wilde said all art was perfectly useless, he was making propaganda for uselessness, for nonutilitarian, nonedifying beauty. The paradox is that such uselessness is supremely useful, that such beauty is of itself edifying.

G. S.: You have said that sex badly needs to be demystified, to be "scrubbed clean from stigma at the one end, and from false kinds of glamour at the other." How?

E. B.: I can answer this in a single word: propaganda. Someone else might say: art. A third might say: education. The three of us mean the same thing.

G. S.: How do you take away a stigma?

E. B.: Darker pigmentation of human skin carried a stigma in nineteenth-century America. How has this stigma been removed? By someone saying "Black is beautiful." This was propaganda, poetry, and education. Malcolm X made a contribution by a witticism. He pointed out that white folks go sunbathing "because they all want to look like us." The key word in the phrase you cite from me is *scrubbed*. Stigma does not blow away. It has to be scrubbed. Work has to be done—by artists among others. Brainwashing, if you like. Strange how brainwashing is always put down! Great idea, really. We all need re-educating. For which we have first to be de-educated. The arts could contribute, though in general they are used for just the opposite purpose: most art is soap opera, the opium of the people.

G. S.: How about glamour?

E. B.: I took exception to false glamour. The remedy is true glamour. With this in mind, D. H. Lawrence penned *Lady Chatterley's Lover*. E. M. Forster seems to have had similar intentions for his book *Maurice* which, yes, I praised. But I cannot praise it in the present connection, because the love of Maurice and Alec lacks glamour.

G. S.: When can we find a glamorous homosexuality in literature?

E. B.: A lovely question! But not an easy one. There have been many attempts, but often, in the result, the glamour is false, or at least strikes some false notes. Read the gay poetry of Oscar Wilde's generation as conveniently anthologized in Brian Read's volume, *Sexual Heretics*. Even nonglamour, or sordid raciness, as in mid-twentieth century novels à la John Rechy, turns out to be glamour of a sort: false glamour, the dubious fun of slumming, of suburban *nostalgie de la boue*. I sometimes think the best attempt at homosexual glamour has been in works of little or no artistic pretension, classified as pornography, such as the story *Song of the Loon* or the movie *Dust unto Dust*. While most pornographic fictions I have seen or read tend to ugliness and brutality—and patently belong to a world that is sleazy in style and venal in motive and method—this subclass of pornographic works is dedicated to a fantasy romantic and soft and, to a degree, genuinely glamorizing. Beyond that degree, no. These are *corny* fictions. Insincerity is not only permitted but encouraged. Behind the sentimentality, if rather well hidden much of the time, is the same cynicism that supports the tough school of pornography too. The romance, unfortunately, is tongue in cheek: "We don't really mean it, but it would be nice if. . . . "

G. S.: What *great* artist has done most to glamorize homosexuality?

E. B.: Walt Whitman.

G. S.: But he also denied his homosexuality in the famous letter to John Addington Symonds.

E. B.: He may just have been denying anal intercourse. In any case, I'll stand by my answer, and add that Whitman may well have made the calculation that, in his time, one could only glorify the homosexual mentality while denying that any physical activity followed in its wake. Nineteenth-century men could not but be entangled in nineteenth-century contradictions. At his trial, Oscar Wilde was applauded for his eloquent improvisation on the "Greek" love of an older man for a boy, yet in his own defense he used a lie—the denial that he had sexual intercourse with boys. Even heterosexual intercourse couldn't be glamorized until the 1920's and even then only in a banned book—*Lady Chatterley*, again. But Wilde did glamorize homosexuality, as did Whitman. In their cases, it is not the glamour itself that is false, only some of their "statements to the press." By contrast, such a writer as Symonds made no false statements, but glamorized homosexuality falsely in his poetry.

G. S.: Whitman. Wilde. Are there distinguished figures in this area of perhaps less tremendous stature?

E. B.: Marguerite Yourcenar. Mary Renault. *Hadrian's Memoirs. The Persian Boy.* These two books have a lot in common, even in being different. One author identifies herself with the boy, the other with the great man, yet in each case it is a woman speaking, and speaking about a great man and his male lover.

G. S.: How come the male writers didn't get to that subject first?

E. B.: They did. Alexander's homosexuality, and Hadrian's, have been written about since ancient times.

G. S.: But with such all-out sympathy—with the desire to glamorize homosexuality?

E. B.: No. Then again, these two women might deny the intent to glamorize.

G. S.: Would you deny it?

E. B.: No. But I'd point out that that is not all they are up to. They are both, also, on a power trip. Madly identifying themselves with male power. If it is remarkable, in this day and age,

to make much of Antinous and Bagoas, it is even more remarkable that a woman should make much of Alexander or
Hadrian.

G. S.: Would these be instances of women's liberation—or the
opposite?

E. B.: A bit of both, I suspect: an ambiguity properly characteristic of the mid-twentieth century.

G. S.: Do you see any differences between the forms of mystification found in presenting heterosexual and homosexual
love?

E. B.: There is always a difference between the hammer and the
anvil. And between the way things look to the hammer and the
way they look to the anvil. Heterosexuals are "mystified" by
other heterosexuals, whereas we homosexuals have had to
submit to being mystified by *them*: mystification is imposed on
us by our oppressors, the heterosexuals, and we are ordered
to accept their mystifications or go to jail. In jail, we are subjected to their kind of homosexuality—rape by heterosexuals—
but that is another story . . . or is it?

G. S.: But don't homosexuals ever mystify themselves?

E. B.: Never say never! The false glamour of bad gay poetry is
an instance of homosexuality mystified by homosexuals. Even
here, one should add that we are pressured into such self-
mystifications by others. The oppressor is still the oppressor,
the oppressed is still the oppressed, and the oppressed only
gets over his oppression at the moment when he decides on
revolt. Until that moment he is an Uncle Tom—not as Harriet
Stowe depicted Tom, but as the more recent stereotype has
him—the happily acquiescent slave whose ideas and senti-
ments must be such as to prolong happy acquiescence. Much
early gay ideology is only gay Uncle Tomism. For instance, the
idea that a male homosexual is a female soul in a male body.
The definition of *female* is the sexist one: the female is weakly
decorative, "fem," hence a male homosexual is a half-man,
half of a human being. Compare the blacks in sexist-racist
movies like *Gone with the Wind*: they are servants by their very
nature, life for them *cannot* be the full-blooded adventure that
it is for the Clark Gables and Vivien Leighs. Incidentally, the

authors of books like *Gone with the Wind,* are the really important reactionaries, far more important than the official "con-
federates" and conservatives.

G. S.: Could you apply that thought to the gay struggle?

E. B.: Yes: a liberal like Norman Mailer can be more of an enemy
than any conservative you can name.

G. S.: Are you assuming then that all art that "mystifies" is bad,
whereas all art that "demystifies" is good?

E. B.: No, but that is a complicated matter because mystification
and demystification exist side by side in the same work. In the
Aeneid, Virgil "mystifies" Rome, creates the "mystic" entity of
Rome, much as Kipling would help create, sustain, and en-
large the myth of the British Empire nearly two thousand
years later. At the same time, Virgil is what we today call
"brutally frank" about the methods used, and his battle scenes
"demystify" mystic Rome considerably. Something similar can
be said of Dante. On the one hand, his poem constructs and
confirms the very idea of a Catholic culture and a Catholic
universe, sanctifying and glorifying as it moves along. On the
other, we encounter, in his inferno especially, the people we
know and the world as it is: stripped naked, "demystified."
Literature builds up *and* tears down, mystifies *and* demystifies.

What we are witnessing today is the decline of the West, the
twilight of the capitalist gods. At such a point, literature can
aim at the crassest kind of mystification—outright falsifica-
tion, refusal to concede that conditions are as they are—or it
can insist on the truth with the special vehemence that stems
from a sense of crisis, as the great modern literature has done.
It's true that many of the great moderns are reactionary, but
only as Balzac was, of whom Karl Marx approved. Balzac
would read you a reactionary sermon but in his depiction of
people and circumstances he would falsify nothing. On the
contrary.

G. S.: Other examples?

E. B.: Ezra Pound. Reactionary as can be in his stated opinions.
Also in many of his actions. But finally more artist than fascist,
exposing himself as fool, and hence exposing his fascism as an

aspect of his folly. Read the life of Pound; it will demystify fascism for you.

G. S.: Proust, Gide, and Genet: Have they demystified homo-sexuality for you?

E. B.: I wonder. There is a period quality about their treatment of the subject—yes, even Genet, though he is still very much alive. It has dated. One has to smile as much as at the *Picture of Dorian Gray* with its Victorian chatter of "unmentionable vices," and in what comes through as "period quality" there is mystification of homosexuality, sometimes extreme. I call mystification extreme when it is nothing less than a cover-up: pretending that Albert is Albertine, for example.

G. S.: In your *College English* interview on homosexuality [November 1974], you remarked that that was not a cover-up only, that Albertine became something of a woman, and was an example of the power of Proust's creative imagination.

E. B.: Life is seldom simple; art, never.

G. S.: Doesn't that also apply to the homosexuality in Proust's novel that is, after all, shown directly—especially through Charlus?

E. B.: Indeed. But from the standpoint of gay liberation, Charlus was an unfortunate choice for Proust to make, an unfortunate creation for him to bring to birth, setting further stigma on homosexuality or at least confirming the stigma already there, perpetuating one of the grosser mystifications of sexism: namely, that there is something demonic (daemonic, daimonic?) about "perversion." This is false glamour of another sort. "Homosexuality is evil but fascinating." Of which proposition the corollary is: "Homosexuality is fascinating but evil."

G. S.: If that is your interpretation, what redeems Proust?

E. B.: The original sin—the original non-sin—of the artist: irony. The Baron isn't all bad. He is the advocate of a devil who is not all devil: the evil is often "evil" in quotes—i.e., what "straight" convention has classified as evil.

G. S.: Is your own standpoint on this matter not, finally, that of gay liberation?

E. B.: Well, if by gay liberation one means, as I did a moment ago, a political movement with short-term tactics to consider as well as long-term strategies and aims, then one is compelled to have a double set of standards, and what is opportune and even necessary at this moment may be unnecessary and inopportune in the long run. Politics resists irony as much as art welcomes it. If censorship is ever right, we would be right in demanding that much good art be censored, at least for a while, since in politics its ironies will not be understood and the residue (the work minus the irony) is harmful.

G. S.: Are you suggesting that Proust should be banned?

E. B.: Let's say I *would have* supported such a ban—except for my opposition to censorship as such—during the period of history just ended. I think enough progress has now been made in gay liberation to render such censorship unnecessary—again on the premise that censorship is ever necessary.

G. S.: I am still very confused on this. Would the ground of such a ban have been that Proust was wrong about homosexuality? Or only that he would have been misunderstood by persons lacking in ironic sense?

E. B.: Well, I think even persons not entirely lacking in ironic sense could get the wrong idea about homosexuals from Proust, at least during a period when such wrong ideas were rife and stood largely uncorrected by any better ideas. I think, too, that his period gave Proust certain verbal formulas in which he imagined homosexuality could be caught—but he was wrong. Today his wrongness lies open to the view. Yesterday it did not.

G. S.: Would you comment on the following remark by Christopher Isherwood: "For me as a writer, it's never been a question of 'homosexuality,' but of otherness, of seeing things from an oblique angle. If homosexuality were the norm, it wouldn't be of interest to me as a writer."

E. B.: Isherwood is being perfectly sensible (isn't he always?) when he decides to make out of an imposed predicament a special opportunity, making, if you will, a virtue of necessity—always nice work if you can get it. Which is only to say we are in history, we do not decide when and where we are born, the best we can hope for is to be able to turn the given disadvantages of our position to advantage. If you are not the Establishment but can make your way only as a rebel against the Establishment, then, yes, you had better make a case for rebelliousness and show the world the merits of rebellion, dissent, unorthodoxy, etc. The world may not care; but then again you may change the world.

G. S.: Would you comment now on this? When Gide suggested that Proust seemed to have wanted to stigmatize homosexuality in his novel, Proust protested. "And eventually I understand," writes Gide, "that what we consider vile, an object of laughter or disgust, does not seem so repulsive to him."

E. B.: I am not impressed by these words of Gide. Who are *we*? (I always want to know who are *we*, pronoun beloved of the self-assured.) If Proust were really not repelled by what *we* consider vile, he would not call it vile himself, would not work so hard on creating a climate of vice. The impression given by *A la recherche du temps perdu* is, on the contrary, that Proust finds vileness even viler than we (I) do, or maybe he finds homosexuality vile, whereas we (I) do not. By the way, what's wrong with your French homosexual writers? (I am addressing myself now to all you owners of French literature in the Departments of French.) Can't French writers play the homosexual without at the same time playing the heel? Gide the "immoralist"! And *liar*, too, I think we must judge him in his reports on Oscar Wilde! Genet the professional thief and jailbird! Not to mention Proust yet again. I am not saying that the cult of the demonic is totally uncalled for. I'm asking who called for it, and why. Has it been anything but a disservice to homosexuals? Do we need it?

G. S.: Whether needed or not, it's there. It's part of a cultural and literary tradition shared by everyone. And if the French writers are as demonic as you say, could they help but reflect that tradition?

E. B.: That question suggests a more fruitful approach: we should not challenge these people, we should probe them. In the nineteenth century, when the homosexual was indeed an

outlaw—a felon by nocturnal habit, a veritable crime-*addict*—
his imagination flew to the poles: north and south. North: the
dandy, the queen, the "uranian," the sissy, the exhibitionist,
the play-actor, in a word the Oscar Wilde of the period before
Reading Gaol. What makes Oscar the symbolic figure that we
all know he is is that, as of Reading Gaol, he fled southwards to
the other pole and became Sebastian, Christian martyr stuck
full of arrows, Melmoth, wandering goy of Gothic fiction, outcast, Satan. Skipping to the beginning of Wilde's century, we
may say it offered us two other avatars: Beau Brummell and
Byron. And Byron is of interest here because we now know he
was far more homosexual than the nineteenth century cared
to think, and also that he was the founder of the satanic-
demonic tradition in its modern form. Byron's Cain and Man-
fred and the rest had their source in *him,* and he was bisexual,
the homosexual strain very strong indeed.

G. S.: You sound almost enthusiastic about Byron's demonism.
Why not Proust's, Gide's, Genet's?

E. B.: Different times demand different responses.

G. S.: Are you implying that the moderns were not responsive
to their time? Or were not entitled to the response they did
make to their time?

E. B.: Well, now I'm in my probing vein, let me say that they
had their reasons for continuing in the Byronic tradition but
that in doing so they were also headed for trouble.

G. S.: Trouble with you—in this interview?

E. B.: Not only.

G. S.: That's your last word, then, on the giants of modern French
literature?

E. B.: My first word would be more like it. Having got *that* off
my mind, I'd like to go on and enthuse about all three. They
have meant a lot to me, Genet less than the other two. It *pains*
me to call Gide a liar, though, on the occasion cited, I'm afraid
he was. As for Proust, I read all through *Remembrance of Things
Past* in the summer of 1945 as the atom bombs fell. It was one
of the great experiences of my life. And I have gone back this
year and reread most of it. Shall probably get through it all.

Am re-rereading many passages. You see, I'm an unashamed Proust freak, maniac.

G. S.: You and Plato would ban nothing but the best.

E. B.: That's it. What do the worst matter? Can I say something else about Marcel?

G. S.: By all means.

E. B.: I disagree with Roger Shattuck about him and agree with an opinion of Edmund Wilson's which Shattuck derides: that *Remembrance* is "one of the gloomiest books ever written." And this, as I see it, is because Proust repudiates Eros. Finds him a cheat. Now the erotic experience that drove Marcel—the real-life Marcel—was all homoerotic. Which makes his work doubly sad for the homosexual reader.

G. S.: Shattuck contends that it is a positive book: "a great comic tale," and ending in affirmation.

E. B.: The gay reader is not likely to agree with him: the message *he* receives is different, and he receives it in the gut. Who can really go for Proust's affirmation anyway? The cure for the disease of loving is to write a masterpiece? And even Proust who wrote a masterpiece, how could he have lived on when *Remembrance* was finished?

G. S.: Are you saying his reflections on Eros are untrue or only that you can't face the truth in them?

E. B.: I think they take in much of the truth, but that one must face the untruth in them.

G. S.: Had Proust been straight, would he have been more optimistic?

E. B.: Racine wasn't. He had to leave Eros for—was it religion?—at the same point where Proust left him for Art.

G. S.: Has anyone really answered what Proust says about Eros?

E. B.: Not in the form of Proust criticism. But I've read answers elsewhere—in *On Love* by Ortega, even in our own Alan Watts's *Nature, Man, and Woman*.

G. S.: In general, what are critics going to do now about homosexuality?

E. B.: Live out their historic destiny as Dunces of Clio's endless Dunciad. Betray the prime obligation of intellect—which is not to be intellectual but to be intelligent—and put themselves, as usual, at the service of the opportune, the expected, and the "trendy," progressive or reactionary. Mind has never had anything like the human appeal of simplemindedness, and so for a while we must expect that "gay criticism" will be pretty much on the plane of Communist criticism in the thirties, saying up with the good guys, and down with the bad. And just as the response of the Others, in the thirties, was to pretend Communism didn't exist, so now the Others will pretend homosexuality doesn't exist. The only closely argued response to the *College English* gay issue was a letter that argued that homosexuals are not a category of any importance to gentlemen and scholars.

G. S.: And yet you have been praising a scholar, Simon Karlinsky, for what he has written on Gogol.

E. B.: Yes. Simon is not just saying: "Hurray, hurray, Nick Gogol was gay!" He is using his special knowledge of gay experience to identify as homosexual certain experiences of Gogol's and thus to give transparency to certain otherwise opaque passages in Gogol's works. If a homosexual biographer, a homosexual critic, can see beyond the immediate circumstances of the gay liberation movement, and make subtle use of his own gay knowledge and experience, he may hope to offer special insight into a Gogol, a Wilde, even a Proust, a Gide, a Genet.

G. S.: Straight critics you leave in outer darkness?

E. B.: Outer darkness? Thus creating my own inferno, and formulating my own demonism? No, no. I would just advise sexist teachers, rabid male supremacists, to lay off Shakespeare's sonnets. . . . More seriously speaking, that is, thinking of the long haul, I don't really wish to place homosexual writers off limits for heterosexual critics, if only because they could then logically ask us to stay away from heterosexual writers. We won't. So we won't ask them to stay away from "ours." Shakespeare's sonnets should be left in the syllabus after all, and at the mercy of straight teachers! Maybe they will bend a little.

G. S.: They didn't always in the past.

E. B.: The times they are a changin'—from the old polarity to the new unisex. Or back to the original bisexuality, if you prefer. Or the polymorphous perverse.

G. S.: Because, according to you, the polymorphous is not perverse, is that right?

E. B.: That is very right.

Jean-Paul Aron and Roger Kempf

Triumphs and Tribulations
of the Homosexual Discourse

Q. Since the Christian era began, there has been a constant repression weighing on homosexuality in the West. Actual places and situations figure only as anecdotes in this process of rejection. What, then, is the particular situation of homosexual literature in the nineteenth century within this wider historical context?

A. It is invariably unhelpful to stifle modes of expression in the strait jacket of closed systems and to treat them as pure forms having neither past nor future. But here, even if one wished, it would be impossible to abstract literature from the diachronics and meaning of the moral ideology which from the French Revolution onward (if not from the 1750's on) views sexuality, and in particular sexual perversion, as the most radical danger. One has therefore to see how the homosexual discourse manifests itself in the nineteenth century and how it expresses itself. Let us say briefly that it scarcely puts two words together until the bourgeois triumph of the Second Empire: there is no organized expression, no body of concepts for this dangerous subject matter. When it expresses itself through the language of the day, it does so almost imperceptibly in legal reports or very furtively, very elliptically in medical treatises. The reporters, the magistrates, the practitioners who evoke these "nauseating phenomena," dwell upon their reluctance to discuss the matter and complain that their pens are being defiled. And if they manage to get the better of their revulsion and to consecrate a few dozen lines to the subject, as Dr. Fournier-Pescay did in the *Dictionnaire des sciences médicales* in 1819, they then proclaim that throughout this ordeal their pens have remained chaste.

Given this ambience, it is hardly surprising that literature, having declined all connivance with other languages (medical, judicial), being economically subjected to and bound to acquiesce in the interests of the dominant social group, should give only the smallest of space to sexual inversion, at least up to 1880. Witness the case of Custine, which caused a great scandal in the summer of 1824, for there are moments when the outcry of public indignation forces the barriers of secrecy, the silence of occultation and shame. Custine, aristocrat, dandy, well-known writer, friend of Chateaubriand, picking up soldiers in the Bois de Vincennes, stripped and beaten by them, left naked on the public highway, fascinated the world of literary Paris and gave rise to various forms of narrative fiction, from the Duchesse de Duras's *Olivier* to Stendhal's *Armance,* via another *Olivier,* this time by Thibaut de Latouche, and Astolphe de Custine's own *Aloys*—but homosexuality is here prudently disguised as impotence, that bizarre attempt on male honor which nonetheless preserves bourgeois esteem.

The audacity of Balzac, his tenderness, and his violence, in the next two decades seem all the more striking. He dares have Louis Lambert say: "We became used, as two lovers, to thinking together, to communicating our dreams to each other."[1] He dares have in the service of Godefroid de Beaudenord "a little boy, called Paddy or Joby or Toby (at will)," a child with blond hair and rosy cheeks, "secretive as a prince, aware as a retired lawyer, ten years of age and the fine flower of perversity, playing and swearing, devoted to jam and punch." Employed by a lord

---

1. *Louis Lambert,* in *La comédie humaine* (Paris: Pléiade, 1948), X, 378. All translations are our own.

who was very fond of him, Toby was dismissed when an English journalist, who found this angel too pretty to be a tiger,

> offered to bet that Paddy was a tamed tigress. The description threatened to get more venomous and *improper* in the highest degree. *Improper* is a superlative that leads to the gallows. His lordship was much praised for his circumspection by Mylady. Toby was unable to find a position anywhere, after having his civil status in British zoology contested. At this time Godefroid was flourishing at the French Embassy in London where the story of Toby, Joby, Paddy came to his ears. Godefroid took hold of the tiger whom he found sobbing over a pot of jam. . . . On his return Godefroid de Beaudenord brought home to us England's most charming tiger and was known for his tiger as Couture was for his waistcoats.[2]

In *Illusions perdues* and *Splendeurs et misères des courtisanes,* even though blurred by a determined heterosexuality, the mysterious relationship of Rubempré and Vautrin constitutes a veritable subversion, the exploding of an obstinate taboo in full Louis-Philippe puritanism. When Herrera appears on the road to rescue Lucien from his thoughts of suicide, the stakes are down. The rather too well dressed vagabond, the lovely victim of the schemes of Paris, gives himself up to his terrifying protector. The Balzacian discourse expresses itself on two levels. The priest tells a story: Biron, a wheedling secretary, favorite of the Baron de Goertz, condemned to death for swallowing a treaty between Russia and Sweden, escapes and takes refuge in Courland. The canon observes: "If you think this pretty fellow, condemned to death for eating a treaty relating to Finland, will break with his depraved tastes, then you have no idea of the empire of vice over men; the death penalty cannot stop him when it is a question of a sensual pleasure he has created for himself."[3] Proust, in *Contre Sainte-Beuve,* notes that "each word, each gesture has . . . undercurrents to which Balzac does not alert the reader and which are of an admirable depth."[4] Is it indeed a question of *papyrophagia?*

2. *La maison Nucingen,* in *La comédie humaine,* V, 607–8.
3. *Illusions perdues,* cited by Roger Kempf, *Sur le corps romanesque* (Paris: Seuil, 1968), p. 139.
4. Kempf, pp. 138–39.

When the canon declares that Lucien is more beautiful than Biron and that he himself is superior to the Baron de Goertz, does he not transport us toward a sort of second level of writing where passion in priest's garb states its true identity? Take the prettiness of his speech: "And we are honorable to the tip of our delicate little boots"; the wheedling caresses in his behavior: "'Little rascal,' he said, smiling and taking his ear to tweak it with an *almost regal* familiarity. 'If you are ungrateful to me....'" One thinks of Charlus pinching the narrator's neck with a vulgar laugh.

It is again with an air full of implications that Judge Camisot in "la dernière incarnation de Vautrin" (the fourth part of *Splendeurs et misères*) asks the priest to "disclose to him the causes of [his] affection for Monsieur Lucien de Rubempré...." Already Vautrin has done the necessary translation and supplied what is missing, but will the reader stop at the implications of the words *causes, affection, Monsieur,* as at the silence of the suspension points indicated by the author? Certainly Balzac does call a *queen* a *queen* and, to be properly understood, does recount the story of Lord Durham visiting one of the main jails in Paris:

> The director, after having shown the whole prison, the yards, the workshops, the dungeons, etc., pointed with a gesture of disgust to a certain building.
> "I shall not take Your Lordship there," he said, "it is where the *queens* hang out...."
> "Hao!" said Lord Durham. "And what are they?"
> "They are the third sex, my Lord."[5]

Even here Balzac does not intend giving more than a "vague idea of the nature of the character whom the inmates, warders, and guards call a *queen*." The distance is then no longer from the spoken to the unspoken, but from the spoken to the experienced, and the distance is terrifying. For it is no more a question of understanding, but of belonging. For the bourgeois who is not *one of them*, the twilight world of homosexuals will always remain unintelligible. Balzac reveals a perversion that is elusive unless practiced.

5. *Splendeurs et misères des courtisanes*, in *La comédie humaine*, V, 1055.

Nonetheless, writing in France, in the whole range of its assignments, touches on homosexuality only with economy and reticence. In 1857, with Ambroise Tardieu's *Etude médico-légale sur les attentats aux moeurs,* a mutation sets in. Expression takes organic hold of homosexuality. Medicine is ahead of literature. Proudhon condemns inversion in terms that confessors' manuals would not have disowned.[6] The Goncourts treat the subject with irony and condescension.[7] And one has to read Flaubert's correspondence with a magnifying glass to discover that this is something that was neither unknown nor detestable to him. The reader is indeed rewarded for his efforts. On 15 January 1850, Flaubert writes to Louis Bouilhet from Cairo:

> Since we are talking about young boys, here's what I know of them. Here it is extremely well carried off. One admits one's sodomy, one talks about it at the *table d'hôte.* Sometimes one denies it a little, everyone tells you off, and in the end all is admitted. Traveling for our instruction and charged with a government mission, we consider it a duty to give ourselves over to this sort of ejaculation. The opportunity has not yet presented itself but we are nevertheless looking for it. It is in the baths that it goes on. One books a bath for oneself (five francs, inclusive of masseurs, pipe, coffee and towels), and one takes one's lad into one of the rooms.[8]

And in another letter, dated 2 June: "You ask if I have consummated the work at the baths. Yes, and on a young fellow who was pockmarked and who had an enormous white turban. It made me laugh, that's all. *But* I'll do it again. For an experience to be truly complete, it must be repeated."[9] But such confiding of secrets is rare. The literature of the Second Empire, although detached from itself, seeking its foundations other than in inspiration and introspective psychology, remains attached to the im-

6. *De la justice,* cited by Jean Borie, *Le célibataire français* (Paris: Le Sagittaire, 1976), pp. 119-21.

7. *Journal, mémoires de la vie littéraire* (Paris: Fasquelle-Flammarion, 1956), I, 433, and III, 453.

8. *Correspondance* (Paris: Pléiade, 1972), I, 572.

9. *Correspondance,* I, 638. Cf. Roger Kempf, *Moeurs: ethnologie et fiction* (Paris: Seuil, 1976), pp. 71-95.

ages of actual experience. For a writer to talk about homosexuality would mean taking on himself something no one would risk assuming in a strictly moralistic society.

A doctor, on the other hand, guardian and good samaritan of the bourgeoisie, above all suspicion, can speak of filth without fear of getting himself dirty. All the more so as the society which has placed these ethical responsibilities on his shoulders sees him as its guiding light. Explaining monstrousness and vice does not aim at absolving them, it is a means of limiting the ravages they could cause. This is how science proceeds when faced with biological scourges, epidemics which are still fatal in the nineteenth century. The doctor who unveils to his petrified readers the atrocious admissions of sodomites is not their accomplice. Impassive, he listens, notes, comes to conclusions. But once his scrupulous exegesis is completed, he assumes once more his liberty as an offended citizen, he pursues these malefactors without quarter. This distortion of everyday and scientific language has an essential epistemological value. In the field of history we have during the last fifteen years or so given a privileged position to the most accomplished theories, the most elaborate knowledge, the most eloquent speech. The precariousness of such a choice is that it eludes other languages that are not reducible to systems and have their own lexicon and grammar. For example, there are naive statements in trials on public decency which, in both town and country, keep the exact measure of the scandal and the repressive suit within the closed walls of the palaces of justice and beneath the dust of archives. There are informal statements, abrupt and interrupted, pervaded with noise and anger, as in a certain garden in Lyon in 1837, when an old man is surprised by passers-by in the process of seducing a little boy. There are statements which are scarcely pronounced in the paragraphs of the *Gazette des tribunaux* beating about the bush, not declaring their intention, as when on 15 March 1838, for example, a Parisian secondhand dealer was attacked by a gigolo:

> A murder attempt was committed this morning at 17, rue de l'Arbre Sec. Monsieur Vaillant, a dealer in toys and fancy articles, whose shop was so frequently to be noticed in the Place Saint-

Germain-l'Auxerrois, saw an individual arrive at his premises whose acquaintance he had recently made and who came to see him sometimes. Monsieur Vaillant told him that he was unwell and that he felt an unusual heat in his throat. 'Perhaps your tonsils are swollen,' the man said to him. 'Sit in this chair and put your head right back, and I'll have a look at it.' The latter got into this position and the individual took a spoon which he introduced into the mouth of Monsieur Vaillant to proceed with his examination; then, with the other hand, he took a sharp instrument and struck the unfortunate man's neck. Luckily, the latter had at hand a bell-pull which connected him with the porter; he pulled at it and shouted while the murderer hastily made his escape. Monsieur Vaillant was first treated by a local doctor; it is hoped that his wounds will not prove fatal, the force of the blows having been broken by the whale-bone collar he was wearing.

This is, then, an *affaire de moeurs*. Would you have guessed it from the surface of this narration and from this inexpressive commentary? Nor would we, doubtless, if a few days later, on 24 March, the *Gazette des tribunaux* had not reported the following details on this affair:

Vaillant's[10] murderer, about whom we have collected some details, was, it would seem, a certain Leboeuf who, twenty years ago, kept a herbalist's shop with his brother at 3, rue du Vieux Marché St. Martin. Vaillant appears to have made their acquaintance at this period when going to shop at their premises. When the elder brother died, the younger sold the old stock and left for Brazil, where he spent several years. Back in France Leboeuf met Vaillant six months ago at a *table d'hôte* in the rue Saint-Honoré, where they renewed their acquaintance.

Finally the point is made, so discreetly however that it escapes the unalert gaze: "This establishment, which had an extremely bad reputation, was closed by the police in the first days of February and several persons were arrested. Leboeuf and Vaillant, it would appear, nonetheless continued to see each other

10. Notice the sudden elision of "Monsieur"; thanks to a stylistic device, the victim is immediately put on the same footing as his aggressor, and passes surreptitiously to the other side of the fence, into the criminal camp.

and it is as a result of this intimate relationship that the murderer tried to commit his crime." There is a wall of silence: things cannot be said because taboo is for the dominant social group the very condition of security and possibly of survival. Literature in the nineteenth century, even though on the loose, challenging and trouble-making, is directly coupled with the fantasies and anguish of common sensibility. Unless choosing to dishonor itself, it jealously keeps its torturing secrets on the chapter of male homosexuality.

Q. Isn't it curious that as far as sapphism is concerned, literature's vigilance is relaxed? The whole nineteenth century deals with the subject without shame, from Balzac to Pierre Louÿs via Baudelaire and Monnier.

A. Presumably because the weight of blame is much lighter here. A fine demonstration of the polytonality of speech, of the distance between the surface and the substructure of indignation. Apparently the latter is directed at lesbians via male homosexuals. The moral ideology of the class in power confounds them both in the same anathema. Parent-Duchatelet, a public health doctor and author of a famous work on prostitution which appeared in 1834, considers: "Lesbians have fallen to the last degree of vice to which a human creature can attain, and, for that very reason, they require a most particular surveillance on the part of those who are charged with the surveillance of prostitutes, but more particularly on the part of persons to whom the direction of the prisons dealing with these women is entrusted."[11] Listen to the precision which proves that this disgust is sanctioned by the institutions, directly connected to a whole system of dissuasion: "These unfortunate women have, at different moments, fixed the attention of the administrations. Thus, in 1824, it was expressly forbidden for those keeping houses of ill repute to allow their girls to share the same bed; those who at the moment of visits and inspections were found in bed together were punished with several days of imprisonment; in the same way, loose girls in a similar situation were punished severely; and finally one woman's authorization to keep a house

---

11. *La prostitution dans la ville de Paris* (Paris: Baillière, 1834), I, 170.

was taken away from her because she was surprised in bed with one of her girls."[12] But beneath the judicial rigor is a dormant indulgence quite unlike the aversion to male homosexuality. Subject to an emasculating moral code, the nineteenth-century bourgeois seeks pleasure in the evocation of lesbian loves. His virility makes the best of it and even rejoices in it as laying hands on some fantasmagoric possession: he evaluates, thanks to these forbidden games, the superiority of the strong sex. A voyeur with equivocal desires, he projects into revolting scenes his uncontrollable lot of repressed homosexuality and frees himself from it, without striking a blow, through the spectacle, real or imaginary, of servile womanhood.

It is not therefore surprising that the tribunals, despite the laws and the opprobrium, show themselves more kind toward these errors than toward the lewdness of uranians. If a young lady dresses up as a man in 1830, it is a mere bagatelle for Parisian judges: "In a modest room in the rue Bertin-Poirée lived a pretty young girl by the name of Adèle Pecquet who exercised the profession of a burnisher. Normally she wore male dress and this habit which had made her stand out, had called attention to her. Brought before the usual tribunal of police for this slight infringement, she did not appear and was fined three francs."[13] Zola gushes with some tenderness about his sapphic couples, Suzanne Haffner and the Marquise d'Espanet, Nana and Satin. One might think he has sided with the Marquise when, in *La curée,* she begs Hupel de la Noue to bring Suzanne to her. At the same time, observe his prudence as far as male homosexuals are concerned. His intrusions into this domain are few, very few, and without sympathy:

"I was forgetting, I haven't told you the story of Baptiste, Monsieur's valet. . . . Doubtless no one will have to tell you. . . . "
The young woman admitted in fact that she knew nothing.
"Well, you remember his grand, dignified airs, his disdainful glances, you even mentioned it to me yourself. . . . All that was play-acting. . . . He didn't like women; he never came down to

12. Parent-Duchatelet, I, 170–71.
13. *Gazette des tribunaux,* 20 August 1836.

fulfill his functions when we were there; and he even (I can repeat it now) maintained it was disgusting in the salon because of the low-necked dresses. I'm quite sure he didn't like women!"

And she leaned over to Renée's ear. She made her blush at the same time as keeping her own honest placidity.

"When the new stable-lad had explained all to Monsieur, she continued, Monsieur preferred to sack Baptiste rather than take him to court. It seems that these foul things had been going on in the stables for years.... And to think that that great lout of a fellow seemed to love horses! It was the grooms he loved![14]

And that same day Renée, in the procession of familiar carriages in the woods, "had a surprise, a feeling of disgust, on recognizing Baptiste... with white skin and a solemn air," next to the Baron Gouraud's coachman.

Q. Let us attempt a summary. Three sorts of homosexual discourse find expression in the nineteenth century: a common discourse, scarcely spoken; a scientific discourse which is systematized only during the Second Empire; and a literary discourse which is applied to sapphism but more or less freezes over on the subject of male homosexuality. So Jean Lorrain, Pierre Loti, Gide, and Proust, born in the years 1860–1870, bring at the turn of the century an unprecedented homosexual coloring to literature. Does this advent correspond to an overthrow of values?

A. No one doubts that the emergence at the end of the century of a scientific interpretation and of a literature of inversion translates a slackening-off of bourgeois severity. All the same one mustn't let oneself be taken in. The passage from horror to explanation in medicine and, in the novel, from the unspoken to the spoken, does not mean that the collective sensibility at one leap endorses the challenge to what had been established for the space of a century as the one legitimate rule, but simply that it pours into literature a subject pregnant with tensions; that what is said about disorder no longer spills over the barrier of its own tolerance; that it encourages a consensus between scandal and writing to express its accursed share; that the positivism which it

14. *La curée*, in *Les Rougon-Macquart* (Paris: Pléiade, 1963), I, 591.

has not ceased to take as its Bible has borne fruit, permitting it to discern the illness of wickedness in the aberration of vice. It is in fact at the very moment when psychopathology is underlining the amphibology of the word *perverse,* referring concurrently to perversion, that is, to a morbid process, and to perversity, that is, to turpitude, that writers lift the veil from homosexuality.

Gide in particular conveys the difficulties of this revelation through a precautionary distancing, primarily conceptual. The pseudonaturalist philosophy of *Corydon* finds its principal references in the humanism of Antiquity or of the Renaissance, its arguments in judicial affairs and its material in the natural sciences. But who, then, is Corydon? A brilliant individual, a former doctor, and doubtless there is nothing more subversive in Gide than the civil status of his mouthpiece: an unmarried doctor who doesn't hide his being one of them any longer, while his colleagues are, by definition, citizens above suspicion. If the rumor of deplorable morals makes people uneasy about Dr. Corydon, he must also reassure them with his austere home (no trace of effeminacy) and the breadth of his culture. But in the work he is preparing, a *Défense de la pédérastie,* one senses a hodgepodge of edifying demonstrations and specious distinctions: between pederast and homosexual, uranian and invert. These categories, in vogue since Krafft-Ebing, serve as a pretext for Gide, not without a certain amount of courage all the same, not to accept himself truly. In the preface to a new edition of *Corydon* in 1924 he does not hesitate to denounce the confusionism of Proust who, under the bad influence of Dr. Hirschfeld, mixes up irreducible essences, sodomy, sexual inversion, effeminacy and the taste (justified both by history and by nature) for young boys, ephebes who form the subject matter of Gide's work (from *L'immoraliste* to the *Journal,* via *Si le grain ne meurt* and *Le voyage au Congo*) even more so in far-off places than in France. It is a geographical difference that covers a political difference: in those times of triumphant colonialism it is less provocative to plant the decor of illicit loves in Tunisia and Egypt than in Nevers or La Roche-sur-Yon. If he no longer hesitates in *Les faux-monnayeurs* to place the landscape of the transgression in the holy of holies, in Paris itself, he does manage to attenuate the opprobrium by means of class mythology, which is all the more significant as, in its avant-garde flight, the *Nouvelle revue française* is hardly a friend of the aristocracy. At Schlumberger's, when the debate on *A la recherche* is on, everyone is disgusted and everyone is in agreement with Gide when he exclaims, "It's full of duchesses; it's not for us!" Nevertheless, homosexuality is better tolerated in the escapades of the Comte de Passavant than in the deviations of a butcher from La Villette or a stevedore from Bercy. The nobility furnishes the seditious writer at the beginning of the twentieth century with his surety for insolence. It also avoids the usual customs and depictions because it incarnates the ruling class. It distinguishes between two moralities—its own and the other one for everyone else.

The Maréchal de Richelieu recounts the story of a "Greek orgy" which took place at Versailles during the minority of Louis XV, under the very windows of the king. The regent, who was extremely blasé, was nonetheless forced to assemble his council. The quarrel was between partisans of punishment and of smiling reprimand. Among the latter was Condé, second prince of the blood. He suggested that there was hardly any risk to be run in hushing up the affair since it had taken place in the park of the château; that if, by some misfortune, it was to become known elsewhere, there could be no follow-up, as the people did not know anything had happened. The nobility, between 1890 and 1920, is no longer anything but a fossilized species, sublime because vestigial, mythical because disestablished and consequently devoid of all corrosive function. If Proust, whose statements on homosexuality remain the least obliging ones, solicits its anachronistic intercession, it is because the nobility serves him less as a mouthpiece than as a subterfuge. For it is all very well his adventuring into the thick of perversion—he has to have it accepted. The interdict is still far too strong in 1910 for the narrator of Proust's novel to manipulate his subject matter without any precautions. Medicine can afford the luxury of cynicism and declare coldly that it is bound only to the principle of objectivity, even if untutored; through it the dominant social group liberates its instincts as best it can. But literature is responsible to the ideology it stems from, despite what it may sometimes assert; does it not have a public, does it not circulate in a liberal democracy, from hand to hand? The pointer is in people's hearts, despite priests and police. And, at the zenith of the *belle époque,* at the apogee of the scientific method, at the time of Cléo de Mérode, there are compromising things to which the heart cannot consent: "If there is one vice or illness which revolts the French mentality and French health, it is surely, to give things their name, homosexuality."[15]

The world where *A la recherche du temps perdu* unfolds is suited to anaesthetizing the reader's sufferings somewhat. Around Palamède de Guermantes, Baron de Charlus, youngest son of an illustrious house, all sorts of lordly figures revolve, and even yeomen adopted by this degenerated feudal system. Still, it is not enough to transform Charlus into an allegoric, missionary star of the sodomite cause; one must create for him an apparatus of protection, a network of metaphors, a whole symbolism of diversion by means of which he avoids, as much as possible, the tragedy of admissions.[16] Charlus is wrapped up in a vegetable world in which Jupien is a rare plant. To seduce the Baron he sticks his rear out: "He took up this pose with the coquettry that the orchid might have for the providentially arrived bumble bee."[17] Charlus artist, Charlus creator. He "had been able to extract from the surrounding society a sort of poetry in which were to be found history, beauty, local color, comedy, frivolous elegance." Charlus saved by the subversion of laughter, the humor which saps and traps. Charlus, who marks *A la recherche* with his fits of anger and his excesses, which prove irresistible because they are disconcerting, exploring the gulf as in Saint-Simon between the things expressed and the expression—rhythm, register, tonality. In the hall of the Grand Hôtel in Balbec, flanked by a cousin's valet, elegant and effeminate, he does not hide his mortification: he had invited him, having taken him for another, more rustic and more to his taste. The lad's self-esteem is hurt: "No one else works with me except one whom you can't have been eyeing up; he's awful, he looks like a big farm hand." Charlus, so as not to hurt him further, shifts the

15. Ernest Charles, in *La grande revue,* July 1910.
16. Kempf, *Corps romanesque,* pp. 142–48.
17. *A la recherche du temps perdu* (Paris: Pléiade, 1954), II, 604.

line of argument: "But I have not made a special vow of knowing only people in the employ of Mme de Chevregny. . . . Could you not—as you are leaving soon—introduce me in Paris or indeed even here to a lot of your friends from one household or another?"[18] Notice the disparity between the religious vocabulary, the movement of the eloquence, and the unspoken side of the suggestion, the desire for someone rough instead of this whipper-snapper naively imitating people of quality. Comedy in Proust nearly always arises at the intersection of two distortions: of the form and the content of the discourse, of the reality and imagination of the social gulfs. Homosexuality destroys the landmarks. Charlus lowers himself to the rank of servants and waistcoat makers. But these, being very snobbish, reconstitute a hierarchy of their own advantage, raise themselves in their fancy to the level of their partners. Dream replaces initiation for them, they know nothing of a coveted society, its system of kinship, its alliances, its gear wheels, and they commit enormous blunders and suffer unbelievable rebuffs. The valet of Mme de Chevregny in his over-affectation, even proposes to the Baron to bring him the Prince de Guermantes, his cousin! And when Morel, going to a very special reception at the Prince's, notices in the little drawing room the photograph of M. de Charlus, seized by an uncontrollable terror, he flees without asking anything further. Proust tries the cathartic virtues of derision on the sons of Sodom, on the strange fauna of men/women who are to be found in his narration. Nissim Bernard, shortsighted as a bat, confuses his boy, a farm hand, with his twin brother who pays him with sound beatings for his homages. Legrandin plunges meteorically into the very places which revolt him the most, public lavatories or the house of M. de Charlus, for fear of being seen. And the ineffable Jupien starts by saying to the Baron: "You've got a big bum," but very quickly corrects the vulgarity of the exclamation with an affectionate: "Yes, go on, great baby," aping in a few lines the comedy of class conflict—Charlus, at first an object and then no longer seen from behind but from the front, reintegrated in his singular essence at the price of a cer-

18. *A la recherche*, II, 987.

tain amount of shrinking, of a lesson in discipline from a conde-
scending master. However, who is the *subject*? It is not Jupien,
ruling only by substitution, miming the role of arrogant lord.

Finally, mask of masks, Charlus, male, enjoying violent exercises, exhausting himself in long-distance runs, arriving in Balbec on foot: "It was, Saint-Loup said, by spending the night at
farms that his uncle was to make the journey from the château
where he was on holiday." Charlus rediscovering in peasants the
aristocratic roots in the soil, the source, he feels, of true virility.
Charlus, rude, disagreeable, hard on those of his own sex, swift
to chastise them for the slightest error, but a friend to women,
gallant, enterprising, so handsome in his youth that legend says
he had a thousand good fortunes. Saint-Loup, not without
pride, laments the fate of Mme de Charlus: "But I know well
enough that he was unfaithful to my poor aunt." Nobly faithful
to her memory, however, he goes to the cemetery in Paris every
day. And, with all, men and women, he is proud, never daunted,
impetuous, fit to command. One can understand that with such
broad shoulders he gives a thrashing to an impudent fellow who
dared to make indecent suggestions to him!

Q. For the last twenty years discussion on homosexuality has
been progressively liberated. Contestation by a specific literature
has produced a flourishing of works, theoretical and fictional,
where transgression expresses itself unashamedly. Aren't we
witnessing a veritable anthropological upheaval, a massive lifting
of censorship?
A.   Thanks to one of those bizarre things in which French culture abounds, contemporary formalism, the triumph of organization, of function, of the closed system, has taken desire, permanent insurrection, and irresistible breakdown of order, in
hand. We are present at a combat of titans: desire is invading
language, which immediately engulfs it, for it is unfortunately
always the loser. But that does not discourage speakers. Conscious that they are defusing sexuality, extenuating it and burying it alive in rhetoric and jargon, they compensate for it
through redundance and prolixity. Doubtless, they do in fact
translate the contradictions of a society caught between the dis-

closures of eroticism and its vestigial shackles. Consider the
evolution of this language since 1950. At the beginning there are
the second-generation surrealists: Bataille, Blanchot, Klossowski. The tone is set: desire is promoted to universal, poetic,
political, ontological dignity—naked, frenetic desire, the energy
which takes no law other than that of its own whim, no other
finality than pleasure. A frightening change: we have followed
the vicissitudes of writing, outraged, then yielding, then hedg-
ing; here it is now vicious and glorious, the agent of disintegration. But who could be led astray? What writing undertakes has
been stolen from existence. The war of extermination, led since
1955 by the dominant ideology against the chimeras of experience lifts all that is equivocal from this subject. Eroticism is de-
fanged by theory, expropriated by textual semiology, muzzled,
caged up by Lacan-style analysis in the asepticized and distres-
sing space of structure. The words with which the theory runs it
to earth, passed through the sieve of semantic examination, state
its ghostly identity and receive its admissions of impotence and
the echoes of its despair. Homosexuality is caught up in a network of baits, acclaimed, proclaimed and at the same time strait-
jacketed.

Q.   A dead end, then? No opening into the field of literature
for undisguised, undistanced, unrecuperated homosexuality?
A.   This opening is possible thanks to the science of history
which is now benefiting from the abolition of genres, as are
marxology, ethnology, and psychoanalysis. History institutes a
literature of the secret, throws light on the codes and the usages,
on the feast and the tragedy of sexual inversion by placing it in
its authentic context, dismissing face to face the repressed and
the repressors. Of course the trials for morality deciphered in
the memoranda of the archives give the redressers the largest
part of blame and allow the accusers to speak more than the
homosexuals. The latter rarely express themselves except to re-
fute the charges which are marshaled against them. But if the
historian is capable of listening partially, he knows that the silence of the accused reflects the pressure of the interdict, that
the stifled voices nonetheless stand out from the general outcry,
that they ring forth either provokingly or painfully through the

crudity, vehemence, or ambiguity of the witnesses. History re-habilitates what has been lived without falling into the ruts of psychology, assembles information without a wink in the direction of positivism, undramatizes homosexuality without dodging it, and opens up the dossier of desire without annexing it.

Critical Texts

Spent an hour of yesterday evening with Proust. . . . I am taking him *Corydon*, of which he promises not to speak to anyone; and when I say a word or two about my Memoirs:

"You can tell anything," he exclaims; "but on condition that you never say: *I*." But that won't suit me.

Far from denying or hiding his homosexuality, he exhibits it, and I could almost say boasts of it. He claims never to have loved women save spiritually and never to have known love except with men. His conversation, ceaselessly cut by parenthetical clauses, runs on without continuity. He tells me his conviction that Baudelaire was homosexual: "The way he speaks of Lesbos, and the mere need of speaking of it, would be enough to convince me," and when I protest: "In any case, if he was homosexual, it was almost without his knowing it; and you don't believe that he ever practiced. . . . "

"What!" he exclaims. "I am sure of the contrary; how can you doubt that he practiced? He, Baudelaire!"

—André Gide

Le pur et l'impur will perhaps be recognized one day as my best book.

—Colette

[Genet] never speaks to us *about* the homosexual, *about* the thief, but always *as* a thief and *as* a homosexual. His voice is one of those that we wanted never to hear: it is not meant for analyzing disturbance but for communicating it. . . . When reading Genet, we are . . . tempted to ask ourselves: "Does a homosexual *exist*? Does he think? Does he judge, does he judge us, does he *see* us?" If he does exist, everything changes: if homosexuality is the choice of a mind, it becomes a human possibility.

—Jean-Paul Sartre

Jacob Stockinger

Homosexuality and
the French Enlightenment

However divergent their ideological viewpoints may be, historians and sociologists of homosexuality agree that the single most important factor in determining the post-Hellenic status of homosexuality as a persecuted subculture was Christianity. Nowhere else had the Church been so attacked and undermined as it was in eighteenth-century France. Vitriolic political tracts against *l'infâme*, literary satires of the clergy, and sophisticated philosophical works all helped to make the campaign against it effective. Moreover, the attack proved all the more successful because the monarchy was crumbling from internal corruption to such an extent that it was incapable of imposing severe moral standards with any degree of credibility. In short, the concurrent decline of the religious and political bodies that had decreed and enforced moral codes appears by itself sufficient to explain why more intense and diversified thinking about homosexuality became possible.

But the eighteenth century in France was the Age of Enlightenment before it became the Age of Revolution, and it is pertinent to ask to what extent attitudes toward homosexuality were influenced by the ideas as well as the events of the time. Without taking sides in the debate about whether the revolutionaries were influenced by the writings of the philosophes, one can still remark the historical coincidence that existed between the concerns of the philosophes and the political, social, and legal consequences of the French revolution. While prior to the eighteenth century few major writers touched even indirectly on the issue of homosexuality except to narrate its practice or to condemn it, nearly all the great Enlightenment writers did address the question. At times they did so in the most direct manner possible, but even their indirectness was more positive and pertinent, on the very brink of directness, than was the case with their predecessors. Such attention did not, of course, imply personal approval of or participation in homosexuality. But as the philosophes themselves were the first to realize, the success of their efforts in enlightening others depended on transcending their own preferences and on examining the entire range of human behavior without judging any particular deviation. The kind of comment that the subject of homosexuality typically drew from the advocates of open and tolerant inquiry can be seen in Voltaire and Montesquieu.

During his stay at the court of Frederick II, Voltaire experimented once with homosexuality and, when asked by his partner to repeat the act, declared in a now famous quip: "Once a philosophe, twice a sodomite."[1] That Voltaire did not explicitly approve of homosexuality can be explained in part by defensiveness, for enemies tried at least once to implicate him in homosexual intrigues and thereby facilitate either silencing or discrediting him.[2] Yet his personal opinion did not prevent him from giving intellectual priority to understanding rather than judging homosexuality and to demonstrating how homosexuals had been mistreated and misunderstood by intolerant zealots, as the articles "Friendship" and "So-called Socratic Love" in the *Dictionnaire philosophique* (1764) demonstrate:

> The Thebans had the lovers' regiment: a fine regiment! Some
> have supposed that it was a regiment of sodomites. They are

1. Quoted in Arno Karlen, *Sexuality and Homosexuality* (New York: Norton, 1971), p. 148. See also Peter Gay's *Voltaire's Politics: The Poet as Realist* (Princeton: Princeton University Press, 1959), pp. 290–91.

2. *Voltaire's Correspondence*, Vol. I, ed. Theodore Besterman (Geneva: Institut et Musée Voltaire Les Délices, 1953), pp. 303–4.

mistaken. This is to take the incidental for the essential....

How did it come about that a vice destructive of mankind if it were general, an infamous outrage against nature, is yet so natural? It appears to be the highest degree of deliberate corruption, and is nonetheless the ordinary lot of those who have not yet had time to be corrupted.[3]

By contemporary standards, Voltaire's remarks hardly seem liberated, let alone liberal. But if he was not a homosexual apologist, an eighteenth-century Gide, neither was he such a reactionary as to justify the question that one critic has asked: "Voltaire fut-il un infâme?"[4] He did intervene and save a convicted sodomite, the Abbé Desfontaines, from being burned at the stake; with the exception of the satire of the Bulgarians (*bougres* or "buggers") in *Candide*, he used his writings to seek reasons for and even defenses of homosexuality, notably in climatic influences (the incidence of homosexuality, he said, is greater in warm climates) and in the recognition that moral standards are relative and must be evaluated within the specificity of their social context. There can be no doubt that such acts and views marked a substantial advance toward securing understanding and justice for homosexuals.

Politically more conservative than Voltaire, Montesquieu nonetheless also drew a line between personal disapproval of moral behavior and official interdiction of the same behavior. In "Of the Crime against Nature," a chapter in *De l'esprit des lois* (1748), Montesquieu detailed his views. First, of course, he eliminated any uncertainty about his own negative opinion of homosexuality; then he went on to indict the justice of his time for overpunishing the homosexual:

God forbid that I should have the least inclination to diminish the public horror against a crime which religion, morality, and civil government equally condemn.... What I shall say concerning it will in no way diminish its infamy, being levelled only against the tyranny that may abuse the very horror we ought to have against the vice.... It is very odd that these three crimes, witchcraft,

3. Voltaire, *Philosophical Dictionary*, ed. and trans. Theodore Besterman (Baltimore: Penguin Books, 1971), pp. 29; 31–34.

4. Alain, "Voltaire fut-il un infâme?" *Arcadie* 3 (March 1954), 27–34.

heresy, and that against nature, of which the first might easily be proved not to exist; the second to be susceptible of an infinite number of distinctions, interpretations, and limitations; the third to be often obscure and uncertain—it is very odd, I say, that these three crimes should amongst us be punished with fire.... I may venture to affirm that the crime against nature will never make any great progress in society unless people are prompted to it by some particular custom.[5]

Montesquieu, like Voltaire, was obviously not concerned with the homosexual as a special case, but rather as another representative of the disenfranchised and marginal persons who had been stigmatized and unduly victimized by *l'infâme*, the power structure that made deviations out of variations.

What stands out in Voltaire and Montesquieu is their awareness of how any networks of ideas and actions directed toward social reform and critiques of society necessarily involved those whom society had made outsiders in the past. They clearly perceived a lesson that was most explicitly propounded in Holbach's primer of Newtonian ethics, *Système de la nature*: free thinking entails free doing, both in a realistic appraisal of human nature and in an idealistic program of social reform:

> If we examine matters without prejudice, we will find that most of the precepts which religion, or its fanatical and supernatural ethics, prescribe to man, are as ridiculous as they are impossible to practice. To prohibit men their passions is to forbid them to be men; to advise a man carried away by his imagination to moderate his desires is to advise him to change his physical constitution, to order his blood to run more slowly.... To tell a lover of impetuous temperament that he must stifle his passion for the object that enchants him is to make him understand that he should renounce his happiness.[6]

In the *Enquiry into the Principles of Morals,* Hume followed a similar line of reasoning, suggesting that sexual taboos and

5. Montesquieu, *The Spirit of Laws,* trans. Thomas Nugent (New York: Haffner, 1966), p. 189.
6. Quoted in Peter Gay, *The Enlightenment: An Interpretation. Volume II, The Science of Freedom* (New York: Knopf, 1969), pp. 194–95.

shame do not arise from either God or nature, but rather from social utilitarianism.

Of course, neither Holbach nor Hume mentioned homosexuality by name, and it is fairly certain that they would never have openly condoned homosexual behavior. But in this area, as in so many others, the philosophes' liberating influence could not be limited to the ends that they themselves had specified. The thrust of their remarks was evident: a new vision of man and society must be a holistic one which could not a priori dismiss or condemn any facet of human behavior without undermining its own foundation. To that extent, the philosophes' thought was expansive rather than reductive and could easily be extended from majority groups to minority groups without distortion. More than any other single factor, it is this fluidity, with its wealth of implications, which situates the origin of contemporary attitudes toward homosexuality in the eighteenth century. For although a present-day observer can discern the politicization and other "field" or contextual contingencies of homosexuality as far back as the Middle Ages, it was the philosophes who first understood these implications and applied them to their own times. Not only did they recognize, discuss, and tolerate minority morality, but they did so without the impersonal voices or ironic gestures of earlier ages. The nature of their general approach to ethical thought as well as the specific directions of that thought allowed a consciousness of homosexuality—though not yet a homosexual consciousness—to form and emerge with greater safety, assertiveness, and significance than it had ever before demonstrated.

It seems ironic that it should be the Age of Reason that vindicated the moral, emotional, and sexual dimensions of man. But it was indeed an age of reason, not of rationalism. Throughout this effort to sharpen the faculty of reason as an instrument of analysis and action, the primacy of the human passions was not, for the most part, denied. Man was asked only to better what he was, not to become something he was not, and the concern with reason remained sufficiently undogmatic to include the study and acceptance of human affectivity. In speaking about the "passionate naturalism" of the Enlightenment, Peter Gay has succinctly resolved what appears to be the glaring and, at first, irreconcilable contradiction of the eighteenth century: "The dialectics of history confronted the Enlightenment with an apparent paradox which was, in actuality, a magnificent opportunity; as the power of conscience had grown, the passions had become safer; as reason had tightened its hold, sensuality improved its reputation. It was precisely the growth of the superego in Western culture that made greater sexual freedom possible."[7]

The two philosophes most attuned to this particular note struck by the general movement of the Enlightenment were Diderot and Rousseau. Diderot's most penetrating critique of the morality of his time was the *Supplément au voyage de Bougainville* (1772). Using Tahitian mores as a contrast against which both the truth and the social utility of the Judeo-Christian moral code could be measured, Diderot composed a searing indictment of the status quo of Western ethics. It is true that homosexuality was not specifically mentioned. But it didn't have to be, for two reasons: first, Diderot gave the Tahitians a convincing defense for incest, a moral crime that certainly rivaled and probably surpassed homosexuality in its ability to arouse abhorrence; and second, he stated his observations in such an all-embracing way that no reader could possibly ignore the implications for an overall revision of the moral concepts of the time:

> Is there anything so senseless as a precept that forbids us to heed the changing impulses that are inherent in our being? . . . When we are born we bring nothing into the world with us except a constitution similar to that of other human beings—the same need, an impulsion toward the same pleasures, a common dislike for the same pains: that is what makes man what he is, and the code of morality appropriate to men should rest on no other foundation. . . . Religious institutions have attached the labels "vice" and "virtue" to actions that are completely independent of morality. . . . But the untamed heart will not cease to cry out against its oppressors.[8]

As Diderot reiterated in *Le rêve de d'Alembert*, the *Pensées philosophiques,* his letters to Sophie Volland, and other works, the

7. Gay, *The Enlightenment*, Vol. II, pp. 204–5.
8. Diderot, *Oeuvres philosophiques*, ed. P. Vernière (Paris: Garnier, 1964), pp. 455–516 *passim*.

enlightened mind will not refrain from joining the heart in mutual expressions of outrage against the damaging arbitrariness of moral codes. And the persuasiveness of his view stemmed as much from his tone, which seemed lyrical and almost loving in contrast to the sharp irony of Voltaire's remarks on the same subject, as from his argumentation. Diderot's work, in short, had the double appeal of being a metacritical as well as critical liberation of affectivity.

Rousseau, although also firmly committed to freeing the human sensibility from the unreasonable and unrealistic restraints that had been imposed on it, remained a curiously enigmatic and, at times, equivocating figure. In many ways he was less daring in his views on moral reform than Diderot. When compared to Diderot's *Supplément*, for example, Rousseau's *Julie, ou la Nouvelle Héloïse* seems timid in its treatment of a subject which could have justified a much greater frankness concerning human sexual nature.[9]

In other ways, however, Rousseau proved to be more brazen and more pertinent to minority concerns than any of the previously mentioned authors. In "Book II" of *Les confessions* (1770), Rousseau recounts in explicit terms a scene in which he, a young adult undergoing preparations for a conversion to Catholicism, is subjected to the homosexual advances of a Moor. Whether he was feigning a naiveté he did not have will never be known, but the test makes the incident traumatic to an extreme. Escaping from the man's advances, Rousseau witnesses the orgasm he inspired: "My stomach turned over, and I rushed on to the balcony, more upset, more troubled, and more frightened than ever I had been in my life."[10] The following morning he relates the incident to one of the principals. To his surprise, however, the reaction is not exclamations of indignation or a wish for chastisement, but rather a plea for tolerance and understanding:

9. For an excellent discussion of Rousseau's contribution to a freer expression of sexuality, see "Three Stages on Love's Way: Rousseau, Laclos, Diderot" in Peter Gay's *The Party of Humanity: Essays in the French Enlightenment* (New York: Norton, 1971), pp. 133–61.

10. Jean-Jacques Rousseau, *The Confessions*, trans. J. M. Cohen (Baltimore: Penguin Books, 1954), p. 71. All references are to this edition.

> I listened to the wretch with redoubled astonishment, since he was not speaking for himself but apparently to instruct me for my own good. The whole matter seemed so simple to him that he had not even sought privacy for our conversation. There was an ecclesiastic listening all the while who found the matter no more alarming than he. This natural behavior so impressed me that I finally believed such things were no doubt general practice in the world, though I had so far not had occasion to learn of them. So I listened without anger but not without disgust. [72]

The consultation obviously does not change the emotional effects of the episode, since Rousseau suspects—and not without cause—that he is being subjected to an attempt at a kind of apologetic seduction. On the contrary, the outcome of the whole experience in his sexual life seems a prototypical case of reaction formation: "My memories of the self-styled African transformed the plainest of sluts into an object of adoration." But however negative the episode remained for Rousseau himself, it was important to the depiction of homosexuality for several reasons.

First, although Rousseau's attitudes and reactions did not undergo a significant transformation, he nevertheless questioned and at least somewhat modified them. This represented a limited triumph of reason over irrationality in a concrete personal situation and not merely in philosophical abstractions. Moral libertarianism, rhetorical in Diderot's Tahitians, had been strengthened by being put into practice as an active mediating force in Rousseau's own life. Tolerance of homosexuality was shown to work, however incompletely or imperfectly, on an existential plane as well as a philosophical one.

Rousseau implicitly suggested what Kinsey's research would verify two centuries later: that even as an ordeal or an experiment, homosexuality belongs to a continuum on which all forms of sexuality are interrelated; that homosexuality plays a role in the lives of non-homosexuals. That being the case, it can also be integrated into literature and made meaningful to essentially non-homosexual readers. Rousseau had indirectly begun to delineate the dialectic by which majority and minority concerns became profoundly pertinent to each other. It was a crucial step, for within the process of literary transmission it gave both homosexual senders and non-homosexual recipients a broader base for communication, and expanded the signifying potential of literature.

Finally, the episode is central because it marked the first time in French literature that an explicit and detailed account of homosexuality had been set down with at least some defenses to match the usual condemnations. Rousseau obviously did not advocate homosexuality, but even a second-party, third-person advocacy represented a bold innovation in the treatment of the theme. And at least the first-person voice of the narrative experienced and evaluated the homosexual episode in a sincere, if condemnatory, manner, which was also novel in French literature.

Although Rousseau himself gave no first-person endorsement of homosexual experience, it was he who, more than anyone else, prepared the way for such an endorsement. It was of prime importance to writing on homosexuality—and, of course, to the whole modern sensibility as well—that from the very first page of *Les confessions* Rousseau, generally recognized as the originator of the modern confession, memoir, and autobiography, emphasized being different as the source and measure of individual worth. Just as the essential lesson of Montesquieu's *Lettres persanes* could be learned only by taking the famous question "But how can one be Persian?" and substituting other adjectives denoting minority or socially marginal attributes for the word "Persian," so too the quintessence of Rousseau's contribution lies in the expansive suggestiveness of his "pre-Romantic" aspect: the cultivation, and perhaps even cult, of uniqueness. "I am like no one in the whole world. I may be no better, but at least I am different"—the celebrated opening paragraphs of *Les confessions* were a challenge to the classical collective reality, serving as a call to all misfits, outcasts, and deviants to come forth with authentic accounts of their own private subjective realities. By deed and declaration, then, Rousseau promulgated a literature of revelation that would be therapeutic to the repressed reality and correctively enlightening to the repressing reality.

Voltaire, Montesquieu, Diderot, and Rousseau—each contributed in his own way to a new context for thinking about homosexuality. Despite differences in their degree of commitment to radical reform, they did arrive at a common conclusion:

the reevaluation of society necessitated a corresponding
reevaluation of human nature, and any kind of social reform
was inextricably linked to ethical concerns. In that sense, the
philosophes formulated a new majority political awareness that,
for the first time in European history, directly involved
minorities. Its lesson was simply that the previous conceptual
basis of government must be reversed, that true justice meant a
system of jurisprudence that would accommodate itself to
human nature and behavior, and not the contrary. It was a revolutionary idea in the strongest sense of the term. If homosexuality itself was not a choice—a belief that radical homosexuals
would eventually challenge—at least there existed a choice of
attitudes with which it could be viewed, which in turn engen-
dered the possibility of intracommunity exchange and contention. In short, the eighteenth century not only made the
homosexual's act of speaking out possible, but also prepared us
to give a new importance to his words; for the homosexual
would pass from being the accused to being the accuser.

It seems ironic that these new potentials for discourse were
created by non-homosexuals. Homosexuals themselves did not
adopt such attitudes until long after their theoretical determination largely because ideological justifications offer few concrete
reassurances of protection as long as the structure and uses of
political power remain unchanged. Moreover, homosexuals did
not, as a group, possess enough unity or strength to realize the
potential significance of their sexuality or to act on that knowledge. In the eighteenth century, as today, the interruption of
subculture organization and communication was a highly effective means of oppression because it prevented any sense of
community solidarity out of which could arise the impetus to
conceive and assimilate new modes of analysis and behavior.

In various ways, the general intellectual and cultural milieu of
the eighteenth century reinforced the concerns that had been
voiced by the philosophes. As Lester G. Crocker has remarked:
"French philosophy in the eighteenth century becomes the
pseudoscientific expression of egoism and the search for pleasure, at the same time that it sought to establish a new ethics. It is
obvious from the data we have examined that the sexual activities were one of the foci of the revolt against cultural limitation.

The sexual act, in the eighteenth century, was at the center of art, gastronomy, fashion, and literature."[11] The eighteenth-century apologists for Eros did not generally turn their attention to homosexuality. But that fact must be understood within the context of qualifications which made eighteenth-century literature, no less than philosophy, hospitable to the homosexual presence.

First, whenever the expression of heterosexual concerns is expanded and liberalized, an increased awareness of minority sexuality invariably follows. This was particularly true with the eighteenth-century novel. No less than in Bayle's articles on "Eve" and "Hélène" in the *Encyclopédie,* Helvétius's *De l'esprit,* or La Mettrie's rhapsodies, in Duclos's *Madame de Luz,* D'Argen's *Thérèse philosophe,* Prévost's *Manon Lescaut,* and especially Laclos's *Les liaisons dangereuses* love and eroticism were portrayed as supreme drives that will not be denied. Such fictional accounts were given added verisimilitude by the exotic journals and reports of explorers like Lahontan and Bougainville who, through their experiences with primitive societies, found that "natural" sexuality was indeed a free and aggressive sexuality which violated the civilized standards of sexual conduct, and that cultural and moral relativism was a reality, not just a philosophical construct. And in spite of its outright condemnation of homosexuality as unnatural and unsatisfying, Rétif de la Bretonne's quasi-pornographic work had the indirect effect of encouraging others to explore the full range of sexual experiences and thus to examine the very aspect it had itself dismissed.

Even the eighteenth-century theater, which can hardly be described as heterosexually, let alone homosexually, hard core, can be viewed as an invitation to a frank examination of eroticism. Beneath all the refinements of language and gesture in Marivaux, for example, there lurks a latent admission of the primacy and pervasiveness of eroticism in private and public human relations. And the lusty candor of Beaumarchais went beyond courtly conceits of love and highly stylized or idealized models of amorous comportment and brought the public an

11. *Nature and Culture: Ethical Thought in the French Enlightenment* (Baltimore: The Johns Hopkins Press, 1963), p. 356.

encounter with the earthy realities of sexuality. As history so often suggests, a candid confrontation with heterosexuality in art is tacitly preparatory to the artistic integration of homosexuality, and in eighteenth-century France the transition from one to the other was almost immediate.

Admittedly, the minority sexual act was at times presented in eighteenth-century literature in such a way as to emphasize the perversity of the act rather than to redeem its sexuality. The most famous example is probably Diderot's *La religieuse,* in which the inattentive or biased reader could easily miss the point that it is the context of the homosexual acts—the hypocrisy and failure of the attempt to repress natural instincts within the convent—rather than the acts themselves which gives the work its apparently sensational and condemnatory aspects. More often, however, homosexuality was treated either descriptively, such as in Saint-Juste's poem *Organt,* or even prescriptively, such as in Barrin's *Vénus dans le cloître.*

On the other hand, the eighteenth-century in France presented several major obstacles to the development of homosexual concerns. The first of these is one of the most important events in the modern history of all minorities: the birth of the asylum. Although the mental institution in France actually dated back to 1656 and a royal decree establishing the Hôpital Général, it was the eighteenth century which, as Michel Foucault has detailed in *Histoire de la folie à l'âge classique,* became the "age of confinement" and first established a reciprocal connection between madness and minority status. This development allowed the medieval myth of the homosexual as a heretic and a criminal to be revised into a form that survives to the present day. In a move that could be regarded as the dialectical response of repressive forces to the philosophes' liberalizing influence and gradual success in combatting Christianity, sin became sickness and the role of the ecclesiastical authorities as consulting partners to the civil authorities was passed on to the medical community. No longer seen as a moral aberration, homosexuality was now viewed as a psychopathological dysfunction that required "curative" as well as punitive measures, both of which were administered in places such as the Bastille and Bicêtre. Moreover, the long-held belief that homosexuality was contagious was reinforced by what Foucault has called "the great fear," the widespread apprehension that madness, like germs, was escaping from institutions and infecting the surrounding populace. It was, in short, a new and more sophisticated kind of witch hunt with patients replacing sorcerers. In many ways this updated version of the medieval homosexual stereotype was—and still is—the most difficult one for homosexuals to overcome insofar as it was self-perpetuating, with the unconscious complicity of homosexuals themselves in the destruction of their self-image. For, as Foucault has so clearly demonstrated, it grew from a cluster of deeply rooted authority mystiques which the physician embodied and which themselves were reinforced by the increased autonomy that medicine obtained with the popularization of science during the Enlightenment.[12] And the homosexual was as susceptible to that kind of diffuse and seemingly well grounded basis for persecution as anyone else, perhaps even more so given the dynamics of internalizing guilt.

The second major obstacle was the persistence of past patterns of oppressive and repressive behavior. Much of the thinking about moral and sexual reform was so directed to the future as to qualify as utopian. In almost every way, the daily realities were harsher than even the most modest of the philosophes would admit. Sources indicate that the clergy continued its practice, already established in the Middle Ages, of protecting its own homosexuals while persecuting others for homosexuality, and official records show that many homosexuals were publicly executed. In the seventeenth century homosexuality had become an aristocratic privilege and clandestine societies had been formed, the most famous being the "Ordre des Sodomites" and the "Société des Amis du Crièce." The eighteenth century saw a proliferation of lesbian societies, one of which "Les Vestales de Vénus," was reputed to have chapters throughout the nation.[13]

12. Michel Foucault, *Madness and Civilization: A History of Insanity in the Age of Reason*, trans. Richard Howard (New York: Vintage, 1973), pp. 269–77.

13. For a discussion of secret male homosexual organizations in the seventeenth century, see Marc Daniel's *Libertins du Grand Siècle* (Paris: Arcadie, 1960), and on eighteenth-century lesbian orders, see Jean de Reuilly's *La Raucourt et ses amies: étude historique des moeurs saphiques au XVIIIe siècle* (Paris: H. Daragon, 1909).

Insofar as these continuing regressive tendencies produced an intellectual and organizational inertia, they were important from the very beginning of the century. But they took on an even greater significance as the century advanced and France experienced the full effects of its political and social crises, for they aggravated what could be called "the revolutionary problematic."

Revolutions are born in antithetical desires: to destroy and to create, to play and to work, to absorb and to exclude, to praise and to punish, to indulge and to purify. In many ways the revolutionary ethic is a classic example of what contemporary psychology calls "a double-bind situation," and the relationship between homosexuality and the French revolution is a striking example of that problematic in action. On the one hand, homosexuality had to be condemned because it represented behavior of the privileged classes and *libertins* and was therefore counterrevolutionary. That is why even the most tolerant minds frequently used the issue of homosexuality in their diatribes against the clergy and the aristocracy. By provisionally ignoring their own pleas for tolerance and sexual reform and by subordinating any commitment to homosexuals to their larger commitment to the struggle against Christianity and the monarchy, the revolutionaries, who were astutely political in both the ideological and practical senses of the word, could undermine the support of their enemies and rally support for themselves. On the other hand, homosexuality had to be somewhat tolerated and protected, if not encouraged, for its defense was inextricably tied in theory to the expansion of human rights and civil liberties. Furthermore, the defense of homosexuality and other minority concerns held a certain polemical value insofar as it was proof of the desire to appropriate what had been the privilege of a few and make it the right of all.

The issue of moral choice was, then, ambiguous, and it was usually treated according to the demands of circumstances and the public. The outcome of such ambivalence was a dilemma: homosexuality was alternately extolled as a revolutionary morality and damned as a reactionary one. It was a situation that would arise again, especially in the twentieth century: first, in the early years of the Soviet revolution when Lenin abolished all laws against minority sexuality because such laws were counter-revolutionary, but Stalin subsequently reinstated them because such morality was counterrevolutionary; then, during the Cuban revolution when homosexuals were sent to detention camps; and finally, during the disagreement among militant black leaders in America in the late 1960's over the possibility of forming a coalition with the gay movement.

Of course, these four instances of the revolutionary problematic were not identical in their consequences. The situation in France was complicated by the role of the bourgeoisie in the revolution. Not adhering strictly to any ideological viewpoint but only to its self-interest, the middle class wanted to displace power from the aristocracy and the clergy without establishing a truly egalitarian society. With compromise in favor of itself as its only creed, the bourgeoisie silently consented to the possibility of minority reforms only as long as the issue might help to subvert the powers it wanted to replace. Once the bourgeoisie had firmly consolidated its own position in the early nineteenth century, minority sexuality became a threat to its moral standards and repressive measures were quickly instituted.

Despite the divisiveness about minority sexuality on the part of nearly all the participants in the French revolution, however, one fact stands out as dramatic evidence of the liberating influence of the philosophes: France had gone from the last public burning of a homosexual in 1784 to placing homosexuality on a more or less equal basis with heterosexuality in the Constitution of 1791. It was a step without parallel in Western civilization, providing homosexuals with legal sanction for the first time since the Roman Empire.

No fair assessment of the complex status of homosexuality in the eighteenth century can be made without taking account of the figure who comes closest to being the personal embodiment of it: the Marquis de Sade. At once an anomaly and a prototype, Sade seems to derive his importance and interest from his persisting status as an enigma, typified perhaps by the way in which he was simultaneously creating and created by what we may now begin to designate as a homosexual "tradition."

In many ways, Sade belongs more to the twentieth century

than to the eighteenth, for it is this century which, starting with
the research of Apollinaire and Maurice Heine and culminating
in the 1950's and 1960's with the criticism of Beauvoir, Paulhan,
Blanchot, Klossowski, and Bataille, has brought his texts and
significance to light. He has, for the most part, passed from
incomprehension as the infamous marquis through culthood as
the "divine marquis" and can finally be viewed as a writer and
thinker. Even today, however, he inspires paradox, for although
it is literary critics who have largely undertaken the restoration
of Sade, most of their criticism has concentrated on his thought
rather than his writings. Such work has been invaluable, for
readers can now perceive unity in a body of work which once
seemed hopelessly chaotic and impenetrable, and Sade himself
can be seen in relation to the intellectual currents of the Enlightenment. But the philosophical and ethical reevaluation of
Sade has not been complemented by a literary one. He has generally been accepted into philosophy-as-system to a much
greater degree than into literature-as-system.

Obviously the two domains are not mutually exclusive even
though emphatic differences between them exist. In "Faut-il
brûler Sade?", Beauvoir seems on the verge of defining a conjunction between philosophical and literary appreciations when
she correctly asserts that "Sade's sexuality is not a biological matter. It is a social fact"[14] and that "his chief interest for us lies not
in his aberrations but in the manner in which he assumed responsibility for them. He made of his sexuality an ethic; and he
expressed this ethic in works of literature" (6). In a particularly
suggestive passage, Beauvoir describes the transformation of the
conservative young marquis: "On the verge of his adult life he
made the brutal discovery that there was no conciliation possible
between his social existence and his private pleasures" (7). Using
some basic principles of contemporary formalist criticism,
Beauvoir's largely sociological and philosophical observations
can easily be extended in a more literary direction and made to

14. Simone de Beauvoir, "Must We Burn Sade?" in The Marquis de Sade, *The
120 Days of Sodom and Other Writings*, comp. and trans. Austryn Wainhouse and
Richard Seaver (New York: Grove Press, 1966), p. 4. All references are to this
edition.

yield certain insights: that Sade's sexuality was a literary fact even more than a biological or social one; that his works created, not merely expressed, his ethics and his sexuality; and that writing may well have been the one way for Sade to find the conciliation that reality denied him. Moreover, if he is viewed as fundamentally homosexual—and Beauvoir clearly sees sodomy as Sade's primary mode of sexual behavior (23) and not just another aspect of an essentially bisexual or "polymorphous perverse" identity—one could apply Laud Humphreys's analysis of artistic activity as a form of homosexual "passing" to Sade's career as a writer.[15]

Yet even this kind of criticism remains on such a general plane that it still leaves Sade as an anomaly in literary history, and denying him any participation in the larger literary context distorts Sade. The problem is that he must be considered in terms not of a tradition but rather of a subtradition, for a minority tradition provides the necessary mediation between the totally collective and the wholly individual. In short, the difficulty in defining Sade's position in literature is directly related to the delay in defining a homosexual tradition.

The mutual influences between Sade and this tradition can be shown by demonstrating how important homosexual stereotypes entered into and were reinforced by his work. Like the medieval and Enlightenment sodomite, Sade was considered a criminal, heretic, and madman. He spent more than thirty years in the most infamous institutions in France, the Conciergerie, the Bastille, Bicêtre, and Charenton, and lived much of the rest of his life in flight from prosecution (he was condemned to hang in effigy by a court in Aix) or in countryside exile imposed by the king. As his letters to Madame de Sade prove, Sade was the first to realize that it was the solitude of his social and moral marginality which drove him to become a writer who could find both redemption and revenge through his works. He was born an aristocrat and, despite his later political convictions, he could never purge himself of an aristocratic penchant for privilege

15. See "Skills of the Oppressed" in Laud Humphreys's *Out of the Closets: The Sociology of Homosexual Liberation* (Englewood Cliffs: Prentice-Hall, 1972), pp. 63–77.

and self-indulgence, which brought him close to the guillotine during the Terror. During the last part of his life, however, others joined him in the recognition of the radical political, social, and ethical implications underlying the surface obscenities of his work; and in the postrevolutionary period, Sade was received as a celebrity and made director of the Section des Piques.

Sade's recapitulating of the development of a homosexual tradition belongs as much to his literature as to his life, however. Even while he was personally enjoying status and esteem as a revolutionary, his works remained outlawed, and the many volumes of Sade that have survived represent only one-fourth of his total output. Yet the neglect and destruction his work suffered at the hands of others was only a superficial and expected aspect of the work's criminality; more striking is the way in which Sade himself affirmed its criminality. He frequently asserted that he wrote not to attract but rather to alienate and provoke his readers: "And now, friend-reader, you must prepare your heart and your mind for the most impure tale that has ever been told since our world began, a book the likes of which are met with neither amongst the ancients nor amongst us moderns.... Many of the extravagances you are about to see illustrated will doubtless displease you, yes, I am well aware of it."[16] As his "Last Will and Testament" shows, Sade fully expected a criminal's fate. He even participated actively in establishing the criminality of his works, using articles like "Reflections on the Novel" and "Notes Concerning My Detention" in order to condemn critically and then deny authorship of his most prized work, *Justine*.

That Sade's writings should be judged criminal by nonliterary standards seems self-evident. But Sade was guilty of more, for he committed not only literary crimes against society but also literary crimes against literature. If such a thing as a "criminal style" can be said to exist, Sade's is certainly that style. Weak characterizations, the lack of verisimilitude in his plots, his vocabulary, his formlessness and repetitiveness, the excessively black and grotesque humor which surpassed even the most cynical of the Enlightenment satirists, and the general lack of clarity

16. Sade, *The 120 Days of Sodom and Other Writings*, pp. 253–54.

in the exposition of his thought—these were the literary violations that would bring condemnation and neglect from scholars and intellectuals as well as from the general public and the civil authorities. Sade's criminality was complete, for, by committing crimes against the classical style, which even the most radical of philosophes had never abandoned, he cut himself off from a literary tradition that otherwise offered a refuge for *poètes maudits*. Sade was consciously too much the condemned man and too little the poet to find acceptance on either side of the society/arts alternative.

Nothing could seem further from the distorted and excessive world of Sade than the proportioned and learned art of the Renaissance. Yet his works do possess certain Renaissance attributes. Sade's philosopher-libertines not infrequently refer to the manners of the Greeks and praise them for the realism of their relatively unrestricted and unrestrictive view of human morality. The cult of physical beauty is also found in Sade: despite the abundance of repulsive sexual details and descriptions in his works, he often viewed the well-formed human body from an aesthetic perspective and accorded it the admiration that a Renaissance poet might have held for a perfect sonnet on a theme from classical mythology. Of course Sade pushed his vision to an extreme, and the characters who receive such names as Cupidon, Narcisse, Adonis, Hercule, and Antinoüs usually merit them not because of a beautifully proportioned neck or trunk but because of perfectly, if outrageously, proportioned genitals. Finally, the bisexuality of Sade's works cannot be denied, Beauvoir's view of his homosexual preference notwithstanding. It is obviously not accompanied by the glory and joy that have been attributed to Renaissance artists, but Sade's sexual explorations do demonstrate a strong inquisitiveness about the possibilities and limitations of human nature.

The presence of a secret homosexual aristocracy that forms an underground elite, as in the seventeenth century, is the most common aspect in all of Sade's writing. The very core of his writings and thought involves the search for a new outlet for "the will to power" and for a substitute sovereignty that will be both personally and philosophically meaningful. In *Les 120 jours de Sodome* (1785), the *encyclopédie raisonnée* of vice which Sade considered to be the theoretical basis of his entire work, the Duc de Blangis apprises the participants in the exhaustive experiments in criminal pleasure of their situation:

> Give a thought to your circumstances, think what you are, what we are, and may these reflections cause you to quake—you are beyond the borders of France in the depths of an uninhabitable forest, high among naked mountains; the paths that brought you here were destroyed behind you as you advanced along them. You are enclosed in an impregnable citadel; no one on earth knows you are here, you are beyond the reach of your friends, of your kin: insofar as the world is concerned, you are already dead, and if you breathe, 'tis by our pleasure and for it only. And what are the persons to whom you are now subordinated? Beings of a profound and recognized criminality, who have no god but their lubricity, no laws but their depravity, no care but for their debauch, godless, unprincipled, unbelieving profligates, of whom the least criminal is soiled by more infamies than you could number. [250–51]

It is a passage which can justifiably be regarded as a "primal scene" in Sade, for, in addition to conveying his imperiousness and personal absolutism, it defines the temporal, spatial, and human relationships that dominate his work and recall the closed world of the secret orders of the seventeenth century.

There are moments, however, when Sade transcends his concern with private pleasures and the larger consequences of his sexuality come into view. The most striking one is the speech "Yet Another Effort, Frenchmen, If You Would Become Republicans," inserted into the fifth dialogue of *La philosophie dans le boudoir* (1795). Richer in ideas and more polished in form and style than any of Sade's other works, it is a plea for his countrymen to consummate the revolutionary destruction of the *ancien régime* with the revolutionary construction of a new moral code that will prevent the reestablishment of dictatorial government. In "Religion," the first part of the work, Sade lays the groundwork for a natural ethics by arguing that the church-state hegemony must be dismantled forever and that the new age of republicanism demands atheism.

In terms of a homosexual tradition and Sade's own work, the

most important part of the tract is the second section, entitled
"Manners." Sade himself realized its significance when he reminded his readers that, of the two parts, "this article is the more
crucial, for the laws to be promulgated will issue from manners,
and will mirror them."[17] And it is especially in this section that
Sade assumed his place as the first revolutionary homosexual, a
role theoretically defined earlier by the philosophes.

His premise sounded simple and reasonable enough: "Frenchmen, you are too intelligent to fail to sense that new government will require new manners" (307). By mixing seemingly
paradoxical commitments to personal aristocracy and republicanism, Sade derived surprising conclusions. The same man
whose name became legendary and synonymous with the love of
crime, pain, and bloody rituals found that "in fact there are very
few criminal actions in a society whose foundations are liberty
and equality" (307) and that even those few crimes did not merit
capital punishment. In an analysis that anticipated the sociology
of class conflicts, Sade refused to condemn theft, asking
"whether that law is truly just which orders the man who has
nothing to respect another who has everything?" (313). And in
the final part of "Manners," Sade included a defense of sodomy
of unprecedented length and detail. Strictly speaking, the passage must be classified as a third-person apology for homosexuality since it is delivered by a character, the Chevalier de Mirvel.
Yet the narrative veil is so thin as to be transparent, and no one
can doubt that it is Sade himself who is really speaking. Thus he
is responsible for the first authentic first-person defense of
homosexuality that went beyond mere tolerance in French literature.

Actually, Sade prepared the way for his defense of homosexuality earlier, in the fifth dialogue when, anticipating the Marxist
analysis of how sex is exploited through reproduction toward
socioeconomic ends, Dolmancé exclaims: "Ah! far from outrag-
ing Nature, on the contrary . . . , the sodomite and Lesbian serve

17. Sade, *Justine, Philosophy in the Bedroom, and Other Writings,* comp. and trans.
Richard Seaver and Austryn Wainhouse (New York: Grove Press, 1965), p. 307.
All references to "Yet Another Effort, Frenchmen, If You Would Become Re-
publicans" are to this edition.

her by stubbornly abstaining from a conjunction whose resultant progeniture can be nothing but irksome to her. Let us make no mistake about it, this propagation was never one of her laws, nothing she ever demanded of us, but at the very most something she tolerated" (276). In "Manners," however, the defense is expanded to incorporate legal, historical, and ethical considerations and to be even more militant in its declarations:

> But sodomy, that alleged crime which will draw the fire of heaven upon cities addicted to it, is sodomy not a monstrous deviation whose punishment could not be severe enough? Ah, sorrowful it is to have to reproach our ancestors for the judiciary murders in which, upon this head, they dared indulge themselves. We wonder what savagery could ever reach the point where you condemn to death an unhappy person all of whose crime amounts to not sharing your tastes.... Let us abide in our unshakable assurance ... that it makes absolutely no difference whether one enjoys a girl or a boy, ... that no inclinations or tastes can exist in us save the ones we have from Nature, that she is too wise and too consistent to have given us any which could ever offend her.
>
> The penchant for sodomy is the result of physical formation, to which we contribute nothing and which we cannot alter. At the most tender age, some children reveal that penchant, and it is never corrected in time. Sometimes it is the fruit of satiety; but even in this case, is it less Nature's doing? Regardless of how it is viewed, it is her work, and, in every instance, what she inspires in us must be respected by men. [325–26]

As an avid reader of Voltaire, Diderot, Rousseau, and other contemporaries, Sade was familiar with natural ethics and philosophy and their derivation from objective Newtonian cosmology. It should not be surprising, then, that his own work pursued a similar direction and transformed "unnatural love" into natural love by redefining nature, both human and nonhuman, as amoral existence. The pertinence of Enlightenment thought to minority sexuality had at last become manifest.

Sade also brought historical and sociological data into his argument, touching on the Greeks, Romans, American Indians, Turks, the Amasians of Crete, the blacks of Benguela, and the seraglios of Algiers. The catalogue of precedents is impressive, but while it makes his case superficially more persuasive, it does less to strengthen its substance. Still, there are more severe limitations and qualifications to Sade's defense of homosexuality.

First, the homosexual's gain in Sade cannot be considered completely and consistently revolutionary because of the extreme misogyny that clearly emerges in his comments on prostitution. Insofar as he accords women the freedom to do with themselves as they wish, his views are compatible with those he expressed on homosexuality; but more often he defends prostitution for the wrong reasons, all having to do with a belief in a "natural" male sovereignty which obviously conflicts with the unhierarchical and amoral view of nature he espoused in his defense of sodomy. Second, one cannot help but regret that such progressive ideas about homosexuality were expressed within the very kind of context—shockingly obscene works which continued to outrage intellectuals as well as the bourgeoisie for more than 150 years—most likely to ensure the repression rather than the dissemination of such views.

Yet it is the essence of the Sadean enigma that these contradictions and many others should coexist in the same body of works and that their philosopher-pornographer author should defy easy comprehension and classification as much today as he did in the eighteenth century. If one tries, for example, to establish for Sade the kind of textual-contextual homology that Lucien Goldmann has devised, the results are even less satisfying than those obtained by viewing Sade within the perspective of a homosexual tradition. For Sade's homologies seem to extend in every temporal direction: backward to the seventeenth century and earlier; certainly to the intellectual and socioeconomic currents of his own time; and forward to the Decadents of the nineteenth century and the homosexual apologists and militants of the twentieth.

Yet all the problems in dealing with Sade cannot diminish his originality. It is a difficult originality, difficult to grasp and difficult to accept, but it is originality nonetheless. The judgment that Sade "was never more than a caricature of the Enlightenment whose heir he claimed to be"[18] is invalid if only on the basis

18. Peter Gay, *The Enlightenment: An Interpretation. Volume I, The Rise of Modern Paganism* (New York: Random House-Vintage Books, 1968), p. 25.

that no other voice in the eighteenth century had the boldness to
address the issue of minority morality so directly and forcefully:

> Now that we have got back upon our feet and broken with the
> host of prejudices that held us captive; now that, brought closer to
> Nature by the quantity of prejudices we have recently obliterated,
> we listen only to Nature's voice, we are fully convinced that if
> anything were criminal, it would be to resist the penchants she
> inspires in us, rather than to come to grips with them . . . , we
> must demand enough wisdom and enough prudence of our legis-
> lators to be entirely sure that no law will emanate from them that
> would repress perversions which, being determined by constitu-
> tion and being inseparable from physical structure, cannot render
> the person in whom they are present any more guilty than the
> person Nature created deformed. [316, 329]

Written on the eve of the nineteenth century, Sade's words
announced that a homosexual tradition had come of age. It was
a mature and active tradition to the degree that, by the end of
the eighteenth century, it had found a sureness of voice and
vision which would allow it to pass from passive withdrawal to
assertive commitment. Literature's homosexual heritage was no
longer just an accumulation of short-lived trends or isolated
works and writers. It had evolved into a spectrum of analytical
and creative possibilities which now seemed to exhibit diachronic
growth and to provide a broad enough base of common givens
to engender and assimilate widely differing perspectives. Moreover, structural cohesion and exchange marked not only the
elements of this homosexual tradition, but also the relation of
that tradition to the larger literary and extraliterary contexts.
For these specific reasons, then, as well as for the encouragement of minorities generated by the period's pervasive mood of
social, political, and philosophical experimentation, the Age of
Enlightenment and the Age of Revolution proved to be the
pivotal century for a homosexual literary tradition in France.

It would be erroneous, however, to see the homosexual legacy
of the age solely in terms of liberation. The ironies of the time
are simply too glaring to allow such an interpretation. Whether
we look at Voltaire's simultaneous denigrations and defenses of
sodomy, Montesquieu's commitment to both private abhorrence

and public acceptance of "the crime against nature," Rousseau's lessons in tolerance within the very Church whose intolerance united the philosophes in outrage, or the discrepancy between the Sadean mode and the Sadean message, the entire century seems to partake of contradictory attitudes which found their most overt expression in "the revolutionary problematic." To that extent, the French Enlightenment did not overcome the condemnatory perspectives and homosexual stereotypes of previous epochs so much as it countered them by providing a set of comparatively more positive viewpoints and models that set the old and new homosexualities into dialectical opposition. The change marked by the French Enlightenment is not, in brief, an exchange of absolute positivity for absolute negativity but rather the creation of ambivalence. Ambivalence was the true heritage of the age, for just as it formed the condition of the philosophical and sociopolitical pertinence of homosexuality in the eighteenth century, it became the basis for the appeal of homosexuality to art, the very process of which seeks out and reworks ambiguity, in later periods. Perhaps more than any other factor, it is the ambivalence of the Enlightenment that accounts for the unparalleled homosexual participation and presence in nineteenth- and twentieth-century French literature.

Gerald H. Storzer

The Homosexual Paradigm in Balzac, Gide, and Genet

Balzac, Gide, and Genet have in common their obsessive pre-occupation with the relationship between homosexuality and criminality. In accepting that relationship, at least as a point of departure, they espouse a traditional view of the homosexual that has important implications. What is criminal is ultimately defined as anything that is not part and parcel of the accepted ideas and conventional mores of society. Thus the homosexual, because he is perceived as criminal in this larger sense of the term, if not always in actual fact, is the outsider living beyond the confines of rigid social structures. Within those structures the self exists as a social personality or mask that is a denial of authentic being. To wear a mask is to experience a form of death as sexuality is repressed, along with the instinctive responses, the emotive reactions, the spontaneous and creative approaches to the other and to reality that are associated with it. In refusing to allow his sexuality—and consequently the very nature of his being—to be structured by social forces, the homosexual figure comes to represent a major revolutionary force both within and without the fictional universe. His disruptive sexuality becomes emblematic of the attempt to safeguard individuality and creativity in the face of stifling exigencies imposed by the social and cultural milieu.

It is evident that the homosexual figure does not stand alone in his position as outsider, social critic, and defender of the creative self. However, to the extent that this view of the homosexual-criminal serves as the point of reference in relation to which an author develops the concepts of self and society that constitute the foundation for his fictional world, one may speak of a *homosexual paradigm* in his works. In such cases the notion of homosexuality is transformed into a kind of literary construct. It serves to evoke, almost spontaneously, the complex network of metonyms and correlates we have described. That construct can be used as a device and convention as long as the assumptions of the original paradigm are accepted as viable and operative.

It is to be emphasized that we are dealing with a paradigm that exists for the most part in the mind of the writer and is not necessarily translated into homosexual characters or situations within the fictional universe. Our task is not primarily, therefore, to categorize characters and situations, or even the author, according to sexuality. Nor is it to prove tenuous relationships between fictional events and the author's own real-life experiences, if any, with homosexuality. Rather, our interest lies in demonstrating that in the case of Balzac, Gide, and Genet, the author's concepts of self and society have evolved from this basic homosexual paradigm. That endeavor necessitates the use of a kind of structural thematics which will permit us to show how the various themes, emotional associations, philosophic notions, and narrative techniques connected with homosexuality are fused in a unique vision for each of the authors.

Balzac's royalist and conservative prefaces to the *Comédie humaine* and to the individual novels misrepresent his vision of society by ignoring the real problems raised by the work. At bottom, the *Comédie* is not a study of traditional social institutions at all, but of the new industrial society that was flourishing before Balzac's very eyes. At the heart of each of the novels lies the same basic struggle between corruptive materialism and individual integrity. In terms of literary geography the *Comédie* divides France into Paris and the country, the center of rampant materialism and the beyond, which are summarized thematically in the struggle between the "social" and the "natural" states of man.[1] At other times the metaphorical division is drawn in terms of legality and criminality, opposing the social state to the natural life of the criminal. At the eye of the hurricane, on the line of demarcation between the social and the natural, stands the homosexual figure, Vautrin—police chief and underworld boss.

The character is the last incarnation, after Argow le Pirate and Ferragus, of a figure by whom Balzac was obsessed. Vautrin incorporates the traits of his two predecessors and adds one: homosexuality. The portrait of the natural man, evolving beyond social laws and institutions, would not be complete without some form of disruptive or natural sexuality. Vautrin's homosexuality transforms him into the prototype of Balzacian characterization. In Vautrin are illustrated the essential precepts governing Balzac's concept of self: (1) that true sexuality is always asocial in nature: (2) that it is the source of vital energy; (3) that passion is a form of sexuality in the sense that it represents a concentration of sexual energy; and (4) that natural sexuality—sexuality experienced outside the limitations and repressions fostered by the social order—is the only source of authentic being.

For Balzac, vital energy is an extension of sexuality. He speaks, for example, of the savage energy that is released during the orgy in *La Peau de chagrin* (453). The flow of sexual energy within the individual can be understood completely only when one compares Vautrin to his counterpart, la Zambinella in *Sarrasine*. Both characters evolve beyond readily accepted norms for masculine and feminine and in this sense might be considered androgynous. However, the castrato is devoid of sexuality, therefore completely lacking in energy (266–67). True an-

1. Honoré de Balzac, *Splendeurs et misères des courtisanes* in *La comédie humaine*, ed. Pierre-Georges Castex and Pierre Citron (Paris: Seuil, 1966), p. 432; cf. *Goriot*, pp. 287–88. Each of the novels is cited in the Intégrale (Seuil) edition, indicated in my text by a simple abbreviation of the title of the work. All translations into English are my own.

drogyny is sterile. The castrato represents a negation of being: his very presence connotes death.[2] In the creation of such characters as Vautrin and Margarita-Euphémia Porrabéril, on the other hand, Balzac uses homosexuality—which emphasizes the sexuality of a character in a way that simple heterosexuality might not—to point up their savage energy and their eminently forceful and viril temperaments (*Goriot,* 221-22, 249-50, 268; *Splendeurs,* 400-01, 436-38; *Fille,* 128-29). Although sexual in nature, such energy is not necessarily expended in the sexual domain. Vautrin's force and emotivity, for example, seem to be inversely proportional to actual sexual activity.[3]

Most commonly, sexual energy is translated into passion through the metaphor of desire. Passion itself is nonsexual. It is a form of hope in the sense that it is a dissatisfaction with the everyday and a striving toward the ideal: "Passion [in the realm of love] is the intuition of love and of its infinity toward which all suffering souls aspire" (*Langeais,* 90). However, the manifestation of the need to transcend the ordinary—in any domain—is a form of desiring and, consequently, a manifestation of sexuality. Indeed, passion and desire exist in metonymic fusion in the *Comédie humaine,* except when the latter is used to designate dispassionate sexuality within the social order. For Raphaël, for example, passionate involvement of any sort is equated with desire, and uses up the brute sexual energy at the center of his being (*Peau,* 441, 472). One might properly speak of passion as the sublimation of sexuality, the channeling of sexual energy— and the unconscious, libidinal needs associated with it—into a very personalized effort of transcendence.

In terms of characterization, sexual energy is the source of being, and its concentration in a passion is the basis for individuation. Lucien's suicide negates Vautrin's sexual desire by depriving it of its object and thus destroys the criminal's vital energy. Simultaneously, that suicide neutralizes Vautrin's passion and consequently dissipates the effort—which was the mark of his individuality—to realize a certain superhuman form of being. Thus, to rob Vautrin of both sexual desire and passion is not just

2. *Sarrasine,* p. 275. See also Roland Barthes: *S/Z* (Paris: Seuil, 1970).
3. *Lambert,* pp. 298-303, 321; *Splendeurs,* p. 345.

to deprive him of his energy, but to destroy as well the distinguishing traits of his personality: "Right now [with Lucien] they
are burying my life, my beauty, my virtue, my conscience, all of
my strength! Imagine a dog from which a chemist has drawn out
the blood . . . I am that dog" (*Splendeurs*, 458). Passion is most
often manifested as an imperious emotion. Such emotions, as
the source of authentic individuality, tend to explode the outer
mask to reveal true, inner identity. The scene in which Vautrin is
captured by the police, by its perfection and impact, stands as a
model for the innumerable instances throughout the *Comédie
humaine* in which assumed identities are destroyed to reveal the
true nature of the character to the reader—and occasionally to
the character himself. In the case of the Duchesse de Langeais,
for example, an unsuspected capacity for passion leads to self-
discovery and, through love, she becomes the woman she really
is (90).

Passion, and by extension sexuality and authentic being, are
asocial and thus criminal in the larger sense of the term. Vautrin
cannot be integrated into society until he has experienced the
loss of passion and sexuality that coincides with his figurative
death and the end of his criminality: "I am that dog. . . . That is
why . . . I am giving myself up!" (*Splendeurs*, 458; cf. 425; *Goriot*,
268). In a similar way, the characters who experience deep
loves—a form of passion—exist outside the social realm by virtue
of the fact that their loves are defined in opposition to the sexual
roles imposed by society. In love, both male and female characters transcend masculine-feminine dichotomies, and many of
them experience loves that are either totally nonsexual in nature
or purified of sexual desire: the paternal loves of Goriot,
Ferragus, Vautrin, and LaPeyrade, the fraternal love between
Pons and Schmucke, the religious loves of the Duchesse de
Langeais and Mme de Mortsauf.[4] Goriot's protestations that his
daughters are destroying the values of paternity, family, and
country are ironic (302). Goriot has himself rejected the sexual
power structure and thus placed himself outside society: he has
refused to accept the delimitations of the paternal role, and tries

---

4. *Ferragus*, p. 42; *Langeais*, pp. 71, 75, 76; *Splendeurs*, pp. 291, 296, 297, 300,
425, 427; *Lys*, pp. 303, 304, 320, 355, 387.

instead to transcend pragmatic realities through a superhuman form of love. Since their passions are incompatible with the ordered hierarchy established by sexual roles in the industrial society, it is not surprising that so many Balzacian characters should live their loves like monks and nuns in a world apart. Though most commit no criminal act, these passionate beings are ideologically in league with the prostitutes and criminals who represent "two living protestations, male and female, of the *natural state* against the *social one*" (*Splendeurs*, 432). Thus the Duchesse de Langeais would willingly be branded with the mark of criminality to emphasize the degree to which passion has divorced her from social institutions (88). This relationship between asocial passion and criminality is made explicit in *Splendeurs et misères*, where Balzac pinpoints the channeling of energy into passionate love as one of the distinguishing characteristics of the criminal type, and cites it as the source of seven out of ten crimes (433).

Within society, on the other hand, passion cannot exist and authentic being is stifled. People are transformed into lifeless masks through the desexualizing influence of a theatrical milieu. In choosing the title for his work Balzac is perhaps less indebted to Dante than to modern notions of game- and role-playing. Comedy for Balzac is theater, theater that connotes gratuitous, meaningless action. Although the notion of theater is occasionally applied to life in general, it is usually reserved for the play of ambition and vanity within the microcosm of industrial society that Paris represents (*Fille*, 125; *Splendeurs*, 406, 460). Like the masked ball which opens *Splendeurs et misères*, Paris is a landscape of swirling travesties and false appearances. The prelude to *La fille aux yeux d'or* is a scathing indictment of this theatrical society in which the self is reduced to a series of empty poses adopted and discarded according to the demands of institutionalized status-seeking and greed (104–08). The social self is a form of nonbeing. It is a castration of the self through the formulaic gesture, the calculated maneuver and the controlled emotional reaction (*Peau*, 453). Even love and sexuality can be "socialized." Love can be feigned and added as an accoutrement to the mask (*Peau*, 471). Sexuality is relegated to the confines of limited social roles or becomes a conquest for social ends. The self is lost as sexual energy slips its moorings in deeply felt passion: "In Paris, no emotion resists the flow of events, and their current necessitates a struggle that dissipates passion: there, love becomes [simple sexual] desire" (*Fille*, 104). Foedora, whose character is developed almost exclusively through the theme of the mask, exemplifies the woman who has used social poses to negate inner being and deny her sexuality (*Peau*, 478–80). She is described as an androgyne (*Peau*, 475). In her masklike frigidity she is like La Zambinella. Her whole life is reduced to the surface of the role she plays, and La Zambinella's cry could easily be her own: " 'I have no heart!' she cried out in tears. 'The stage on which you saw me, that applause, that music, that's my life, I have no other' " (*Sarrasine*, 273).

Passion, on the contrary, allied as it is with free-flowing sexual energy, exists beyond the rational and the control of the conscious mind. It invariably involves free and spontaneous emotional reactions and intuitive modes of cognition. It constitutes a kind of diabolism composed of intuition, psychic powers, and moments of intense physical strength, and the passionate character is often compared to God or to the devil; Vautrin, for instance, is both god and devil (*Lys*, 355; *Goriot*, 243, 249, 259; *Ferragus*, 37, 43; *Langeais*, 85, 90; *Fille*, 120; *Splendeurs*, 207, 338, 417). Children of Cain, these characters evolve beyond good and evil, fusing both in a synthesis that affords them an occult and intuitive knowledge of the universe. That knowledge places them beyond the rigid laws of cause and effect governing the Balzacian world.[5]

Such diabolism spawns creativity. The poet's conceptions are based upon needs inspired by passion: his genius consists of the power to use the imagination to give form to ideals that are glimpsed at the unconscious level of desire (*Splendeurs*, 296, 410). The lover, the social revolutionary, the debauched man, and the monomaniac, among others, are like the poet. All belong to a category of men apart, for whom existence is a passionate involvement in the creative striving to move beyond accepted norms in the search for perfection. They are all de-

5. *Pons*, p. 206–08; cf. *Goriot*, p. 253; *Splendeurs*, pp. 386, 416, 425, 448; *Peau*, p. 465. See also E. R. Curtius, *Balzac* (Bern: A. Francke, 1951).

scribed as poets (*Peau*, 438, 491; *Splendeurs*, 296, 410; *Goriot*, 251, 268).

Vautrin's passion is, of course, specifically defined as homosexuality (*Goriot*, 268), and his potential for diabolism and creativity is thereby accentuated, for Balzac singles out homosexual passion as the one which, above all others, incarnates the thirst for the ideal that is characteristic of creative temperaments (*Splendeurs*, 290). However, while the other Balzacian psychics are absorbed in a kind of cosmic fatality or in personal obsessions, Vautrin possesses the unique capacity to deploy energy in the social arena in order to further the goals dictated by inner passion. That ability constitutes his peculiar genius (*Goriot*, 251; *Splendeurs*, 295, 410). It allows him to assume a privileged position in relation to the microcosmic Parisian society and establishes an implicit parallel between him and the persona of the poet-narrator.

Balzac's concepts of plot and semi-omniscient narration are based on the notion of a social reality that is only appearance. The novel in Balzac's hands becomes a "drama" as the narrator discovers and communicates the truths lurking below the surface realities. Now, theater and drama are not to be confused: the term *comédie* is reserved for the play of masks that is society, while the term *drama* always indicates the process by which the mask and the surface appearance are exploded to reveal true realities underneath.[6] In his elucidation of reality, the semi-omniscient narrator is obliged to sniff out information or to follow the lead of a character-observer, like Rastignac, whose curiosity enmeshes him in clandestine intrigues. Thus in *Ferragus*, the semi-omniscient narrative voice highlights the activities of Maulincourt as he ferrets out "the causes, the interests, the nodus hidden behind the mystery [of Mme Jules]." That mystery is described as "a novel to be read, or better a drama to be played, and in which [Maulincourt has] his own role" (20). Because of the detective work he engages in and the control he exercises over this society, Vautrin's position is similar to that of the elucidating narrator: "God does not understand the means

6. For this concept of the novel as drama see, for example: *Goriot*, pp. 220, 246; *Ferragus*, pp. 14, 17, 20; *Langeais*, p. 55; *Splendeurs*, pp. 320, 384, 448.

and ends of his creation any better than this man grasped the slightest differences in the mass of events and people" (*Splendeurs*, 382). In terms of creative powers Balzac, as writer, through this structural parallel between the criminal and the poet-narrator, allies himself with Vautrin more than with any other character in the *Comédie humaine*.

By associating a disruptive sexuality with the character of the passionate outsider as he moves from Ferragus to Vautrin, Balzac is able to reinforce the dichotomy of the sexual and the asexual (natural/social) that is at the basis of his characterization. Vautrin illustrates the principle out of which are created the sexless androgynes—the Foedoras, the Mmes Vauquers, the Nucingens, even the treacherous Poirets and Michonneaus— who trade authentic being for empty social identities and sacrifice humanity to avarice. Out of that same principle are born the passionate beings—the "group of the 13," the monomaniacs, the great lovers and criminals and poets—in whom liberated sexual energy leads to a creative affirmation of the self in defiance of the social order. Because Vautrin's particular passion is sexual and disruptive in nature, the character illustrates as well the peculiar relationship between natural sexuality and passion that distinguishes characterization in the *Comédie*. In a broader sense, Vautrin's disruptive sexuality becomes the vehicle for Balzac's attack on the dehumanizing materialism that he perceives in the flourishing industrial society. Vautrin's homosexuality serves to crystallize into a concept the various elements which compose Balzac's view of the self and society. In that sense one can say that the homosexual paradigm is of central importance in the *Comédie humaine*. It summarizes the Balzacian notion of authentic and creative individuality freed from the constraints of capitalism.

Gide's writings demonstrate an amazing continuity, which stems directly from his preoccupation with defining the homosexual self in its relationship to the social milieu. In his struggle with the moral dilemma posed by homosexuality, Gide very early adopts two apparently contradictory stances that pervade the process of characterization in his works. On the one hand, like Balzac, he views disruptive sexuality as the source of being for an "idiosyncratic" self—a self which constitutes an ontological truth, and which is basically asocial and amoral. Gide proposes jealously to safeguard the integrity of this intimate self against all impingements by the social and cultural milieu. Thus the bulk of his writing is devoted to examining the process by which the inner self is manifested and the various ways in which it may be distorted and falsified by the individual or by his environment. On the other hand, Gide finds it inconceivable that the idiosyncratic self cannot and should not be integrated into society, a stance which implies a rejection of the notion that homosexuality should ever be totally disruptive. Consequently, his works contain as well a detailed examination of the obstacles that must be overcome if the idiosyncratic self is to function meaningfully within social structures.

The notion that sexuality is the source of being is already developed in *Les cahiers d'André Walter.*[7] In the struggle between mysticism and sexuality that consumes him, Walter comes to the realization that he is dealing with two protean transfigurations of the same vital energy (*OC*, I, 171). To deny the sexuality he finds unacceptable is to destroy his very being: "The enemy is within us: that is what is so frightening. Escape is not possible"

7. I shall confine my analysis to the *récits, soties,* and *romans,* with particular emphasis on the *Cahiers, L'immoraliste* and *Les faux-monnayeurs.* All notes concerning the *Cahiers* and *Si le grain ne meurt* refer to the NRF edition of the *Oeuvres complètes* (Paris, 1932–38), indicated by *OC* in the text. The notes for the *Journal des faux-monnayeurs* refer to the NRF edition of that work (Paris, 1927). The notes concerning the other works refer to *Romans, récits et soties, oeuvres lyriques* (Paris: Pléiade, 1958), indicated by an abbreviation of the title of the work quoted. The *Journal* is also quoted in the Pléiade edition: *Journal, 1889–1939* (Paris, 1948). All translations into English are my own. The following translations of the quoted works might be consulted by the reader: *The Counterfeiters with the Journal of the Counterfeiters,* trans. Dorothy Bussy (New York: Knopf, 1959); *If It Die: An Autobiography,* trans. Dorothy Bussy (New York: Random House, 1957); *The Immoralist,* trans. Richard Howard (New York: Knopf, 1970); *Lafcadio's Adventures,* trans. Dorothy Bussy (New York: Vintage, 1960); *Marshlands, and Prometheus Misbound,* trans. George D. Painter (New York: New Directions, 1953); *Narcissus* in *The Return of the Prodigal, Preceded by Five Other Treatises, with Saul, a Drama in Five Acts,* trans. Dorothy Bussy (London: Secker and Warburg, 1953); *The Notebooks of André Walter,* trans. Wade Baskin (New York: Philosophical Library, 1968). To the best of my knowledge no translations exist of *La tentative amoureuse* and *Le voyage d'Urien.*

(*OC,* I, 172). Walter's sexuality is an a priori truth, the mysterious "cuttle-fish egg that grows and hatches" within one for no apparent reason (*Tentative,* 79). It represents one's most intimate and spontaneous impulses; it is a kind of Freudian libido.

Sexuality is the source not only of being, but of the idiosyncratic nature of individual being. Walter's sexuality is idiosyncratic, not in terms of specific acts, nor yet in terms of the objects of desire, but in terms of the quality of desire before it has been categorized and defined in the conventional terms of acts and objects. Gide himself is still slightly unclear on this point in *Les cahiers.* However, a close reading of the text confirms that, Gide's protestations notwithstanding (*Grain, OC,* X, 301–02), Walter's problem is not onanism (the manifestation of sexuality in any specific act) or even repressed homosexuality (sexuality defined in terms of the object of desire). Rather, Walter is troubled by the unique quality of his sexuality, a quality that permeates the personality whether or not acts are engaged in or objects chosen. One is one's sexuality. Every act and idea that the phenomenal self displays in the real world is colored by this inner source of being. Thus, the young Gide translates the problem of homosexuality into a problem of idiosyncratic sexuality and, in the process, redefines *disruptive* in terms of the subject, rather than the object, of desire.

The idiosyncratic, sexual self is a quality of being. For Gide, this inner self, which is the source of all values, is consistently equated with the notion of a deity (for example, *OC,* I, 95; *Tentative,* 85; *Paludes,* 1478; *F-M,* 1208–12). And the conviction that the social personality must be sacrificed to the expression of this inner truth, no matter how disruptive that truth may seem, is quickly transformed into a moral imperative (*Narcisse,* 9). In *Les cahiers* the inner self is expressed in spite of all obstacles. From the *Narcisse* on, Gide is primarily concerned with how that self can be manifested with the least distortion.

Contact with the intimate self can be made only through the emotions which spring directly from it and which are, like it, spontaneous and formless. The problem is that if emotional realities are to be manifested concretely in the phenomenal world, they must be given form through actions and thought, and that process of structuring necessarily deforms and truncates. The enemy of the emotions is the conventional: the accepted modes of conduct, the stereotypic views of the self, and the linguistic structures that incorporate and establish the hegemony of those limiting patterns (*OC,* I, 118, 130, 135). Bernard Profitendieu of *Les faux-monnayeurs* is the only Gidian character who confronts and succeeds in liberating the idiosyncratic personality. Gide very carefully shows him rejecting the religious influence of the pension, the pedantry and rigid logic fostered by the schools, the constant self-analysis associated with rationalistic approaches to the self, the patterned psychological reaction, and the programming influence of language (1088–96, 1110, 1149–50). Above all, Bernard is able to avoid the rigidity of the attitude of revolt that is in itself a false structuring of reality for such characters as Armand: Bernard is able to return home. His success hinges upon his ability to preserve intact the sexual and emotional self. He does not begin to "ring true" until he has rejected false purity (resulting from the repression of sexuality in his love for Laura) and false sexuality (experienced with Sarah). Like Dmitri Karamazov, he is guided by his passionate nature: "Bernard no longer listened to anything but his heart" (1248; cf. 1084, 1093, 1141–42, 1144, 1215).

The idiosyncratic self, though asocial in nature, exists in complete interdependence with the social and cultural milieu. Within that environment the conventional—which may take many forms, one of which is the unconventional—insidiously allies itself with the individual's own capacity for rationalization to create inauthenticity: the idiosyncratic self is repressed. However, the inner self will not be diverted, its needs will be satisfied by one means or another. In the individual who does not consciously take those needs into account in establishing his relationship to the environment, the intimate self becomes an autonomous force capable of wreaking havoc. As Gide develops this notion of a *je qui est un autre* he begins to equate the idiosyncratic self with the devil as well as with God, particularly in *L'immoraliste, Les caves du Vatican* and *Les faux-monnayeurs.*

The term *diabolism* designates this complex psychological mechanism by means of which the individual, through a combination of programming and unawareness, acquiesces in the repression of idiosyncratic needs. Michel, for example, speaks of the "somber god" he serves, of the "demon more forceful than himself" who motivates his actions (459, 467). In Michel of *L'immoraliste,* however, emerging homosexuality is diabolic only to the extent that he avoids a lucid confrontation with it and thus creates a situation in which he is pushed into an irrational and uncontrollable destruction of himself and others. His very revolt against the conventional turns into a conventional pattern of escape from the self: the theories on the value of individualism and the harmful effects of culture and property are, in Michel's case, rationalizations and diversions that allow him to ignore his own inner being. Obviously, the pitfall of diabolism is most clear-cut and threatening for the individual who, like the homosexual, is engaged in an attempt to come to terms with an openly disruptive sexuality (cf. Walter, Michel, the pastor of *La symphonie pastorale,* Olivier, Edouard). However, very early Gide transforms the psychological mechanism into a generalized element of characterization.

In terms of techniques of characterization, the presence of this mechanism is often marked by the creation of a dichotomy between dream and emotion (*Narcisse,* 10; *Urien,* 56, 68; *Tentative,* 71; *Journal,* 40–41). The dichotomy is implicit rather then explicit in some works, for instance *Le Prométhée* and *L'immoraliste.* In *Les caves du Vatican,* however, Lafcadio's whole life is presented as a dream and his most significant acts are always performed in situations that are colored by a dreamlike atmosphere. At the end of the novel the possibility of true emotional involvement with Geneviève provides him with the opportunity finally to shake off the dream in order to establish an authentic relationship with the real world: "But how could she explain to him that she too, until now, had tossed about as if in a dream? . . . He listens, bent over her, through the fragile sound of her breathing, to the vague stirring of the city already shaking off its lethargy" (872–73). The characters of *Les faux-monnayeurs* live in a similar dream world and pass alongside true emotions and the true self. Sophroniska forces Boris to "dream out loud" and thus plunges him irrevocably into the oneiric world of guilt and sin from which he never truly emerges (1075). Olivier, in his indecision and false bravado, fights with Dhurmer as if in a dream (1174). Vincent, unable to come to terms with himself, spends his days dreaming in Africa (1233). Edouard experiences an obsessive need to live through his journal or other people. His idiosyncratic self never achieves authentic contact with the reality around him: he "moves as if in a dream" (1057). Only Bernard succeeds in shaking off the dream to get back to true emotions and authentic sexual needs (975, 1084, 1091, 1144).

One of Gide's most innovative gestures is to broaden this notion of diabolic unawareness to include an examination of its consequences on the level of interpersonal relationships. *Les faux-monnayeurs* is conceived as a kind of treatise on the devil, who becomes its principal character (*Journal des f-m,* 29). Under the devil's influence Vincent represses all emotional impulses as he renounces his original altruistic motives toward Laura and falsely interprets his victory at the gambling table as a sign that he was right in forsaking her (1045–46). That action will lead to madness for Vincent, but more important, it sets in motion the complicated network of events that will end in Boris's suicide. Vincent's act brings Edouard back to Paris and the latter, through false and unthinking generosity, brings Boris to the pension: "Behind the most disinterested of motives is often to be found an ingenious devil who knows how to profit from what we thought we had denied him" (1109). Directly or indirectly, through his own special form of unawareness, each character in the novel provokes other characters who in turn react with equal lack of lucidity. Together they form a counterfeit society which is the real diabolic force in the novel (*Journal des f-m,* 76–77). The counterfeiting that occurs at all levels of this society eventually is concentrated, through a series of coincidences, in the Azaïs pension, where it is responsible for the death of the innocent Boris. Using a concept developed originally in relation to homosexuality, Gide creates a very complex vision of interpersonal relationships based upon the notions of diabolism, coincidence, conjunctive action and reaction, and multidimensional motivation. That vision is responsible in turn for a novelistic universe in which the traditional concepts of cause and effect and of linear action are destroyed.

Through the theme of the mask, *Les faux-monnayeurs* raises again the fundamental question of being and nothingness that Walter had formulated in relation to his own disruptive sexuality

(*OC*, I, 150, 173). The pervasive nature of both personal and social diabolism makes authenticity well-nigh impossible for the characters in the later work. All of them are transformed into masks: "As if each of us were not acting, more or less sincerely and consciously. Life, my friend, is nothing more than a comedy" (1229). The real subject of the book is suicide and assassination, for the counterfeiting these characters engage in is a daily annihilation of the idiosyncratic self. Armand's theory of insufficiency makes the theme explicit: "That line of demarcation between being and nonbeing, I am intent on tracing it everywhere.... As for me, I am like the Arab in the desert, who is going to die of thirst. I am reaching that precise point, you understand, where a drop of water could still save him ... or a tear" (1163). A tear—an authentic emotion—could save any one of this cast of characters, all of whom are poised on the thin line between being and nonbeing. A liberation of the emotional and sexual self could mean life for each of them. Most die in a figurative suicide, choosing the existence of the mask as they succumb to counterfeiting and diabolism. Boris's death is at once the result and the concretization of this process of spiritual suicide.

Homosexuality is not disruptive in the sense that it criminalizes the individual and places him outside the social milieu. In *Les faux-monnayeurs* all the characters engage in some form of illegal activity, yet each remains an integral part of society and cannot escape its influences. In a world where all men are both guilty and innocent, homosexuality is disruptive because it raises the possibility of idiosyncratic being—without guaranteeing it—amid a sea of masks. A single moral law governs this fictional universe and defines criminality: "any man who does not manifest is useless and bad" (*Narcisse*, 8). Michel remains an *immoraliste* and a criminal in the domain of the amoral because he has transgressed that basic law.

By redefining criminality as inauthenticity, Gide seriously weakens the system of metonyms and equivalences created by the romantic myth of the homosexual. Homosexuality in and of itself no longer connotes criminality or asociality. Nor does it serve any longer as an automatic correlate of authentic being and creativity. Michel, Olivier, and Edouard, for example, are no more criminal, asocial, authentic, or creative than most other

Gidian characters. Thus, homosexuality ceases to be perceived as a defining category of being. Such categories are after all only cultural codes and just one more manifestation of the conventional. Being is determined less by the object of desire than by the manner in which sexuality is manifested (or repressed), lived out as an idiosyncratic mode of being. Through the concept of diabolism, originally associated with the homosexual dilemma, Gide places the major emphasis on the problems involved in the struggle to integrate the personality and to realize its uniqueness within the confines of society. In the process, as the source of disruption is transferred from the object to the subject of desire, Gide comes to conceive of all individual modes of sexuality as essentially idiosyncratic and disruptive.

In the notion of self that Genet develops during his early career, homosexuality and criminality are perceived as givens and are so intertwined as to be almost indistinguishable. The homosexual paradigm is an integral part of the effort to give pure and meaningful form to the unstable, protean, criminal-homosexual self. The self achieves permanence in the "image," a kind of prototype or objective model that borders on the stereotype. Certain characters in Genet's novels may be called images: they have achieved, usually in death, the status of archetypes and serve as the model in reference to which a given role is to be conceived. The most important of these characters are Harcamone (*the* Criminal) and Divine (*the* Homosexual). Other characters, such as Querelle, may at times ascend to the level of images. As a state of being, the image is at bottom a form of impersonality in which the body is emptied of immediate sensations and emotions so as to better assume the poses and gestures that will give it meaning by placing it in the realm of the hieratic. The relationship of the self to the image changes drastically as Genet's career progresses.[8] It is in that evolution that the homosexual paradigm and its importance for characterization in both the novels and the plays is best perceived.

8. Most of the criticism that has appeared to date on Genet's works imposes on the novels the vision that is communicated through the plays. The development of Genet's thought thus is obscured, and the positive value that the image has in

The theory of images and the ethics of evil represent an attempt to transcend the phenomenal self through the realization of some archetypal form of the outcast. On the surface, the novels seem to support Sartre's contention that the ethics of evil is a simplistic effort to glorify as a conscious choice a role that has been imposed upon the individual by society's accusing gaze (*Saint-Genet*, 27, 51). It is evident that, for a character like Divine, criminal and homosexual tendencies unfold at least partly because the adolescent has been "objectified" as a thief and a homosexual. However, Genet's use of ritual in the novels suggests that such images may not be mere social stereotypes, but archetypes surfacing from the collective unconscious. The gravest manifestations of criminality and homosexuality are invariably perceived as ceremonial functions in the novels. Village becomes an officiant in a ritual as he kills Sonia and encases her body in bricks (*Notre-Dame*, 105–06). The beginning of the author-narrator's sexual relationship with Divers is sanctified by

---

the novels is negated or embroiled in confusion. See, for example, Richard Coe, *The Vision of Jean Genet* (New York: Grove, 1968), p. 183. See also Jean-Paul Sartre, *Saint-Genet*, trans. Bernard Frechtman (New York: New American Library, 1964). Sartre's generally unsympathetic interpretation of the role of archetypes in the novels stems from his refusal to recognize as valid their positive value within the frame of reference Genet has established. In my own interpretation I am indebted to Jaclyn R. Veneroso's doctoral thesis entitled "The Concept of *Jeu* in the Novels of Jean Genet" (Brown University, 1976). There is, of course, no good standard edition of Genet's works. *Notre-Dame des fleurs, Pompes funèbres* and *Querelle de Brest* are quoted in the NRF edition: Jean Genet, *Oeuvres complètes* (Paris: Gallimard, 1951. *Notre-Dame:* Vol. II, 1969 printing; *Pompes* and *Querelle:* Vol. III, 1970 printing). *Miracle de la rose* (1946), *Les nègres* (1958) and *Les paravents* (1961) are quoted in the Arbalète edition. *Le funambule* is found in *L'atelier d'Albert Giacometti. Les bonnes, suivi d'une lettre. L'enfant criminel. Le funambule* (Décines, Isère: L'Arbalète, 1958). The *May Day Speech* was published by City Lights Books, San Francisco, in 1970. All translations into English are my own. The reader might wish to consult the following translations of the quoted works (all are by Bernard Frechtman except for *Querelle of Brest*): *The Balcony* (New York: Theater Recording Society, 1969); *The Blacks: A Clown Show* (London: Faber & Faber, 1967); *Funeral Rites* (New York: Grove, 1969); *The Maids and Deathwatch: Two Plays* (New York: Grove, 1962); *Miracle of the Rose* (New York: Grove, 1966); *Our Lady of the Flowers* (London: Blond, 1964); *Querelle of Brest*, trans. Gregory Streatham (London: Panther Books, 1969); *The Screens* (London: Faber & Faber, 1963); *The Thief's Journal* (New York: Grove, 1964). *Le funambule* has not been translated.

a marriage ceremony of amazingly serious proportions. These rituals are the means by which unconscious images are released and given form. During the execution of Métayer, for example, the children are transformed into criminals, not through an effort to correspond to society's stereotypic notion of them, nor yet in an attempt to imitate consciously an objective ideal, but rather by the frenzy of a ritualistic act in which unconscious violence and cruelty are unleashed (*Miracle,* 181). Genet consistently compares such ceremonies to the cultural manifestations of ancient Greece in order to emphasize the notion of an eternal, collective unconscious carried within the individual.

The energy released during the ritualistic act is sexual in nature. The boys at Mettray quite naturally equate the satisfaction of sexual instincts with the murder of Métayer. Querelle's sudden urge to murder Vic is felt as a form of sexual attraction, and the satisfaction of that urge includes the propositioning of Vic in a kind of sexual foreplay to the murder (245–46). The objects which serve as an extension and magnification of the self that emerges during the ritual are a concretization of the sexual energy being expended: Querelle associates the jewels that consecrate the murder with his own testicles and virility (247; cf. *Miracle,* 23). Such criminal and homosexual acts are fortuitous and occasioned by the most insignificant details (*Pompes,* 79; *Querelle,* 247). Yet "necessity" is always an integral part of the ritual. Necessity is internal and consists in the imperious need the individual feels to play out the role lying dormant within him. In playing out that role he recreates his being. He attains a purity of essence that can be taken for nonchalance and an absence of emotion (*Miracle,* 185; 197). That illusion stems from the fact that petty emotions and cares are negated as one submits to deeper and less conscious forms of emotivity: "Querelle felt the presence of the murder throughout his body. . . . Nothing of Querelle was present in his own body. He was empty. . . . The murderer has just attained perfection" (245–47). The ritual is a metamorphosis in which the self becomes other to exist as image beyond phenomenological time and space. That process is inextricably intertwined with the release of libidinal impulse. For the ritual—with its satisfaction of sexual desire, its spontaneous, animalistic necessity, its ability to place one in contact with the deepest realms of the unconscious, and its momentary negation of the phenomenal self—must be defined, in some obscure way, as a form of sexual activity. Genet's notion of ritual seems to grow out of a kind of nostalgia for the plenitude of being that can sometimes be experienced in sexuality. In the novels that plenitude is realized through a criminal-sexual act transformed into a ceremony.

In criminal sexuality lies the source of creative power for Genet. The endless rituals and images described in the novels represent the private sexual fantasies of the lonely imprisoned homosexual. The characters of *Notre-Dame* are recreated from "real-life images," the photographs the author-narrator has affixed to the wall of his cell, which serve as the point of departure for solitary orgies (12–13). In *Miracle,* the process by which Harcamone and the other characters have been created from the fantasy of the galley is examined in detail. Narrative rhythm parallels the rhythm of the author-narrator's own sexuality: "I won't be able to stop singing of [Mignon] until my hand is sticky with released pleasure" (16). If, on the one hand, the characters in the novels strive to attain the status of images, on the other, it is the author-narrator who portrays that striving and who is the creator of those images. The novel is specifically defined as a product of the psychic energy, primarily sexual in nature, that is released through the powers of the creative imagination in the process of fantasizing. That process is a ritual in which the author-narrator becomes other to live through the images he has created (*Notre-Dame,* 13).

The self finds its reality in the interstice between the two modes of being, in the consciousness it has of moving from the everyday self to the image and back again. Thus, in *Le funambule,* which codifies Genet's early conception of creativity, the tightrope walker, to exist consciously, must exaggerate the discrepancy between his life as a bum and his life as pure image on the rope. His being is, precisely, his potential for metamorphosis (*Funambule,* 183–84). Similarly, the stereotypic surface appearances through which Divine's homosexuality is manifested are an expression of her identity (creative sexuality) to the extent that they are a product of her capacity for imaginative metamorphosis (cf. *Notre-Dame,* 95–96). For the novelist, the self is found not in the cell, nor even so much in the novel, but in the creative power that allows one existence to be transformed into the other. Whence the rhythm of construction and destruction that is so characteristic of Genet's style: the creativity involved in the construction of an image is apparent only when the image is destroyed to reveal the emptiness out of which it came (*Miracle*, 44). The homosexual-criminal does not revolt against society merely by accepting an inverse system of values. His revolt lies not in those values at all, but in the burst of creative sexuality (antisocial because it is homosexual and criminal) through which the outsider becomes artist. That creative sexuality is his being, the only part of him that society has not been able to objectify and destroy.

This notion of creativity and self is dealt a fatal blow in *Querelle de Brest*. Although Querelle displays a great talent for incarnating images, he is described as being without imaginative powers (396). Ultimately, he is incapable of creating roles out of the impulses coming from the depths of inner being. Rather, he is a docile puppet who, in fleeing from role to role, obligingly incarnates the images suggested by others. In a sense he is dominated by Seblon, whose image of the ideal Sailor he incarnates (310–11). However, Seblon is no more creative than Querelle and is in turn dominated by the visually oriented consumer society around him. The Lieutenant's fantasy of *the* Sailor is nothing more than the embellishment of an advertisement he had glimpsed: "I, too, am a victim of posters" (405). He who creates images is no creator at all but, like everyone else, a submissive consumer programmed by posters and advertisements. And he who incarnates images is a puppetlike mask who plays out the sterile, surface roles concocted by ad men.

Sexuality is intellectualized and sterilized as the programming process substitutes nonsexual goals for sexual ones. For instance, Seblon's programmed fantasy posits a basic sadomasochistic relationship in which the Hitlerian lieutenant at once dominates *the* Sailor and submits to him. By succumbing to the fantasy Seblon has displaced the source of sexual satisfaction which for him lies, not in the satisfaction of libidinal desires, but in the realization of a predetermined scenario. That satisfaction is intellectual in nature, not sexual. Thus, Genet's attempt to create

novels out of sexual fantasies leads him eventually to the notion
of the transposition and sterilization of sexual energy. Such
transposition can occur on the level of sexuality itself—as in the
case of Seblon and Querelle. On another level, transposition and
sterilization occur when the energy that is basically sexual in
nature is subsumed by the empty social role and channeled into
the institutionalized power games of society. In both cases creative sexual energy is destroyed and authentic being evaporates.

The brilliance with which roles and masks are used to negate
and dissipate the real self in *Les bonnes, Le balcon, Les nègres* and
Les paravents has been analyzed in detail. Sartre's early essay on
Les bonnes stands as one of the most perceptive summaries of that
process (*Saint-Genet,* 654–69). This is a theater of sexual politics
and of sexual consumerism. Here, Genet's cruelty is no longer
really that of Artaud, the surfacing of the repressed unconscious
in gesture and ritual. Rather, we see the negation of sexuality
and the unconscious, as psychic energy is channeled into social
games born of repression and sublimation. Maids dissipate their
sexuality in sterile love-hate relationships with mistresses, judges
too timid to love ensconce themselves in their roles as browbeat-
ers of wenches, Blacks and Whites too bland to meet or to separate squander their being in false confrontations—all looking for
death and absence through rigidly controlled scenarios in which
real sexuality and emotion are squelched. Genet has discovered
the falseness of his images, and he turns them back against a
society he abhors: they become a virulent vehicle for his social
criticism. The creators of images are no longer, as was the
homosexual novelist, outsiders and artists. They are the procur-
ers of this society, the sexless Irmas who have lost contact with
their essential sexuality, whose images are not born of imaginative fantasy but hatched from consumer demand and carefully
calculated by the greed for monetary gain. The "break" in the
image through which lovers in the novels glimpsed the sorrow-
ful, lonesome, sexual self—the index of creative power—has become in the plays the "false detail." It reveals nothing beyond the
role. It serves only as a constant reminder that the ritual is faked
and can be bought for a price in any good bordel. These
scenarios are consumed by impotent men who anesthetize themselves in the acting out of production-line fantasies—fantasies

born of a collective unconscious that has been vitiated and im-
mobilized in outdated institutions and shallow publicity.

The process by which gimmicky imagery infiltrates subcon-
scious being and determines the very fabric of sexual energy is
inevitable and irreversible. It is true that Village and Vertu
momentarily glimpse the possibility of transcending social programming to rediscover authentic sexuality and imaginative
powers: "For you I could invent anything . . . but gestures of
love . . . still, if that's what you really want . . . " (*Les nègres,* 180).
Querelle and Seblon also seem to move beyond roles and images
for a split second: real sexuality is liberated in Querelle's abandon and the "true essence" of his being is revealed (414). As late
as 1970, the Yale *May Day Speech* is still optimistic in that revolution, defined as the destruction of social images and symbols,
appears viable (14). Generally, however, the notion that one can
escape imagery to experience creative individuality beyond the
confines of the social realm is abandoned. Saïd, though not himself a homosexual, is the last incarnation of the character growing out of the homosexual paradigm, the outsider by abjection
and choice. In his struggle to protect inner being—as incarnated
in Leïla—from the onslaught of images, he is annihilated. The
only path open to him is the future Genet envisioned for himself: oblivion (*Les paravents,* 260; *Playboy,* April, 1964). The self
exists only through the charades it plays out, and beyond the
roles is nothingness. Genet is truly revolutionary not because of
the image of the criminal and the homosexual he created in the
early works, but because of the conclusion to which he is eventually led: sexuality cannot serve as the basis for authentic being
and the source of individuation, for one's sexuality is not a
product of free choice and will.

The homosexual paradigm we have tried to delineate is a
literary construct. It serves as a convenient nucleus around
which gravitate a series of metonyms and correlates concerning
the self. The paradigm is based upon several assumptions that
might well appear quaint today. (1) It assumes a kind of schizophrenic division of the personality into a social and an asocial self,
presupposing that authentic being is impossible in one who accepts social structures and institutions completely. (2) It con-

ceives social structures (institutions, laws, cultural and moral codes, and the like) as a monolithic, well-defined, and static entity against which the individual is capable of reacting *in toto.* (3) The paradigm assumes further that the self is defined by its sexuality. All three authors pinpoint basic sexual energy as the source of being and individuation. (4) A correlative of this third assumption is that sexuality is at some point or another a matter of choice and free will. Although a character like Vautrin may be born a homosexual, his individuality is affirmed by the choice he makes to assume and live out that sexuality. (5) The paradigm always assumes that it is not homosexuality, but sexuality in general, that is disruptive. Sexuality, when it is authentic, is always experienced by the asocial self in the realm of the criminal. The experience is perceived as unstructured, spontaneous, emotional, total, and animalistic. (6) Finally, the sexual experience is invariably perceived as a form of creativity. Thus, the paradigm has a definitely romantic flavor about it. Indeed, it grows out of the romantic myth of the individual who, through a combination of personal will and mysterious libidinal energy, transcends the limitations of his environment to affirm his creative selfhood.

Although *homosexuality* serves as a catchall term summarizing a certain view of the self that serves as a point of departure for the thinking of all three of our writers, the differing attitudes they adopt toward the various elements of the paradigm indicate a gradual erosion of the assumptions upon which it is based. In Gide's novelistic universe, for instance, social structures are not viewed as one monolithic and static entity. Consequently the notion of a schizophrenic self existing first within, then without, the society is greatly attenuated, and Gide replaces that concept of self with the notions of authentic and conventional being. Genet's evolution is of particular interest. His early view of the homosexual represents an almost total acceptance of the various correlates upon which the paradigm is based. However, as the notion of a nuclear self is replaced by the notion of dispersed being existing only through roles activated by external stimuli, the concept of an individualizing and disruptive sexuality is rendered inoperative. In the mindless and behavioristic universe of the plays, the very notions of social and asocial selves, of willed sexuality, of creativity, are anachronistic. Genet's work could easily be viewed as a conscious attempt to invalidate the homosexual paradigm as a literary construct.

Indeed, that paradigm appears to lose all significance and value after 1960. In the modern novel the self is invariably reduced to a kind of residual consciousness and a potential for being that is rarely realized. Personal will is dissipated as the self is acted upon rather than exerting dominance. Within that context, the very notion of definitive sexuality is destroyed. The self submits to sexuality. Protagonists often move unthinkingly from one mode of sexuality to another. The self is drowned in its obscurely felt desires—as it is in its obscurely perceived environment. Outside of literature, in the domain of psychology, for instance, or in the realm of cultural codes, homosexuality may still be viewed as disruptive and vaguely criminal. In contemporary literature, however, the paradigm we have delineated no longer seems to have any currency.

Isabelle de Courtivron

Weak Men and Fatal Women: The Sand Image

The woman who always wants to be like a man, a sign of great depravity.

—Baudelaire

The strong woman should remain a symbol; she frightens when seen in reality.

—Balzac

It is not so much George Sand the writer who concerns us here as Sand the image. Her provocative personality and her life-style, the legends to which these gave rise, the fascination she exerted, and the fears she evoked dominated the French imagination for a large part of the nineteenth century. She left an indelible imprint on the consciousness of many important writers of her time and, through their work, on the popular mind as well. Tracing the ways in which Sand's personality, or the transformations projected onto it, may have influenced various works from Balzac's *La fille aux yeux d'or* to Barbey d'Aurevilly's *Les diaboliques* would obviously demand a highly detailed analysis. Yet it can be said, more generally, that she is in fact partially responsible for the strange and fearsome transformations of the female image during the nineteenth century. Indeed, she may be the very prototype for the exotic and satanic version of the *femme fatale* which dominates French art and literature from the 1830's on. Mario Praz remarks in *The Romantic Agony* that during the earlier part of the century it is the Fatal Man (the Byronic hero) who is depicted as the dominant, and dominating, character until slowly this role is taken over by the Fatal Woman. As the hero grows weaker, more vulnerable and masochistic, the heroine gains in cruelty and power, eventually reaching the extremes of vampire, bloodthirsty empress, and *diabolique*. An important aspect of Praz's well-known thesis, and one which has been somewhat neglected, lies in the following comment: "For a type—which is in actual fact a cliché—to be created, *it is essential that some particular figure should have made a profound impression on the popular mind*. Some chronic ailment has created a zone of weakened resistance and whenever an analogous phenomenon makes itself felt, it immediately confines itself to the predisposed area until the process becomes a matter of mechanical monotony."[1]

If we read Sand as this "particular figure,"[2] what "predisposed area" did she invade? On the most obvious level the social threat she posed was in her independence, in the way she assumed the heretofore male prerogative of complete freedom, thereby anticipating the feminist movement of 1848. She also invaded the jealously guarded domain of intellectual creativity, proving that one didn't need a phallus to write energetically and copiously. Hadn't Balzac himself contended, through his character Camille Maupin, in reference to artistic talent, that "only men possess the rod which props one up along these precipices, a strength which turns us into monsters when we possess it"?[3] It should be noted in passing that Camille Maupin, the heroine of *Béatrix* whom Balzac created as a frigid and asexual version of Sand, is described by the writer as "an amphibious being who is neither man nor woman" and in whom "everyone is afraid to encounter the strange corruptions of a diabolical soul."[4] This connection between Sand and Satan would be echoed by Baudelaire twenty-five years later in *Mon coeur mis à nu*, in a much more direct and violent manner: "THE DEVIL AND GEORGE SAND . . . I cannot think of this stupid

1. Mario Praz, *The Romantic Agony* (London, New York: Oxford University Press, 1970) 2d ed., p. 201, my emphasis.

2. Apart from mentioning that "thanks especially to George Sand, the vice of Lesbianism became extremely popular" (p. 333), Praz does not make explicit connections between Sand and the *femme fatale*.

3. Honoré de Balzac, *Béatrix* (Paris: Classique Garnier, 1962), p. 101, my translation.

4. Balzac, pp. 55 and 80, my translation.

creature without a certain shudder of horror. If I met her I could not help but throw a basin of holy water at her head."[5]

Then of course there were the trousers, the cigars, Marie Dorval, and Lélia's outspoken confessions in which Sand established herself as the cold, sadistic, fatal woman. All of these, however, inscribe themselves within a greater context and involve a fear that goes far beyond the one attached to an active, creative woman who defied the limiting norms of bourgeois morality. What Sand seems to have embodied is a pattern that deeply shook the collective imagination; indeed it was to recur and become increasingly exaggerated throughout nineteenth-century literature and art until it had reached its most grotesque forms in the Decadent period. It is this pattern—namely, that of the fatal woman destroying weak, delicate men—which I shall attempt to delineate and connect with the impact of the Sand image.

Sand, it appeared, turned men into objects. Despite her conscious search for a lasting love, she wandered restlessly from one lover to the next, leaving each behind in a state of desolation. What may have been and has been interpreted as nymphomania, frigidity, Sapphic tendencies, or all three, manifested itself in her recurrent attraction to frail and gifted men like Sténio (the young poet in *Lélia*) whom she dominated and frequently came close to destroying: Sandeau, Musset, Chopin are but the more famous. An analysis of what really happened between Sand and her young lovers would be irrelevant here. After all, most of them were not obscure, held their own in terms of psychological warfare, were already fragile in health and nerves before they met her, and could be considered inferior creatively only in terms of quantity of output. What is significant is the distorted reputation that was imposed on her as a result of these much publicized affairs. They were judged more severely than ordinary society scandals primarily because of the reversal of roles involved (symbolized by Sand's masculine clothing) and because of the fatal effects she seemed to have on the young men in her life.

5. Charles Baudelaire, *Oeuvres complètes* (Paris: Pléiade, 1961), p. 1281, my translation.

I suggest that it is precisely this reversal of sex roles and its fatal consequences that gives us the clue to the "zone of weakened resistance" mentioned by Praz, as well as to the origins of the nineteenth-century *femme fatale*. At the time Sand became notorious, numerous fantasies connected with destructive and virile women were already beginning to inflame the Romantic imagination. Women were dressing like men in order to engage in adventures forbidden to their sex, and Sand was only the most famous to follow this shocking new fashion. Madame Marbouty, a friend of Balzac's, wore men's clothing when she accompanied the writer on his travels in 1836. In fiction also, masculine and sadistic heroines were appearing. Mathilde de la Môle's semi-necrophiliac episode with Julien Sorel's head (1830), Balzac's amazon Marie de Verneuil in *Les chouans* (1829), the hermaphroditic Camille of Latouche's *Fragoletta* (1829), who passed herself off as an officer and seduced her lover's sister, all of these corresponded to fears and fantasies that were becoming prevalent in the society of their time. Meanwhile, the Romantic heroes were being depicted as increasingly beautiful, frail, and effeminate creatures. Joseph Péladan, fascinated by this phenomenon, which he glorified in *La décadence latine, éthopée,* was to attest: "The number of women who feel themselves to be men grows daily and the masculine instinct leads them to violent action, in the same proportion as that in which the number of men who feel themselves to be women abdicate their sex and, becoming passive, pass virtually on to a negative plane."[6]

What needs to be followed carefully, in the creative imagination of the times, is the emergence of a new image of the *femme fatale* that resulted from this increasing confusion of socially defined sex roles. Fatal women had always existed, but in widely differing versions. The figure which appears during the Romantic period and lasts until World War I comes under the guise of an exotic, dominant, sadistic, and masculine woman, foreshadowed perhaps by the Marquise de Merteuil (*Les liaisons dangereuses*) but certainly a far cry from the Manon Lescaut type. While the latter destroyed men through traditionally "feminine" channels, the lethal females of the nineteenth century clearly

6. Cited in Praz, p. 334.

exert virile power. This is symbolized by their status of ruler, their frequent appearance as princess, queen, or empress.

Such was the climate of the time when Sand entered the scene with her masculine ways and her man-devouring reputation, thrusting herself forcefully onto what was becoming an increasingly vulnerable terrain. Probably because both she and her "victims" were so well known, and because she was a serious personage in her own right rather than a passing fashion, she overshadowed the other existing models. Sand managed to crystallize around her various ill-defined and free-floating fantasies stemming from the sexual ambiguities of the Romantic period. Because she, for one, did not stop at fantasy but actually lived out the reversal of roles (that is, went from "wish to be man" to "acting like man"), she forced the opposite fantasy into becoming reality.

In many male writers, these fantasies seem to point to a phenomenon we shall call the "wish to be woman," which is often manifested in a fascination with lesbianism. It appears most explicitly in Baudelaire's lesbian poems, in Verlaine's *Les amies*, in some parts of Diderot's *La religieuse*, and in paintings of the time such as Courbet's *Les dormeuses* and Ingres's *Le bain turc*. In these Sapphic or homoerotic scenes, several characteristics immediately stand out. The passive, amorphous poses of all the women described (bathing, reading, reclining, or most frequently, sleeping) appear at first to be the banal continuation of their traditional "feminine" posture. Baudelaire's "femmes damnées," for example, are likened to "passive cattle stretched out on the sand" with "deadened eyes," "idle tears," "stupor," and "gloomy voluptuousness." Those of Verlaine recline on "deep cushions" under "languid lamps." Diderot's abbess and her nuns are described as round, static, and half-asleep.[7] On closer scrutiny, it becomes apparent that what is expressed here is more than conventional femininity. The focus must be placed

7. It is admittedly difficult to take the "convent scene" out of context in order to link it to our theme. However, I think it is correct to state that the fantasy I have been describing is also present in *La religieuse*. What might confirm this statement is the fact that Baudelaire is known to have been partially influenced by Diderot's lesbian scenes when writing his own poems.

on the position of the writer vis-à-vis this mass of voluptuous, lethargic, female bodies, and this position is clearly that of a hypnotized voyeur. Moreover, he is both attracted and repulsed by the scenes glimpsed, whether these be Sapphic or only implicitly homoerotic in that they take place in convents, harems, baths, girls' schools, or other contexts where groups of women are enclosed.

The element of attraction is conveyed in various ways: in direct form—for example, in "Ballade Sappho," where Verlaine pretends to make love to his mistress as one woman would make love to another; in quasi-participatory form—Diderot describing the convent scene through the eyes of Suzanne Simonin, who is a participant in it and conveys her reactions; and particularly in Baudelaire's claim that he has been chosen to sing of Lesbos, not only because of his special empathy but because he has been initiated into its mysteries.

The scenes that depict lesbians frequently involve women *in groups* (as in "Lesbos"), as *bodies* (they are always nude or barely clad), and amorphous to the point of appearing in a state of *drugged stupor*. Moreover, they are usually *enclosed* in spaces which exude an almost tangible thickness, an all-pervasive sensuality. All of these conditions seem to indicate that what these women are indulging in is an inner voyage through the rhythms, the pulsions, and the secret voices of their own bodies. It is this status as a fully eroticized body that the poet desires, this voyage that the poet appears to envy and wish to join.

On the other hand, he is also aware of an inherent element of danger and madness lurking in this forbidden territory. A sudden glimpse of "blood-colored hair," of a "fatal eye," the allusion to "dark mystery," "yawning chasms," or "howling fevers" convey the cruel and demonic qualities of these "monsters," as they are frequently called. This continual movement of attraction and fear, envy for the experience of these "poor sisters" followed by horror for the "monsters and martyrs," makes up the rhythm of many lesbian poems, especially in Baudelaire. Since it is necessary that the poet retain the distance of voyeur in order to avoid the lurking danger—and we shall return to this danger—he frequently exploits the exotic element (hence the harem and drug motifs), the *là-bas* where fantasies can safely be indulged in. Given this condition, the female homoerotic scenes seem to provide the necessary domain for acting out certain projections while leaving the voyeur in the advantageous position of a man observing women.

What seems to attract the poet in this vision of female sensuality is the temptation of passivity, the promise of dissolving into a greater and undifferentiated erotic experience, made clear by the emphasis on static bodies and on groups. Such experiences would free him from the limitations of the purely aggressive, phallic, and one-to-one heterosexual attitude expected of him.

While this "wish to be woman" or "wish to be body" should not automatically be equated with the wish for homosexuality, there exists an undeniable connection between such wishes in that they represent different facets of a complex network of fantasies. Certainly, the links between androgyny, homosexuality, bisexuality, and transsexuality were not precisely defined in the nineteenth century; they are difficult to distinguish even given our present state of psychoanalytic knowledge. It would therefore be dangerous to categorize any literary character as explicitly homosexual or transsexual. Yet it is also true that from our perspective we can see in much of this earlier literature the dramatization of desires, the imaginative acting out of fantasies which, although impossible to delineate clearly, are equally impossible to ignore.

An important aspect of this complex nexus, and one which connects the "wish to be woman" with the *femme fatale* figure, involves androgyny. Usually described as an abstract, aesthetic ideal, it is a concept which contains many ambiguities. Its prevalence in the nineteenth century points to the already mentioned confusion of sex roles, which probably stemmed from a general frustration with the limitations that this role-playing involved. But androgyny also has homosexual and bisexual implications, although they are usually minimized in its numerous interpretations, and this is what I wish to stress as a vital aspect of its power to fascinate. Indeed, if one finds reunited in the self a balanced set of dual pulsions, characteristic emotional qualities, it follows that this duality should apply to the sexual realm as well. In most cases, androgynous heroes or heroines do in fact show definite tendencies to cross the limits of sexual norms, even if such tendencies are expressed through very indirect channels.

This sexual ambiguity is demonstrated in Gautier's *Mademoiselle de Maupin* by Madeleine, one of the most authentically androgynous characters in nineteenth-century literature (which usually tended toward abstract versions of this theme—statues, angels, or asexual creatures like Balzac's Séraphita). To recapitulate briefly Gautier's plot, Madeleine de Maupin, like George Sand and Jeanne d'Arc, two other well-known heretics, dresses like a man in order to satisfy what seems, at first, curiosity regarding men's true nature. She dons masculine garb so as to be admitted within the unsuspecting intimacy of male comradeship and to observe their conduct at first hand. It soon appears that her actions stem from a much deeper impulse and that the element of curiosity is but a pretext. The switching to clothes of the opposite sex is in fact an initiation rite which allows her gradually to lose the consciousness of her sexual identity: "Because I kept hearing everyone calling me Sir, and because I saw myself treated as if I were a man, I forgot imperceptibly that I was a woman."[8] This change is reminiscent of the converse process undergone by Woolf's Orlando, whose personality changes unwittingly to suit the self created by her response to society's treatment. In *Orlando* too, Woolf tells us that the change of clothes is a symbol of the much deeper impulse toward androgyny. Gautier's Madeleine manages to cross over the danger zone, unlike certain other "masculine" heroines such as Balzac's Camille Maupin or Stendhal's Lamiel, who remained paralyzed in a sort of asexual void. What she finds on the other side is the acceptance and concretization of her true androgynous impulse, that is, of her bisexuality. Because she has grown so comfortable in her male persona, she is able to examine women through eyes liberated from the taboos associated with such closeness. Rosette, unaware that Théodore/Madeleine is not a man, makes such provocative advances that Madeleine's desire is aroused and she cannot refrain from responding. At the end of the novel,

8. Théophile Gautier, *Mademoiselle de Maupin* (Paris: Garnier Flammarion, 1966), p. 293, my translation.

Madeleine dresses once more as a woman and makes passionate love with d'Albert; then she crosses over to Rosette's bedroom where she repeats the performance.

What is important here is that the novel also contains a male homoerotic element, but it is projected onto the female. The hero, d'Albert, has so much in common with Madeleine, even to the extent of sharing the same mistress, that it soon becomes evident they represent two halves of one personality. D'Albert is also androgynous, but only *potentially*. He is frail, refined, criticized because of his ornamented, effeminate clothes, his long curly hair. He sees in his mistress no more than a "delightful comrade," a "lovely fellow"; he longs to change sex, addresses his most tender letters to his dear friend Silvio; finally he falls in love with Madeleine when he thinks she is a man, admitting to Silvio that "what is strangest of all is that I hardly think of his sex any longer, and that I love him with perfect assurance."[9] Yet, owing to the stronger social, psychological, and personal taboo of male homosexuality, Gautier can go no further than to project the homo- and bisexual fulfillment onto the female character—or the female half of his hero's persona. In leading her to the furthest stage of sexual androgyny, Gautier permits the acting out his hero's forbidden and repressed longings, while managing to avoid what would prove a theatening self-confrontation.

While these two fantasies, the "wish to be woman" in the lesbian poems and the projection of homosexual desire in *Mademoiselle de Maupin,* are not identical, it is clear that they represent complementary and intermeshing aspects of one major desire, that of eluding the trappings of the societally defined "masculine role." Moreover, they frequently overlap and merge in a variety of infinitely subtle and complex ways. As d'Albert admits, the reason he longs to change sex is in order to acquaint himself with new voluptuous sensations. A very fine line of demarcation may be said to exist between this longing for "voluptuous female sexuality" and the repressed desire to be made love to by another man. Or else they may represent one and the same thing.

9. Gautier, p. 212, my translation.

La fille aux yeux d'or is another novel in which these same fantasies converge, once again projected onto lesbianism and androgyny. What is crucial here is that in Balzac's novel the hero takes a first step on the path from fantasy to reality, from the safe position of voyeur to the dangerous one of participant. This has disastrous consequences. For the first time the *femme fatale* makes her appearance as an important symbol. As she does, it becomes clear that her function is to punish the man for concretizing his dangerous fantasy.

La fille aux yeux d'or presents two characters who resemble each other physically and love the same person, Paquita. Both are androgynous. De Marsay, the young dandy, the Don Juan who until this episode had been a fatal man, wavers between the so-called "masculine" and "feminine" traits. He is described as an angry young man who "had in hand a sceptre more potent than the one belonging to modern kings," and who has an "assurance of action, a certainty of power, a leonine consciousness which concretizes for women the kind of strength which they all dream about."[10] On the other hand he has the typically Romantic appearance of a young girl, a soft and modest manner, a thin and aristocratic waist. He spends hours preening himself in front of his intimate friend Paul and does not seem particularly shocked to wear a woman's gown before making love with Paquita. What is most important is that he actually *enters* the lesbian fantasy, symbolized by the exotic boudoir of Paquita and Margarita, where he is led *blindfolded* and *passive* as if to forgo responsibility for this move. Then he is dressed up as a woman, thereby being initiated into the secret erotic life of this all-female world.

Opposing him is his sister and look-alike, the Marquise de St. Réal, who combines feminine beauty with extreme violence, and loves another woman. Balzac, like Camille Latouche and even more explicitly than Gautier, splits his character into male and female halves by using the brother-sister or twin symbolism frequently associated with androgyny. Yet here again, the bisexuality is acted out *in fact* by the female character only, although the

10. Honoré de Balzac, *La fille aux yeux d'or* (Paris: Pléiade, 1952), pp. 299–300, my translation.

hero takes a definite step into the "wish to be woman" dimension.

In this novel, one of the first battlegrounds (and probably one of the bloodiest until Flaubert's *Salammbô*) is established on which the *homme fatal* and the *femme fatale* struggle for power. Wanting to remain true to the conscious glorification of virility, Balzac chooses to give the sexual victory to de Marsay. Paquita, recognizing in him the true answer after having sampled the attributes he possesses, rejects the Marquise, who lacks them. The phallic, heterosexual principle is meant to be victorious. But on a more significant, symbolic level, it is the Marquise who has the last word. Not only is it her name which Paquita cries out in pleasure when making love with de Marsay, but it is the Marquise who, by murdering the young girl before de Marsay has a chance to seek revenge, literally becomes the fatal element in the story. This is still indirect, for it is not the young man she murders; but by acting before and for him, she renders him momentarily impotent. The "feminine power" Paquita had warned him about earlier in the story ultimately wins the combat—as it will in many other works to follow.

This split between the Marquise and de Marsay, their battle, and her "victory" can be interpreted as the discovery of the hero's deeply hidden feminine self, as Geneviève Delattre proposes in her comparative study "De 'Séraphita' à 'La fille aux yeux d'or'."[11] But it can also be seen as the struggle between the forces of virility and those of feminization in a much broader context. The *femme fatale* not only represents the feminine side of the hero's being, but she also punishes him for having ventured too far into this realm. She renders the hero impotent for having transgressed the laws of voyeurism, for having usurped the forbidden territory of what he sees as feminine sexuality and, dressed as a woman, for having participated in its dangerous rites. In this particular work, the line has become blurred between the narrator-hero as mere spectator who indulges in pure fantasy, and the narrator-hero who participates and suffers the consequences. De Marsay takes a first step into the languid and violent

11. Geneviève Delattre, "De 'Séraphita' à 'La fille aux yeux d'or'," in *L'année balzacienne*, 1970, pp. 183–226.

domain of feminine love, inside the mysterious dimension of the body and of the demonic. It is as if, by coming too close to the tempting but dangerous scene, the hero had suddenly found himself drawn irresistibly into it. As a result he is rendered impotent (and in most cases this will assume the form of castration) at the hands of the powerful female element.

To what extent George Sand may have influenced Gautier is unknown, for the latter is said to have modeled his heroine after a seventeenth-century historical figure. But it is certain that Balzac's Marquise de St. Réal was inspired by the Sand-Dorval episode. Since both novels were written around the same time and since it is suspected that Gautier and Balzac discussed Sapphism together,[12] Sand's influence may be much more pervasive than is usually believed. Still, it must be repeated that I am not claiming she is the unique model for all *femme fatale* characters, only the most influential. Also, without wanting to overemphasize the biographical element, one must inquire here to what extent the Sand-Sandeau affair, which was highly publicized at the time (as were the Dorval and Musset episodes), affected Balzac and influenced his writing. After all, Balzac did give shelter and tender care to "le petit Jules" in 1832, when the latter in despair was rejected by Sand for his various inadequacies. It is this same Sandeau who served as one of the models for Lucien de Rubempré, the most effeminate of Balzac's young men and, it must be noted, the one who is beloved by Séchard and Vautrin, both of whom bear a certain resemblance to their creator. We also know that Balzac, when writing *La fille aux yeux d'or,* locked himself up in a white studio decorated with cashmere, muslin, and oriental draperies, similar to the one he describes in his novel, a boudoir that led Sandeau to exclaim upon first entering it: "it is womanlike; but beautifully, gracefully womanlike!"[13] Clearly, the author and his hero merge in this story, for what Balzac lived out by locking himself up in an exotic decor which mirrors the one he created in his imagination involves the various fantasies we have discussed. On one level, there is the homoerotic desire which might have been inspired by Sandeau

12. R. Bolster, *Stendhal, Balzac, et le féminisme romantique* (Paris: Lettres Modernes, 1970), p. 152.

13. Cited in Delattre, p. 205.

and which is projected onto the lesbian (Sand-Dorval) couple. On another level, there is the "wish to be body" lived out by both de Marsay and Balzac in their corresponding boudoirs, and traceable once again to the lesbian fantasy.

The impact of George Sand on Balzac's writing, then, may partially stem from the meshing of biographical elements, from the Sand-Dorval, Sand-Sandeau, Balzac-Sandeau, Balzac-Sand interactions. The broader principle that underlies the *femme fatale* phenomenon, however, cannot be explained by the Sand personality per se or by Balzac's possible homoerotic sublimations. The biographical references merely serve to demonstrate the extent to which living figures can catalyze, and force to the surface, greater and more general undercurrents. Nor are we dealing with linear cause-and-effect or chronological action-reaction processes. Baudelaire was writing his lesbian poems two decades after de Marsay had made his entry into the territory of the fatal woman. In the poet's work both the "passive exotic lesbians" and the "evil vampire women" coexist. We must speak, then, not of a simple progressive development but of a nexus of psychological currents which continue to interact throughout the century. This is verified by the fact that both Balzac and Baudelaire demonstrated similar strong reactions— or overreactions—to the Sand phenomenon. What did increase with history, however, was the intensity of the reactions and the cruelty of the combat.

It has been my suggestion throughout that the Sand image was fashioned from both the latent desires connected to the reversal of sex roles and the powerful fears that derived from such desires. By refusing woman's traditional passivity and submissiveness, by "taking over" and becoming the active, aggressive element, by appearing to objectify her lovers and exploiting frigidity in order to refuse any man's control over her (hence the frequent references to the theme of the "cold woman" in the literature of the time), Sand adopted the masculine pose and forced men into the feminine one. In doing this she gave what was an existing but forbidden desire a semblance of reality, and consequently also came to embody the punishment for those who transgressed the limits of their "masculinity." Symbolizing both sides of this inescapable pattern, she was seen as both the catalyst and the consequence: hence her power. What remains to be understood is what fears were actually involved; why being forced to realize an existing wish, in this case the wish for what was imagined as passive female sexuality, should have led men into such traumatic situations.

The fear is obviously traceable to that of castration. This is not only directly implied in the "wish to be woman" but is also symbolized by the form of punishment that awaits the heroes who have indulged too realistically in this wish. Increasingly, men are portrayed as *mutilated* while the heroines, feeding off their partners' blood, their sperm, and their strength, establish themselves as the mutilating powers. This process, it would seem, gained an impetus of its own, adopting a mechanical repetitiveness that eventually lost any direct connection to the plot. The young heroes were automatically created as weak and masochistic and the women as *femmes fatales*. By the end of the century, in literature and in painting (and here we think of Gustave Moreau), we meet only "Herodiases, Salomes, Judiths . . . women from Thrace tearing apart the body of Orpheus or dreamily contemplating his severed head . . . the man, or what is left of him—his head beautiful, painful and asexual—is therefore each time the victim of a woman as if this had been predestined by his celestial aspirations and his ambiguous nature."[14] It is with the analysis of this fear of castration that we must conclude, for it forms the basis of all that has been discussed so far. Two theoretical interpretations, both by women, will serve to clarify some of the psychological and philosophical roots of this phenomenon.

Karen Horney has explained the fear of castration as a wish for castration (and she defines this fear as a neurotic symptom), something I have suggested in its nineteenth-century version. She tells us that in man "this wish to be woman is not merely at variance with his conscious narcissism but is rejected for a second reason, namely because the notion of being a woman implies at the same time the realization of all his fears of punishment centered on the genital region." On the other hand, in a

---

14. Françoise Cachin, "Monsieur Vénus et l'ange de Sodome," *Bisexualité et différence des sexes* (*Nouvelle revue de psychanalyse*, 7, Spring 1973), p. 64, my translation.

woman "the identification with the father is confirmed by old
wishes tending in the same direction and it does not carry with it
any sort of feeling of guilt but rather a sense of acquittal."[15]
Whereas some of Horney's theories may appear slightly out-
moded, this one seems still to be viable for as recently as 1973, in
La nouvelle revue de psychanalyse, Robert Stoller stated that "the
feeling one has of being male, and its ulterior development,
masculinity, are somewhat less solidly rooted in men than the
feeling of femaleness and of femininity in women."[16] In saying
this, Stoller confirms Horney's thesis that the tendency toward
feminization, under the guise of a "wish to be woman" (wish for
castration) is a much more threatening psychological process
than its opposite, and is therefore more likely to undergo severe
punishment from the ego. This may explain why it was easier for
Sand, psychologically at least, to reverse the roles than for the
men around her. If we accept that the masculine castration anxiety which leads to the fear of punishment is partially explained
as the ego's response to a secret "wish to be woman," the whole
pattern outlined above becomes clearer. In this case, the Sand
figure, by feminizing men, would bring out the latent wish acknowledged by Horney while at the same time representing the
psychological danger connected with this wish-fulfillment.

Hélène Cixous, in *La jeune née,* deepens our insight into the
nature of this psychological danger by exploring the connection
between feminization and death (which is also seen in the general association of Eros with masculinity and Thanatos with
femininity). Her main thesis, for which she acknowledges her
debt to Jacques Derrida, is that systems of thought have always
been based on a structure of *opposition.* The opposed elements of
each couple constantly engage in battles which are systematically
resolved by the victory of the half identified with the masculine
element. This hierarchization of opposites is what has allowed
the masculine "active" principle to dominate continually the
feminine "passive" one. To Cixous, then, all philosophy has been
constructed on the basis of the subordination of women to the

15. Karen Horney, *Feminine Psychology* (New York: Norton, 1967), p. 53.
16. Robert Stoller, "Faits et hypothèses," *Bisexualité et différence des sexes,* p. 153,
my translation.

masculine order through just such a system of opposition. The basic couple from which all others derive is formed by the active-passive elements. This can be extended to sexuality. Masculine desire, Cixous explains, has been constituted from lack, or loss, and consequently depends on what she calls the "law of return." Man appropriates; he brushes with death (as during orgasm) in order to come back to himself somewhat aggrandized and having gained what she calls "a supplement of masculinity, a surplus of virility, authority, power, money or pleasure."[17] This is why "the other"—that is, woman's body—is necessary, and why it must be colonized and conquered: "It is necessary that she recognize him and by recognizing him, during the moment of fulfillment, that she disappear leaving him a profit—or a imaginary victory."[18] Such is the reason, Cixous suggests, why what is thought of as "female sexuality" is considered a necessity in man's partner, but lethal if it threatens to contaminate him. What she interprets as man's demand is: "Belong to us, excite us, do not make of us passive, feminine beings. *Your style of love is death for us.*"[19] This process, which consists in woman resisting long enough to let herself be conquered, then abandoning herself and allowing her partner to return to his being with an appropriated dose of virility, is precisely what Sand and all the strong females she symbolized never accepted. Not only did she refuse this, but she apparently stood it on its head. Having no chance to "reappropriate," the man was left in the void, in the feared domain of loss. Woman who had always been seen as *being* (as opposed to man *having*) suddenly was *and* had. Since masculine desire, by identifying itself with the penis and relying solely on the active-passive opposition, was denied its habitual victory, what was left was loss, or death. We can now couple this with the fact that what Praz calls a certain "predisposed area of

---

17. Catherine Clément/Hélène Cixous, *La jeune née* (Paris: Union Générale d'Editions, 1975), p. 161, my translation. Portions of Cixous's section of this book have been translated by Keith and Paula Cohen: "The Laughter of the Medusa," *Signs,* 1 (Summer 1976); also by Anne Liddle: "Sorties," in *The Newly Born Woman,* to appear in *New French Feminisms,* ed. Elaine Marks and Isabelle de Courtivron (University of Massachusetts Press).

18. Clément/Cixous, p. 146.

19. Clément/Cixous, p. 123, my emphasis.

weakened resistance" may have been the very wish for castration
(or to be woman) which, for as yet unexplained reasons, seems to
be a prevalent characteristic of Romantic sensibilities. One can
also see how when the two intersected—the latent wish-fear
(Praz's "chronic ailment") and the (Sand) figure of catalyst-
punisher (the "analogous phenomenon"), and these can also be
combined as wish-catalyst and fear-punishment—they set off a
rather dramatic chain of consequences.

What Cixous suggests is simply one more explanation for the
fear of castration and does not have to be accepted as absolute
truth, but it is one which sheds a considerable amount of light on
the idea of the *femme fatale* and the reasons she was considered to
exert such power. After all, even if she was dreamed up only as a
warning against the eventual concretization of an appealing but
destructive fantasy, it might still explain her recurrence
throughout the Romantic and post-Romantic period—at least
until World War I had furnished men with a new dose of active
misogyny through the writings of Montherlant, Malraux, Sartre,
Saint-Exupéry, and other influential advocates of *camaraderie
virile*.

The tradition of the cruel, sadistic, and exotic *femme fatale* was
indeed to continue through the Romantic, post-Romantic, Symbolist, and Decadent periods. It included Mérimée's Carmen,
Musset's Countess Gamiani,[20] Flaubert's Salammbô and
Hérodias, Gautier's Cléopâtre, Daudet's Sapho, Barbey d'Aurevilly's Diaboliques, Péladan's Princess d'Este, Mendès's
Méphistophéla, and many others of lesser stature. Although
Sand alone certainly does not account for all these, we are dealing here with a phenomenon of which she was undeniably a vital
part. Even if she did not initiate this phenomenon, nor inspire
directly its many transformations, she certainly played a major
role in crystallizing around her many of the desires and fears
associated with this tradition, thereby perpetuating it forcefully.

20. This book has been attributed to Musset and is said to represent a satirical
portrait of George Sand. Praz questions this attribution, but because it is a pornographic work full of "Lesbian lecheries, bestialities, and sadistic pleasures"
(Praz, p. 183) and because it was identified in the readers' minds with the life of
George Sand, it undoubtedly reinforced her general image.

If she was not a direct model for all the fatal vampires of the *fin de siècle* (significantly referred to by some as *fin de sexe*), it seems increasingly evident that her influence, which to this day continues to fascinate, stretched far beyond the simplistic clichés attached to wearing top hats and smoking cigars.

Paul Schmidt

Visions of Violence:
Rimbaud and Verlaine

Jakob Boehme, the German mystic whose obscure writings gave Hegel his celebrated dialectical "triad," liked to say that "In Yea and Nay all things consist." Liminality may perhaps be regarded as the Nay to all positive structural assertions, but as in some sense the source of them all, and more than that, as a realm of pure possibility whence novel configurations of ideas and relations may arise.
—Victor Turner, *The Forest of Symbols*

We are about to discuss the sexual relationship of two of the greatest Nay-sayers of Western literature, and to locate that relationship beyond one of the severest of Western taboos. Let us, however, see it constantly as a moment of what Victor Turner calls liminality, as a moment of passage from one conception of the world to another. Let us see it constantly, that is, as Rimbaud and Verlaine saw it: as an experiment in radical opposition to the patterns and structures of life, whose resolution was to be something as yet unseen and unimagined—*New Love.*

This is an essay about sadomasochistic homosexuality, considered not as an object of scandal, but rather as a record of the consequences of images turned into experience: of words made flesh.

When two people are lovers, words get passed back and forth as a part of love-making, like saliva, from mouth to mouth. There is a double resonance to such words, to words that are shared. They reverberate longer and larger in our lives—that is why, I think, we believe what our bed partners tell us the way we believe no one else. We cannot conceive that someone to whom we have revealed that part of ourselves, someone who has seen

228

that, does not know us in a profounder way almost than we can know ourselves. We seem to know ourselves more truly, some- how, in the sight of us that only a lover has, and to define ourselves somehow by the words a lover uses with us. And the shared language of love is a poetic one. It is hyperbolic, synec- dochic, metaphoric. It can be incantatory: redundant, in that it is an invocation of what is already there (or perhaps sometimes evocation, meant to conjure up what is not there). What then of this shared language in the case of two supremely gifted poets— two individuals, I mean, for whom language is the primary real- ity? What can we learn about love, and about poetry, from the language they shared?

We begin by observing that Rimbaud and Verlaine in fact shared a vocabulary, one documented in their poetry. I do not mean to speak of stylistic influences from a common source, or merely of borrowings back and forth, although these exist. Rather I want to point to certain words that both poets used, centrally and repeatedly, in their writings. They had a language of their own, apart from, cut out of, the ordinary language. Its words were among the most ordinary, but used by them almost as fetishes, as evocations, meant to conjure up certain images. And how tightly these words cluster around the central image of marriage and the family! *Orphan. Child. Mother. Marriage. Widowhood. Widow. Widower.* And the phrases, particularly Ver- laine's, but used by Rimbaud: *older sister, friend (l'amie,* feminine).[1] Verlaine: "And I think of a Friend, a Sister . . . but she is dead, and now two little girls in dark dresses play 'mama,' their favorite game, 'til bedtime" (*Pr.* 83, 84). Rimbaud: "Your heart tells you the truth—they have no mother. No mother in the house! And a father far away! . . . The children are alone in

---

1. All quotations from Rimbaud in this essay are taken from my own *Arthur Rimbaud: Complete Works in Translation* (New York: Harper & Row, 1975). Page numbers following quotations from Rimbaud refer to this edition, which is in- dexed in both French and English. There is no standard English edition of Ver- laine's writings; all the quotations from Verlaine in this essay are in my own translation. Page numbers following quotations from Verlaine refer to the origi- nal French texts, in these editions: Verlaine, *Oeuvres poétiques complètes* (Paris: Pléiade, 1951), cited as *Po.*; Verlaine, *Oeuvres en prose complètes* (Paris: Pléiade, 1972), vol. 1; cited as *Pr.*

the icy house: orphans at four." (13) They are both, in their
imaginations, orphans lamenting a family, which had to vanish
for them to come into being. They are widow and widower lamenting a marriage, the spouse whose absence makes them what
they are. And the denial of reciprocal love that those words
imply—widow and orphan: love lost, or love never had—is for
them a fundamental state. Absence becomes a presence; deprivation becomes a kind of having, and gives substance to denial.
Lack becomes pregnant with possibility. Certainly this is true for
Rimbaud; Verlaine, less free, mourned his lack all his life, and
celebrated it in himself, in the dissolution of his later years, in his
features blurred by alcohol, in the wretched body that was
picked up again and again out of gutters and carted off to hospi-
tals.

Yet for both of them, the heart of the matter is marriage: the
sexual union that engenders the family; the center of kinship. It
is, I am convinced, the deep image upon which their poetry and
their life together was founded. It was an image infinitely and
complexly elaborated and distorted by both poets; the leitmotif
of their lives. Rimbaud was to parody his life with Verlaine as a
perverse kind of marriage in *Une saison en enfer,* as the union of
the Foolish Virgin and the Infernal Bridegroom. But earlier,
and less consciously perhaps, Rimbaud had worked out an almost diagrammatic vision of marriage and the extended family.
I think of that group of poems he wrote in the spring and summer of 1872, in Paris, the Ardennes, and Belgium: "Mémoire,"
"Larme," "Comédie de la soif," "Bonne pensée du matin,"
"Bannières de mai," "Chanson de la plus haute tour," "Eternité,"
"Age d'or," "Jeune ménage," "Bruxelles," "Fêtes de la faim,"
"Entends comme brame . . . ," "Michel et Christine," "Honte."
All of them are written soon after Rimbaud's first intimacy with
Verlaine, and the stylistic similarity between the two poets' work
at this period has long been evident; these poems are full of
terms shared with Verlaine and references to him. And their
thematic core, their central images, their "cast of characters,"
their preoccupation, is marriage and the family: the structures
and relations of kinship.

It is with ego that these poems begin. Constant in all of them is
the speaking persona, isolated and separate from what sur-

rounds it, using the pronouns *je* and *moi*, or speaking with grammatical forms that imply the distinction between ego and others: imperatives, hortatives, vocatives. In "Mémoire" the nuclear family is made visible in the course of an extended comparison between the fecundity of a river bed and the marriage bed ("O Wife, your conjugal faith!"), where the actors are *Madame* and the *children*, and *He, She*, and *I*. In "Comédie de la soif," the constant speaker is *I*, and the interlocutors expand the family into previous generations; they are the *forefathers*, and *grandparents*. "Bannières de mai" concludes with one of the most moving passages in all of Rimbaud:

> We laugh with our parents when we laugh in the sun,
> But I will laugh with nothing, with no one;
> And I will be free in this misfortune. [146]

"Chanson de la plus haute tour" uses Verlaine's terms *widowhood* and the *poor soul* in a stanza that concludes with a reference to two of Verlaine's lines:

> Ah! Widowed again and again
> The poor soul
> Who has only a picture
> Of the Mother of God!
> Can one really pray
> To the Virgin Mary? [147]

"Age d'or" includes a dialogue between brother and sisters, and the refrain: "this flowering wave / is your own family!" "Jeune ménage" is also full of references to Verlaine; the room it describes reappears later in Verlaine's "Le poète et la muse" with the same specters, the same cobwebs and patterns on the walls. Verlaine's term *l'amie* is here, and the actors include the *young household, the husband*, and *godmothers*. "Bruxelles" was surely written in Verlaine's company, and is rare in Rimbaud's work, with its tone of excitement and delight, its almost campy exaggerations. Again, the *little widow* and *sounds of children*. The first line of "Fête de la faim" ("Ma faim, Anne, Anne") echoes the dialogue between the heroine of Perrault's *Barbebleue* and her sister: "Anne, sister Anne." "Michel et Christine" is a strange poem, but the seventh and last stanza tops the grandiose swirls of the preceding six like the ornament on the top of some weird wedding cake—the "blue-eyed Bride," the "red-faced bridegroom," and "at their feet, the white Paschal Lamb." It is an idyll done in icing. "Honte," finally, echoes the plaintive voice of ego abandoned that marks the last stanza of "Mémoire": "This child, this bother, this mindless beast . . . Yet when he dies, O God— / Let someone say a prayer."

In Verlaine's poetry the relations of kinship are less clearly articulated, because they are presented in idealized terms: *La bonne chanson* is a hymn to bourgeois felicity, and somehow vitiated by the facts of the marriage that it celebrated. But the lack of such relations is made clear in a text that is at the center of Verlaine's poetry. It was his signature; in his last years as a luminary of the Latin Quarter it was inevitably the poem he would recite when admirers insisted on hearing something. His image for his own ego was the mysterious orphan Kasper Hauser—*Pauvre Gaspard*. Gaspard is hopeless and helpless:

> Was I born too soon, or too late?
> What am I doing in this world?
> All of you, my misery is great:
> Pray for poor Gaspard! [*Po.* 183]

Verlaine wrote a scenario for a ballet based on the life of Gaspard Hauser, in which Gaspard murders his adopted father and becomes a revolutionary; in his notes we find these descriptions:

> Abandoned child. Parents too poor. Knows nothing about anything; can't even talk. Have pity on poor Gaspard. . . .
> Once the unspeakable crime has been committed, Gaspard, all innocence, accepts it, and ratifies it with the help of the constant Frédérique by revolting, together with his beautiful young friends (all of them in drag) against SOCIETY. [*Pr.* 98, 100]

The image of the abandoned child dominates both poets' imaginations; the desperate search for kinship fails, and what remains is the child cut loose, left behind, left alone. We know that Verlaine and Rimbaud were model children when very young. And by "model children" we always mean children modeled on adults, children forced into the world of adult behavior: repressed aggression, repressed hostility, frustration. Children deprived of the freedom to express themselves, above all deprived of the freedom to express anger. Being forced into the mold of adult behavior, they were never able to perceive it as a goal, as a pattern to admire and eventually to accept. What they discovered when they met was surely the child in each other, and the ecstatic possibilities of the childhood they had both been denied. Together they tried to invent a childhood, and the love that they imagined went with it. But it was all too late, coming as it did on the very edge of adulthood. They were never either adults or children. Deprived of childhood by being made mock adults, they spent the crucial moments of their adult life as mock children.

Their behavior together, then, from one point of view, was totally infantile; but let us remember that this behavior was a desperate attempt to attain something *beyond,* some state of being, a state of happiness that both knew existed, but never having experienced had no feeling for—no sense of its dimensions, its delineation, its requirements, its limitations. They were like blind children trying to conceive of color. Rimbaud at least imagined it from time to time in his writing as a state full of possibilities, above all the possibility of vision: that child drifting as a drunken boat might someday "see what men have only thought they saw." But for Verlaine the child poet is resigned, ironic even: "Thus the Poet, who is only a child after all, a bit less consciously perverse, perhaps, than the others" (*Pr.* 95). The only seeing Verlaine can conceive is totally passionless—detached, voyeuristic. He is the widower: "A man as free, as independent, as unencumbered, as disinterested, as egotistical, for example, as a widower: the perfect spectator" (*Pr.* 84–85). But Rimbaud is the *voyant,* the visionary; his seeing is born out of a passion, and born in the heart of something else: disorder. "The disordering of all the senses." Visions of rebellion are born out of the dark corners of order.

That order, for both poets, was the image of a disastrous marriage—for Verlaine, his own; for Rimbaud, his mother's. Out of the darkness of his mother's life, what visions of violence were born? What words, even, from the darkness of her mouth—"Shadow-mouth," Rimbaud called her—or from the folds of her stiff dark clothes, for she dressed as a widow from the day her husband left her, and thought of her children as orphans. The phrase constantly in her mouth is the one Rimbaud uses to characterize her: "Such a pity."

For Verlaine, too, the same metaphors were compelling, obsessive. Surely his marriage began for him as a search for order. But his images for himself, the words he uses constantly to describe his state, are the leftovers of marriage—*widower, widow, orphan.* There must first have been a marriage, the order of marriage, and now there must no longer be one, the disorder of nonmarriage, for there to be widows and orphans. They are the relicts, objects of pity. But Rimbaud proposed an attack on such order, and an attempt to reach something beyond pity—a kind of strength. *Something new.*

Into the order, then, that Verlaine tried to establish in his life, the order of marriage, came Rimbaud, a child with a question, and an answer:

> What do we care, my heart, for streams of blood
> And fire, a thousand murders, endless screams
> Of anger, sobs of hell, order destroyed in a flood
> Of fire? Nothing! [85–86]

A destroyer, sixteen years old. And with him a savage dialectic that was to be a struggle to the death, a dialectic to be carried out in flesh and bloodshed.

It was the disordered life that Verlaine entered with Rimbaud, and its great disorder was homosexuality. A life of liminality, a life lived permanently in-between, a life incomprehensible in terms of the society he inhabited as a married man.

> Understand it how you will, that's not what it is;
> You good people cannot understand the sense of things.
> I tell you it is not what you think. [*Po.* 253]

An outlaw? Yes, for his in-laws at least. Because marriage is the primal structure and the ultimate order. That at least they do understand, the good people. What is it then that they don't understand, that they cannot know? Precisely what Rimbaud proposed to Verlaine: a voyage—a trip, as the children say about hallucinogenic drugs—to arrive at the unknown. To arrive at what was not known because only the voyage made that knowledge possible, and had never been known because the good people had never made the trip, had never been aware that there was a trip to be made, that there was another side of things to voyage to. To be good means not to perceive the other side of things. And the other side of things, for the good people, the ones who marry, is homosexuality.

To be homosexual, even bisexual, is to be constantly aware of one's life in a way that heterosexuals are not forced to be. It is to be aware of another possibility, another dimension. Not merely aware of it—heterosexuals are certainly aware of it—but to know that it is knowable, and then to know it, necessarily. *Forcément.* To be forced to know it. It is the inescapable other knowledge. It is the unknown made known. It is the knowledge that lies beyond the bite of the apple, the attraction, the compulsion, fatal or otherwise, toward another world. That world may be sensed only, and perhaps only dimly; it may be written about, or acted out. It may even, with difficulty, be lived. It is real.

Homosexuality, then, in the program of Verlaine and Rimbaud, is one of a number of *disorderings of the senses* which free us from our everyday perceptions of the world. But it is the most important of them, and radically serious because it makes us question the world we live in, and question it precisely in its basic assumption—the inevitability of generation. Homosexuality is an alienation introduced into the very root of the social order, into sex as procreation. We say usually that the opposite of homosexuality is heterosexuality, but that's not quite it. The opposite of homosexuality is marriage. Homosexuality is a permanent extension of a period of in-betweenness, of liminality. It questions the social order that liminal states usually prepare us for and lead us to. It is an alienation from the order of society, and it provides, as all alienations do, a view of that order from outside, from the other side. But being permanent, it is more—it is a refusal of that order. It is indeed a radical denial of all human order, in that it denies kinship and its rules and obligations. By denying generation, homosexuality denies time, and fruition in time; and it rejects them in the name of the instant, the instantaneous in perception and experience. By disengaging itself from the flow of generations it is able to constitute itself an exemplary and natural state of exaltation. It is thus one with states of trance, of contact with the extraordinary. From this point of view, homosexuality may well be seen not as a psychological aberration but as a cultural possibility—a state of permanent quest for vision. Not that this quest is inevitably actualized, or even made conscious. In practice it is more likely to be a quest for experience, or more often than not for mere sensation. Still, homosexuality contains within itself a virtuality: it can be a source of instantaneous illumination. In a larger sense, indeed, homosexuality may be one of a number of patterns by which a complex, fragmented culture provides an initiation that is not collective but individual, one that may easily be made permanent, and one that thus provides the culture with an ongoing posture of critical vision. But it operates, as all initiation rites and all vision quests do, in terms of individual enlightenment, self-knowledge. Both *widower* and *visionary*, no matter how different their styles and natures, seek reflexive vision. "I is an other. I am a spectator at the flowering of my own thought: I watch it, I listen to it" (102). The reflexivity of this vision removes it from the reciprocity of human society; it opens and keeps open a realm beyond the social, a realm of abstraction, of "pure possibility whence *novel* configurations of ideas and relations may arise." Newness, here, is all, and homosexuality is a method, rigorous and unavoidable, for attaining it. To plunge into the gulf is *by that act alone* to find something new. But to return with it, to carry it back intact and to persuade the good people that it is indeed new—that's the difficulty. The problem for the alienated viewer, for the prophet in the desert or the drunk in the gutter, is to find a way to announce what he sees. The visions of the *other* are not often available to the good people because a voice and a vocabulary are lacking. But Verlaine and Rimbaud, out of the most profound lack, created both voice and vocabulary.

Yet now we must ask the question Verlaine and Rimbaud tried to answer: what novel configurations of ideas and relations are possible? The flesh exists: how can we carry it into a realm of pure possibility? It is solid: how can we apply abstractions to it? Beyond kinship, outside the family, outside the social order, what kind of relations are possible? Where the rules of kinship don't apply, what does?

We must begin with the flesh, but the flesh of two artists, Rimbaud and Verlaine. Now, one of the possible disasters of an artist's life is that he is capable of making love as he makes art. I mean that the act of love may become for him, like the act of art, an act whose consequences, whose boundaries even, are an integral part of the act itself. And yet the central nature of the act of human love is very precisely that it cannot be just a moment; it entails commitments and liabilities beyond the mere act. An artist's conception of the immediacy of his work, and of its self-sufficiency, its self-containment, must always come to grief upon the complicated consequences of loving and being loved by other people. It is here that the idea of instantaneous illumination fails; reflexive vision darkens in any long run. Verlaine writes of Rimbaud (few lovers have ever written so clearly about each other):

> You go with a mind darkened by the image
> Of a happiness that for you must be immediate.... [*Po.* 150]

Yet is not happiness defined only when no end to its extent is imagined? Can it ever be immediate? Does it not inevitably require time to come to fruition? Immediacy, happiness, and human flesh is an impossible concatenation. Outside of kinship, then, what extended relationship is possible? And for these two poets, each carrying his metaphors and images of the world toward the other, what relationship obtains?

Two relationships are possible, it seems to me, and they reflect each other like mirrors throughout both poets' writings. They may well be, in fact, only two aspects of one single relationship; all relations outside of kinship may be merely one, that has two opposed manifestations. The first is a relation based on affection, a relation between equals, a relation conceived horizontally. This seems to me to be the kernel of what Victor Turner calls *communitas*. The second is a relation based on control, a relation between nonequals, a relation conceived vertically. This seems to me to be the kernel of hierarchy, of structure and order. The radical image of the first is two children playing together, the radical image of the second is master and slave. And over and over, in the many texts in which the two poets describe their relationship, these are the ubiquitous images. But these were more than just images in words; both poets intended to make them images incarnate. The word was to become flesh.

Now, the image of two children playing harmoniously together is very much a projection of the adult imagination, but as an image it has had a long life, and as a vision a high credence. To act it out, though, is something else; playing at being children together is difficult for adults; it's a tiring game. Rimbaud seems to have had little affection for anyone, and less patience; what feeling he had for Verlaine in the early days of their relationship seems quickly to have disappeared, and when affection disappears, control takes its place. "I was never strongly enough in control of that undertaking," Rimbaud was to write later in *Vagabonds* (220).

The prime example of perfect equality may well be two children playing together. But the great horror, and the primal image for the sadomasochistic imagination, is the beaten child—beaten because alone, without equals, without kin, therefore unloved, therefore unprotected, therefore the perfect subject for dominance and the threat of annihilation. The helpless orphan. *Poor Gaspard.* The child who is not loved, or is made to feel unworthy of being loved, is the source of the ambivalent hatred-of-self and hatred-of-other-for-reflecting-self-and-still-being-other that is at the heart of sadomasochism. And this was eventually the pattern of Rimbaud and Verlaine's relationship. We must admit it finally, I think: the violence that has always seemed a metaphor in the texts was more than that. "We make love like tigers," Verlaine announced to the guards at the Belgian frontier, and showed them the cuts and bruises on his chest. Stories tell of Rimbaud deliberately stabbing Verlaine's hand in a bar one night, of Rimbaud beating Verlaine senseless and abandoning him on a riverbank near Stuttgart. There is, in the police records, Rimbaud's astonishing casualness after Verlaine shot him—the entire afternoon spent together, with the bullet in his wrist, before going to the hospital; and going off together that evening to the train station, with Verlaine still drunk and carrying a loaded pistol. Verlaine was given a medical examination after his arrest, and the report speaks of "marks of active and passive pederasty"; on the face of it this seems farfetched, but I wonder. Might not those wounds brought brazenly across at the frontier be understood at last in the capital as a dangerous kind of contraband?

Certainly the texts which describe the relationship are soaked with blood and sexual violence. Verlaine:

> a breast stamped twice with the mark of a fist,
> and a mouth, a wound still red . . ., [Po. 186]

And this:

> The happiness of bleeding on the breast of a friend. . . . [Po. 360]

Rimbaud:

> Convulsed with wounds . . . racked . . . by tortures. . . . [235]

And this:

the terrible shudder of unpracticed loves, on the bloody ground. [167]

And this:

> Eyes flame, blood sings, bones begin to swell,
> tears start, and networks of scarlet ripple and throb. [159]

Blood and wounds are constant in both poets' work. There is, finally, the evidence of the two great central pillars of *Une saison en enfer*, the two "Deliriums," in which Rimbaud performs for us two characters: Verlaine first, as the Foolish Virgin, and then himself as the deluded poet finally rejecting their joint enterprise. Verlaine's confession begins: "I am the slave of the Infernal Bridegroom." It is a moving mixture of tears and blood, of cruelty and submission, and at its heart is a despairing cry for

the opposite state, for the innocence and happiness of children
at play: "I used to imagine that we were two happy children. . . . Oh, that wonderful world of adventures that we found
in children's books, won't you give me that world?" Yet the
maudlin rambling contains moments of the clearest perception
of what was at stake: "Love has to be reinvented, we know
that. . . . No man before ever had such a desire. I was aware—
without being afraid for him—that he could become a serious
menace to society. Did he, perhaps, have secrets that would *remake life*?" The idea is astonishing, that out of all that violence
and torment was to come a vision of New Love and a new life.
We are forced to pass beyond the idea of pain as mere voluptuousness and think of it as a method of piercing through into
another world, into another vision. It is a means of creating the
unknown.

Part of this method was, I think, frankly magical. Rimbaud's
readings in nineteenth-century mystic writing have been documented; certainly *magic* is a frequent word in his writing during the time he spent with Verlaine. Now, sex *as* magic is largely
ignored in our speculations on either subject; since Freud we
no longer connect the two practices. But Antiquity, the Middle Ages, and the seventeenth century certainly did—and we
know that Rimbaud read Michelet's *La sorcière*. Let us remember
another case in French history of sadomasochistic homosexuality
as a kind of magic: the matter of Gilles de Rais. Consider the
acts and words of sex as incantation: we perform certain acts,
handle certain objects, and say certain words, in an attempt to
transform ourselves: to partake of another being, another world.
This is magic, by definition. Rimbaud and Verlaine certainly
practiced it, together. And there seems no question that sadomasochistic sex, with its rituals, its cult objects, its litanies, is intended as magic. A black mass is magic, but its intention is the
same as that of a white mass: to unite the participants in a mystical union, a mystical body, forever, world without end. Does not
all magic attempt to *recover eternity*?

It is at this point that Rimbaud's quest fits into another pattern, the pattern of a more familiar quest *to remake life*. "The one
who will create God" can hurt others, and Verlaine suffered; but
Rimbaud writes that "the pitiful thought of Christ crucified

turns in my head" (194). We finally rejoin the great central image of the sadomasochistic vision, the crucifixion: the acceptance of annihilation by the all-powerful—out of love. It is, moreover, the purest image of the abandoned and suffering child. And was not the crucifixion the great historical moment of the introduction of another New Love into the world? Rimbaud and Verlaine are, after all, two profoundly religious poets. Now there are two strains to what we describe as religious. One is the social pattern, religion as *religio,* what is passed on within a social framework, symbolic patterns which justify and sanctify an order we impose upon ourselves and understand as we imagine it reflected in what surrounds us. The other is the pattern of vision: what each of us experiences as transcendent within us and seeks merely to ratify in our perception of what surrounds us. The two are linked inasmuch as the patterns we perceive in the world around us tell us how to recognize the shape of the divine. Yet most records of mystical experience reveal a necessary rejection of *religio,* of the bonds that unite us with others; only out of this gesture of refusal can come recognition of the divine. What divides Rimbaud from Verlaine—and what may have eventually divided them in fact—was the different lengths to which each was willing to go in order to separate himself, to make that gesture of refusal. To recognize, that is, the state of otherness, of in-betweenness, of liminality, which was a prerequisite for vision. Verlaine had been indulged; his experience of the world was too pleasant for him to give it all up. Rimbaud had less experience of pleasure to abandon; Verlaine's voluptuousness was foreign to him. When the moment came to recognize the failure of the joint enterprise, the hopelessness of any kind of relation that might replace the lost ties of kinship, it was Rimbaud who recognized it. Verlaine pursued the patterns of their joint imagination—veering ever more wildly between childish helplessness and violence—until the moment came when imagination must yield to the fatality of fact, and Verlaine shot Rimbaud. Annihilation is the ultimate stake in the balance between dominance and submission.

Weak and vicious, a critic wrote of Verlaine. We can pardon the vice, but not the weakness. It is the strong Rimbaud who has always attracted the modern imagination—"te voilà, c'est la force," he wrote in *Une saison en enfer*: "you exist, that is strength." The phrase has an astonishing simplicity, and a supreme confidence despite its despairing context. The weak Verlaine we treat with contempt. Freedom is our god, and Rimbaud was free, defined freedom for us as perhaps no one else ever has. Verlaine was enslaved—to drink, to sex, to Rimbaud. Perhaps we can only pity him, as Rimbaud did—it was with the word from his mother's mouth that he described Verlaine: "Pitiful brother!" What sounds in Verlaine is the last cry of the wounded animal; what sounds in Rimbaud is the first clang of the machine. Verlaine possessed every human weakness, Rimbaud sought inhuman strength. To be weak is to be ultimately human, and so deserving of pity. To be merely strong is ultimately to give up being human, and so even more deserving of pity. But do they not both deserve more than pity? Let us imagine them as one poetic entity, weakness and strength locked together: they were thus as a couple exemplarily human, and so profoundly deserving of our admiration and gratitude. They were joined in the essential homosexual paradox, the problem of trying to establish a relationship beyond the patterns of kinship, and within a state that is defined precisely by the denial of bonds and ties: by separateness, apartness, in-betweenness, individualization and reflexivity. And by vision, ultimately: the vision of Otherness. And they both knew it. What was it Rimbaud sought? "To possess the truth within one body and one soul." And yet it is Verlaine who understood, profoundly, the pain of the paradox:

> . . . Do I even know why
> We are caught in this trap
> And are still here, though we've been exiled
> And have gone far away? [*Po.* 125]

Wallace Fowlie

Sexuality in Gide's Self-Portrait

To American students of my generation, who reached adult-hood about 1930, the case of André Gide was famous and unique. If we acknowledged the importance of his writings, first to ourselves, and then to our friends, and finally, a few years later, to our students, we knew we were taking a stand that had extraliterary implications. We were praising and defending a writer, a great writer—of that we were certain—who in his early books had written deftly and evasively of his sexual nature, and who then, in *Corydon* (1924) and *Si le grain ne meurt* (1926), had forcefully and unquivocally described and accepted his homosexuality.

For readers of Gide today, as well as for critics, and for teachers discussing his books in a classroom, the sexual problems are still complex and varied. They have undergone some changes, some modifications through the years, but on the whole they remain fairly steadfast. The argument to which they have given rise might be summarized as follows.

(1) The sexual proclivities of Gide himself and of his charac-ters have nothing to do with the literary value of his writings. Why discuss biography and psychological references in a work that stands by itself? This approach is the aesthetic one, and

Gide himself advocated it in a sentence that has been endlessly used by those critics who declare they are looking solely at the work and not at the man who wrote it, but who almost never cling to their announced stand.

(2) The exact opposite view might be stated in the following way. Gide's sexual nature is the total explanation of every line he wrote. Every work, from *Les cahiers d'André Walter* (1891) to the final entry in his *Journal*, June 1949, is an expression of his homosexuality. The thesis is clear and could be defended convincingly (although, as far as I know, no one has done so): each book of André Gide's is an approach to his central problem of a physiological and psychological nature, exacerbated by the time and by the mores of the country in which he lived, and by his contacts with other countries of mores different from those of France.

(3) The third position might be phrased in this way. The very name André Gide has become synonymous with the practice of homosexuality in a world which still, on the whole, condemns the practice, or looks down upon it, or derides it. No other writer I can think of has known this fate: certainly not Proust, whose novel draws attention to its massiveness and historicism; certainly not Cocteau, who moved swiftly from genre to genre, covering up his traces with ever new and varied exhibitions; certainly not Jean Genet, who has not reached the universality of Gide. Acknowledged or unacknowledged, it is the first "tag" attached to his name, the first designation used by those who like him and by those who do not like him; by those who read him and by those who do not read him; by those who consider him a major writer and by those who, without possessing a shred of evidence, consider him a perverter of the young. Homosexuality is central to him, in the view of friend and foe alike. This first became apparent in 1926, the year when all doubts were dissipated, and Gide's friends and literary associates either remained friends, as in the case of Charles Du Bos, and took a strong stand against his philosophy, or, as in the case of Claudel, gave up their friendship and denounced him.

Such news travels fast in our society. It has only to be whispered hesitatingly, quizzically, and it is fixed forever in the mind of the one who hears it, and who forthwith communicates it to others, usually in a tone of apology and commiseration. The sexual nature of a man, when revealed, even if the revelation comes from a source that is not authentic or dependable, takes first place in the world's estimate of the man's temperament and activities, more important than his politics, his philosophy, his family and his class situation, his race, his learning. And if his sexual nature is homoerotic, according to hearsay or to evidence or to confession, then the news, in the form almost of a conviction, is welcomed as titillating and dramatic, and is destined to last the man's lifetime—and if he be a writer, to last as long as his work survives.

Important reasons and very complex explanations lie behind this state of affairs. Morbid curiosity is a facile interpretation; the truth is more closely related to society's primordial need to designate a scapegoat of sufficient stature to bear its fantasies about the sexual acts that are forbidden the stolid, so-called "normal" members of society. Not even the dignity and the intellectual brilliance that Gide displayed both in his life and in his writings were able to protect him. He was vulnerable, and more than most men. Did he willfully lay himself open to attack? Did he solicit attacks, under the cover of his word "sincerity," through some deep-seated masochistic tendency? Was his frankness a sign and a proof of his courage? These are some of the questions I would like to consider, but, as far as is feasible, consider them in the light of changing attitudes in society, in the differing reactions of young readers and older readers, and in terms of some perennial problems of literary criticism.

Gide left to the world a voluminous work which is, more than anything else, a self-portrait. I propose to look, once again, at the purpose and the subtle candor that seem to be present in his various exercises of introspection. It would be comparatively easy to limit myself to the autobiography *Si le grain ne meurt,* and to the volumes of the *Journal,* but the resulting picture would be inaccurate. All Gide's writings are mirrors of himself where he watched himself and facets of the self-portrait he wanted to leave to us and to readers after us.

Traits of Gide's temperament are, of course, visible in his *Journal,* but they are also to be found, and in a more profound treatment, in Edouard's journal of *Les faux-monnayeurs,* in Alissa's journal of *La porte étroite*, in rhapsodic passages of *Les nourritures terrestres*, in the play *Saül*, and in the letters to Claudel and Valéry.

We in America, who are of another literary tradition, find this unique insistence on the self to be particularly French. Our students, when they begin reading Gide, are initially more attracted to the *récits*, to *L'immoraliste*, for example, than to the personal writings. They need something like an objective structure to reasure them in order to feel at ease when they are trying to follow Gidean themes.

What saves the Frenchman in his inordinate concern with the self is his critical turn of mind, his skill in self-criticism, which almost makes his egocentrism seem objective. Analysis accompanies egocentrism and raises it above the purely personal in the journal-confessions, whether the writer be Rousseau, Chateaubriand, Amiel, Constant, Gide, Julien Green, or Jean Genet. In a word, analysis endows confession, or seeks to endow it, with universal significance. Gide wrote with the belief that he was in connivance with his readers, especially with his younger readers, helping them to rid themselves of uptightness, helping to dissolve prejudices and fears, trying to convince them that the sexual needs of their nature were right for them. The drama of the Gidean hero, in book after book, arises precisely from the hesitation of a young man to accept the sexuality of his nature.

I am thinking here of Montaigne's sentence in the essay *Du repentir* (III, 2), one of the best known sentences in all of French literature, part of which is used by Malraux as the title of his third novel: *Chaque homme porte la forme entière de l'humaine condition.* This sentence about each man bearing the form of humanity, of all the states of man, is appropriate to recall here, not only because of its application to Gide's self-portrait and because Gide used it, but because of its strong religious resonance.

I see the sentence as justifying Gide's insistent will to explore himself. Its overtones are markedly Christian. The verb *porter* in this context, *to bear,* would seem almost to mean *to be born with.* This is what we have to bear. Human nature is our fate. The mystic would say, "The cross is in every life." Montaigne in the sixteenth century and André Gide in the twentieth are examples of French writers who explore the self as it changes and who acknowledge indirectly, inadvertently at times, the religious meaning of life.

The habit of introspection in Gide is so allied with the habit of articulation, of speech, that the one cannot be distinguished from the other. And this again is a specifically French trait— "Intensely audible," as Henry James once said of the French. Gide often seems to be thinking aloud as he writes in his *Journal*. Introspection and speech are married here. This love of speech brings with it the danger of facile rhetoric, although in Gide's case the temptation was not facility of speech, but rather that of elegant speech, in keeping with subtlety of analysis. I know no other French writer who used this inheritance of elegance of speech and subtlety of analysis more brilliantly than he did.

Everything in Gide's life was directed toward his art, toward the articulation and the writing down of his thought. Every experience and every observation, no matter how commonplace, was something to be converted into a sentence or a paragraph or a book. How erroneous it is to think of Gide first as a homosexual and then as a writer. The reverse is true. He was first and foremost a writer, in the fullest sense of the word, and then a man whose sexual inclinations were pederastic.

The literal sexual acts in Gide's life were brief, infrequent, and clandestine. As a boy, he was attracted to other boys, but he masturbated almost always alone. Feelings of guilt over onanism harassed him throughout childhood and adolescence. His strict Protestant upbringing, and especially the example of his mother's constant denunciation of any sexual indulgence, and even of any sexual thought, maintained young André through his mid-twenties in a state of worry and apprehension. It was precisely in the years when his sexual drives were the strongest that he struggled the most against any indulgence.

Then came the turning point, clearly marked in the autobiography. The Arab boy Ali, in Soussa, in the Tunisian desert, gave himself freely and exuberantly to Gide. The Calvinist from Normandy was twenty-four when he had this first sexual relationship in North Africa, with a dark-skinned native boy who felt no scruple, no hesitation, and who understood in his simple way that this Frenchman—a tourist—desired his body.

From that time on, sexual activity for Gide was associated with exotic or unusual places and with boys whose sexual instincts were easily aroused and quickly satisfied. Gide was not a sodomite. He was, if one can say this, totally uncomplicated as a sexual partner. He was satisfied with caresses and with self- or mutual masturbation, in hotel rooms, in movie houses, in train compartments, on deserted stretches of beach. The encounter was usually unexpected, a furtive experience, where therefore the sexual feeling was intense and capable of quick culmination. It was not unlike a hygienic exercise which, when carried out, would then liberate him for note-taking and writing. On the whole, sex was not for the houses of his family, not for Cuverville, nor for the Paris apartment on the rue Vaneau run for him by his elderly friend Mme Théo van Rysselberghe. Sex was not associated with love, except in the case of Marc Allégret, and perhaps those of two or three other adolescents whose families Gide knew and saw frequently.

Love both complicated his daily life and enriched his writing. Such experiences were very few in Gide's life; there were perhaps not many others after that with his wife Madeleine Rondeaux, which endured for many years without any sexual component, and that with Marc, of few years' duration where sexual love turned into love and loving companionship. In other words, Gide's relationship with Marc Allégret, and not his marriage with Madeleine, was the classical case of a successful marriage. But when the "marriage" reached the phase of love without sex, there was no commitment and no need or desire to live together.

Gide always felt the need for detachment from any bond that would constrict the freedom he deemed necessary for his work. The secretive, spontaneous, and even unhoped-for sexual encounters suited the pattern of his life. A strong aesthetic experience: the sight of a beautiful boy, active in his movements, at times criminal in his actions, would provide Gide with an experience having sexual overtones, an experience worthy of being noted in his *Journal* and later narrated in *L'immoraliste* or *Les faux-monnayeurs*. Gide the entomologist and the naturalist was the same man as Gide the voyeur, the cerebral lover who, like Aschenbach, never touched Tadzio. Aschenbach had one Tadzio, but Gide had many, in Amalfi, Taormina, Tanger, Biskra, Nice, Algiers.

The attraction that Michel feels for Moktir in *L'immoraliste* and that Edouard feels for Olivier in *Les faux-monnayeurs* is the literary form of Gide's real-life sexuality. In the *récit* and the novel, the two experiences are more developed and analyzed, and more related to surrounding secondary actions, than the similar encounters that were lived briefly and then replaced by other similar encounters. These are two of the best remembered and most frequently referred to episodes in Gide's published work because they are the most revealing and the most shocking in terms of the heterosexual love that might have developed, but did not, between Michel and Marceline and between Edouard and Laura. Even the most casual reader becomes fully aware of the importance of such episodes. Michel and Edouard find excitement and intensity in their sexual thoughts and acts, but they find no stability in them, no hope for any permanent love situation. It is clear, without Gide the writer expressing it, that neither Michel nor Edouard wants any permanent situation of erotic love. Michel prefers Moktir to his wife Marceline because a rapidly passing infatuation with the lithe seductive Arab boy will help him recover his health. And Edouard prefers Olivier to a wife, because a man-boy relationship interferes less with his writer's vocation. The point here is that the characteristics of Gide's homosexuality were peculiar to him, were developed in terms of his career as a writer, and are lucidly depicted in his fiction.

One is struck by the difference between his life—uneventful, peaceful, not at all extraordinary—and the boldness of his writings. Gide's entire life (1869–1951) was devoid of any monetary problems. He lived as a *rentier,* and from time to time expressed a feeling of shame at not having to earn his living. I have found no trace of any influence of this financial independence in his writing. We can also say, I think, that the many meaningful friendships he enjoyed never affected his work. There seems to have been a total separation between the writer and the friend, between the writer and the man in his social life. His day-by-day existence never revealed, as his writings reveal, his burning de-

sire for authenticity and his belief in self-exposure. I am trying
here to translate the word Gide used so often to describe the
state of the self he wished to create and expose: *dénuement.*

In his self-exposure, or what I am calling more politely "self-
portrait," Gide returned periodically to the theme of the difficulty of living. By this he did not mean the practical difficulty of
living, but the difficulty of living authentically. Gide's merit in
this was confessing the difficulty as a self-observer. Like
Montaigne and Stendhal, he derived no particular delight from
the art of confession. And he did not do it from any vulgar wish
to attract the curious. He was courageous in analyzing errors in
his life, errors that were due to temperament. Already in literary
history, Gide's name has become associated with "sincerity." In
kinship with Rousseau, he made claims to sincerity and centered
his autobiography on a deliberate effort to be sincere. But sincerity about any such complex experience as a man's life has to
be selective. Gide was not a philosopher and was wise in choosing
such a word as sincerity rather than truthfulness.

If, however, he was discouraged over any hope of reaching
truth, even about himself, at least he was concerned with ways of
discovering truth. And more than that, with ways of presenting
truth. He was almost sixty years old when in his *Journal* he wrote
the sentence: *"Je deviens celui que je crois que je suis"*—I am becoming the man I think I am.[1] This passage, from October 1927, is
rich in definitions and contradictions. He proposes that man is
perfectible (meaning, I suppose, modifiable), that he can end by
experiencing a sentiment that once he pretended in a social
sense he was experiencing. He reminds us that some people
remain virtuous simply to correspond to the opinion that they
believe other people have about them. Gide says in this same
passage—it is a line often quoted and one very close to a
Montaigne formula—*"je ne suis jamais, je deviens."* If I enlarged
the sentence, it would seem to mean: "I am never one thing; I
am always becoming something else."

What did remain steadfast was the general pattern of his existence, the way he lived, the friendships he cultivated and those
he avoided or discouraged, his sexual life, his method of writing,

1. *Journal: 1889–1939* (Paris, Pléiade, 1960), p. 852.

and finally, a defect, called by friends who loved him, by acquaintances who observed him, and by members of his family, Gide's avarice.

This habit of avarice—not a pleasant one—was unavoidable in Gide's life, as it is in the case of anyone, rich or poor, who lives as he did, in a pattern of work that involves a daily accretion of minute particles—in the case of a writer, a daily accumulation of words and sentences. This kind of labor necessitates a life in which the most fertile hours of the day are spent separated from any human companionship, and where one is quite literally a prisoner of the self, concentrated on an observance of the mind and of memory. The richest hours are those when the spending of money is impossible. To preserve the intactness of such a rigorous routine, visits with friends have to be carefully planned so that conversations will not be invasions into the sacrocanct hours of work, and when there will be as little expense as possible of time and money.

Avarice also is the characteristic of the masturbator whose sexual release is easy to accomplish and often represents a reward for the hours of solitary work. With a young sexual partner, a boy or an adolescent who has perhaps learned to "trick" several times in a day, there is little time wasted in "making out," no money spent in preliminary courting, a small sum involved, or no sum at all if the partner is flattered by such attention and wants his own sexual satisfaction.

Gide's way of life was fashioned around his way of writing. That came first. His house in Cuverville was run by Madeleine until her death in 1938. His Paris apartment, 1bis rue Vaneau, was run by Mme Théo, whose daughter Elisabeth van Rysselberghe was the mother of Gide's daughter Catherine. Gide accepted gifts gratefully and delightedly, but never gave any, not even to his grandchildren. He lived as if he were exempt from the duty and pleasure of giving presents, meals, invitations. He gave . . . advice, conversation, spiritual and moral gifts that involved no money. He husbanded the wealth he had inherited, and added to it by economizing in every way possible. This was much more than a habit of stinginess. It paralleled and strengthened his habit, in writing, of economizing on words, as it accounted for his sexual life.

At the end of one of his earliest books, *Les nourritures terrestres,*
Gide the narrator and initiator into all the enjoyments of the
earth, says to his young disciple Nathanaël, "Throw away my
book (*Jette mon livre*). My book should instill in you desire to
leave your family, your room, your past, and open you up to the
new experiences awaiting you." Gide's message and the beauty
of his writing are in those sentences. He argues that everything
should be sacrificed to a life of the senses, to a daily re-education
of the senses where a man falls in love with a momentary sensual
experience: the sound of water, the color of a cloud, the coolness
of the air, the taste of a pomegranate, the beauty of a youth's body,
and the swiftly reached orgasm of love-making on the desert
sand.

The ambiguities of Gide's teaching in such a book are flagrant,
when, on the one hand, he advocates a hedonistic way of life
where all the senses of a man will be aroused and satisfied, and
where, on the other hand, he urges his disciple toward an ascetic
life in which all love of worldly possessions will be castigated,
where the bonds of responsibility to class and family will be severed. Hedonism and asceticism are fused in Gide: in his extraordinary attentiveness to every minute experience of the senses and
the mind, and in his plodding daily methodical habit of writing
about such experiences. Such extremes cohabited in him without
friction because one extreme, the writer's vocation, was stronger
than the other.

I know of no passage in Gide's writing where he specifically
described the self that he wanted to become. But he does speak
of the ideal image of himself as the image Madeleine Gide would
have endorsed. His wife's was the only approval he needed or
wanted. Very often Gide described one manifestation of his personality when he was aware of it. But of course no one manifestation accounted for the whole. There were too many versions of
the self that contradicted one another.

His autobiography emphasizes this point over and over again.
The subject of an autobiography is created in the same way that
a fictional character is created. Gide tended to become what he
said he was when he traced a portrait of himself. In discussing
this process, he often used the word *dédoublement.* He watched
himself as if he were simultaneously the self who watched and the

self who was being watched. With a grain of humor he once said that on the point of dying, he would still be watching himself and would probably say: *"Tiens! il meurt!"*— Look! he's dying![2]

The last pages Gide wrote in the *Journal* are among his finest. They are, as always, pages of self-judgment wherein he states, without modesty or immodesty, that the charge of coquettishness so often leveled against him was no longer valid. That element had been burned out and replaced by what we, as continuing readers of Gide, might possibly call his final elegance of mind and sensitivity, that final state of serenity that did not depend on a neglect of struggle or a relaxation of inner discipline, but on the acquisition of a final wisdom.

Where the self-criticism is stringent, especially in those comments that help us, in a negative way, to see the self-portrait, Gide reveals the anxiety of a moralist, the suffering that comes from not living in accordance with the regimen he had set himself. His worry was usually over somnolence, emptiness, inactivity. He counted the number of hours that gave him nothing, those hours therefore when he was not living. But no one can be a writer twenty-four hours a day. The work he had set himself was too arduous, too exacting to allow him any freedom, any relaxation that might dull his sharpness.

Among the many worries about himself which he clearly articulated, however, there is no mention of his sexual preference. As soon as it was clear to him that he was homosexual, and that he could live as a homosexual, he accepted that fact, never denied it, and never believed that he could or should make any attempt to change it. His sexual activity occupied much less of his life than is usually believed. But it sharpened and marked his sensibility because of the age in which he lived and the country in which he lived for the most part. He knew that by most people he was looked upon as one who should live in exile from normally constituted society or be forced to conceal his sexual desires. He refrained from discussing these matters with his many intellectual friends, probably to avoid embarrassing them. Only with a very small number of people was he able to speak of inversion: friends such as Jacques Rivière, Julien Green, his son-

2. *Journal*, p. 1164.

in-law Jean Lambert, and a few others whom he saw infrequently: Klaus Mann, Maurice Sachs, or visitors from other countries who came seeking advice and help from the master who had publicly taken his stand.

In full knowledge of what he was doing, Gide called attention to himself in *Corydon,* a treatise-defense of homosexuality, and, more subtly, in such books as *L'immoraliste* and *Les faux-monnayeurs,* where he studied, as a creative writer, problems of the homosexual temperament, and then, finally, in his autobiography and in his *Journal,* where in brief passages he was unabashedly frank. In all these writings, Gide treated his subject with grave seriousness. He himself was the example he used, but he was always concerned with the bigger social and moral problems of homosexuality in the modern world.

Gide wrote movingly and sympathetically of the case of Oscar Wilde, of the Irish writer's humiliation and dramatic trial. But Gide never manifested any of the "camp" behavior for which Wilde was notorious and which ultimately militated against him. Probably—and this is more surmise than fact—Montaigne's case is closest to Gide's in the annals of French literature. Biographical details are lacking, as are specific comments by Montaigne on his sexual habits. But although it is difficult, and dangerous perhaps, to read between the lines of such a complex writer as Michel de Montaigne, some of the passages on his love for Etienne de la Boétie, for example, are as passionate as those that any man has ever written about a woman.

The many parallels between Gide and Montaigne are striking. The importance of daily writing and the habit of writing about whatever subject solicited their attention at the moment, topics usually suggested by the massive doses of reading each absorbed, chosen in the works of important writers—this was the background of their two lives. No financial problem troubled either, and no urge to possess material things preoccupied them. Both enjoyed traveling; it was one of the many ways in which they satisfied some of the curiosity about themselves and defined traits of temperament different from the make-up of most men. The only persistent problem for Montaigne and Gide seems to have been the preservation of independence. Each lived apart from his wife, and each was fairly indifferent to children and grandchildren. Each had little to do with the "running" of the castle or the apartment. Each enjoyed frequent encounters with friends and also chance encounters with people seen only once. Each enjoyed discussing with himself, and then consigning to paper, passages from favorite authors. Each lent himself generously and warmly to an understanding of the leading philosophical and social problems of his day, and each spoke his own mind about such problems.

The sexual nature of a man, whether it be strong and demanding, or passive and undemonstrative, provides the fundamental explanation of his character and his work. If we have considerable knowledge concerning Gide's sexuality, we can only guess at Montaigne's, we can only surmise that it was similar to Gide's. But more significant than this surmise and this knowledge, is the fact that each gave himself to the vocation of writer and, through constant and meticulous self-examination, attempted to study mankind and bring to mankind some degree of relief, of illumination, of understanding.

Far too intelligent to be simple about anything, Gide, during sixty years (and Montaigne during a span of thirty years), almost daily consigned his thoughts to paper. These thoughts might be grouped under two major headings: those that were efforts to find the truth about himself, and those that were efforts to find the truth about others. Both aspects of this project, by their very nature, were destined to fail, to be incomplete. With some degree of envy, Gide watched Paul Claudel who, once his position was chosen, did not budge. For Claudel, the fixed position was everything. For Gide, mobility was the only possible state.

Wherever Gide was—I am thinking here, first, of simple geography—he was ill at ease, either mildly or extremely. All his life he was looking for a home. He is the outstanding wanderer in French literature, far more intent on moving from place to place than the professional wanderers such as Valery Larbaud or Blaise Cendrars. I have never known what to call this "drive" in Gide's nature, this endless need to search for places in which to live briefly. I have tried various words: "imagination," for example. Did his imagination need the stimulus of new places? "Empathy" is another word that might be applied. His power of empathy was exceptional, and he was able, it seems, to project a possible self in a new set of circumstances. The lands he visited became his books. But of course they are not the travelogues of a tourist. His absorption in nature was as profound as his empathy for human beings and human situations.

That need for change, that very capacity for change, that ceaseless mobility of feelings and even convictions, made Gide vulnerable to attack. His enemies were many and the attacks were often massive, leveled at his Protean character and often couched in such terms as "duplicity" and "hypocrisy." But the real attack, not always explicitly stated, as in the writings of Henri Massis and François Mauriac, was on his homosexuality. From an early age Gide manifested a great zest for experience which often took the form of a remarkable receptiveness to knowledge. The many voyages corresponded to that constant impulse in his nature toward new experience. It was not experience in itself, not a mere curiosity about picturesqueness or exoticism, but experience for nourishment of his spirit and thus nourishment for his work.

This wandering pattern of life is often the homosexual's, especially in the modern world where a permanent relationship is not possible, not feasible, and perhaps not even desired. Mobility, whether it be on a vast scale such as Gide's, from country to country, or on a small scale, from bar to bar, for a man confined to one city, has a definite relationship to sexual habits where no enduring attachment is imaginable.

His need for mobility is again reflected in his attitude to his finished work. Completing a book liberated Gide for the next book. This release, to which he often referred, is also the sexual pattern of a man who, either through desire or through a necessity imposed by social customs, moves from one adventure to the next. In speaking of one of his earliest works, *La tentative amoureuse* (which he once called *Tentation amoureuse*), completed in 1893, Gide recorded in his *Journal* that a book, when finished and separated from him, changed him and altered his existence: "*Il nous change, il modifie la marche de notre vie.*" This is a moving notation on the equilibrium Gide always maintained between the art of living and the art of writing. Temperamentally his nature was often divided between an impulse of revolt and a familiar

impulse of submission. And the books too followed these alternating movements of revolt and acceptance, of a moral dilemma
which is resolved in the literary form he gave it.

Because of the sharpness of these conflicts, and the way Gide
exposed them, which often resembled boldness, his readers and
critics have raised a central question it is difficult to answer: were
these apparent contradictions in his temperament exposed and
analyzed so that he might know himself better, or so that he
might show himself and indulge in a form of exhibitionism?
This kind of accusation is inevitable. It is not difficult to feel that
on many of his pages Gide is making himself visible in order to
make himself vulnerable. No other French author has so persistently concentrated all of his writings on himself. In all his
genres: *récit, roman, sotie, théâtre, autobiographie, journal, essai,* and
throughout a very long work, Gide never abandoned his own
dramas, his own revolts, his own justifications.

The sexuality of a man, whether it is directed toward a girl or
a boy, toward a woman or a man, is primarily fantasy. And it is
inevitably a private fantasy. But if the one fantasizing is a writer
possessing the skill of a Gide, a Proust, a Genet, or of a Balzac, a
Stendhal, a Flaubert, the fantasy, as it appears in the work, is
universalized and recognizable to readers of all faiths. When a
critic writes of Gide, if he is a critic in the highest sense of the
calling, he installs us, his readers, within Gide's fantasies. He
does not clarify Gide for us, he clarifies the fantasies. Thus
Gide's neuroticism, expressed in his obsessions and fantasies and
personal myths, is doubled when a good critic writes of him,
because that critic's own neuroticism and obsessions are added to
Gide's. This is the triumph of the new semiotic criticism being
written today where the criticism is often more interesting, from
the viewpoint of fantasy, than the literary work under inspec-
tion.

A very young child plays with simple objects, and continues to
play with them day after day because he imagines them to be
things they are not. His mind transforms them into wondrous
mysterious objects. For an adult, fantasies have replaced the
objects of his childhood, and he lives with these fantasies, with
their enduring reality. The writer, of all men, is closest to the

child, because the words he puts together have replaced the playthings of a child, and they translate his fantasies. The literary work is thus totally mythical.

The more active literary members of the gay liberation movement today persistently use André Gide as an example, and Gide's writings as a guide, without always knowing or remembering that the *Essais* of Montaigne form the most convincing work that mankind has on the subject of tolerance, on the ways to reach and comprehend and practice tolerance. Tolerance Gide often called *disponibilité,* and in using Gide, almost too recklessly, the gay liberationists have narrowed his work and his message. Gide the man narrating and confessing a deeply personal struggle, was at the same time the artist achieving a form of art born out of constraint, out of labor, out of a self-investigation that did not leave him free.

During the years since his death, Gide has become more firmly than ever the artist whose books, while providing a series of self-portraits, offer to new readers today, to young people in colleges and universities, a portrait of the artist. It is the artist without personal traits, whose life appears discontinuous, unstable by virtue of the irregularity and the unpredictability of inspiration. Rather than finding a self-portrait of the author in Gide's books, the new generation of readers is finding in them the problems of the creative artist of every age who is eternally seeking to reintegrate himself in society and to find for himself a moral justification.

The readers of his day—I am thinking of the younger readers who were influenced by him, Julien Green and Albert Camus, for example—found in his books a subtlety that delighted and even entranced them. Young readers today—I have noticed this often in my own students—do not find Gide a subtle writer, and they are not influenced in the same way the earlier generation was. Today young readers find in him, I would say, lucidity. This shift from subtlety to lucidity now seems to me less mysterious than it once did. It is somewhat thanks to Gide's subtlety that the moral problems he discussed are clearer, that certain of his assumptions, especially his sexual assumptions, are more acceptable to today's world. I have in mind his lesson, everywhere expressed in his books, on man's need to become more and more involved with his own conscience, on the hypocrisy of social patterns, on the dishonesty that comes from compromise.

Gide's sense of moral honesty might best be defined, obliquely perhaps, by pointing out the special relationship he felt and tried to establish with his public. Like most writers, Gide wrote in order to be read, but he had in mind that very special segment of the reading public, the young. While he knew they would not necessarily follow him or agree with him, he felt instinctively (because of his earliest desires and ambitions, both sexual and literary) that the young readers he wanted to reach would be at least stimulated, and possibly changed, by him. His real sexual conquests were his countless youthful readers who derived from his pages an excitement of their senses and an assurance that their fantasies were not absurd or perverted or unfamiliar. If at one time, Gide was admired by the young for his ability to cultivate ambiguities, today he is admired by readers of the same age-group for his clear-mindedness about problems that still concern the young, a clear-mindedness that has no trace of misanthropy, or stark pessimism, or class prejudice, or self-adulation. The letters Gide most enjoyed receiving were not those from Francis Jammes or André Suarès or Jean Schlumberger. They were those typified by the warm frank letter from an unknown youth who had gained from *Les nourritures terrestres* a new confidence and a new acceptance of himself.

Early admirers of Gide wanted to find everything in him: a literary artist and an original thinker. Readers today have more perspective on his work, and young readers have greater wisdom about human nature and sexual motivations. This wisdom is somewhat owing to André Gide. I chose the title for this paper because it seems to represent what the young now find in Gide: not the originality of a thinker like Sartre, not the artist with a prodigious inventive capacity like Proust, but a writer who has left a self-portrait more sincere and more meticulously studied than any other self-portrait in literature.

If I were asked to define André Gide in just one sentence (this embarrassing situation sometimes arises in the classroom), asked to reduce all my meandering thoughts to one principal thought, I would say: Gide is the writer who felt and illustrated the attraction of beginnings. This trait explains for me both the *Journal* and *Les faux-monnayeurs*. This particular attraction explains in the novel the perpetual transitions from episode to episode, from character to character, from Paris to Switzerland, and back again to Paris. Traditionally in the composition of novels, the use of letters and diaries is an artificial device, but in Gide's novel it is the basis for key adventures. It is the means for revealing the homosexuality of Edouard, the protagonist-novelist who in the novel is writing a novel, and who observes around him the many characters who are "counterfeit" because they perpetuate lies about themselves. Edouard, because he is a bachelor, mysterious, mobile, seemingly detached from all those who have responsibilities and commitments, appears to most of the characters he encounters at the beginning of the book rather forbidding, enigmatic, even awe-inspiring. But gradually he begins exerting a great power of attraction. He is both understanding and kind. Most of the characters end by using him as a confident and adviser.

Both Gide the writer and Edouard his protagonist are Socratic. They are teachers at all times, and lovers briefly, episodically, jealously, in accordance with a pattern that is discernible in every age of humanistic culture. The leading examples are artists who were both pedagogues and lovers, but who always subordinated their transitory loves to their work: Socrates, Plato, Shakespeare, Michelangelo, Whitman, Gide, Proust. . . .

This Socratic aspect of Gide's art is still audible today in the dialogue he continues to carry on with his reader. In the same way that he enjoyed the beginning of an episode or a drama, the first impulse of a sentiment, the first encounter with an unknown figure, so may the reading of Gide today instigate in the reader a fresh start in some awareness of himself, a desire to begin again with a new perspective on some familiar ambition. Jean Delay, in his carefully documented psychoanalysis of *La jeunesse d'André Gide,* draws the conclusion that Gide because of his complexion and complexes was destined to the genre of the journal. By definition a diary is a rebeginning each day or each week, of thought, sentiment, or activity. The act of writing is comparable to the daily exercise of an athlete in training.

Writing is also the act of loving after literally making love.

Without ever losing the pederastic fixation of his sexuality, Gide wrote in the way he did, thanks to an energy liberated by a release from possessions, prejudices, and personal ties. The most astringent exercise Gide ever wrote is *L'immoraliste,* a beautifully constructed *récit* that accurately illustrates the Gidian *dénuement,* perhaps best translated as "traveling light."

Much of the *Journal* may be explained by the phrase I am using: the attraction of beginnings. There Gide looks at himself in order to be seen by others. But he keeps reminding us of the horror he feels at seeing any one portrait of himself, of fixing his features in a permanent picture. This diversity of portraits seems to have derived from the need to be understood, but not to be followed as a master is followed. Gide wanted to be accompanied for a while, but it was a simple companionship he hoped for and not a permanent relationship. A disciple would be, in Gidian terms, a prisoner. So would a husband or a wife.

Ever since eternity took hold of Gide, he has grown into himself, with the full array of enigmas, almost like a character in a play, like Alceste who has turned against humanity and yet who loves a flirtatious woman, or like Hamlet who claims to his mother he has "that within which passeth show." In a word, Gide has grown into the kind of character we usually watch on a stage, who has many enigmas that irritate us and delight us. He confirms today the paradox once stated by Valéry: those who die with a sense of mystery about them are surer of survival than the rest: *les obscurs survivent mieux.*

J. E. Rivers

The Myth and Science
of Homosexuality
in *A la recherche du temps perdu*

Of the many different traits Proust assigns to homosexuals in *A la recherche du temps perdu,* one of the most broadly suggestive is the concept of the homosexual as "homme-femme," or "man-woman." And yet this idea has received very little attention in Proustian criticism. Critics either tend to accept it automatically as universally valid truth; or they tend to reject it as an absurdity easily disproved by the most cursory consideration of historical, cultural, and anthropological research on homosexuality.[1] Both reactions treat Proust, wrongly, as if he were primarily a theoretician of sex and only secondarily a creative artist. But Proust's concept of the man-woman is much more than an attempted theoretical explanation of homosexuality. It is also an artistic strategy which helps articulate and unify three important dimensions of the novel—the mythological, the scientific, and the aesthetic.

1. For the former case see Dr. Robert Soupault, *Marcel Proust du côté de la médecine* (Paris: Plon, 1967), p. 195 and *passim;* for the latter see J. Z. Eglinton, *Greek Love* (New York: Oliver Layton Press, 1964), p. 407 and *passim,* and André Gide, *Corydon* (Paris: Gallimard, 1948), p. 9, n. 1 and *passim.*

In *Sodome et Gomorrhe I* (II, 601–32),[2] where Proust first explicitly introduces the theme of homosexuality, he also undertakes an elaborate mythopoeia of the homosexual personality. Among other things, he rewrites the biblical story of Sodom to create his own etiological myth of homosexuality. In Proust's version of the story, some of the Sodomites were able to escape the judgment of heaven and people the earth with their descendants—and these descendants are the present-day homosexuals. Further, the epigraph that stands at the beginning of *Sodome et Gomorrhe* presents the men-women and the descendants of the ancient Sodomites as two interrelated aspects of the same mythography: "Introducing the men-women, descendants of those of the inhabitants of Sodom who were spared by the fire from heaven." In this way Proust establishes the mythic tone. And throughout *Sodome I* he maintains that tone with appropriate mythological allusions. The female spirit coming to life in a homosexual is like the slow vivification of Pygmalion's statue. The lonely homosexual, waiting on the beach for an unknown lover, is "a strange Andromeda whom no Argonaut will come to free." And Jupien and Charlus recognize each other as men of similar tastes because "the gods are immediately perceptible to one another, as quickly like to like, and so too had M. de Charlus been to Jupien."

But, side by side with this carefully planned myth-making, we find the recurrent suggestion that what we are reading is not myth but science—an attempt to observe the homosexual in an objective, almost clinical way, and formulate the general laws of his personality and conduct. The narrator watches Charlus and Jupien in the same way that a naturalist would study plant life. And, in fact, he is waiting to see whether a bee will come to pollenate the rare orchid of the Duchesse de Guermantes when

2. References are to *A la recherche du temps perdu,* ed. Pierre Clarac and André Ferré, 3 vols. (Paris: Pléiade, 1954). Quotations in English are from *Remembrance of Things Past,* tr. C. K. Scott Moncrieff, 2 vols. (New York: Random House, 1934), with quotations from the last volume from *The Past Recaptured,* tr. Andreas Mayor (New York: Vintage, 1971). My occasional alterations of the standard translations are enclosed in brackets. Original translations from the French are marked with my initials (JER).

the drama of homosexuality begins to unfold before him. Having just reflected that "the laws of the vegetable kingdom are themselves governed by other laws, increasingly exalted," he realizes that Charlus and Jupien are conducting themselves according to a similar set of laws and rituals. The devices Jupien uses to signal to and attract the Baron are, the narrator points out, not unlike the special adaptations which help orchids attract bees. And then, in a famous *morceau de bravoure,* Proust metaphorically transforms Jupien into the beckoning, coquettish flower and Charlus—noticing, approaching, happily whistling—into the curious and questing bee. The narrator, observing and interpreting all this, is like a botanist of human nature. "Failing the geologist's field of contemplation," he says, "I had at least that of the botanist." And he concludes that Jupien represents a subvariety of homosexual which "every collector of a human herbary, every moral botantist can observe in spite of their rarity."

So the language of myth and the language of science run parallel in *Sodome I.* But how, precisely, do myth and science conjoin in the image of the man-woman? They do so partly because this concept is of ambiguous provenance, partaking at once of the mythic and the scientific traditions. A very likely mythological source for the image is Plato's *Symposium,* a dialogue Proust knew well.[3] In the *Symposium* Aristophanes expounds a half-comic, half-serious myth to account for the origin of homosexual, heterosexual, and lesbian love. The first humanity, according to Aristophanes, was composed of three sexes. Each gender was circular in form and endowed with two faces, four hands, four legs, four ears, and two sets of sexual organs, back to back. Some of these twofold beings were male-male, some female-female, and some male-female. They were creatures of prodigious strength and great pride, who challenged the sovereignty of the gods, causing Zeus to weaken them by splitting them in half. This, says Aristophanes, explains the three varieties of love. Men formed from a cutting of the male-male gender seek out a male complement in an attempt to regain

3. For Proust's knowledge of the *Symposium* see George Painter, *Proust: The Early Years* (Boston: Little, Brown, 1959), pp. 140–41.

their original state; women formed from a cutting of the female-female gender seek out female partners; and men and women who are cuttings from the original androgyne are heterosexuals.

One of the points of Aristophanes' myth is playfully to confuse the whole concept of gender and sexual identity. Aristophanes is careful to point out, for instance, that before the three dual genders were split down the middle there was no sexual intercourse and propagation as we know it. Instead, primal humanity "[begot] and brought forth not with each other but with the ground." The point, of course, is that when gender is interwoven, duplicated, and reduplicated to such a degree, the concept of partial and separate sexual roles simply does not exist. The sexual division of the primal beings is really Aristophanes' version of the Fall of Man. Gender and sexual separation are punishments, inflictions that make humanity imperfect, incomplete, and less happy than it once was and would like again to be. This is why love of all sorts is such a potent force. It arises, says Aristophanes, from man's constant desire for "bringing together the parts of the original body" in order to "heal the natural structure of man."

We shall see in a moment that the treatment of the man-woman in *A la recherche*—and, indeed, the treatment of sexuality in general—follows in several ways the pattern and spirit of Aristophanes' myth. But first we should notice that the concept of the man-woman, in addition to its mythic resonance, is also the basis of a particular scientific attitude toward homosexuals to which Proust alludes in the novel. It was a commonplace of nineteenth- and early twentieth-century sexology to regard homosexuals as spiritual hermaphrodites. The idea seems to have originated in the work of the German jurist, Latinist, and pioneering sexologist Karl Heinrich Ulrichs, now little known, but one of the most significant influences on the great outpouring of sexological research which characterized the last decades of the nineteenth century. Ulrichs's most important work was *Memnon* (1868), in which he defined the male homosexual character in the Latin formula "anima muliebris virili corpore inclusa" ("the soul of a woman enclosed in the body of a man"), and the converse for female homosexuals—"anima virilis muliebri corpore inclusa."[4] Now the imagery with which Proust describes the blending of the masculine and feminine in the homosexual temperament makes it evident that he was familiar with Ulrichs's ideas, whether directly, by reading the texts themselves, or indirectly, through their survival in Magnus Hirschfeld, Krafft-Ebing, Havelock Ellis, and practically every other important sexologist who came after Ulrichs. The interior psychology of Mlle Vinteuil, a conflict between "a shy and suppliant maiden" and an "old campaigner, battered but triumphant" (I, 161), recalls Ulrichs's theory. And Morel is said to have a "girlish air enshrined in his masculine beauty" (II, 1007). In other sections of the novel the echo of Ulrichs's formula is direct and explicit. The narrator speaks of "the woman whom a mistake on the part of Nature had enshrined in the body of M. de Charlus" (II, 908). He attributes the effeminacy of homosexuals to the fact that "for long years a certain number of angelic women have been included by mistake in the masculine sex" (II, 908, 967). And he states that in practically every aging homosexual one can discern "beneath all the layers of paint and powder, some fragments of a beautiful woman preserved in eternal youth" (III, 991).

This background allows us, I think, to understand something of why Proust chose to advocate the man-woman theory in his novel. He wanted, as the imagery of *Sodome I* plainly shows, to be mythically suggestive and scientifically precise at the same time. And the man-woman theory (also called the "*Zwischenstufen,*" the "third sex," or the "intermediate sex" theory) was in Proust's time the most widely accepted theory of homosexuality. It was, of course, not the only theory. Even in Proust's day there were those who held that homosexuality is a natural and universal component of human sexuality. There was, in fact, an early homosexual rights movement under way in Germany which, in 1907, underwent a split between those who advocated the popular man-woman view and those who had decided that this view

4. Karl Heinrich Ulrichs, *Memnon: Die Geschlechtsnatur des mannliebenden Urnings* [*Memnon: Sexual Nature of the Man-Loving Urning*], Part II (Schleiz: C. Hübsch'sche, 1868), p. vii and *passim*.

had little to do with the facts. Benedict Friedländer led the splinter group; and John Lauritsen and David Thorstad describe Friedländer's position as follows:

> The *Zwischenstufen* theory was attacked by Friedländer as "degrading and beggarly . . . pleading for sympathy." He ridiculed the notion of "a poor womanly soul languishing away in a man's body, and of the 'third sex.'" Friedländer insisted upon a historical approach which also took into account anthropological evidence; he wrote, "A glance at the cultures of countries before and outside of Christianity suffices to show the complete untenability of the [*Zwischenstufen*] theory. Especially in ancient Greece, most of the military leaders, artists, and thinkers would have had to be 'psychic hermaphrodites.'"[5]

Now Proust's correspondence shows that he was aware that there was more than one way of understanding homosexuality. But it also shows that he had decided, by the time he wrote *Sodome et Gomorrhe,* that the most widely accepted theory—that of the psychologically disordered man-woman, men who should have been women, and women who should have been men—was also the true one. And part of his mission as an artist, he thought, was to communicate the truth in his art, no matter how unpleasant it might seem or whom it might offend. In a letter to André Gide, Proust said of *Sodome et Gomorrhe:* "Unfortunately, the attempt at objectivity I made there, and everywhere, will render this book particularly hateful. In the third volume, in fact, where Monsieur de Charlus . . . plays an important role, the enemies of homosexuality will be revolted by the scenes I shall depict. And the others will not be any more pleased at seeing their ideal of virility presented as the consequence of a feminine temperament."[6] And he wrote to Louis de Robert of his obligation in *Sodome et Gomorrhe* to "dissect" homosexuality and report the results "with the good faith of a chemist."[7]

5. John Lauritsen and David Thorstad, *The Early Homosexual Rights Movement, 1864–1935* (New York: Times Change Press, 1974), p. 50.
6. Marcel Proust, *Lettres à André Gide* (Neuchâtel and Paris: Ides et Calendes, 1949), p. 40. (JER)
7. Louis de Robert, *Comment débuta Marcel Proust* (Paris: Gallimard, 1969), pp. 64, 66. (JER)

Myth and science, science and myth, revolve around each other in Proust's conception as if they, too, were two halves of some primal whole. But how do they bear upon and interrelate within the aesthetic dimension of the novel? What, in other words, does the man-woman have to do with the central theme of time and the overarching scheme of the narrator's development as an artist?

Most basically, the homosexual as described in *A la recherche* serves as a prototype and model for the narrator's developing creative personality. For in order to create, the narrator has to become in a certain sense androgynous, to become like those men-women who make their appearance at the midpoint of his novel and stand in every sense at its symbolic center. Since the publication of Carolyn Heilbrun's *Toward a Recognition of Androgyny* (1973), we have, of course, been hearing a great deal about "androgynous literature" and the "androgynous vision." Indeed, now that these labels have become fashionable, we often find them attached to works which offer very little explicit justification for them—books as unlikely and diverse as *The Odyssey* and *The Brothers Karamazov*.

But in all the talk about androgyny Proust—one of the most clearly and unmistakably androgynous of all writers—has been strangely ignored. Heilbrun says he is "marvelously androgynous," but this is, quite literally, all she says about him.[8] To be sure, Gilles Deleuze and Lisa Appignanesi have made some perceptive comments about the androgynous implications of *A la recherche*.[9] But there remains a great deal to be said, especially with regard to the aesthetic and cultural reverberations of Proust's portrait of the man-woman. For the idea of androgyny, as I shall try to show, underlies some of the most fundamentally important aspects of Proust's understanding of life and art.

As was suggested above, the narrator, in order to write his book, has to recapture and exploit the feminine side of his per-

8. Carolyn Heilbrun, *Toward a Recognition of Androgyny* (1973; rpt. New York: Harper Colophon, 1974), p. 87.

9. Gilles Deleuze, *Marcel Proust et les signes* (Paris: Presses Universitaires de France, 1971), pp. 144ff.; Lisa Appignanesi, *Femininity and the Creative Imagination: A Study of Henry James, Robert Musil, and Marcel Proust* (New York: Barnes and Noble, 1973), pp. 205ff.

sonality. I say recapture, because the separation of his personality into masculine and feminine parts is one of the first examples of the fragmentation of the self we witness in the novel. On the fourth and fifth pages of the Pléiade edition, in the narrator's famous description of his half-waking, half-sleeping state, we read:

> Sometimes, too, just as Eve was created from a rib of Adam, so a woman would come into existence while I was sleeping, conceived from some strain in the position of my limbs. Formed by the appetite that I was on the point of gratifying, she it was, I imagined, who offered me that gratification. My body, conscious that its own warmth was permeating hers, would strive to become one with her, and I would awake. The rest of humanity seemed very remote in comparison with this woman whose company I had left but a moment ago; my cheek was still warm with her kiss, my body bent beneath the weight of hers. If, as would sometimes happen, she had the appearance of some woman whom I had known in waking hours, I would abandon myself altogether to the sole quest of her. . . . And then, gradually, the memory of her would dissolve and vanish, until I had forgotten the maiden of my dream.

In a certain sense this is a précis of all the love affairs to follow, in which the narrator thinks he is loving outside himself but is mainly loving projections of his own imagination and sensibility. In other words, throughout most of the novel he looks outside and beyond himself for the feminine complement to his personality, when actually it has been within all along.

His love for Albertine is a desperate and disappointing attempt to reconstruct in life a version of the primal mythic unity which obtained before Adam and Eve were separated, before man and woman became separate beings and separate concepts. Now there is a rabbinical tradition with which Proust may have been familiar which holds that Adam was in fact a hermaphroditic creature, half man and half woman, and that God created woman by simply dividing his original bisexual creation. It was even thought by one ancient writer that Plato had read the creation account in Genesis and thereby got his idea for the myth of the primal, twofold beings he assigns to Aristophanes in the

Symposium.[10] Though there is no explicit reference to a hermaphroditic Adam in *A la recherche,* something like this idea is certainly implied in Proust's fascination with the symbol of Adam and Eve as the masculine and feminine modalities of a single personality. In the narrative of the Albertine affair, Proust reverts three times to the Adam-Eve image of the opening of "Combray," underscoring the narrator's perpetual desire to recreate a situation like that which existed before the first division of the sexes, a situation in which the feminine constantly infuses the masculine, and the masculine the feminine. At first the allusion is in the comic mode. Proust prepares for the visit of Albertine in *Le côté de Guermantes* by having the narrator describe his frame of mind on the chilly day as that of "a shivering Adam in quest of a sedentary Eve" (II, 346). But later on in this section the language takes on a tone of high seriousness. The narrator says that his desire for Albertine "made me dream . . . of mingling with my flesh a substance different and warm, and of attaching at some point to my outstretched body a body divergent, as the body of Eve barely holds by the feet to the side of Adam, to whose body hers is almost perpendicular, in those romanesque bas-reliefs on the church at Balbec" (II, 354). Later the rhetoric becomes even more rhapsodic, as the act of sex with Albertine is explicitly presented as an attempt to undo the work of the Creator by rejoining the sexes: "O mighty attitudes of Man and Woman, in which there seeks to be reunited, in the innocence of the world's first age and with the humility of clay, what creation has cloven apart" (III, 79).

This semi-blasphemous attempt to compete with God as creator, even to undo and remake God's creation, is, for Proust, one of the traits of the successful artist. Elstir's studio strikes the narrator as "the laboratory of a sort of new creation of the world"; and he says of Elstir's use of visual metaphor that "if God the Father had created things by naming them, it was by taking away their names or giving them other names that Elstir created them anew" (I, 834–35). In this regard it is surely no

---

10. Marie Delcourt, *Hermaphrodite: Myths and Rites of the Bisexual Figure in Antiquity,* tr. Jennifer Nicholson (London: Studio Books, 1961), pp. 72–74.

accident, as Justin O'Brien has pointed out,[11] that when the narrator discovers the secret of metaphor in Elstir's studio, he discovers at the same time a portrait of ambiguous sex, *Miss Sacripant,* depicting a young woman dressed in such a way as to appear simultaneously male and female. It is a portrait, the narrator says, in which Elstir has raised the intermingling of sexes in the dress and demeanor of the model to the level of an aesthetic principle, "[fastening] upon those ambiguous points as on an aesthetic element which deserved to be brought into prominence, and which he had done everything in his power to emphasize" (I, 849).

The suggestion of androgyny in *Miss Sacripant* touches something fundamental to the way people have felt about art and inspiration throughout the ages. In the ancient world, cross-dressing was a common feature of religious rites and rituals. Through it, the powers peculiar to each sex were symbolically combined to make for a fuller, a total humanity. Marie Delcourt comments that "transvestism . . . had power to promote health, youth, strength, longevity, perhaps even to confer a kind of immortality."[12] Furthermore, the concept of androgyny was closely associated in classical times with the origins of art. The Dionysian revels from which tragedy and comedy developed featured an exchange of dress between the sexes; and Dionysus himself, the god of the theater, was sometimes represented as an androgynous deity.[13] In Aristophanes' *Frogs,* Dionysus descends into Hades in search of a *gonimon poieten,* a "fecund poet," one who incarnates the spirit of true artistic creativity. Significantly, the costume Aristophanes thinks appropriate to such a quest is a mixture of masculine and feminine garb: he has Dionysus appear wearing the lion-skin of Heracles over a saffron gown.[14]

In *A la recherche* the relation of the primitive dream of an-

11. Justin O'Brien, "Albertine the Ambiguous: Notes on Proust's Transposition of Sexes," *PMLA,* 64 (1949), 950.

12. Delcourt, p. 22.

13. Ibid., p. 12; Walter F. Otto, *Dionysus: Myth and Cult,* tr. Robert B. Palmer (Bloomington: Indiana University Press, 1965), p. 176.

14. Aristophanes, *Frogs,* 45ff.; 96ff. And see Cedric Whitman, *Aristophanes and the Comic Hero* (Cambridge, Mass.: Harvard University Press, 1964), p. 236.

drogyny to the creative power of the artist and the truthful illusions embodied in art is reflected not only in *Miss Sacripant*: it also materializes in the art of the heavily made-up, effeminate dancer the narrator notices rehearsing backstage at Rachel's theater: "a young man in a black velvet cap and hortensia-coloured skirt, his cheeks chalked in red like a page from a Watteau album, who with his smiling lips, his eyes raised to the ceiling, as he sprang lightly into the air, seemed . . . entirely of another species than the rational folk in everyday clothes, in the midst of whom he was pursuing like a madman the course of his ecstatic dream." The movements of the dancer, the total freedom of his body, are examples of pure theater, recalling at once the origins and the highest achievements of the art. Simultaneously Apollonian and Dionysian, they are ecstasy and madness carefully structured and controlled. They seem both to break free of the laws of nature and to fuse the natural and artificial in "winged capricious painted oscillations." Rachel comments: "Isn't he too wonderful with his hands. A woman like me couldn't do the things he's doing now" (II, 177–79).

But perhaps the most significant thing about the performance of the effeminate dancer and its relation to Proust's men-women is that it represents a recapturing of lost time, evoking the idea of something "anterior to the habits of . . . civilisation" (II, 177). Here and throughout *A la recherche* androgyny functions as a means of reversing, or escaping from, the forward thrust of chronological time. Dreams, for Proust, are a means of access to our atavistic past, a way of contacting the phylogenetic history of the race. And dreams, appropriately, are inhabited by a "race [that] . . . is, like that of our first human ancestors, androgynous. A man . . . appears a moment later in the form of a woman" (II, 981). We see an example of this primal, oneiric androgyny when, in Swann's famous dream toward the end of *Un amour de Swann*, Mme Verdurin suddenly sprouts a mustache. Similarly, speaking of homosexuals who would trace their ancestry to the ancient orient or to classical Greece, the narrator states that "inverts . . . might be traced back farther still, to those experimental epochs in which there existed neither dioecious plants nor monosexual animals, to that initial hermaphroditism of which certain rudiments of male organs in the anatomy of the woman and of female organs in that of the man seem still to preserve the trace" (II, 629).

Here Proust is drawing once again on the science of his day, on the Darwinian concept that the ancestors of the vertebrates were hermaphroditic and on the several attempts which were made to explain homosexuality with reference to this idea. Proust's immediate source may be the summary of this type of work in Krafft-Ebing, who writes as follows:

> Later researches... proceeding on embryological (onto- and phylogenetic) and anthropological lines seem to promise good results.
>
> Emanating from *Frank Lydston* ("Philadelphia Med. and Surg. Recorder," September, 1888) and *Kiernan* ("Medical Standard," November, 1888), they are based (1) on the fact that bisexual organization is still found in the lower animal kingdom, and (2) on the supposition that monosexuality gradually developed from bisexuality. *Kiernan* assumes in trying to subordinate sexual inversion to the category of hermaphroditism that in individuals thus affected retrogression into the earlier hermaphroditic forms of the animal kingdom may take place at least functionally. These are his own words: "The original bisexuality of the ancestors of the race, shown in the rudimentary female organs of the male, could not fail to occasion functional, if not organic reversions, when mental or physical manifestations were interfered with by disease or congenital defect."[15]

So, in order to recapture lost time in art, in order to make his work a history of the race as well as a history of an individual life, the narrator must rediscover and exploit in his book something of, on the mythic level, the androgyny of primal humanity, and, on the scientific level, the hermaphroditism of the first plants and animals. And then he must show how the two relate. This he does in *Sodome I,* in the famous comparisons of the homosexual courtship of Charlus and Jupien, those two androgynous inhabitants of the mythical city of Sodom, to the processes of mating and fertilization which occur in nature. Jupien has been placed

15. Richard von Krafft-Ebing, *Psychopathia Sexualis,* tr. Franklin S. Klaf (New York: Bell, 1965), p. 226. See also Havelock Ellis, *Sexual Inversion* (1896), in *Studies in the Psychology of Sex,* 2 vols. (New York: Random House, 1936), I, 311ff.

on earth for the specific purpose of serving the needs of older homosexuals, just as certain hermaphroditic flowers exist for the sole purpose of fertilizing other hermaphroditic flowers which otherwise would be doomed to sterility, "remaining as indifferent to [the advances] of other young men as the hermaphrodite flowers of the short-styled *primula veris* so long as they are fertilised only by other *primulae veris* of short style also, whereas they welcome with joy the pollen of the *primula veris* with the long styles."

Technically, of course, the love of the two homosexuals, unlike the mating of the flowers, *is* sterile. But according to the narrator a special kind of fertilization can occur in homosexual love, a spiritual fecundity comparable, though he does not directly draw the comparison, to the impetus toward the quest for ideal beauty which homosexuality inspires in Plato's *Symposium:* "here the word fertilise must be understood in a moral sense, since in the physical sense the union of male with male is and must be sterile, but it is no small matter that a person may encounter the sole pleasure which he is capable of enjoying, and that every 'creature here below' can impart to some other 'his music, or his fragrance or his flame.'" One homosexual supplies what the other lacks, and together they form a unit more complete and productive than either represents separately. Later in the novel, for instance, the talents of Charlus as an accompanist are viewed as the perfect complement to the musical genius of Morel (II, 953). And of Saint-Loup and Morel the narrator says: "It is possible that Morel, being excessively dark, was necessary to Saint-Loup in the way that shadow is necessary to the sunbeam" (III, 705). One thinks immediately of the partial beings of Aristophanes' myth, of the quest of each half for the other and thus for the primal union that will "heal the natural structure of man."

In Proust's vision, of course, there is the additional complication that in homosexual love each of the two men who come together to form the union is himself androgynous. This means that the Proustian combination of male with male simultaneously involves a combination of male (Charlus—bee—seed) with female (Jupien—flower—egg). It also involves a combination of female with female, since both homosexuals, as the narrator points out, have female souls, carrying within themselves an embryo of the feminine sex which they cannot fertilize themselves but which can be fertilized by another androgynous man. At this point the concept of separate and polarized genders becomes so fluid and ambiguous as practically to vanish altogether. We are surrounded once again by the spirit of Aristophanes' myth, which depicts primal humanity, humanity in its strongest and most perfect state, as a kind of triply-reflecting mirror in which we see, simultaneously, man-man, woman-woman, and androgyne.

But Proust's statements on the cross-fertilization of hermaphrodites are not simply a product of the mythic imagination. They are, as we have already seen, also based on processes which exist in nature and can be scientifically described. The union of Charlus and Jupien reproduces a situation "such as we find in so many hermaphrodite flowers, and even in certain hermaphrodite animals, such as the snail, which cannot be fertilised by themselves, but can by other hermaphrodites" (II, 629). Indeed, the process by which Jupien finds himself attracted only to older homosexuals is "a phenomenon of correspondence and harmony similar to those that precede the fertilisation of heterostyle trimorphous flowers like the *lythrum* [*salicaria*]" (II, 628). Proust alludes here, as in the reference to the pollenation of the *primula veris* quoted earlier, to Darwin's treatise on *The Different Forms of Flowers on Plants of the Same Species*. Describing in that work the manner in which the three hermaphroditic forms of the *lythrum salicaria* pollenate each other, Darwin expresses a similar sense of wonder at the complexity and perfection of a "marriage-arrangement" involving "a triple union between three hermaphrodites." The scheme, Darwin concludes, "is perfect; there is no waste of pollen and no false co-adaptation."[16]

In keeping with the Darwinian allusion, this section of *Sodome I* is rife with words such as "miracle," "marvellous," "beauty," "correspondence," "harmony," words evocative of the intricate

16. Charles Darwin, *The Different Forms of Flowers on Plants of the Same Species* (New York: D. Appleton, 1896; rpt. New York: AMS Press, 1972), p. 138. Rina Viers has previously pointed out Proust's debt to this work in "Evolution et sexualité des plantes dans *Sodome et Gomorrhe*," *Europe*, nos. 502–503 (1971), pp. 105ff.

symmetry Darwin and other nineteenth-century naturalists were continually pointing out in the fertilization patterns and mating rituals of nature, words through which the narrator, in turn, invites us to see a unique formal beauty in the laws of yet another kind of "marriage-arrangement." Proust intends our reaction to *Sodome I* to follow the same course as the narrator's changing feelings about the jellyfish. When he saw the animal at Balbec, the narrator says, he was instinctively repelled by it; but if he looked at it, as did Michelet, "from the standpoint of natural history, and aesthetic" it became a thing of wonder—"an exquisite wheel of azure flame" (II, 626). Similarly, the narrator says of the scene of homosexual courtship between Charlus and Jupien that "this scene was not, however, positively comic, it was stamped with a strangeness, or if you like a naturalness, the beauty of which steadily increased" (II, 605). *Etrange beauté*, strange beauty—Proust is here fulfilling one of the most basic duties of the artist, to reveal beauty where little has been thought to exist, and in places where we have been previously ill inclined to look for it.

But Proust insists on preserving the strangeness as well as the beauty. His comparison of homosexual love to the larger processes of nature is not aimed, as some have thought, at showing that, contrary to the opinion of conventional morality, homosexuality is natural and good rather than unnatural and evil. This Gidean argument is foreign to Proust's whole tenor of thinking. What interests Proust about homosexuality is the paradox by which, in homosexual love, that which is natural and that which is against nature constantly reflect each other, the dialectic of *physis* and *antiphysis*.[17] In Proust's realization the homosexual is the nexus, at once repugnant and fascinating, hideous and beautiful, grotesque and harmoniously conceived, of all the unnamed and dimly imagined potentialities of nature. Speaking of the comparisons drawn in *Sodome I* between the courtship of Charlus and Jupien and the courtship rituals of nature, the narrator remarks that "the multiplicity of these analogies is itself all the more natural in that the same man, if we examine him for a few minutes, appears in turn as a man, a

17. Cf. Marcel Muller, "*Sodome I* ou la naturalisation de Charlus," *Poétique*, 8 (1971), 476.

man-bird, [a man-fish, a] man-insect, and so forth" (II, 606). In a similar vein, the narrator later compares the homosexual to a centaur (II, 614).

These passages make it plain that, while Proust's vision is clearly androgynous, it cannot be reduced to androgyny alone. Androgyny for Proust is simply one aspect of the overall coalescence of ontological planes which characterizes his artistic vision. Man-woman, man-bird, man-fish, man-horse, man-insect—the vision is of a piece. It suggests and constantly illustrates man's cosmic potential for recapitulating within his own life the totality of the biological and the mythological history of the race.

This is the sense in which the narrator strives toward androgyny. His futile attempts to contain Albertine in the same way Adam contained Eve are, as we have seen, partly attempts to find and strengthen the feminine element within himself. But they are more: they are also attempts to absorb and understand the world at large, the "infinity of all the points . . . in space and time" symbolized by Albertine and the other *êtres de fuite* in the novel (III, 360). The love affair with Albertine fails. But Albertine as a symbol, as a source of inspiration, as an impetus toward the penetration of the limitless, remains a constant presence in the narrator's final act of creation.

In *Le temps retrouvé* the narrator suggests that in order to carry his project through he will need the combined powers of man, woman, and god. In creating his book, he will have to "accept it like a discipline, build it up like a church, follow it like a medical regime, vanquish it like an obstacle, win it like a friendship, cosset it like a little child, create it like a new world" (III, 1032). He feels himself grown big with "this work which I bore within me. . . . anxiously embraced with the fragile protection of its own pulpy and quivering substance" (III, 1036–1037). And Leo Bersani has pointed out that "there is, in fact, a process suggesting the stages of pregnancy: the joyful conception of the idea at the Guermantes *matinée,* the weakness and dizziness on the staircase sometime later, and a painful delivery."[18] For the artistically pregnant narrator of *Le temps retrouvé,* the most pressing appointment is no longer an appointment with Albertine, or with

18. Leo Bersani, *Marcel Proust: The Fictions of Life and Art* (New York: Oxford University Press, 1965), p. 55.

any of the other women he has pursued. It is "a supremely important appointment with myself" (III, 986). Androgyny and the ontological expansiveness it implies have become a state of mind, an inner resource, a quality of vision.

According to certain mystical traditions, Adam was not only androgynous in the garden of Eden, before the creation of Eve and the Fall; he will regain the androgyny of his original state at the end of time, when all things are restored to their original perfection. This is the doctrine, as Marie Delcourt phrases it, of "androgyny both initial and final"; and it is one of the most important of the several mythic patterns attached to the narrator's development as an artist, moving as it does from the initial splitting of his personality into a symbolic Adam and Eve, through the long and painful quest to find that Eve again, to the recovery of the androgynous feeling and vision in *Le temps retrouvé*. In *Le temps retrouvé* the narrator is like the Adam of the mystical tradition, who regains his androgyny in Paradise at the end of time. But he is simultaneously like those bisexual creator gods who unite with their feminine halves and from that union create the universe at the beginning of time.[19] In the cyclical Proustian myth, the end is the beginning, and the ripening of experience is the inception of creation. So, once the masculine and feminine aspects of the narrator's personality reunite, he is able to begin dividing himself once again, this time to create the world of the novel and people it with characters some of whom are male, some of whom are female, and some of whom are male-female—like those novelists who, as the narrator says in discussing the doubling which occurs in Swann's dream, distribute their own personality among all the personalities they create (I, 379). From the perspective of *Le temps retrouvé* the narrator presides over his work in the same dual role the poet Valerius Soranus assigned to Zeus: *Progenitor genetrixque*.[20] And in this way he is able to realize something of what he calls early in the novel "that possible multiplication of oneself which is happiness" (I, 794).

19. On these myths see Delcourt, pp. 67ff.; 82–83; 101. See also Edward Carpenter, *Intermediate Types among Primitive Folk* (New York: Mitchell Kinnerley, 1914), pp. 71–72.
20. Quoted in Delcourt, p. 71.

René Galand

Cocteau's Sexual Equation

Mathematical metaphors abound in Cocteau's writings. Their
function is obvious: they create the feeling that the universe is
subjected to laws as rigid and uncompromising as a theorem in
geometry. In Cocteau's world nothing is left to chance. Each
event in a human life is the result of operations as predictable
and unavoidable as the computational steps leading to the solution of an algebraic problem. In *La machine infernale,* the god
Anubis offers this explanation: "Look at the folds of this material. Press them together. Now, if you pierce this mass with a pin,
if you remove the pin, if you smooth out the material until every
trace of the creases is gone, do you think that a country bumpkin
could believe that the innumerable holes which occur every now
and then are the result of a single thrust of a pin? . . . Human
time is but folded eternity. For us, it does not exist. From his
birth to his death, the life of Oedipus is laid out under my eyes,
all flattened out, with its succession of episodes." And the Sphinx
will watch Oedipus "running from one trap to the next, like a
brainless rat." For Cocteau as for Pascal, man's only possibility
for greatness is the lucid realization of his predicament. Man is
not the master of his fate. He can at best come to see that the
universe in which he exists is a machine built for his "mathematical annihilation." Poetic revelation comes to Orpheus in the

form of numbers because the poet is, according to Cocteau, the privileged (or accursed) man to whom fate has granted some understanding of "celestial computations."[1] It is therefore no surprise that Cocteau identifies poetry with calculation, that is, with the calculated workings of the fateful forces which determine human behavior. The poet is the individual in whom and to whom these workings are most clearly visible.

For Cocteau, artists are not entirely of this world. They live in a kind of no man's land. In some cases, drugs (opium, for instance) enable them to establish positive contacts with material reality. Like deep-sea divers who must wear heavy boots in order to walk on the bottom of the ocean, artists require artificial means to remain at the level of ordinary men. In other cases, however, drugs carry off these buoyant souls into another dimension. Nitrous oxyde or peyotl, not to mention opium, push them across the frontiers which separate the world of everyday experience from the unknown. So do their dreams. Such dreamers enter a realm which, from our world, can only be characterized as supernatural. Their condition is similar to that of a sleepwalker. They are manipulated by powers which rob them of their will and compel them to do their bidding. Cocteau often mentions "the occult forces which want us to be passive," "the gods which inhabit us," the "unknown forces" of which he is only the vehicle, "the strange force which hides in darkness," the "night" from which he takes his orders, the "darkness" which

1. *La machine infernale* (Paris: Livre de poche, 1964), pp. 13, 106–9; *Orphée* (Paris: Editions de la Parade, 1950), p. 41; *Opéra* (Paris: Stock, 1959), p. 17. Unless otherwise indicated, quotations are taken from the original French texts and the translation is my own. Many of the works referred to in this essay may be found in the following English translations: *The Journals of Jean Cocteau*, ed. and trans. Wallace Fowlie (New York: Criterion, 1956); *Professional Secrets*, ed. Robert Phelps, trans. Richard Howard (New York: Farrar, Straus, and Giroux, 1970); *Cocteau's World*, ed. and trans. Margaret Crosland (New York: Dodd, Mead, 1972); *My Contemporaries*, ed. and trans. Margaret Crosland (Philadelphia: Chilton, 1968); *The Infernal Machine and Other Plays*, trans. Albert Bermel, John Savacool, Dudley Fitts, W. H. Auden, Mary Hoeck, E. E. Cummings (Norfolk, Conn.: New Directions, 1963); *The Hand of a Stranger*, trans. Alec Brown (New York: Horizon, 1959); *The Holy Terrors*, trans. Rosamund Lehmann (New York: New Directions, 1957); and *Two Screenplays*, trans. Carol Martin-Sperry (New York: Orion, 1968).

occupies him, "the starry night of the human body," "the nocturnal self" who commands him.[2] He also takes great pains to differentiate this nocturnal self from Freud's concept of the unconscious: "One must not confuse the night of which I speak with the one which Freud invited his patients to visit. Freud burgled poor apartments. He would carry out some mediocre furniture and a few erotic photographs. He never consecrated the abnormal as transcendence."[3] Freud considered the sexual drive as the inner fatality by which his patients were governed. This, according to Cocteau, was his mistake. He failed to see that sexuality is only the tool of a higher power, which it masks. The Sphinx in *La machine infernale,* like the Princess in the film *Orphée,* appears in the form of a seductive woman to indicate the sexual component in the protagonist's drama. Cocteau clearly indicates, however, that they are only instruments in the hands of higher gods. Freud should not have stopped at the sexual level in his search for the ultimate answer to the human riddle. He believed he could inventory the night of our unconscious, which is unfathomable. Freud is thus indicted by Cocteau for his failure to recognize the metaphysical significance of his findings. He took no notice, for instance, of the similarities which may be observed between human beings and animals or plants. If Freudian psychology cannot account for the spots on the skin of a leopard or the petals of a flower, for the stripes of a bee or a tiger, it cannot claim to plumb the mysteries of human behavior. Wars are waged between animals and germs as well as between men, and accelerated films prove that plants lead lives as murderous and erotic as human beings. The word "vice" is commonly used by society to designate acts which may actually be required by nature. If living organisms sought sexual pleasure only for reproductive purposes, overpopulation would occur in every reign and destroy the balance of nature. Practices which are considered social disorders may therefore be part and parcel of the natural order. This is why sexual instinct is blind: from a purely sexual viewpoint, that is, at the instinctual level, a normal

2. *Journal d'un inconnu* (Paris: Grasset, 1953), pp. 18, 26; *Poésie critique II* (Paris: Gallimard, 1960), pp. 183, 227; *Opium* (Paris: Stock, 1930), p. 23; *Poésie critique I* (Paris: Gallimard, 1959), pp. 9–10.

3. *Journal d'un inconnu,* p. 39.

man will find sexual gratification with any person or object. The means do not count. Among sailors, for instance, homosexual practices would be no vice: they would merely be a normal response to prolonged sexual segregation. Cocteau's remarks lead to an obvious conclusion: human beings are no more responsible for the peculiarities of their sexual behavior than is the flower for the mechanism which, every night, forces it to close its petals.[4]

Let us not hasten to accuse Cocteau of Sartrian bad faith. Cocteau is not the author of *Corydon*. He makes no special plea for greater sexual tolerance on the part of society or its law enforcement agencies, he does not beg for indulgence on the grounds that homosexuality is a physiological condition beyond the control of human will. Nor does he appear vitally interested in any scientific or rationalistic explanation which might be found for the stripes of the tiger or the complex workings of our instinctual drives. What concerns him most is the strange power which manifests itself through such phenomena. Cocteau is well aware that this power may originate in man himself. He is not unfamiliar with psychological projection, as is clear from the following passage: "If the savage experiences fear, he sculpts a god of fear, and he asks the god to take away his fear. He is afraid of the god born of his fear. He expels his fear under the form of an object which becomes a work of art through the intensity of his fear, and which is taboo because this object, originating in a moral weakness, is changed into a force which orders him to reform."[5] The sculpture is a human artifact: it can, however, radiate a numinous aura which is the reflection of the psychic energy expended in its creation. In point of fact, any object may strike the beholder in a similar fashion. Cocteau has defined poetry as the experience in which the most common thing, a dog, a carriage, a house, takes on a miraculous appearance: "Such is the function of poetry. It shows in all their nakedness, under a light which shakes our torpor, the surprising

4. *Journal d'un inconnu*, pp. 42, 80, 106; *Poésie de journalisme* (Paris: Belfond, 1973), pp. 85–86; *La difficulté d'être* (Paris: Morihien, 1947), pp. 229–31; *Poésie critique II*, pp. 103, 124; *Opium*, pp. 136–37; *Les enfants terribles* (Paris: Livre de poche, 1960), p. 80.

5. *Journal d'un inconnu*, p. 17.

things which surround us and which our senses registered automatically."[6] The phenomenology of religions gives an identical description of the sacred as it is perceived in primitive cultures: any object, an animal, a plant, a stone, may become a repository for magical-religious forces.[7] The artist, for Cocteau, appears to be the individual whose perception of the world remains closest to the experience of archaic man. His creations, like the work of the primitive sculptor, concentrate the occult forces which pervade the universe just as an electric eel accumulates electricity. He does so unconsciously, by instinct: "A great artist is nonhuman, plant-like, animal-like."[8]

Cocteau does not question the existence of these forces. If the unconscious of children, as he believes, has the power to create poltergeists or cause voodoo-like deaths, why couldn't the unconscious of the artist give birth to creations which provoke similar results? And Cocteau lists in all seriousness the intriguing coincidences that accompanied the performance of his play *Orphée*.[9] We may not quite believe, as he also appears to do, that the paintings of Chirico can cast a spell over the unsuspecting spectator and drive him to suicide, but their haunting power is not to be denied. At any rate, the point is not whether a work of art can actually set magical forces in motion. When Cocteau describes poetry as "a secret weapon, a dangerous weapon, precise, quick-firing, and which sometimes reaches its target only at incalculable distances," he truthfully describes what he himself knows of poetic illumination: he has personally experienced the murderous effect of beauty.[10] In the depths of his own self, he has met with the numinous Other who can only be a messenger from the unknown, he has seen the Angel. Cocteau can therefore state in all sincerity that poetry inclines man toward the supernatural. The poet is for him what Claudel considered Rimbaud to be, *un mystique à l'état sauvage*.

To sum up: for Cocteau, the poetic experience is the revelation of beauty, and beauty is the encounter with a numinous

---

6. *Poésie critique I*, pp. 49–50.
7. Mircéa Eliade, *Traité d'histoire des religions* (Paris: Payot, 1964), pp. 24–25.
8. *Poésie critique I*, pp. 51, 152.
9. *Opium*, pp. 58–63; *Journal d'un inconnu*, p. 54.
10. *Poésie critique II*, p. 177.

force which is both fascinating and terrifying. This fascination is clearly linked with sex: Cocteau writes that the beauty he is talking about causes "an erection of the soul."[11] The innumerable angels he has drawn or painted are figures of desire, just as the idol sculpted by the savage was a response to fear. Cocteau's encounter with the Angel Heurtebise is a metaphorical description of sexual possession and fecundation leading to the birth of the poem: "The Angel Heurtebise with an incredible / Brutality jumps on me. For pity's sake / Do not jump so hard / You beastly boy. . . . " "The angel did not care about my rebellion. I merely was his vehicle, and he treated me as a vehicle. He was preparing for his coming out. My attacks came more often, and became a single one comparable to labor pains. But it was a monstrous delivery."[12] In the figure of the Angel, the power of Thanatos is inextricably united with the fascination of Eros. The vision of his beauty can destroy the beholder: " . . . the angel has his place just between the human and the nonhuman. He is a young animal, full of charm and vigor, who passes from visibility to invisibility with the powerful shortcuts of a diver, with the thunderous wings of a thousand wild pigeons. . . . A perfect example of athletic monstrosity, for whom death has no meaning. He chokes the living and tears out their souls without any emotion." "Gracious monsters, cruel, terribly male and androgynous, such is the idea I had of angels. . . . What comes closest to it would be what was seen by the crew of Superfortress #42.7353 after they dropped the first atom bomb."[13] In his meeting with the angel, the poet experiences a loss of self, a kind of death reminiscent of sexual ecstasy or mystical rapture. Cocteau's work may well be summed up in the equation: poetry = sex = death.

For Cocteau, the poetic visitation thus seems to repeat the drama of his childhood, the crisis in which he discovered his doom. It appears impossible to ascertain the exact circumstances of this drama. We can only attempt to reconstruct the general form of the original event. What Sartre wrote of Genet applies equally to Cocteau: "He is a man of repetition—the dull empty

11. *Poésie critique I*, p. 244.
12. *Opéra*, p. 51; *Journal d'un inconnu*, p. 51.
13. *Poésie critique I*, p. 38; *Journal d'un inconnu*, pp. 46–48.

time of his everyday life ... is transfixed by fulgurating epiphanies which bring back his original passion as Holy Week brings back the Passion of Christ."[14] Cocteau's writings provide a number of mythical representations which seem to be based on a single underlying pattern. The clearest and most detailed of these representations may be found in the novel *Les enfants terribles*. In the opening pages, the protagonist, Paul, a young schoolboy, is in love with another student, Dargelos: "This love, which preceded any knowledge of love, was all the more destructive. It was a vague pain, an intense one, a chaste desire, sexless and aimless." During a snowball fight, Paul seeks Dargelos: he wants to prove himself in Dargelos's eyes, but as he approaches, Dargelos throws snowballs at him and hits him in the mouth and in the chest: "A blow strikes him full in the chest. A dull blow. A blow struck by a marble hand. A blow from a statue. His head empties." Dargelos is described as an idol surrounded by acolytes, bathed in a supernatural light. The scene is repeated in the film *Le sang d'un poète*, where the following poem serves as a commentary:

The marble blow was a snow ball
And it made a star on his chest;
And it made a star on the smock of the victor,
A star on the dark defenseless victor.
He stood stupefied, stood
In his sentry-box of solitude,
His legs bare under the mistletoe, the golden walnuts, the holly,
Starred like the blackboard in the study-hall.
Thus often there come from school
Blows which cause the blood to flow
The hard blows of snowballs
Which beauty throws at the heart, as it goes by.

The incident exemplifies the chaos that Dargelos's insolent beauty could provoke in schoolchildren "so unversed in the riddle of the senses, and utterly defenseless against the terrible damages inflicted upon any sensitive soul by the supernatural sex of beauty."[15]

14. *Saint-Genet, comédien et martyr* (Paris: Gallimard, 1952), p. 12.
15. *Professional Secrets*, p. 25.

Dargelos makes another appearance in Cocteau's unacknowledged novel *Le livre blanc*. The protagonist, who is also the narrator, happens to meet him in the fourth form of the Lycée
Condorcet, the school Cocteau himself attended with the real
Dargelos:

> One of the boys, called Dargelos, possessed a virility far in ad-
> vance of his age, and enjoyed great prestige as a result. He exhib-
> ited himself in cynical fashion and would do so, even for boys of
> other forms, in exchange for rare foreign stamps or tobac-
> co. . . . His open-collared shirt revealed a broad neck. A strongly
> curled lock of hair fell over his forehead. His face, with its rather
> thick lips, slightly narrow eyes and somewhat flat nose, was
> characteristic of the type which for me was to prove fatal. When
> fatality appears in disguise, it gives us an illusion of freedom and
> in the end always leads us into the same trap.

The impression of fatality is reinforced by the fact that the narrator's homosexual inclinations may be an inherited trait: his
father is also a homosexual, although he has remained all his life
unaware of his true sexual preference. As far back as the narrator can remember, he has felt attracted to boys. In each case,
the same pattern is repeated. In the first incident, as a very
young child, he caught a glimpse of a young farmboy taking a
horse to have a wash. It was a hot summer day, and the boy had
undressed so that he could enter the water with the horse without getting his clothes wet. The sight of this naked body had an
extraordinary effect on the narrator: "My ears buzzed. My face
flushed. My legs felt weak. My heart pounded as though I had
committed a murder. Without realizing it, I fainted." A similar
incident occurs one year later: "I was going for a walk with my
nursemaid. Suddenly she pulled me away, calling out to me that
I mustn't turn round. The heat was blinding. Two young gypsies
had taken their clothes off and were climbing the trees. The
sight of them terrified my nursemaid, and my disobedience gave
the scene an unforgettable aura."[16] These scenes clearly complement the parallel incidents in *Les enfants terribles* and *Le sang
d'un poète*. The snowball thrown by Dargelos appears as the ma-

16. *Cocteau's World*, pp. 123–27.

terial representation of the sexual impression made on Paul by the boy's virile beauty. Merely looking at male nudity is felt to be a sacrilege, a transgression punishable by death.

In *Le livre blanc,* the narrator recounts his successive love affairs and comes to realize that fate has indeed caused him to fall repeatedly into the same trap, which lies in wait for him everywhere, even in the abbey where he eventually tries to seek refuge: "The porter arranged for me to be conducted by a monk, beside whom I walked in silence beneath the vaults.... He lowered his hood. His profile was silhouetted against the wall. It was that of Alfred, H, Rose, Jeanne, Dargelos, PAS DE CHANCE, Gustave and the farmhand."[17] Each of his previous love affairs has ended in death or suffering: could it be otherwise in the monastery where, once again, the ghost of Dargelos returns to haunt him, under a monk's hood this time, after appearing successively in the guise of a farmhand, a male servant, a sailor, a bisexual parttime actress, a young whore and her pimp, a bisexual young man, and a boy who shot himself because he refused to share the narrator's love with his sister? Similarly, in *Les enfants terribles,* Paul discovers that the movie stars, the gangsters, and the detectives whose photographs are pinned to his walls all resemble Dargelos. In Racine's Phèdre, in her love for Hippolyte, Cocteau finds a true image of human love: "Legally one must be faithful to a person, humanly to a type. Phèdre is faithful to a type. It is not an example of love, it is *the* example of love.... It is lawful that Phèdre should respect Thésée and that Thésée should love Hippolyte. It is human that Phèdre should love Hippolyte and that Thésée should hate him."[18]

For Paul, as for the narrator of *Le livre blanc,* the revelation of beauty inevitably leads to its loss. Cocteau has noted that fate took from him the men whom he loved: "Garros's plane catches fire. He falls. Jean Le Roy arranges my letters on top of his footlocker. He grasps his machine gun. He dies. Typhoid fever robs me of Radiguet. Marcel Khill is killed in Alsace. The Gestapo tortures Jean Desbordes to death."[19] Is this why, in his

17. *Cocteau's World,* p. 147.
18. *Opium,* p. 47.
19. *La difficulté d'être,* p. 86.

works, love usually leads to death? Renaud's kiss will be the cause
of Armide's death, in the play *Renaud et Armide*. Forcing Stanis-
las to stab her is the only way left to the Queen to express her
love for him, in *L'aigle à deux têtes*. Lancelot and Guinevere are
united in death, in *Les chevaliers de la Table Ronde*. The wife, in
Pauvre matelot, finds no other means of proving her love to her
husband than murdering him. The love of Nathalie and
Philippe brings about their death, in *L'éternel retour*. Paul's love
for Dargelos reaches its climax in the moment of his death, in
Les enfants terribles, a death caused by the ball of poison which was
a present from Dargelos. The equation love = death is the very
heart of the film *Orphée*, of the mimodrama *Le jeune homme et la
Mort*, of the essay *La corrida du premier mai*. Let us add for good
measure Cocteau's adaptation of Shakespeare's *Romeo and Juliet*
and his film script based on Mérimée's *La Vénus d'Ille*, in which
the bridegroom dies in the embrace of the statue for whom he
has unwittingly betrayed his fiancée. The association of love
and death, of Eros and Thanatos, has of course become a cliché
in the Western literary tradition. Few writers, however, have
been more consistent than Cocteau in their use of this topos.

For Cocteau, sex itself is often linked with physical suffering
and death, or at least with the inflicting of metaphorical wounds.
He has offered this explanation of the Chinese custom of bind-
ing the feet of women: "A broken foot remains sensitive where
the fracture occurred. This place need merely be touched in
order to inflict torture. That is the true motive of this fascinating
custom, which, along with other refinements, is coming to an
end.... Young Chinese brides need no longer dread the conjugal device which wrung from them, at the crucial moment,
spasms and shrieks of pain."[20] Like the ancient Chinese, Cocteau
cannot conceive love without a concomitant suffering. Through
his masterful use of metaphor, a lover and his mistress are
turned into a killer and his victim: "Then, contemplating this
Desdemona flung backward on the bed, dying near the pillow,
so frightfully pale with her teeth uncovered, he heaped up
shameful memories on her face and withdrew from her like a
knife."[21] Sexual possession is disguised murder. No wonder that

20. *Professional Secrets*, p. 160.
21. *Le grand écart* (Paris: Stock, 1947), p. 59.

Cocteau should so often call "chambre du crime" the hotel rooms where lovers meet. The impulse to kill exists even in the most tender of lovers: "Their kiss is only a weakened form of the vampire's bite, a rite which figures the act of appropriating the blood of the beloved. . . . This yearning for the blood of another becomes still more evident when the lips suck the skin so as to work like a cupping-glass and to leave a black and blue mark which adds exhibitionism to vampirism. This spot proclaims that the person who wears it, on the neck usually, is the prey of a creature who loves her so that he wants to draw out her vital spirit in order to mix it with his."[22] Cocteau readily believes that inflicting or receiving death can bring about sexual gratification: ejaculation takes place when a bullfighter makes the killing thrust or when a criminal is executed by hanging.

This identification of sex with the death impulse is also made in the episode of the Hermaphrodite, in *Le sang d'un poète*. The hand of the Hermaphrodite is seen lifting the cloth over his sexual organs. It unveils a placard bearing the words, "Danger of death." The same association may be created through less direct means. The hotel room in which the Hermaphrodite holds his desperate assignations has been alluded to earlier in the film: "In the early morning, Mexico, the moats of Vincennes, the Boulevard Arago, a hotel room, are equivalent." Famous executions have taken place in the moats of Vincennes. It was there, for instance, that the Duke of Enghien was shot upon Napoleon's orders. The Mexican scene presented in the film is also an execution by firing squad. Assuming that Mexico = the moats of Vincennes = the hotel room, it follows that if the sexual encounter which takes place in the hotel room leads to death, the execution of the Mexican represents a sexual conquest. The Mexican, after his execution, rises again to face the firing squad once more. Cocteau thus seems to suggest that man is doomed by his sexual drives to undergo many a death. A statue of the Virgin placed next to the Mexican is shattered by bullets. What is taking place is a sacrilegious act, a transgression of the sacred. In addition, the broken Virgin points to the victim's secret femininity as well as to his sexual violation. The phallic significance of the rifle barrels in the foreground is unmistakable. They under-

22. *La difficulté d'être,* pp. 217–18.

line the homosexual character of the episode (males are the agents of a male's death), which is made still more obvious through the association of the Mexican with the Hermaphrodite.

One should not leap to the conclusion that, for Cocteau, only the male can take the role of lover-executioner. In the sexual encounter, woman may become the instrument of death, the agent to whose phallic-like power the passive partner has to defer. On more than one occasion Cocteau has mentioned the praying mantis, which devours the male during coitus. Judith and Holophernes are the subjects of one of his most famous tapestries. The female of the species assumes a similar role in his evocation of the young women who, at the time of the Russian Revolution, transported bombs under their dresses. Their breasts thus became living instruments of death, capable of killing on contact, "a star of lightning and love."[23] In Cocteau's writings, female characters often appear more virile than their male counterparts. This is why the male narrator of *Le livre blanc* has fallen in love with a girl: "Jeanne was a boy; she loved women, and I loved her with the feminine part of my nature." Conversely, in the sailors' bars of Toulon, "the most brutal jailbird, the roughest Breton, the most savage Corsican" will appear as "tall, flower-decked girls with low décolletés and loose limbs who like dancing and lead their partners, without the slightest embarrassment, into the shady hotels by the port."[24]

In the moment of poetic inspiration, the poet plays the passive role. For Cocteau, the poetic trance is obviously a transposition of sexual possession. His writing of the poem *L'ange Heurtebise* is described as "some sort of parthenogenesis, a couple made up of a single body and which gave birth."[25] We can therefore understand why, in his film *Le testament d'Orphée*, he chose the hibiscus flower as his symbol. Its peculiar shape suggests bisexuality, since it appears to be made up of a concave calix containing an erect stamen. Its destruction and recreation imitate the alternance of death and rebirth. This rhythm espouses the cycle of sexual desire, which dies as it reaches its goal, but only to be

23. *Les enfants terribles*, p. 161.
24. *Cocteau's World*, pp. 130, 133.
25. *Journal d'un inconnu*, p. 51.

reborn. Cocteau's symbol of the Phoenix, the fabled bird which is reborn of its ashes, has similar implications. When Cocteau stated that "writing is an act of love," he gave the words their fullest sexual meaning.[26] The Muse is the praying mantis which devours her male in the act of copulation. She is a female, but with distinctly phallic attributes. After her murderous visitation, the poet calls for her return in these revealing lines:

> Give me back this murderous
> Companion This praying
> Mantis This love
> Which devoured me Her beak
> Her long legs of a green
> Amazon her Palladian eye
> Behind the slits of her helmet.[27]

His encounter with the Muse, whom he identifies with the goddess Pallas Athene, receives its most striking expression in the film *Le testament d'Orphée*. After a long wait, the poet is finally admitted into her presence. Her flawless female form (the part was played by Claudine Oger, a Miss France competition winner) is set off by a clinging black rubber suit, of the kind worn by divers, but the suit itself, with its armorlike appearance, her helmet, her shield with the Gorgon head, and her spear tend to make her look like a young Greek warrior. She hurls her spear at the poet: it pierces his back, right between the shoulders, goes through his body, and comes out of his chest. He dies, whispering words that echo Kurtz's final utterance in Conrad's *Heart of Darkness*: "The horror . . . the the horror . . . the horror."

The figures which appear in Cocteau's writings as symbols of poetic visitation share similar androgynous traits. The Princess who has enabled Orphée to renew his inspiration is of course a feminine figure, but she gives orders in a most male fashion, and her aides are motorcycle riders who appear almost as caricatures of virility in their semi-military uniforms, complete with helmets, goggles, wide leather belts and gloves, and heavy boots. More

---

26. Quoted by Louis Nucera, *Cocteau-Moretti. L'âge du verseau* (J.-C. Lattès/ Edition spéciale, n.p., (1973), p. 25.

27. *Le requiem* (Paris: Gallimard, 1962), p. 171.

often, poetic visitation takes the form of the Angel, whose androgynous features are made quite obvious in Cocteau's drawings. His sexual ambivalence is strikingly underlined in this stanza of the poem *A force de plaisirs* . . . , which must perforce be given in the original French:

> Sous un tigre royal la rose aux chairs crispées
> Meurt de peur; il est vrai que ce tigre a des ailes.
> Mais l'ange gardien qui casse nos poupées,
> A des ailes aussi comme une demoiselle.
>
> Under a royal tiger the rose with wincing flesh
> Dies of fright; it is true the tiger has wings.
> But the guardian angel which ravages our dolls,
> Has wings too, like a dragon-fly.

Demoiselle has of course the dual meaning of "damsel" and "dragon-fly." The alternate version of the first two lines is equally revealing: "Sur un tigre royal la rose aux chairs crispées / Se referme." ("Around a royal tiger the rose / Closes its wincing flesh.") In spite of its murderous power, the flying tiger is eagerly welcomed by the timid rose.

During the poetic trance, the poet ceases to exist: he becomes absorbed by the conquering Angel. He dies, but only to live in another form. Poetic possession thus accomplishes the process of vampirism which Cocteau considers to be the ultimate goal of sexual desire. In the novel *Le grand écart*, the hero, Jacques Forestier, is obsessed with the "desire to be those whom he finds beautiful, not to be loved by them" (p. 14). Cocteau is still more explicit in *Le Potomak*: "The Christian eats his God. / I remember the first pangs of desire. / I was ignorant of desire. / My desire, at the age when sex does not yet influence the decision of the flesh, was not to reach, not to touch, not to embrace, but to be the loved one."[28] We understand why Cocteau so often describes death in terms of sexual (or, to be more precise, of homosexual) possession. In the film *Le sang d'un poète*, the black Angel of Death lies face down on the body of the boy who has been struck down by Dargelos's snowball and absorbs it into his own sub-

28. *Le Potomak* (Paris: Stock, 1950), p. 314.

stance. When Jacques Forestier attempts suicide, he feels on his body "a weight of cork, a weight of marble, a weight of snow. It was the angel of death accomplishing his work. He lies flat on the body of those who are about to die. . . . Death sends him; one could take him for one of these Ambassadors Extraordinary who take the place of princes at royal weddings. . . . The angel works coolly, cruelly, patiently, till the final spasm. . . . His victim sensed him to be pitiless, like the surgeon who administers chloroform, like the boas who, in order to swallow a gazelle, dilate their bodies like a woman in labor."[29] In the poem *L'endroit et l'envers,* death also appears as a lover who comes to claim his bride:

> You come like an angel of snow
> Heavier than bronze, lighter than cork
> To lie on the lover whose spasm
> At last brings you pleasure.

Cocteau makes use of the same imagery in his essay *La corrida du premier mai.* The bullfight is described as a wedding between the torero and the White Lady of Death, who is represented by her Ambassador Extraordinary, the black bull. The bullfighter is the royal bridegroom on his way to the powerful bride to whom he is destined. In this encounter, two males are face to face, and yet there is only one law governing the couple they form, "the law of insects, when the female copulates with the male and devours him. But who is the male? . . . The great mystery of the Fiesta consists precisely in the paradox of adversaries who by turn become female and take back the prerogatives of virility. . . . If the bullfighter wears the bright colors of the male and the bull the modest dress worn by the female in the animal kingdom, at the end of the love act the male will have to change his sex and, by virtue of his grace and of his dancer's costume, become again the female who kills."[30] A similar exchange of sexes takes place in the poetic trance. The poet thus accomplishes his childish wish, to be transformed into the object of his desire: he is both I and Other, possessor and possessed, bridegroom and bride,

29. *Le grand écart,* pp. 141–42.
30. *La corrida du premier mai* (Paris: Grasset, 1957), pp. 89–91.

royal tiger and wincing rose, armed Minerva and transfixed
Cocteau, and art is born of their conjunction.[31]

The purpose of this essay was to examine the constitutive
elements in Cocteau's equation sex = death = poetry. One problem remains: how in the first place did the equation come into
being? To solve it, one would have to launch a full-scale
psychoanalysis of Cocteau based on what is known of his life as
well as on his writings. Significant attempts have already been
made in this direction, notably by Milorad.[32] One readily agrees
with him that the suicide of Cocteau's father, who shot himself
when the boy was only eight, must have been a determining
factor in the child's psychological development. His essays, however, leave many questions unanswered. We would like to know,
for instance, the meaning of the strange dream that was to haunt
Cocteau's nights for many years after his father's death: "My
father, who was dead, was not dead. He had become a parrot at
the Pré-Catelan, one of the parrots whose racket remains
forever linked, for me, to the taste of fresh foaming milk. In this
dream, my mother and I sat at one of the tables at the Pré-
Catelan farm, which mixed several farms with the terrace of the
cuckatoos at the Jardin d'Acclimatation. I knew that my mother
knew and did not know that I knew, and I guessed that she tried
to find out which of the birds my father had become. I woke up
in tears because of her face which had attempted to smile."[33]
Genet had Sartre: Cocteau still awaits his exegete.

31. "Art is born of the coitus between the male and female elements which are
our constitutive components" (*Opium*, p. 137).

32. Milorad, "La clé des mythes dans l'oeuvre de Cocteau," *Cahiers Jean Cocteau*, II (Paris: Gallimard, 1971), pp. 97–140; "Le mythe orphique dans l'oeuvre
de Cocteau," *Revue des lettres modernes*, nos. 298–303 (1972), pp. 109–42.

33. *Opium*, pp. 220–23.

Frank Paul Bowman

The Religious Metaphors of a Married Homosexual: Marcel Jouhandeau's *Chronique d'une passion*

Marcel Jouhandeau is almost unknown outside France (despite Havelock Ellis's appreciation of him) and even in his native land only one major study has been done on him—a very good one, by Jean Gaulmier.[1] Rumors circulate about his "behind-the-scenes" powers in the literary world, and a small "in" group maintains that he is a remarkable writer, superior to Gide, to be ranked with Proust, but such a group can be found for almost anyone in Paris. The comparison with Gide is tempting; both share the subject of the married homosexual, and write "confessional" literature in an artificial style in order to create a kind of moral ambiguity; in both, the debate about homosexuality eventually becomes a debate about the nature of God, thanks to recourse to metaphoric constructs. Jouhandeau, however, a Catholic, is more explicit and more ironic and, unlike Gide, does not alienate reader from hero; rather, through the artifices of language and authorial commentary, he seeks a *comprobat ridendo mores* full of awareness but devoid of guilt.

---

1. Jean Gaulmier, *L'univers de Marcel Jouhandeau* (Paris: Nizet, 1959); see also José Cabanis, *Jouhandeau* (Paris: Gallimard, 1959) and Jacques Danon, *Entretiens avec Elise et Marcel Jouhandeau* (Paris: Belfond, 1966).

"No, no one has seen with his eyes as well as you have Mr. Godeau in person; irony and ecstasy mixed to that extent at the corner of a human mouth and in the depths of a look, where, in a supernatural light, all disputes ceasing, one wonders who is present, the Devil or God"?[2] So Jouhandeau describes the portrait of himself as cleric, done by his lover J. St. The marriage of irony and ecstasy is an apt description of the style and of the ethical content of the *Chronique d'une passion*. That style at times waxes lyric in a strangely apostrophic, unnatural way, about the joys of homosexual love or about the virtues of heterosexual marriage. At other moments an irony bordering on the comic attacks not only Elise, the spouse, jealous, irrational, uncomprehending, but also homosexuality, infidelity, self-justification—and the Church, which is the pretext and excuse for all of Elise's evil-doing but which also solves the dilemma and prevents the tragedy that threatens from the book's very beginning. It is not, however, a matter of irony and ecstasy alternating stylistically, with one tone providing relief or controlling the other; instead, they are blended, even married in a way many readers, unaccustomed to emotional ambiguity, find unpleasant. That emotional ambiguity reflects a moral ambivalence where it is impossible to say which is God's side, which the Devil's. Jouhandeau neither justifies nor condemns homosexuality; or rather he does both, and at times for the same reason. The author of the *Algèbre des valeurs morales,* which includes an "Apology for evil" but also a "Defense of hell," in *Chronique d'une passion* illustrates not an ethics of ambiguity but the ambiguity of all ethics, and does so not by a series of propositions and learned citations from the Church Fathers, as in the *Algèbre,* but by an action and by the highly literary, quite particular style in which that action is recounted.

Chronique d'une passion, unlike many of Jouhandeau's books,

<hr />

2. *Chronique d'une passion, récit* (Paris: Gallimard, 1964), p. 109. All references are to this edition. The first edition was published in 1949. All translations in the text are my own. Selections from *Chronique d'une passion* and from other texts by Jouhandeau about his marital problems may be found in *Marcel and Elise,* trans. and intro. Martin Turnell (New York: Pantheon, 1953; London: Longmans Green, 1955). The only other work by Jouhandeau available in English (though he has been much translated into Polish, German, Spanish, Italian) is his life of *Saint Philip Neri,* trans. George Lamb (New York: Harper & Row, 1960).

has a plot. It is not a very complex one, and Jouhandeau presents it through rather unusual techniques and gives its parts curious proportions. Marcel, the hero-narrator, becomes friends with J. St. ("Jacques") who has admired him and wanted to know him for years, but whom he rebuffed at their first meeting. Soon the friendship blossoms into a passion, Jacques shows his body to Marcel, they make love, and Jacques, a painter, gives Marcel the talisman-portrait he did of him ten years before. Marcel takes the portrait home, where it becomes the center of attention, dominates the household. His wife Elise learns of Jacques's existence and of Marcel's affair with him, and makes his acquaintance. The affair itself follows an irregular, comic course; Marcel suffers first from Jacques's permissiveness, then from his infidelities with butcher boys, Africans, and the like, but he learns to accept these as not of the same category as their passionate love. Elise's jealousy becomes violent when she discovers that Marcel's passion for Jacques is not simply physical. She seizes a butcher knife and announces that she intends to kill Jacques, goes to his hotel but does not find him, then lacerates the portrait. Marcel, in dire straits, calls in Elise's beloved Dominican, Fr. J., who finally gets the knife from her, after forcing Marcel, for the sake of peace, to vow that he will never see Jacques again. The last fifth of the book is taken up with a discussion by Elise and Marcel of the affair and of Marcel's guilt or lack thereof.

This plot Jouhandeau has used, with variations, elsewhere: in *Du pur amour,* where the beloved betrays him with women and gets married; in the *Chroniques maritales,* where the homosexuality is less explicit; endlessly, and more comically, in his *Journaliers.* And Elise herself wrote a novel, *Le lien de ronces,* which gives her version of the story told in *Chronique.* If *Chronique* stands out among Jouhandeau's writings, it is because the conflict among Elise, Marcel, and the other man is here quintessential, and viewed in all its consequences, because the outcome is such a total disaster, ending the relationship definitively, and finally because of the extensive use the novel makes of religious metaphor. Through that religious metaphor the novel effects a moral examination of Marcel's conduct, of love, of homosexuality. Jouhandeau's style is "precious," but here the almost sacrilegious preciosity of the religious references gives the book an

ethical dimension. Jouhandeau is elsewhere a professional
moralist (or, if one prefers, immoralist); his treatise *De l'abjection*
was published while the events described in *Chronique* were
occurring—but here he succeeds in combining the roles of
moralist, novelist, and autobiographer. However, before the
moralist is analyzed, the artifices of form and style must be defined, for they control the impact of what ethical propositions
the book contains.

Chronique d'une passion is full of artifice in plot and structure.
The central device, the portrait of Marcel by Jacques, which is of
a supernatural beauty and sows dissension in the household, and
which Elise destroys, is reminiscent of many another magic portrait or totem in Hoffmann, Charles Nodier, Oscar Wilde. Not
that Jouhandeau attributes any real magic to this portrait, which
possesses strange qualities only because of the imagination or the
exaggerated language of the characters, but the device is nonthe-
less venerable. Other such devices include the use of letters, of
chance encounters. The proportions of the novel are also artificial and do not try to correspond to "lived reality." The book
contains only 224 small pages; the crisis, in which Elise decides to
kill Jacques, occurs on page 155. It then takes fifteen pages to
disarm Elise, and the rest of the book is really epilogue, describing the modus vivendi Marcel and Elise work out. Major events
are telescoped or briefly alluded to and attention given to reactions to the event, subjective or even lyrical; commentary on the
action is more important than description of it. But this is not the
only way in which Jouhandeau breaks the traditional mold of the
novel.

The opening of *Chronique*, for instance, is very strange indeed.
It is a brief but bitter attack on Elise and her book, *Le lien de
ronces*; he accuses her of misrepresenting the events, in part for
aesthetic reasons, but mostly because of deficiencies in her
character. She is unable to grasp nuances, and "always acts with
the same brute unawareness." She offers a striking illustration of
how egotism, once it goes beyond a certain point, resembles
blindness. Elise lies; and even though the example Marcel gives,
of how he used a Louis-Philippe chair to break into her room, is
suspiciously irrelevant, everything leads the reader to expect a
tale which will end in divorce, and will explain and justify the

rupture between husband and wife. Jouhandeau carefully sustains this expectation for four-fifths of the novel, but the ending is the opposite; Marcel and Elise are still married to each other. This is a constant in Jouhandeau's autobiographies, and even his essential theme; the conclusion of each novel should be divorce, but instead the marriage bonds are tighter than ever.

After this attack on Elise comes a series of brief paragraphs, which seem to pose moral problems or provide precious proverbs (excommunication by a friend is a desert where a man forges his moral armor; everything looks tragic at times, but what is the tragic?). Following a page of this sort of thing there appears the mysterious sentence, "He had hardly left; I called him back." Then a new series of meditations, even more abstruse and more interrogative than the first, which conclude this time with: "Prey to him, to 'Danger' once more, but which has taken on a new face, that of J. St." Then we gradually learn that Jacques wanted to meet the narrator ten years earlier, that when they finally did meet the narrator was fascinated by him and that they are physically attracted to each other. The opening pages are quite confusing to someone who does not know in advance what to expect. Nor does this opening clarify the text's moral "lesson." The style is too mysterious, too metaphoric, too interrogative. "Frail face high on his staff and his hands like moss and fringe. Under the ash of his coat did I glimpse the fire of a diamond?" Who and what, the reader asks. Only later does he realize that this is his first vision of the object of the narrator's love. The text is a puzzle to be solved by the reader, for the activity of solving the puzzle maintains the tonal ambiguity and the moral ambivalence of the text.

The crisis of the tale is provoked not by any major event, but by something rather minor and quite unexpected; there is a kind of inevitable tragedy about the whole affair, but the catalyst is haphazard and even irrelevant. Elise seems resigned until the day when Jacques commits his big mistake, which is to invite her to lunch. The invitation plunges her into melancholy, then despair, then anger, for she feels that in daring to do this Jacques shows that he is stronger than she, that he is her triumphant superior. The consequences of the meal are even more disastrous, but those disasters largely stem from his use of the pronoun "we" when talking to her about himself and Marcel. Her homicidal outburst is provoked not by any new discovery of infidelity, as would be traditional, but because she learns that Marcel's attraction to Jacques stems from passion, not just lust. This is the essential irony in the book's delineation of homosexual love; it is the less base (passion, rather than lust) which provokes the greater punishment. Marcel's quite noble sentence, "It may astonish you, I find no trace of evil or anything impure in what I feel, since I've met J. St., because I love him" (155), turns Elise into a mad avenger. The basic plot structure is almost trite, but what provokes act or peripetia is unexpected and impertinent. Since it is Elise who does most of the acting—in every sense of the word—this device serves to accuse the unjustifiable nature of her conduct. It also helps create the atmosphere of the ludicrous and absurd which Jouhandeau mixes, but never blends, with his story of love and tragedy.

Jouhandeau does not always write in this manner. In his texts reality is always stylized, even caricatured, but the degree and the modes vary; he is a master at the many artifices of style, whose prose is always idiosyncratic but not always the same. Take his portraits of the village of Chaminadour; *Chaminadour* is full of realistic, comic anecdotes and imitates to an extent popular language. *Binche-ana,* even with its dream scenes, is more poetic and more subjective, describes three personalities in depth; the "Terebinthe" episode of *Astaroth* is purely fantastic, the events recounted and personalities presented exaggerated beyond the range of possibility in a masterpiece of satirical caricature. *Cocu, pendu et content* is a dry, distant, economical recounting of an almost Aeschylean tragedy. Yet all four works describe the same world. Jouhandeau's vision of the self is equally multiple and complex, the perspective adopted varies from book to book and within each book. *Du pur amour* in many ways resembles, in subject, *Chronique,* but its style is less lyric, more blatantly comic, less dense. In *Chronique,* although a degree of psychological realism remains, he mixes the tragic and comic, sympathetic and satiric attitudes toward the self in a manner which is apt to perplex a reader who prefers his emotions straightforward. There is little if anything straightforward about Jouhandeau. He avoids the straightforward primarily by the use he makes of metaphor, which creates the stylistic irony of his text.

In a novel that describes the homosexual passion of a married man and the jealousy of his wife, it is curious that religion should be evoked roughly every third page. These religious metaphors eventually serve to define the relation between the two loves— not homosexual and heterosexual, but sacred and profane—and the ethical status of Marcel's "illicit" passion; but many only set the tone or create an atmosphere. These include such pre-monitory incidents as the gypsy making the sign of the cross a multitude of times, or the movie theater showing the *Three Children in the Fiery Furnace,* surely to be identified with Marcel, Elise, and Jacques, each praising the Lord and burning in his manner. Yet such references are so numerous that they create a texture where religion and love are confused. The title itself serves that end, especially since *Passion* is usually capitalized in the text and the pun is on occasion made quite explicitly (133). Jacques early compares his body to "the carriage of the Blessed Sacrament," suggesting he is Marcel's God (22); later, Marcel concludes that though he is separated from his love, "I feel him always standing nude beside me, as Adam stands nude in the mind of God" (202); the sacrilegious tone creates a veritable confusion of the sacred and the profane. Jouhandeau gives these evocations an ethical content. The comparison of Jacques's room with paradise is typical: "I am on the point of throwing myself against the door. No, with his steel blade, an Angel bars my way, it is me refusing myself Paradise" (90). If Jacques's room is paradise where Marcel will know joy, the Angel of the Lord (a form of Marcel himself) prevents his access to the Promised Land. This passing reference evokes the whole problem of the novel. The same is true of the portrait of Marcel, significantly entitled the "Prelate" and described in either/or terms where the "either" is religious: "cardinal in disgrace" or "royal vagabond," "his strange headgear hesitates between the egret tufted cap of Don Juan and the ecclesiastical biretta. . . . Probably a fallen Prince of the Church, definitively a prey to himself, unless you are that Prince of Darkness in person" (220). This description gives a clue to the function of religious metaphors in *Chronique*; they assess Marcel's effort to reconcile the two loves, to turn his passion into a way of knowing God, and the defeat of that effort by Elise. The prelate is finally not a pilgrim, but the disgraced Prince of the Church who has not found the grace he sought. Frequent as the metaphors are, they avoid the blatantly scandalous in which Jouhandeau elsewhere delights—for example, *Journaliers* XX (1974), 210, a quite remarkable comparison of the male prostitute to the priest at mass.

Several extensive passages of *Chronique* compare the love of God and homosexual love. Some declare, almost dogmatically, the religious value of homosexuality. Another series treats the parallel in a comic manner, using the sacrilegious for satirical ends. A third set reasserts the identification of religion and love in a panegyric of homosexual passion. The final set proposes that to refuse such identification means preferring lust to passion, and that this is indeed the way and the will of God's Church.

Thus, in his first "religious" meditation on his love Marcel claims that Passion puts us in a state which "partakes simultaneously of Sanctity and Damnation," in a divine *imprudence* as close to perversity as it is to perfection; the object of love receives that combination of terror and voluptuousness which should be reserved for God (26). Such Passion creates, not Heaven, but a "delectable Hell." As his passion for Jacques intensifies, its religious aspects become more pronounced: "To love for me was to pray without ceasing on love and to have my own organ master. Ecstasy is the goal of Love; Ecstasy: to be outside oneself" (35). Love's total absorption of the being in devotion to another makes it a properly religious ecstasy. The next identification of love with religion goes a step further to assert that Jacques is in a sense Christ, the object of Marcel's worship as much as of his lust. Despite Jacques's imperfections, Marcel sees in him the image of the Incarnation: "My religion is 'you' such as you would have deserved being, if you had wished; you, without the deformations of life, as you came out of the Hands of the Eternal and a copy of which remains in His breast. The original, the essential, the only true, this 'you,' nothing can hide it from me, neither wounds nor stains could disfigure it in my eyes, as his wounds, the Blood and Mud spread on him, decorate and crown better than precious stones and any purple, for the devout, the body of their Jesus Christ" (38). The sins of Jacques, in this instance his infidelities with blacks and butcher boys, are thus compared to the marks of Jesus's passion—and here the comic tone seems absent.

The next theme orchestrated is that Marcel's love for Jacques is of such a nature that it constitutes a love of God. "Jacques, if I loved God as I love you, I would be a Saint, but because I love you in this unique way, it is impossible for God not to be enveloped, included with us in my love for you" (44). The love of Creator is known through the love of the creature precisely because the creature is idolized, turned into a God. Thus Marcel can assert that thanks to his passion, "I have become reconciled with the flesh of Jesus Christ" (56).

Before any examination of the consequences of this union, which indeed sacralizes Jacques more than it turns God into someone beloved, the comic treatments of the theme must be noted, for the problem of tone is here very grave indeed. Jouhandeau may be sad on the feast of the Trinity because he thinks of his lost innocence, but that does not prevent a comic treatment of the Mystery in which he introduces his passion. "Trinity: this familiar converse introduced into the heart of the divine Unity . . . the Son in the Father's arms, and the Bird of Venus going from the One to the Other and whispering in their ears" (65). Many statements about the fusion—or confusion—of the two loves are manifestly comical. "God does not always bear his Name. God sometimes wears a mask, and, transvestite, traverses our festivals. When one has conceived for any being such a perfect love that it would only worthily have perfection as its object, whom does one love?" (84). The alliteration, the image of God disguised at a masked ball, makes the confusion comic. To see God in one's lover finally becomes a way of depriving religion of any moral content. Most of the casual, metaphoric references to religion and love are in the comic vein. This is especially true of the recurrent image of the statue of the Trinity. "God the Father is always seated, in a cope, on a little wooden bench, solemnly wearing a mitre, and his two little dancer's feet spread apart, the Son in his arms. Between the two faces there is just room for the Dove, which more and more resembles a screech owl. 'You alone understand me, Companion of the first and last hour, oh Eternal, my image and whose attitude resembles mine: the Passion in your arms' " (91). The Holy Ghost as screech owl is less disquieting than Jouhandeau holding Jacques in his arms as God the Father holds Christ, the two Passions.

Other passages proclaim with some seriousness the identity of the love of God and the love of Jacques. Jouhandeau asserts that he was born to contemplate God and Christ on his cross, and that all love for him eventually has that one Object (104). Thus, he prays God, "may I lose myself and find Him and find You in him" (112). He explains the sense of this prayer later in his discussion with Elise's priest, where he defines his doctrine of love as abnegation. It matters not what the object of love is, provided that love is exclusive and absolute. "One keeps nothing for oneself, everything is given away, no one counts except for one being, and God himself as a function of that being. Then love aims so high that body and time are forgotten" (131). To love is to forget the self in the act of giving to God through man. The two loves are fused by that act of abnegation which is essential to any true love, of creature and of Creator. If the two loves are not fused—and this is Jouhandeau's main thesis—then love for the creature can only be lust. The choice is not between loving God and loving man; it is a matter of either losing the self in the love of God and man, or else satisfying lust. Passion alone keeps man in purity; "Suppress passion and I mechanically fall back into vice. I really extol the utility and necessity of passion because it alone lets me go beyond myself, surpass myself" (135). So he can accuse the enemies of his love for Jacques, Elise and Fr. N.: "In reality, they are not in league against my vice, but with my vice against that love which alone could let me triumph over myself" (149). Passion is divine because the absence of passion is vice and sin.

Jouhandeau's dream of uniting the love of creature and the love of Creator finally fails, and Elise wins out. She has her reasons to which Marcel bows, though without agreeing. He composes a dialogue with the Church in which he attacks her argument, which is also that of the Church, and his attacks are countered (185–88); Marcel and Jacques were "guilty toward her" and so should suffer. Someone had to pay, yet God in his mercy demanded only the destruction of the portrait, and in gratitude Marcel and Jacques must give up seeing each other. If this means lying to Jacques and reducing him to despair, so much the better because in that despair he may encounter what would be more salutary than Marcel for him, "the only 'Faithful' in truth, which is Truth itself" (188). Marcel acquiesces, less because he finds the argument convincing than because Elise in her fury is irresistible, because during the crisis only the Church, in the person of Fr. N., came to the rescue, because he had to expiate his own guilt for attacking homosexual love in *De l'abjection* by suffering in that love.

There are two religions in *Chronique,* both sacrilegious. As Marcel himself puts it, he has a *Fils* whereas Elise has a *Père.* The sexual nature of Elise's attraction to the Dominicans, her manner of substituting religion for conjugal affection (just as Jouhandeau does in a way, since he turns his Passion into a religion), are less important than the definition of her religion as a religion of vengeance, wrath, and sacrifice. Hers is the Apocalyptic Vision of the Dreadful Lamb, the symbol of justice. "She claims she is renouncing the Gospel for the Apocalypse. 'That,' she says, 'is the religion I belong to'" (171). Jacques is Satan, Elise is Saint Michael slaying the dragon. And her religion is justified by the Text. "In order to calm her, to reconcile her with love, I try to read the Gospel to her, but I immediately come upon this verse which makes her deception quiver in her. 'It is good that one man perish for the sake of all'" (180). As she herself says, "I have learned that he whom God loves, the lightning is upon him" (197). The biblical *sortes,* present in autobiography since Augustine, here justify the self's enemy.

However, just as Marcel in his Passion substitutes Jacques for God, so Elise substitutes her Idea for God—the Idea of killing Jacques. In *Chronique,* worship takes the form of either sodomy or murder, and one must ask of her Idea, as of his Passion, whether it is the opposite of God or identical with God. In her crisis, she tells God that she will no longer pray, her only love is her hatred, she has renounced heaven in order to kill, and she refuses to call God "Father" because God does not love her. Yet she claims that in wishing to kill Jacques she is doing the will of God, "my hatred is . . . the instrument of His justice, I obey Him in hating Evil" (165). Fr. N. tells her that her Idea is holy, kneels

before her in adoration, and Elise comes to feel that her killing is
religiously justified, partly because Jacques is a Jew. "He represented his whole race, and toward the end not only his race, but
vice incarnate in person, visible in the figure I would crush in
accordance with the mission given me from on High" (175).
There was a "mute, sweet, and terrible" understanding between
her and God, which let her be faithful to Him while hating and
killing. "Hidden mystery: my unfaithfulness to His Law consecrated me to Him more fully than any total fidelity" (176).

This sentence, pronounced by Elise, could perfectly well be
pronounced by Marcel, and the novel suggests that murder is no
worse or better than sodomy, that both offer perfectly good
altars on which to worship the hidden God. But it also suggests
the opposite; either that God should not be worshiped at all, or
that both altars are evil. Jouhandeau preserves this ambiguity
even at the end of the book. The two go to mass together, and,
true to a painterly tradition, "the Sun one moment came to visit
us, after the communion, covering with its golden light only
Elise, transfigured" (199), but Marcel refuses to make his communion and that night a moon beam illuminates his face in bed,
making him seem the image of the destroyed portrait.

As Jean Gaulmier has said, Jouhandeau's major preoccupation is the relation between man and God, or at least man's idea
of God. In this he is typical of his generation: Gide, Mauriac,
Claudel, Henri Bosco shared this preoccupation. But Jouhandeau's attitude is unique, Nietzschean in a peculiar sense. If God
exists, man's attitude toward him should be a declaration of
independence, a preference for the creature over the unjust
Creator; man can thus reduce God to solitude, expel him from
among men and so create true human fraternity. "If man is
God's favored creature, and if he says no to God, then God is
vanquished!"[3] In the Danon interviews, Jouhandeau unabashedly describes his concupiscent reveries on the person of
Jesus as a stage in his homosexuality; for him, such love, far
from being guilty, is admirable as an effort at humanizing God.
"I am love as God is love." A revolt much like that of Pro-

3. Danon, p. 34.

metheus, or of Lautréamont's *Maldoror*, except that Jouhandeau emphasizes not competition between man and God, but the substitution of the human capacity to love for divine love. Yet Jouhandeau is unwilling to deny the existence of God, or to ignore him, because only that existence makes possible the notion of "sin," of the human choice to live in Hell. But Hell is then defined, not as a place of torment and punishment, but in the classical manner; it is where man works out his destiny.

"So I now know what is the mystery of J. St.'s love for me and of mine for him; thanks to the mirage he created between us, I caught myself once and for all, in this world, such as I shall be in the Next, such as I am definitively, absolutely; I contemplated myself in my 'Place,' unique, judged, in that place reserved for me, and in the sovereign attitude destined for me for all eternity at the antipodes of God; I have seen myself in Hell." This exceptionally long, rhythmic, anaphoric sentence concludes *Chronique d'une passion.* For Jouhandeau, passion is the pretext for a contemplation which is essentially linguistic; the passion gives rise, immediately and inevitably, to the chronicle of the passion. As he verbalizes his experience, he turns that Passion into an experience of self-knowledge, or at least self-examination. The object of the chronicle, and of the passion, becomes one of knowing who I am, of discovering identity. This should not be seen as egotistical; Jouhandeau's self-portrait is not flattering and does not claim to be exemplary. Here, indeed, he says that his final position is in Hell. But what is Hell? The antipodes of God, but God in this novel is He who demands the sacrifice of the broken heart, who prefers lust to love. The moral judgment of *Chronique* finally remains ironic and ambivalent. If passion immediately becomes an object of language for Jouhandeau, it is not because of any desire to make money or to display himself, though certainly Jouhandeau welcomes money and enjoys washing his tattered linen in public (in *Chroniques maritales,* he constantly complains of the neglected state of his intimate wardrobe—one of Elise's subtle forms of torture). The strong drive toward confession which leads to his many pages of diaries, essays, novels, an immense production constituting one of the most prolific efforts at autobiography since Henri Amiel, and which creates a play of multiple, complex facets and texts on the self, stems primarily from the awareness that words provide a means to manipulate and judge the self ironically, to preserve ambivalence and thus eventually achieve dignity and self-respect. It is this awareness which leads him to write a very artful, indeed artificial style.

The autobiographical *Chronique* is peppered with the devices of oratory: frequent rhetorical questions and repetition which is most often anaphoric, though he also uses anadiplosis. He plays with assonance and alliteration and imports into prose the license of poetic word order; adverbial prepositional modifiers are placed before the subject, not after the verb. He delights in inversions, prefers putting *jamais* at the beginning of a proposition as in "et jamais le pittoresque ne manque ni dans ce piège l'occasion de se rompre le cou" ("and never has the picturesque been lacking, nor, in this trap, the chance of breaking one's neck"), a typical Jouhandeau sentence where a highly artificial word order culminates in a rather popular metaphor. Ellipsis is frequent; particularly, the reader must often supply subject and verb, and he enjoys complicating the reader's task of tracing antecedents to pronouns, not only separating them widely but introducing other pronouns of the same gender and number but of different antecedents in between. In another archaic affectation, he uses the question mark, as did Balzac, to indicate the dubitative or optative rather than the interrogative. All these devices make the reader attentive, annoyed, and distantly amused.

He doubles adjectives, nouns, and even verbs—not, however, in order to underline by repeating or to make his meaning more precise. Rather, the doubling serves to change the affective level, introducing words which vary in tone and thereby complicate the reader's reactions, obliterating emotional and moral categories. The language is an artificial mask, just as Elise is an actress throughout the novel, just as Marcel states his identity by incessant recourse to metaphor. Indeed, many of the propositions of the text are stated metaphorically, the reader must "translate" to discover what is being said, and the metaphor imposes on the discourse a tonal variety that alters the discourse's value, making it ironic. If action becomes metaphor, at the same time abstraction becomes ideal in the Platonic sense, where only the ideal possesses true reality. Everything else is a play of shifting, kaleidoscopic mirrors. *Passion* and *Amour* are capitalized; in the case of *Passion,* the word creates a sacrilegious confusion between homosexual love and Christ's suffering on the cross (just as elsewhere he took his title from the Quietist *Du pur amour* to describe a homosexual affair). Yet the only objects of devotion not destroyed by metaphor and the ambivalence of stylistic irony are *Amour* and *Passion.*

The very organization of the text serves by its movement to complicate the questions, to multiply the reactions. Jouhandeau has recourse to brief paragraphs, one or several sentences long, often typographically set apart by blank intervals. There is a kind of movement forward from paragraph to paragraph, but each also offers a multiplicity of perspectives and meditations on the event or experience. The paragraphs have a common concern, but otherwise their relation is elliptical and nonsequential; the place from which the object is seen shifts from paragraph to paragraph. Both style and structure multiply the perspectives on the self. Because of these multiple perspectives, even the moral import of Jouhandeau's self-analyses is ironic, both within given works and when one work is compared to another. In the *Essai sur moi-même,* he quotes Fr. Jean Mauriac, the novelist's brother, as saying of him: "M. Jouhandeau cultivates unknowingly a false identity, that of M. Godeau who on the sly supplants in him his own, but the true Jouhandeau is he who is not secure in the state of sin, while the other struts back and forth on a stage with inferno for scenery."[4] But can one be so sure which identity is central? Jouhandeau multiples the autobiographical stances (Juste, Godeau, Théophile, Jouhandeau in the *Essai sur moi-même* or the *Mémorial,* Don Juan in the *Carnets de Don Juan*), and certainly the "real self," whatever it may be, must at the very least be some combination of all these hypotheses. In the *Essai sur moi-même* he describes literary creation as "the efforts man undertakes to create a language for himself" (48) and as he creates a language he necessarily creates a personage. Jouhandeau has chosen to create several languages, a multiplicity of

4. *Essai sur moi-même* (Paris: Gallimard, 1947), p. 76.

personages, a stylistic play behind which any single person can be conceived only as the product of the interplay of these multiple personages.

Sartre is reported to have said of Jouhandeau, "It's not all that grave a matter, having some fun in your room with a young friend."[5] Perhaps so, but Jouhandeau is less concerned with homosexual acts in themselves than with the relation of those acts to the divine and to the conjugal. Jouhandeau has maintained since his youth a personal, direct debate with God (though the Divine Interlocutor may have changed form and substance with the years) and from the time of his marriage on, a debate with Elise, who, as Cabanis says (68), is a figure of Minerva and not of Venus. He has had to find his way—his moral grandeur and his style of life—among these three points of reference: the homosexual, the divine, the conjugal. In that quest, everyone is intensely aware of the harm he can do to others and the self—and within this potential for corruption and pain the characters achieve a stance of dignity and of humanism. Their awareness is complete; the vision, though the Chronicle of the Passion is disastrous and ends with numbing tragedy, is finally a comic vision where the dignity achieved by and through style compensates for the disaster. Autobiography here is creative thanks to a willed and wise exploration of the artifices of language.

In a brilliant essay on Gide, Claude-Edmonde Magny concludes, about the *Faux-monnayeurs,* that the point of the novel is that "there is no non-particular vision of the world"; the novel expresses "man's incapacity to achieve any absolutely impartial view of reality. . . . By thus underlining at the same time the partiality inherent in any point of view, even the novelist's, and the equal legitimacy of all points of view, Gide has drawn that 'figure of transcendence,' the hieroglyphic of the absurd which constitutes being, which all Jaspers's work shows to be both indispensable and impossible for philosophy."[6] Jouhandeau surely

5. Cabanis, p. 64.
6. Claude-Edmonde Magny, *Histoire du roman français* (Paris: Seuil, 1950), pp. 277–78.

aims at the same end Magny ascribes to Gide, but to achieve it he uses the first-person autobiographical narrative in a quite different way from Gide in *L'immoraliste*. First, he lets both his protagonists act, speak, and judge; Elise, as much as Marcel, proposes, provokes, condemns. Other characters also intervene to speak and judge, and though their appearance may be episodic, their statements are often treated as oracular. The priest, the friend at the end of the novel, the visitors who behold the portrait, all pronounce fundamental and even eternal verities, with prescience and acute sensitivity. Jouhandeau also uses *sententiae* and quotations from the Bible to the same end; the moral tradition offers judgments which possess validity. But always these judgments are only partly valid, represent a "surprise" to the narrator (or reader), who reacts to that surprise unwillingly and with incomplete acceptance. The "surprise" with its ensuing moral ambivalence is also created by the turn the action takes; a story which should lead to the divorce of the protagonists instead leads to their semi-reconciliation. Even there, the "double symbolic ending" of the sun's ray on Elise at mass, the moon's ray on Marcel in bed, returns to ambivalence. Finally the style, in imposing a humorous reading on even the most serious propositions, underlines and echoes this ambivalence. Jouhandeau's is the world of Jaspers, but treated in a highly comic vein, where the philosophical ambivalence about the perception of reality, the revelation of the multiplicity of perspectives, becomes a rich and highly amusing moral ambivalence about the ethical stance of the self, where writing becomes a means of playing various personae, wearing various masks, of learning who one is rather than knowing who one is. And where learning requires suspending moral judgment—and remaining witty. So he manages to write of homosexuality in the high style without bathos.

George H. Bauer

Sartre's Homo/Textuality: Eating / The Other

> To eat is to appropriate by destruction; it is at the same time to be filled up with a certain being. . . . When we eat, we do not limit ourselves to *knowing* certain qualities of this being through taste; by tasting them we appropriate them. Taste is assimilation. . . . The synthetic intuition of food is in itself an assimilative destruction. It reveals to me the being which I am going to make my flesh. Henceforth, what I accept or what I reject with disgust is the very being of that existent, or if you prefer, the totality of the food proposes to me a certain mode of being of the being which I accept or refuse. . . .
>
> It is not a matter of indifference whether we like oysters or clams, snails or shrimp, if only we know how to unravel the existential signification of these foods. Generally speaking there is no irreducible taste or inclination. They all represent a certain appropriate choice of being.
>
> —*L'être et le néant*

One of the great eater/readers in Sartre's work is the Self-Taught Man of *La nausée.* His existence shifts between the café and the library, but in both of these ceremonial places this humanist, whose name like that of the narrator in Proust, is incomplete, gobbles and assimilates flesh and text in order to be with and possess men. Ogier (*O chier*—the eye that eats the excremental text-object) P . . . , like his name, remains unfinished in his reading/eating of other men. He is linked in his sexual tastes to several other Sartrean men and boys through his eating, his reading, and the act of writing. In this essay I will focus on just three of these males: Mr. P . . . , Daniel Sereno a/k/a Lalique of *Les chemins de la liberté,* and Jean Genet.

Mr. P . . . 's casual acquaintance with Roquentin is the result of their shared experience of days spent in reading, note-taking, and writing in the library. He has invited the well-traveled bachelor to share lunch with him following a visit to Roquentin's room for a viewing of postcards, debris from years of what he thinks of as adventure. In the Maison Bottanet (*cuisine bourgeoise*), Mr. P . . . forces food on the other man, delighted to have the other to replace the book with which he normally shares his meals. "I usually come here with a book, even though it's against doctor's orders: one eats too quickly and doesn't chew. But I have a stomach like an ostrich, I can swallow anything. During the winter of 1917, when I was a prisoner, the food was so bad that everyone got ill" (*N*, 105).[1] Indeed his eating parallels his reading. His library enterprise has been discovered by Roquentin some time before: Mr. P . . . is devouring the menu of catalogued books alphabetically from A to Z. His secret pleasure, however, is no longer his secret. Roquentin knows. While searching for the name of the author of a book Mr. P . . . has read on Segovia, "Na . . . No . . . Nod . . . ," he is deflated by the revelation that the other has seen that he has only reached Lavergne. Only L. N is impossible. At first reduced to silence and the pack of travel images before him, he suddenly confesses that his reading, his self-instruction, is a necessary prelude to being permitted to join a group of professors and students who annually cruise the Near East. The end of reading, for him, is to make new acquaintances in the hope that something unexpected will happen, an adventure, a real trip in the company of other men.

Roquentin, in this eating experience, clearly has no choice. From a fixed menu he will be served oysters, chicken in a thick gravy, and Camembert cheese—all extra; Mr. P . . . gets radishes and spiced beef, but of course he has manly conversation and men's ideas to chew. As he munches his radishes, Roquentin

---

1. Page references for all subsequent quotations from Sartre's works will be given in parentheses immediately following the quotation. *Nausea*, trans. Lloyd Alexander (New York: New Directions, 1964); *Age of Reason*, trans. Eric Sutton (New York: Vintage, 1973); *The Reprieve*, trans. Eric Sutton (New York: Vintage, 1973); *Troubled Sleep*, tr. Gerard Hopkins (New York: Bantam, 1950); *Being and Nothingness*, trans. Hazel Barnes (New York: Philosophical Library, 1956); *Saint Genet: Actor and Martyr*, trans. Bernard Frechtman (New York, Toronto, and London: George Braziller, 1963); *Situations III* (Paris: Gallimard, 1949). The epigraph is from *Being and Nothingness*, pp. 614–15.

attempts to converse, inquiring as to whether he has straightened out his troubles, the troubles with the Corsican in the library. What troubles? The issue is skirted as radishes rapidly disappear well before the arrival of the other's oysters. Too close. The topic turns to art. Mr. P . . . confesses that aesthetic pleasure is foreign to him. "What I regret is not so much being deprived of a certain taste, but rather that a whole branch of human activity is foreign to me. . . . Yet I am a man and *men* have painted those pictures" (*N,* 108). Mr. P . . . moves to the Beautiful; suddenly he produces a black leather notebook (many blank pages, some penciling, and a few red ink jottings) which he spreads flat on the tablecloth. It contains notes, his maxims, his illuminations, his tentative excretions. His fear, as always, is that they are already in someone else. The one he shares with Roquentin he discovers is—*in* Renan. Sucking his pencil he requests the exact passage and writes, in pencil, the man's name below. "I have come upon Renan! I wrote the name in pencil, but this evening I'll go over it in red ink" (*N,* 109). Stuffing the treasured object away, he returns to silence and eating. He will wait for solitude to transform the excremental into red jelly-text. "But this is a delusion: he imagines that the objects he destroys or disperses *change into his own substance* as food changes into the substance of the one who consumes it. The fact is that they do not, for there is no assimilation here" (*SG,* 262).

The ensuing conversation gives Roquentin the opportunity to express his thoughts on eating with Mr. P . . . ; the laugh is that men eat and drink to preserve their existence but that there is no reason for existing. Mr. P . . . 's rejoinder is that there is after all humanity. In his humanism, the love of men, of man, is the abstract goal. He returns to his prison experience. He does not believe in God; he continues: "But, in the internment camp, I learned to believe in men" (*N,* 114). Two hundred men jammed together: "I don't know how to explain it, Monsieur. All those men were there, you could hardly see them but you could feel them against you, you could hear the sound of their breathing. . . . I almost fainted: then I felt that I loved these men like brothers, I wanted to embrace all of them." Disgust, cold chicken, congealed grease of gravy, the feeling of being. Mr. P . . . continues his itinerary of love of men. First the Mass, a communion of souls (Eating the other together); a remarkable organist; inserting himself in the funeral procession of some unknown: "Whenever I saw men together I would insert myself into their group" (*N,* 115). The next step on the road is joining the Socialist Party, to be with men. "All men are my friends. When I go to the office in the morning, in front of me, behind me, there are other men going to work. I see them, if I dared I would smile at them, I think that I am a Socialist, that all of them are my life's goal, the goal of my efforts, and that they don't know it yet" (*N,* 116). Mr. P . . . gathers that Roquentin does not share his position. He quickly suggests that Roquentin does the same thing in his own way through writing, writing to be with other men. No. Why write then? I don't know. Misanthropy? No. Roquentin's refusal is a refusal to be eaten. He thinks to himself:

> There is a race of beings, limited and headstrong, who lose to him every time: he digests all their violences and their worst excesses; he makes a white frothy lymph of them. He has digested anti-intellectualism, Manicheism, mysticism, pessimism, anarchy and egotism: they are nothing more than stages, unfinished thoughts which find their justification in him. Misanthropy also has its place in the concert: it is only a dissonance necessary to the harmony of the whole. The misanthrope is a man: therefore the humanist must be misanthropic to a certain extent. But he must be a scientist as well to have learned how to water down his hatred, and hate men only to love them better afterwards. I don't want to be integrated, I don't want my good red blood to go and fatten this lymphatic beast. [*N,* 118]

Love. Love. Mr. P . . . eats, reads, and loves all men. The cheese course. Nausea. Roquentin can't, won't eat it. Suddenly he abandons the scene, watched by everyone. Devoured by their eyes, he sees a young woman's mouth as a chicken's ass; no one is eating or talking; no dessert for Mr. P . . . , appetites are gone. Roquentin, threatened from the rear as he flees, turns to give these eaters one hard look at his face before disappearing as a *crab* running backwards from the Maison Bottanet, *cuisine bourgeoise.*

Disenchanted with his project of writing a biography of the Marquis de Rollebon, Roquentin prepares to leave Mudcity. One last trip to the library. There he sees Mr. P... arrive with his usual small white package, containing, Roquentin imagines, the usual fare of a slice of white bread and a piece of chocolate (a bar, as we know, of Gala Peter). Beside these edibles Mr. P... places an illustrated book. This is goodbye, Roquentin reflects: "Tomorrow evening, the evening after tomorrow, and all the following evenings he will return to read at this table, eating his bread and chocolate, he will patiently keep on with his rat's nibbling, he will read the works of Nabaud, Naudeau, Nodier, Nys, interrupting himself from time to time to jot down a maxim in his notebook" (N, 162). But Roquentin will not be eating, reading, or writing. Suddenly it happens. Two boys sit down on either side of Mr. P... and begin looking through the dictionaries they have chosen. Whispers. Mr. P... and the boys are talking, but now all eyes in the library watch. "The boy is drinking in his words" (N, 164). Roquentin moves to extricate Mr. P... from the situation but is interrupted by an irritated glance, followed by silence. Whispers again, then dead silence. The small white hand of one of the boys is exposed on the table before the lover of men. "It was resting on its back, relaxed, soft and sensual, it had the indolent nudity of a woman sunning herself after bathing. A brown hairy object approached it, hesitant. It was a thick finger, yellowed by tobacco; inside this hand it had all the grossness of a male sex organ. It stopped for an instant, rigid, pointing at the fragile palm, then suddenly, it timidly began to stroke it... the finger passed slowly, humbly, over the inert flesh, barely grazing it, without daring to put any weight on it: you might have thought it was conscious of its ugliness" (N, 165). A cough, a warning from Roquentin, does not penetrate the ecstatic smile of Mr. P... whose eyes are closed. The troubles with the Corsican are clear now. This Napoleonic librarian who has carefully monitored the forbidden books of this place shifts his role from defending youth from Gide, Diderot, and Baudelaire to saving them from Mr. P..., the humanist homosexual in the flesh.

The sequence eating/reading is broken. Mr. P... who skips lunch to read, whose most memorable feature is his hand, a fat white worm bringing disgust to Roquentin as he finds the flaccid object in his own, has been transformed into that thick, hairy yellowed organ. He has become that rigid caressing ugly thing, only to find in it his destruction. The Corsican smashes him in the face. Mr. P . . . gropes for his package, bread and Gala Peter, with his left hand; the right wipes the blood running from his nose. Roquentin comes to his aid as the reader/eater is expelled from the library, from boys and men, from loving man. Roquentin's aid results in the violent question from the Corsican: "Est-ce que vous êtes une tante, vous aussi?" (Are *you* a fairy too?—*N*, 168). The *tante* will eat no more books there, he can only cling to his bread and Gala Peter. The unfinished Mr. P . . . is finished. His little black leather notebook of maxims will remain incomplete. Coitus interruptus. The meal unfinished. No assimilation. No excretion. But what is clear is that Ogier P . . . embodies Sartre's observation: "The homosexual attempt can be regarded, despite everything, as an effort to enter into communication with other men" (*SG*, 136). Self-instruction in Ogier's case, however pathetic, had as its goal being with other men. How delicious, through one's reading, one's writing, to be transformed into an object to be taken in other men's mouths, to be permitted to cruise the Near East in their company. But P . . . 's rigidity in sexual *being* fails as surely as Antoine Roquentin's temptation to *be* through writing fails. That bar of Gala Peter and that terrible yellowed organ offending bourgeois morality join Genet's tube of vaseline in its negative poetic being, demonstrating the preposterous outcome of masturbatory humanism and its solitary love of man when it is coupled with the desire to eat to *be*.

In *Les chemins de la liberté*, Daniel/Danielle Sereno, too, is concerned with eating and being eaten. He seeks the tranquillity indicated by his name, permanence of being, of being named. His time is spent in a tension between his gourmet savoring and deconstructing the images projected by others and controlling the gobbling activity of their eyes when they are turned on him. Narcissism is his first step, but in that act of scrutinizing himself before the mirror, he necessarily rejects the reflected image of his own beauty. Evil and ugliness tempt him as he masochistically lops off the head of a pimple in an attempt to disfigure himself. All those eyes that are eating him must be forced to ingest the unpalatable dish he prepares. In this enterprise of self-destruction he will attempt to reach that image in the mirror by drowning his beloved cats; when that fails he dreams of carving his own statue of monstrous dimensions by castrating himself for all to see in the bloody splendor of flesh become thing. Unable to perform this act of self-destruction, he returns to the monstrosity of homosexuality. Permanent pain can be inflicted, he hopes, by marrying his friend's pregnant mistress and thus to achieve a permanent bleeding wound in the presence of the soft flabbiness of hated female flesh and pro-creation. He has succumbed to the temptation of his masculine love before, but he delights in denying himself the furtive pleasure of such activity. He convinces himself that he will just peek in on The Fair and watch the games, to observe "the maneuvers of perverts on the trail," to savor "those half-baked little louts, brutal, coarse, with raucous voices, and a sly cunning all their own, on the look-out for ten francs and a dinner" (*AR*, 164). Eating to eat. Daniel is determined to spoil their pleasure by his detached observation of sexual games.

He is drawn to the place with its turbid light the color of an egg yolk, reminded of a past nausea experienced on a boat to Palermo—a return to "the dull, rhythmic thud of crankshafts" (*AR*, 165) and the yellow light of an empty engine room. "A prick is never the flesh of which it is composed but its power of penetration, its mineral hardness. It is a drill, a pile driver, it will be a dagger, a 'torture machine'" (*SG*, 107). To the accompaniment of pulsing blows falling rhythmically on the leather stomach of the wooden form of a Negro boxer—young toughs measuring the strength of their thrusting fists—Daniel as detached observer/eater is sucked into the machine. A game of chance is being played by a hungry young man who maneuvers a metal crane, trying to pick up some treasure—a flashlight, a Kodak—that tempts him in its inaccessibility on the pile of candies behind the glass. What he gets for his money is only "multicolored sweets that looked as mean and uninviting as dried beans" (*AR*, 166). The lean, hungry look draws Daniel to him; he aches to touch this young Narcissus's arm in order to possess him in his need to eat, in his poverty. Interrupted in this enterprise by the entry of an old queen, he shifts his role to the threatening gaze; he'll pretend to be a member of the vice squad. What he rejects sexually in the old man is his flesh, his plump hips, his fleshy cheeks: "Female flesh as lush as dough" (*AR*, 166). As the old man "licks his thin lips," he encounters Daniel's terrible look. "What a moment! Daniel enjoyed it in anticipation, he devoured with magisterial gaze, his victim's delicate, lined face, his hands shook, and his joy would have been complete had his throat not been so dry; indeed he was agonizingly thirsty" (*AR*, 170). But just then Daniel hears behind him the voice of one of his gaunt, hungry young men: "Monsieur Lalique." His pseudonym calls our attention to the conflict in his homosexual enterprise. He would be both transparent and opaque in these games. Quickly turning around, he discovers another young boy whose catlike leanness had attracted him, only to find not muscle but disgusting fat and the smell of excessive brilliantine. Bobby has lost his job. He is hungry again. "I haven't had anything to eat since the day before yesterday" (*AR*, 174), he tells Monsieur Lalique. The other, the old gentleman in the corset, is freed as he recognizes the "freemasonry of the urinal." Bobby is living with his thin friend, Ralph; he gets his cash (he can eat again), but not without having revealed their current address. It begins again. Daniel abandons the fleshy Bobby, the fleshy old man and the hungry young man, but not before giving the crane game a try. Tempted by a pair of binoculars he had not seen before, Daniel plays: "The crane dropped its claws and began clumsily to rake about in the pile of candy. Daniel picked up five or six in the hollow of his hand and ate them" (*AR*, 175).

That old taste is back again. Out into the street, "Daniel was devoured by thirst, but he would not drink; die, then! die of thirst!" (*AR*, 175). But before he succumbs to his thirst, he chances on his friend Mathieu's "disciple," Boris Serguine as the young man attempts a Gidean theft of a book. "Let us note in passing the resemblance of the universe of theft to that of homosexuality" (*SG*, 281). Here it is not a guide to Algeria, as in Gide, but a dictionary of slang that attracts the young handsome Boris. Before undertaking his theft he stops to weigh himself and is aghast to discover that he has put on weight. Relieved to find that it was only his portfolio, he sets out to steal the seven-hundred-page *Dictionnaire historique et étymologique de la langue verte et des argots depuis le XIVe siècle jusqu'à l'époque contemporaine.* Idly paging the object of his desire, he falls on the entry "A man for; to be inclined towards. A phrase now in fairly common use. Example 'The parson was no end of a man for.' Render: The parson was much inclined towards.... 'A man for men' or 'A man's man' is also used for 'invert'" (*AR,* 186). Sartre's substitution of this book for Gide's guide to Algeria should be related to Sartre's characterization of argot as a language of males: "in its words and syntax and by virtue of its whole semantic content, the permanent practice of rape" (*SG,* 288–89). Argot and the male vocal organs are intimately linked in Sartre's vision of the homosexual Genet; it is in this theft, this appropriation and reading that Daniel catches Boris. He voices the silent question, "Are you a man's man, Serguine?" (*AR,* 186). Of course not, Daniel reassures him, they are soft, Boris is quick and hard. Daniel Sereno (Lalique) proposes private philosophy lessons from Mathieu's disciple in philosophy. Boris could be very strict with his lazy pupil. But it is theft, not "philosophy lessons" that preoccupies Boris. He gets the book, not the man.

What interests us here is Serguine's eye as it falls on Sereno-Lalique in his careful elegance: "In point of fact, there was, in the almost pink tweed suit, the linen shirt and yellow tie, a calculated bravado that rather shocked Boris. Boris liked a sober, slightly casual elegance. None the less, the total effect was irreproachable, though rather lusciously suggestive of *fresh butter*" (*AR,* 187, my emphasis). Daniel as dandy is delicious fresh butter.

Daniel gives in to his "thirst." Bobby knows (but he is a woman). Ralph knows. Mathieu doesn't. The eye that eats, the eye that reads, the eye that counts is the man Mathieu, Marcelle's lover, Daniel's "friend." Daniel is butter, not Lalique. The hard opaqueness of glass escapes him even in the momentary homosexual tryst with tough, lean, muscular Ralph. What Daniel seeks is the permanence of the name homosexual. "The word strikes against its object like a crystal falling into a supersaturated solution. The solution immediately crystallizes, enclosing the word inside itself" (*SG,* 39–40). This is Daniel's desire. Daniel delights in naming others "homo." What he wants is the name for himself. Sartre might well be speaking of his Daniel at The Fair when he observes in *Saint-Genet* the habit of homosexuals who mark others with the name: "I met an old queen..... But the homosexual never thinks of himself when someone is branded in his presence with the name *homosexual*. His relationship to homosexuals is univocal. He is *the one* who receives with horror the name homosexual. It is not one quality among others; it is a destiny, a peculiar flaw of his being. *Elsewhere* there is a category of comic, shady people whom he jokes about with 'straights,' namely the queers. His sexual tastes will doubtless lead him to enter into relationships with this suspect category, but he would like to make use of them without being likened to them" (*SG*, 41). The Fair. The "dirty" encounter with Ralph. What counts is to force the terrible name into the mouth of Mathieu. He goes to him, announces that he is going to marry Marcelle, giving his name to the child resulting from Mathieu's flowering penis: "If it's a boy we'll call him Mathieu" (*AR*, 388). Mathieu Sereno. A marvelous coupling of names. Then the thrust, the confession, "I am a homosexual." "Now that there's someone who *knows*, I—I shall perhaps succeed in believing it" (*AR*, 390). Mathieu's knowing will produce the sense of shame he needs, the shame that will make him feel homosexual. As he tells Mathieu, "I am ashamed of being a homosexual *because I am a homosexual.* . . . All inverts are ashamed of being so, it's part of their make-up" (*AR*, 393). Drinking together, he confesses the delicious truth to make it true. Then the rum is gone. Come have another drink with me at Clarisse's. Mathieu refuses. "I must drink," replies Daniel and leaves.

The satisfaction with the forced naming, of the acceptance of the word, proves to be as evanescent as his sex with Ralph. The butter is still butter. The word in conversation disappears too quickly. Daniel now moves to accept his name, his first name, in order to achieve the permanence, the hardness of *being* he requires: not Lalique—object of opaque glass; not Sereno—the tranquil, the night watchman; but Daniel—God is my judge. Theft, homosexuality, inverted sainthood. He must be seen by the All-seeing Eye to achieve being. The look of God is the look of Medusa. Daniel parallels Sartre's Genet in the "Medusa complex" of petrification. He will place his sin in the eye, in the mouth of God—a hard thing to be sucked. Daniel, like a saint, will attempt to eternalize himself by his destruction, not in the failed castration whose object was the gaze of other men but by

placing his butter-dandy, candy being in the mouth of God, that
perfect "consumer." "In the case of food, fullness of being
emerges at the moment it melts in a mouth and releases its
flavor; moment of death and life, paradox of the instant: though
still objective, the taste is at the same time a subjectivity. And in a
like manner with regard to the saint, who is *sucked by God like a
piece of candy* and feels himself deliciously melting into an infinite
mouth" (*SG,* 196, my emphasis). And that being in the flesh, that
sin of flesh, he would place in God's mouth in the confession of
his homosexuality. He would become a recumbent tomb figure,
an art object, a sculpture seen by God as a thing made through
the word—not an object created through his own suicidal carving of self-castration. But, Daniel being eaten and devoured,
unlike Mr. P . . . eating and devouring, produces a text which he
will require Mathieu to consume. Carefully written, then re-
copied, his conversion-consumption, is squeezed into seven
pages—a wafer, a candy-to-be-sucked, a letter he hopes will be
read and reread, savored in the mouth of the other: only real
when it comes to exist for others. The word to be sucked, to be
eaten, is all. He speaks mockingly of God made man, hanging on
the cross, "open-mouthed," a carp on the cross. He reflects on
the power of the word. He has seen but cannot see himself. "I
seem to be a sort of *flabby mass* in which words are engulfed; no
sooner do I name myself than what is named is merged in him
who names, and one gets no farther (*et tout est remis en question*)"
(*R,* 405, my emphasis). It is through the hatred of the other—his
look, his eating—that Daniel hopes to reach himself, to attain
being. His delight is that God eats, penetrates, him. He recounts
with delectation the sensation of being seen (possessed) from the
rear. The look makes him feel penetrated and yet opaque; like
Mallarmé's Poe he has been taken, changed unto himself. "I am
infinite and infinitely guilty. But I *am.* Before God and before
men, I *am. Ecce homo*" (*R,* 407). "Homo! God sees us. God eats
us. He *reads* in our hearts" (*R,* 408, my emphasis).

Even in this projected reading/eating, something is lacking.
Ironically his text written for the ages—the letter of his
homosexuality in the mouth—is crumpled and thrown out the
window of the train by Mathieu. His homo-textuality will no
more survive than will the superiority of the elite of Mudcity as

official portraits enshrined in the museum. They too melt before the look of Roquentin and are reduced to ashes. Neither Roquentin or Mathieu will hold them in the mouth, sucking their hardness as they melt into substance of being. Matthew refuses to read and reread the Scripture of homo/textual guilt.

The butter problem is still there. Daniel/Danielle's salvation will lie in historical events. The coming of the Germans is the arrival of the thief, the homosexual, and the inversion through which Daniel will seek to be seduced by these new blond gods. He alone remains in the violated city. They are the new sovereigns. He is the new vassal. In his essay on "What is a Collaborator?" (*Situations III*, 43–62), Sartre comments on the charm and seduction of these lovers of French culture. They are the founders of a new love, a new feudal-sexual regime. The collaborator-homosexual in his hatred of heterosexuality, of reciprocity, of a society from which he is excluded, finds his shame glorified by being violated by these conquerors who violate the bourgeois city of heterosexual couples. The collaborator in this essay, Genet, and Daniel will seek anal intercourse with new masters of their own making. Daniel dreams of dropping his trousers before the bourgeois couple hidden behind the windows of an empty Paris. He would turn his ass to that eating look falling from the heterosexual gaze of apartments above, but finds only complete detachment on the part of the respectable gentlemen who make their wives move from the French windows. At The Fair, Daniel sticks his tongue out at the old queen, now he substitutes the flesh of his ass as would-be affront. Still no takers, no eater/penetrator/possessor. But the Germans are coming into Paris. In Genet, Sartre characterizes the burglar entering an apartment in sexual terms: "If all goes well, one *enters a man*, for the gaping, defenseless apartment, naked and paralysed, is a man. It reflects a person, his tastes, his ways, his vices" (*SG*, 260, his emphasis). Here they come. He alone is there to welcome them. "Boldly he returned their stare, taking his fill of their blond hair, of their sun-tanned faces in which eyes showed like glacier lakes, their narrow waists, the unbelievable length of their muscular thighs" (*TS*, 80–81). Daniel's smile (the vassal's) at the new sovereign, his passive stance at this violation elicits a gift of English cigarettes thrown from one of the bare-armed tankers (power of penetration, giver of gifts, mineral hardness, pile-driver, pulsating engine, dagger, torture-machine, tank turret and 100 mm. gun). Butter and guns. "So tightly did Daniel clasp it that he could feel the cigarettes snap beneath his fingers. He was still smiling. An intolerable, delicious thrill mounted in him from his thighs to his temples; he no longer saw very clearly; panting, he said: 'Just like butter—they are entering Paris just like a knife through butter'" (*TS*, 81). Daniel shifts from placing himself in the mouth of God to the sexual devouring being devoured by these thieves, these conquerors, these lovers of things French: "They have come here with the intention to do Evil (*Mal*) to us, the Reign of Evil [*Règne du Mal(e)*] begins. What joy! He longed to be a woman so that he might load them with flowers" (*TS*, 81). Oh the flowering penis! "Pas plus d'armistice que du beurre aux fesses," comments one of the French soldiers at the Front in one of the last lines preceding the episode of Daniel and the entry of the Germans into French cuisine and culture. The vocabulary of the scene that follows echoes and re-echoes the desire that Daniel houses, but for the soldiers (heterosexual fathers of families) it is sexual terror: "Mon cul. Mon cul. Enculé. Enculés. Il nous a traités d'enculés." And whether it is their own troops or the Germans it is the same. Daniel's openness—his embrace—will be a means of possessing the possessors. Unlike the French soldiers, he receives them willingly, *openly*. Their flesh is iron. He will perhaps find his permanent wound at last and experience the same sensation as Ivich, Mathieu's little friend, who stabs her hand: "It's a very agreeable sensation. My hand felt like a pat of butter" (*AR*, 219).

Les chemins de la liberté remains unfinished. Daniel's relation with the Nazis, his collaboration exists only in outline, but we can be sure that, like Moulu (the soft male, the molded one), he didn't lack for gilt-tipped cigarettes, for bread, or for Gala Peter. Daniel, the giver of gifts to hungry young males, was undoubtedly destined to become the receiver of gifts in the *Règne du Mal(e)*.[2]

2. I will not analyze here the relations between the young poet, Philippe Grésigne, and Daniel. Clearly, here, too, Daniel will attempt to convert the young man, stepson of a general (à la Baudelaire) to collaboration and homosexuality

Mr. P . . . and Daniel end inevitably in the "fiction" of Sartre's Genet. I think we can easily recognize Daniel, for instance, when Sartre recounts the steps Genet has taken along the path of eating and homosexuality, of reading, of thievery and writing: Daniel, Ralph, Mathieu, God, Matthew. "He had tried everything, he had attempted to make himself be reflected by a mirror, by the eyes of a lover, by those of the beloved, to have himself possessed by the Other, by himself as Other: each undertaking is a failure. Recourse to art is his final attempt" (*SG*, 489–90). The sexual eatings of the other—the eyes (look), the mouth (eating, reading)—now fellatio, obviously; anal intercourse in which that other mouth voraciously devours; and yes, even masturbation, the frustrated eating of the self—all these that are only implied in Mr. P . . . and Daniel are now voiced in Genet. When Sartre has the good fortune to fall on Genet, the Narcissus, the thief, the homosexual, the writer, he is able to pull together all these threads and speak openly of these cul-inary as-pects, but not as fiction of his own creation—only in the fiction of psycho-anal-ysis do they surface.

Onan and Narcissus. The first stage is the desire to derealize oneself through masturbation. Genet is seen by Sartre in this act to be attempting to be at one and the same time the criminal who

---

after having wrenched him from his desired suicide. Daniel's plan is obvious: take him home to his lair, slake his thirst, get him drunk, feed him the classic texts—those texts defended/protected by the Napoleonic Corsican librarian—from his private library (*L'enfer*). Daniel, the praying mantis of Sartre's Genet, will love, possess—not befriend—young Philippe. He is the first of his desperate, thin, hungry young men that he brings home to eat: "The mad loves of Genet the Victim are rejected friendships. Moreover, he knows this very well, and we have only to let him talk in order to understand how the praying mantis kills its males and eats them in order to absorb them into his own substance" (*SG*, 312). Philippe is, as Daniel proclaims, "My Beauty, My Destiny." The suicide-resurrection will provide Daniel with a dead child to be consumed; Philippe in the flesh will join that object in Daniel's collection: another dead portrait of lost children of his Mexican experience. This is Daniel's fierce young man in the flesh: "Every day Genet, too, causes the death of fierce young men. And their death imparts to him 'a power extracted from their beauty.' Coitus is a grafting. Genet, the praying mantis, devours his male. . . . Those fierce fellows will run into it with their heads down, and then they will become children who die prematurely, like Vergil's Marcellus or the child Septentrio" (*SG*, 129–30). "Tu Marcellus eris!" (*N*, 94).

rapes (steals) and the saint who lets herself be raped, as "both the consciousness that is curdling and the hand that is getting tired churning" (SG, 367). His narcissistic enterprise results in the characters of a solitary fiction far from the world of men and intercourse that he initially fears. These characters are food for his own consumption. "His characters are candies that melt in the mouth" (SG, 367). He cannot be a couple alone. It is a childish act: "Masturbation is the derealization of the world and the person masturbated as well. But this man who is eaten up by his own dream holds up by the virtue of his will" (SG, 368). What is required is the eater/reader/other. This need results in the *making* of poetry rather than *experiencing* it alone. He becomes a writer when he *makes,* in making he becomes an object for others.

But there is a curious ambiguity in this work in relation to the openings of the body, for it, the work made, comes from the mouth, the ejaculating penis, and the anus. "The work of the mind is an organic product. It smells of bowels and sperm and milk. If it at times emits an odor of violets, it does so in the manner of decaying meat that turns into a preserve [*confiture*]; when we poke it, the blood runs and we find ourselves in a belly, amidst gas bubbles and lumps of entrails" (SG, 449). For Genet (and for Sartre) the work of art is shit. In Sartre's essay on Wols, "Fingers and Non-Fingers," the artist is not the praying mantis that devours but a termite that eats his way through the world leaving behind the marvelous pile of excrement that is his termitary. Sartre emphasizes the fact that even though the bourgeois is repelled by the tongue of Marie Alacoque who eats and befouls her tongue, he is fundamentally "Rabelaisian": "He talks about purges and enemas while eating dessert and in his heart he merges the *sexual organs with those of excretion*" (SG, 246, my emphasis). There is a relation between intercourse and eating shit. "Coprophagy is probably not a widespread sexual vice, but the conjugal climate disposes people to it more or less everywhere. Amongst us, coitus does not differ much from the digestive functions; it prolongs them; the couple really tries to become a single animal that smells itself, broods over itself, sniffs at itself, touches itself with its eight groping paws and pursues in the dampness of the bed the sad dreams of absolute immanence" (SG, 246).

But Genet's end-product is a special brand. The bourgeois reader is readily drawn to Rabelais and Zola. The image Sartre uses returns us to the world of eating, of jams and jellies, the making of *confiture*. "It may be that his poetry is the art of making us eat shit, but it is also the art of dematerializing it. Excrement, vomit, stink: all this hardly shocks us in his work; read Zola's *La Terre* or *Pot-Bouille* and you will see the difference between thick, warm, odorous dung and the distinguished icy turds which Genet strews in his books and which resemble candied fruit" (*SG*, 398). But it is not shit-jelly, fart-pearl, spit-diamonds, it is forbidden *metamorphosis* that provokes our nausea. Genet is compared to Alexander Calder who transforms the mundane and the repellent into objects of beauty, not through the use of marble but through the use of bone, tin, and zinc. This excrement is produced to be eaten, yet, in a sense, is perfectly inedible. Sartre asserts that for Genet poetry is the art of using shit and making you eat it: "Genet's art is a mirage, a confidence trick, a pitfall. In order to make us eat shit he has to show it to us, from afar, as rose jam [*une confiture de rose*]" (*SG*, 498).

Sartre has one more trick up his sleeve in the game of eating and homosexuality. If I have insisted on Daniel as butter/Dandy/candy to be eaten, butter facilitating desired anal intercourse, by radically emphasizing what is only latent in *Les chemins de la liberté*, it is with full awareness that Daniel is unable to write, to transform himself into the objet d'art (*objet dard*) of butter that he might have become. Genet will *be* that object, but not butter. He *is* a tube of vaseline jelly, for Sartre. He becomes, in Sartre's fictional Genet, the object of scorn that is confiscated from him by the police, "shining with their gobs of spit, shimmering in the light of their gazes" (*SG*, 488). Genet is transformed—metamorphosis provoking nausea—into an inert sculpture indecently laid on a table, a thing, his thing, his homo-sexuality, a tool used in easing male love-making (best of all metallic container containing translucent, *indestructible* jelly/jam). It embodies a stellar multiplicity of images as an object-poem in the best tradition of surrealist poetry, a poetry of homosexual denial: "The child who was dripping with spit compared himself to a penis wet with sperm; and the tube which he uses to smear his penis with vaseline makes him think of a face sticky with slaver;

[the dream] of smearing the entire body of his lovers with vaseline, and 'their muscles bathe in that delicate transparence...'
Spit, sperm, vaseline: vitreous transparency which protects
bodies and makes them shimmer" (*SG*, 489). The tube of vaseline and the poem here become one, but it is shit. "Such is his
aesthetic purpose: to shit *himself* so as to appear on the table of
the just" (*SG*, 489). In this step beyond the dandyism of Daniel,
he becomes his book as "object-trap" which forces the Others to
see him as he wants to be seen, a strange inedible Lalique Jelly;
Genet's books, Sartre intimates, are just that—tubes of vaseline,
facilitating eating/reading/forbidden intercourse, but finally a
jelly that cannot be eaten, its shimmering absence hidden in the
flaccid-rigid presence of the metal tube and text.

Sartre characterizes Genet's creative act as a summing-up. "*All*
the basic themes of his thought and life are to be found in each
of his works; one recognizes the same motifs from book to book:
would anyone dream of reproaching him for this?" (*SG*, 484).
What I have attempted to demonstrate here is the intimate relation between eating, reading, and writing in Sartre's fascination
with and representation of homosexuality in his works. The
progression is self-evident. Mr. P... eats and reads but his
textual/sexual production is limited to undigested maxims. His
black penciled copying is inadequate; it fails stupidly even when
it is retraced in jelly-red ink. Onan and Narcissus are impotent
gods. Daniel's candies are never sufficiently sucked as his scrawl-
ings lie crumpled beside the train tracks. Homosexual sculpture,
shameful suicide and castration, and homosexual scripture for
Matthew and for God's consuming mouth—the word, *Ecce
Homo*—are insufficient poetic acts/objects. Yes, Genet's jellies
and jams are in fact inedible, but the impossible *metamorphosis* of
excrement into the tube of vaseline jelly best embodies the central problem of the relation between eating, reading, and intercourse (sexual/textual) with other men. "His literary adventure is
not unlike an amorous adventure: while seeking to arouse horror, Genet writes in order to be loved" (*SG*, 550). The responsibility now falls on us as affronted, nauseous readers/eaters because as Sartre writes: "When reading Genet, we are similarly
tempted to ask ourselves: 'Does a homosexual *exist*? Does he
think? Does he judge, does he judge us, does he *see* us?' If he

does exist, everything changes: If homosexuality is the choice of a mind, it becomes a human possibility. *Man* is a homosexual, a thief and a traitor. If you deny this, then renounce your finest laurels" (*SG*, 588). "Are you a fairy, too?" asks the Corsican librarian, protector of texts. The distance between the Self-Taught Man, a negative, comic portrait of the homosexual eater/reader, and the portrait of Genet as a producer of text-objects for our horror and delectation is great indeed, but at the center of both is communication, desire, a love of men—not Man. Masturbation, private eating-consuming is called into question. We now are asked to provide an answer to the impossible enigma of the scandalous beauty of inedible jelly-vaseline, of metamorphosis and difference, in a tube for loving, of eating/of the Other.

Serge Doubrovsky

Sartre's *La nausée*:
Fragment of an Analytic Reading

Nausea, and the Sex of Writing will be the title of a book I hope to publish in the future. For the moment, I will select one insignificant detail from a famous scene: the café scene, the "Rendez-vous des Cheminots," in which Roquentin finally experiences Nausea with a capital N: "Things are bad! Things are very bad: I have it, the filth, the Nausea."[1] Written thus, the Nausea attains in this passage its capital status. Novelistic language is endowed with and doubled by its imperious, even imperialistic, metalanguage which seems a priori to exclude any commentary or, what is perhaps the same thing, to include it. Can one say anything better, or simply say anything more about the Nausea than what is said about it in the text? What remains

1. Jean-Paul Sartre, *La nausée* (Paris: Gallimard, 1938), p. 32. All subsequent page references to *La nausée* will be incorporated in the text and refer to this French edition. The English quotations are based on *Nausea,* trans. Lloyd Alexander (New York: New Directions, 1964). However, it was necessary in many instances to modify this translation in order more nearly to reproduce connotations essential to the analysis. The French will be indicated in parenthesis when no English expression adequately conveys all the meanings of the French. (Translator's note). References to *L'idiot de la famille* are to the Gallimard edition, Paris, 1971-72.

to be seen by the critical eye? Nothing no doubt, except this insignificant detail: the Nausea scene ends with a game of cards described in some detail, and the game itself ends at the very moment Roquentin gets up as a "dog-faced young man" exclaims: "Ah! The nine of hearts." I could therefore call this essay: "The Nine of Hearts: Fragment of an Analytic Reading of *La nausée*."

Sheer realism, one could say, on the level of structural analysis—the verisimilitude of the narrative code requires that in a French café in the provinces one play cards, preferably a game of *manille* or *belotte*. From that point of view, the ace of clubs or the nine of diamonds would have done just as nicely. Psychocriticism begins where other forms of criticism leave off: with the production in the text of an insignificant detail which neither the Sartrean metatext nor other metadiscourses can explain. Sartre could certainly have just as well written: "Ah! The ace of clubs" or "the nine of diamonds" and achieved the same stylistic-narrative effect. But the fact remains that he wrote "nine of hearts," and it is precisely that *remainder* that remains to be examined by the critical eye, all the more so in that, curiously, that card which is displayed right in the middle of the table is *not seen* by the players: "One of the players pushes a disordered pack of cards towards another man who picks them up. One card has stayed behind. Don't they see it? It's the nine of hearts" (40). Here the insignificant is beginning to signify in that the imperceptible which one could hardly miss is perceived only by Roquentin. It is a perception which should in its turn be seen by the psychocritic and, let us hope, seen through.

To be sure, we are not going to do or redo Lacan's text on "The Purloined Letter," play or replay some kind of "instance of the card." Abandoning for the moment this signifier at the end of its sequence (which in this case is ours as well since it closes, exactly, the narrative sequence of the café), we will leave Lacan in favor of Freud and concern ourselves quite simply with sex. As does Roquentin: "I came to screw, but no sooner had I opened the door than Madeleine, the waitress, called to me: 'the patronne isn't here, she's in town, shopping.' I felt a sharp disappointment in the sexual parts, a long, disagreeable tickling" (32–33). Before things start to "whirl about" in his head, it tickles, and disagreeably, in a precise erogenous zone. Like honor, Roquentin's sexual parts are ticklish; and something that is ticklish is, of course, delicate by nature, sensitive to attack. A disproportion strikes us immediately between the releasing mechanism of the Nausea (what one would call in Sartrean terms the "teleological circuit" of fornication: "I came to screw [*pour baiser*]"), and Antoine's usually rather lukewarm feelings toward the patronne: "I dined at the Rendez-vous des Cheminots. The patronne was there and I had to screw her, but it was mainly out of politeness. She disgusts me a little, she is too white and besides, she smells like a newborn child. . . . I played distractedly with her sex under the covers" (87). Without having read Freud, one might well ask why when the patronne *is not there* he feels such a "sharp disappointment" in a zone which when she *is there* is hardly erogenous at all. Why this "long, disagreeable tickling" in sexual parts that are ultimately more ticklish than ticklable? After having read Freud, of course, one can ask if there is a common unconscious denominator in the two complementary and antithetical sequences ("I came to screw"/"I had to screw"), a common "organigram" for pleasure disappointed or received; or, after having read Charles Mauron, one can ask if the two texts are superimposable.

Sequence number two ("I had to screw her"), once the act has been somehow or other performed, produces, to the analyst's delight, a "dream." "I let my arm run along the woman's thigh and suddenly saw a small garden with low, wide trees on which immense hairy leaves were hanging. Ants were running everywhere, centipedes and ringworm. . . . Behind the cactus and the Barbary fig trees, the Velleda of the public park pointed a finger at her sex. 'This garden smells of vomit,' I shouted" (87–88). Not being able to get into the problematics of the written pseudodream, which is not a dream but may be analyzed as if it were (see Freud, *Gradiva*), we will limit ourselves to two remarks. (1) The dream which follows the consummation of the carnal act shows the woman's sex to be a source that is strongly anxiety-producing, more precisely it is the *locus* of a *nauseous* nightmare ("this garden smells of vomit"). (2) If one follows traditional Freudian deciphering, that is, vermin = children in the language of dreams, one understands the nature of Roquentin's "disgust" for the patronne who "smells like a newborn child." The birthing sex of the woman designates in advance the final horror of swooning fecundity (the scene of the chestnut-tree root): "My very flesh throbbed and opened, abandoned itself to the universal burgeoning. It was repugnant" (187–88). *Throbbing, opening and abandoning itself:* Roquentin feels his ultimate nausea as if his flesh had become entirely a *woman's sex,* and what is more, "burgeoning" in gestation. It is the absolute nightmare. For whom? "I came to screw." For a man. Brought back to sequence number one, we discover that the disappointment of a ticklish virility is accompanied by a concomitant symptom: "At the same time I felt my shirt rubbing against the tips of my breasts and I was surrounded, seized by a slow, coloured whirling" (33). Common usage dictates that the word *breast,* especially in the plural, and in the spoken form: "the tips of my breasts" (*le bout de mes seins*), refers to a fundamental signifier of femininity, one of its essential appendages and attributes. A man would speak, rather, of his chest, his breast, or his pectorals (*sa poitrine, son poitrail,* ou *ses pectoraux*). Everything happens, therefore, as if the profound loathing for female sexual parts, projected as a *dream* after the completed sexual act, is introjected as a *fantasy* in the frustrated act; the failure to screw being in no way a failure to have pleasure, but a failure *to prove*: as soon as I cease being able to prove that I am a man, *I transform myself into a woman.* Such is the logic of the Sartrean fantasy that closely regulates the development of the Nausea. One could show in detail the inexorable progression of the fantasy in four successive steps (the scenes of the pebble, the café, little Lucienne, and the chestnut-tree root). It is a progression experienced in the whirligigs of ambivalence, "whirling" from disgust to desire—so many stations of the cross for the man-woman, haunted by the sudden and sustained substitution of a female sex for a precarious male sex: "How strange it is, how moving, that this hardness should be so fragile" (37). It is both disease and remedy, since in assuming a sickening femininity, "the viscous puddle at the bottom of *our* time," entails exchanging a real virility for an imaginary, unassailable virility, inscribed in the symbolic order: the music's "band of steel" (*bande d'acier*, 37) or a story that is "beautiful and hard as steel" (249), in which Roquentin dreams he will transpose himself some day.

Those who would question this analysis can at least take the word of "Sartre by Flaubert," or "Sartre by himself." Thus, in reading Sartre reading Gustave, one rereads, quite precisely, *La nausée*: "The flesh is totally a matter of enduring, suffering. . . . The agent desires and takes: that is the male; according to Gustave, pleasure is born of a swooning abandon, of a happy, consenting passivity; the woman has pleasure because she is taken. She also desires, naturally, but in her own way . . . feminine desire is passive waiting. The text speaks about itself: if Gustave wants to be woman, it is because his partially feminine sexuality clamors for a change of sex that would allow it to fully develop its resources" (*L'idiot de la famille*, I, 685). In that respect, Antoine is Gustave's unhappy conscience. "The text speaks about itself," said Sartre. Yes indeed, especially when it thinks it is talking about the Other. Let's look at Sartre while he imagines Flaubert looking at himself in a mirror: "At first he makes of his constituted passivity the *analogon* of a secret femininity . . . it is possible for him, by effecting a double unrealization—to imagine that he is another man caressing a true woman—himself—on the other side of the mirror. . . . There are here two *analoga*: his hands, his image. Of his image he will apprehend only the caressed flesh, neglecting insignificant details such as his sex or his young male's chest" (*Idiot*, I, 693). In this "Sartre by Flaubert," one surprises Jean-Paul in the act of rewriting quite exactly the progression of the Nausea, that is, the progressive feminization of the flesh, which goes from the *hands* (the pebble scene), to the *face in the mirror* ("An entire half of my face yields . . . the eye opens in a white globe, on pink, bleeding flesh" [31]), preceding the entrance into the café where the narrator suddenly "loses" the insignificant detail of his *sex* and where his *young male's chest* is transformed into "tips of his breasts." A curious intertextuality/intersexuality of novelistic writing and critical writing. In fact, if Madame Bovary is a man disguised as a woman (*Critique de la raison dialectique*, 90), one cannot see why Antoine Roquentin could not be considered a woman disguised as a man. But if one prefers to take the word of "Sartre by himself," we will listen to him directly as he answers (*L'arc*, 61) the formidable questions asked by the formidable Simone de Beauvoir: "So, Sartre, I would like to interrogate you on the question of women. . . . You have never talked about women. . . . How do you explain that?"—"I think it goes back to my childhood. . . . Girls and women formed, in a way, my natural milieu, and *I have always thought that there was inside of me a sort of woman*" [my emphasis].

Only, not as "natural" as all that, as *La nausée* bears witness, and this reticence in regard to the question of women is not at all innocent, analytically speaking (I will leave the ideology to Simone). *La nausée* is there, precisely, on the level of unconscious discourse, to fill the strange lacuna in the writer's conscious discourse. It is well known that the notion of "bisexuality," introduced as a major but poorly defined part of Freudian thought, is a preoccupation of many psychoanalysts. According to a recent report by Dr. Christian David, any successful cure presupposes the integration of the psychic bisexuality of the subject.[2] Conversely, he tells us, "any serious threat to sexual identity or integrity is likely to lead to diverse disturbances of the psychic organization and can even lead to psychosis." And Léon Kreisler, the French psychiatrist, formulates the same idea in a vocabulary that particularly interests us: "Belonging to a sex is one of the most solid cores of the cohesion of our person, and sexuality could be the most primitive and powerful mode of putting forth roots (*enracinement*) in existence." That Roquentin's ultimate Nausea should take place in front of a root (*racine*) that is eminently phallomorphic ("the bark, black and swollen, looked like boiled leather. . . . This hard and compact skin of a sea lion" [180, 183]) indicates clearly that the locus of the subject's existential crisis is where his virility is rooted (*l'enracinement viril*).

The critic, however, is not a psychiatrist, and the diagnosis (what is called the "construction" element) is of interest only if it produces the equivalent of the flow of new repressed material

2. The statements by Drs. David, Kreisler and R. R. Greenson are in a report made by Christian David to the Société Psychanalytique de Paris at its convention in April 1975. An abridged version of this report under the title, "La bisexualité psychique: éléments d'une réévaluation," was published in the *Revue française de psychanalyse*, 39 (Sept.–Dec., 1975).

that Freud gives as the touchstone of a correct interpretation: here, the increasingly urgent integration of metonymically discrete elements of the text into a metaphorically coherent sequence. An analytic reading is, basically, nothing other than the constitution of a rigorous logic of details, to the extent that it places the logic of narrative possibilities back in the functioning of the fantasy. If one brings erotic sequence number one ("I came to screw") to bear on erotic sequence number two ("I had to screw her"), one can say that the completed viril act prevents the sexual identity crisis, if it is true, according to R. R. Greenson's remark, that "the adult neurotic behaves as if the sex of his sexual object determined his own sex." But traces of the first logic of signifiers persist in the second: the Velleda of the public or pubic garden had no sooner pointed to her sex as the sinful party, thus reassuring the male sleeper, than on awaking the latter hears the patronne say to him: "I didn't want to wake you up ... but a fold of the sheet was under my buttocks (*fesses*)" (88). The syntagmatic order is revealing: the lingering "diurnal" detail *immediately* triggers off another "dream" in the novelistic text in which the "buttocks" signifier (*le signifiant fessier*), repressed as a simple "realistic" detail in the waking scene ("fold of the sheet"), proliferates. The obsession is fully revealed: "I spanked (*j'ai fessé*) Maurice Barrès. We were three soldiers and one of us had a hole in the middle of his face. Maurice Barrès came up to us and said, 'That's fine,' and he gave each of us a small bouquet of violets. 'I don't know where to put them,' said the soldier with the hole in his head. Then Maurice Barrès said, 'Put them in the hole you have in your head.' The soldier answered, 'I'm going to stick them up your ass'" (88). We will note the triple associative constellation: a hole in the head, stick up the ass, bouquet of violets, and, in a movement just contrary to the first, we will bring it to bear on erotic sequence number one.

In the café where we left him, we find Roquentin in a total state of Nausea, slouching: "The seat is bashed in (*défoncée*) right where I sat down. . . . I have a broken spring. . . . My head is all limp and elastic, as though it had been simply set on my neck; if I turn it, I will drop it" (33–34). Having become the "little detachable object," the "broken spring," the head that turns so much that it might fall reveals, at the very source of the Nausea, a very strong fear of castration. The cause of Roquentin's dizziness is precisely his head *experienced as a penis,* when he is faced with the castration threat that hits him in his narcissistic identification. "I dropped to a seat, I no longer knew where I was" (33): the text knows precisely where he is; when he (the head)[3] drops down, Antoine sits on the spot where "the seat is bashed in." "To be bashed in" (*se faire défoncer*), in a crude slang expression dear to Sartre, designates the dreaded act which transforms the masculine subject (*le sujet*) into a fag (*une tante*). The fear of feminizing castration brings him back to his fundamental vulnerability: the anus is the vagina of the male. The disgust (desire) of the female sex is interiorized on the fantasmic level as the obsession of possessing a potential female sex, which the Nausea actualizes. The fear of castration is accompanied by a very strong complementary fear of sodomization. We must not forget that when Maurice Barrès asks the soldier to have the bouquet put "in the hole that you have in your head" ("hole" in the soldier's head, Roquentin's "cut-off" head), the answer is "I'm going to stick them up your ass." Now just what, if I dare say it, is one going to stick up this ass? A bouquet of *violets* (*violettes*). The sodomization obsession, felt as a feminization, is marked in the Sartrean text by a privileged signifier, *violet* (*le violet*) since, lest we forget, Roquentin's Nausea is a *colored* dizziness: "I saw the colors spin slowly" (33). An analysis of the thematic "signified" would easily show that in the Sartrean text, that color is the emblem of a lethal, feminine sexuality (thus, the cashier with whom Roquentin spontaneously identifies: "She's red-haired, as I am; she has some sort of stomach trouble. She is rotting quietly under her skirts with a melancholy smile, like the odour of *violets* given off by a decomposing body" [83]). One will no doubt be less astonished than Annie by this aesthetic repugnance of Antoine's: "You swore indignantly for a year that you wouldn't go see *Violettes impériales*" (198). But, what is more important, violet is the Sartrean color for a fearsome female sexuality within the same sequence of signifiers: like *rape* (*viol*), like *violated* (*violé*). After the narrator's identification with the putrefying cashier, his identification with "little Lucienne" confirms this in the next

---

3. Note that *il* is a masculine subject and *la tête* is feminine. (Translator's note)

stage of the Nausea: "Little Lucienne has been violated. Strang-
led. Her body still exists. . . . *She* no longer exists. Her hands . . .
I . . . there I . . . violated. A sweet, bloody desire for rape (*viol*)
takes me from behind" (144). The ambiguity of the expression
"bloody desire for rape" (to rape, to be raped?), which is nothing
other than the ambivalence of the active/passive desire, is momentarily resolved in behalf of a transsexualization fantasma-
tically assumed, by the *place* where the desire takes hold of the
subject: *from behind*. There is an exact symbolic equivalence between the manner in which from then on he experiences his
flesh as feminine ("My body of living flesh which murmurs and
turns gently, liquors which turn to cream . . . the sweet sugary
water of my flesh" [145–46]) and his universal sodomization:
"Existence takes my thoughts from behind and gently expands
them *from behind*: they take me from behind, they force me to
think from behind. . . . He runs, he runs like a ferret (from behind) from behind *from behind*, little Lucienne assaulted from
behind, violated by existence from behind" (146). The "little
Lucienne" who reappears as the final link in the chain of the
verbal delirium, is necessarily "assaulted from behind," if
Roquentin must be able to "become" her. Here, according to the
law Freud assigned to the development of one night's dream
sequences, where the progression goes from the most hidden to
the most obvious, all the elements of the Sartre/Roquentin fantasy structure appear without repression in the delirious writing
(the desyntaxization, degrammaticalization, decodification of
the narrative, indicating the locus wherein the textual work carries out the sexual impulse). We are not yet there, and in the café
scene, those elements barely show through, somewhat obscured,
hesitant: such as cousin Adolph's suspenders (traditional
emblem, if there ever was one, of proletarian machismo, Gabin's
suspenders in Prévert-Carné films), which "hesitate" between
blue and mauve ("You feel like telling them: go on, *become* violet
and let's hear no more about it" [34]). But, at this stage, the
suspenders cannot, do not *want* to become *violet* (*violettes*); and
where Robbe-Grillet once saw a naive anthropomorphism in
Sartre's descriptions, one must see a very sure and precise inscription of the fantasm, which already articulates, in a curious
condensation "the time of mauve suspenders and bashed-in

seats" (37). The desiring or delirious thrust is continued in the appeal to an imaginary virility already mentioned: "This band of steel, the narrow duration of the music which traverses our time through and through" (37). The effect of which is as specifically indicated as the cause: "When the voice was heard in the silence, I felt my body *harden* (*se durcir*) and the Nausea *vanish* (*s'est évanouie*)" (38).[4] The thrust is thus contained, but not without retaining the dangerous, latent feminization, not only in the voice of the female vocalist, but in the reaction of the "veterinarian's little girl" toward the music: "Barely seated, the girl has been seized by it: she holds herself stiffly, her eyes wide open" (37). A phallic little girl, one might say, in whom that which is stiff, in Roquentin's miraculously recovered virility, is a woman's penis. One is less surprised that the final solution of the book is a fetishism of art.

However, the café scene does not end with the disappearance of the Nausea under the effect of the music; it ends with the insignificant card game which came to our attention in the beginning. As it is a game of *manille*, it is, perhaps, less insignificant, if one remembers that the initial nausea is of the *hand* (*main*), and that this same hand will later be punished ("I stab the knife into the palm," 143). The sodomy obsession is exorcized, but the threat of castration must be faced head on in order that the "viril protestation" might be satisfied. It is this second movement of the fantasmatic operation that the card players' scene accomplishes by proxy. When "the big, flushed man" lays his card, diamonds, on the table, the "dog-faced young man" (*tête de chien*) suddenly counters it (better this head, representing a male, domesticated animality, than Roquentin's "limp," "elastic" head): "Shit! He trumped" (39). One trumps (*on coupe*) in a card game; one cuts away (*on coupe*) on an analyst's couch, as well; and, there, one does not cut away from the father. It is precisely the father who now appears, only to disappear, in his most classic form: "The outline of the *king of hearts* appears between his clenched fingers, then it is turned on its face and the game continues. Beautiful king, come from so far, prepared by

4. "S'est évanouie" can also be translated "swooned" or "fainted away." (Translator's note)

so many combinations, by so many vanished gestures. He disappears in turn so that other combinations *can be born,* other gestures" (39). The unexpected lyricism of this passage would hardly make sense on the level of the "realistic" code of a narrative in which Roquentin is not portrayed as being a particularly avid fan of cards or *manille.* On the Other Stage and in the other code, it becomes perfectly logical: the "son" trumps (*coupe*) the "father," liquidates the Oedipus by turning the threat around; so that the son *can be born,* the "king of hearts" disappears, as will M. de Rollebon later on (another imaginary murder of the father). Now that he is dubbed a male, consecrated in his virility, Roquentin is seized by an emotion that is otherwise inexplicable: "I am touched, I feel my body at rest like a precision machine" (39), a rest that is well earned after the transsexual trances. One can understand also the imperious, sudden flow of Roquentin's memories at this precise point in the fantasmatic sequence: "I have plunged into forests, always making my way towards other cities. I have had women, I have fought with men" (39). In line with a henceforth confirmed virility, reassured as to its two essential attributes, the fucker-fighter is at peace with the machine of his body. It is normal that he *see* what the others *do not see,* since it is the place of his fantasy: the nine of hearts (*neuf de coeur* can also be read as "new of heart"). "New of heart," he can go off again ("Enough, I'm going to leave."), and best foot forward, except that he puts his foot in it. The card that was "left behind": "Someone takes it at last, gives it to the dog-faced young man." "Ah! The nine of hearts!" (40) Unless one is "left behind" or, as they say, "retarded," a virility is not "offered," one must take it (*la prendre*) oneself, that is, learn it (*l'apprendre*). Not knowing what to do with it, not yet having decided to transmute it, or "transmale-ize" it in writing, "the young man turns and turns the nine of hearts between his fingers" (40). But, at the same time that there is failure, there is, perhaps, already an indication of the future (re)solution, since next to the young man, "the violet-faced old man (*le vieillard violacé*) bends over a sheet of paper and sucks the end of a pencil" (40).

Translated by Marilyn Schuster

Stephen Smith

Toward a Literature of Utopia

The theme of male homosexuality predominates in all five of the novels this essay will consider: *Killer,* by Yves Navarre; *Le grand amour,* by Antoine Orezza; *Les météores,* by Michel Tournier; *Le voyageur,* by Tony Duvert; and *Le rêve de Job,* by Jean Demélier.[1] In other thematic, technical, and stylistic respects, in their teleologies, and in their ultimate value as literature, these novels offer a diversity as wide-ranging as might be found in any five contemporary fictions chosen merely at random. They thereby elicit the question: Is it legitimate—is it even possible—to categorize literature on the basis of a theme, or must we rather treat that theme, whatever its inherent interest, as one among many formal elements, which together distinguish literature from other kinds of writing?

The immediate and obvious answer, that a sociological or psychological study could justifiably categorize by theme,

1. *Killer* (Paris: Flammarion, 1975); *Le grand amour* (Paris: Gallimard, 1972); *Les météores* (Paris: Gallimard, 1974); *Le voyageur* (Paris: Editions de Minuit, 1970); *Le rêve de Job* (Paris: Gallimard, 1971). All references to these works are to these editions. Page numbers without text identification always refer to the novel most recently mentioned. All translations are my own.

whereas a literary study must concentrate on aspects of form, is less than satisfactory. Georg Lukács, Lucien Goldmann, the Russian formalists, and others have repeatedly demonstrated that links between form and sense are as close-knit as those between theme and significance. Is there, then, a demonstrable connection between formalistic features of these novels and their theme of homosexuality? If so, what relation does that nexus have with the meaning of each work considered in its entirety?

In the search for an answer to these questions, sociological and psychological considerations provide a convenient starting point. How does each author see, how does each work depict homosexuality and homosexuals? Yves Navarre's interpretation is one of unremitting pessimism. In his three "homosexual" novels, *Lady Black* (1971), *Les loukoums* (1973) and *Killer,* his principal homosexual characters hate themselves, despise other homosexuals, and contribute in substantial measure to their own ineluctable doom. On the other hand, Navarre's "heterosexual" novels, *Evolène* (1972) and *Le coeur qui cogne* (1974), contrast strikingly in that their characters realize enduring loves and meaningful lives.

Among the homosexuals, love exists only so long as illusion is retained. The characters in *Killer* all seek a permanent, perfect, reciprocal love, but none ever finds it. The novel portrays the disintegration and destruction of five principal homosexual couples and several lesser ones. Their failure is imposed upon them by the author, who has stated elsewhere: "Whether society tolerates or condemns them, homosexuals seem to me to have a gift for unhappiness. . . . In the long run, . . . each one . . . withdraws into indifference and narcissism."[2] Killer, the central character, fits the description perfectly. Though he professes love for Tony, he is far more interested in his love than in his beloved. As self-loathing as he is narcissistic, Killer makes a great issue of avoiding mirrors. In a moment of revelation near the end he understands that Tony's function in his life has been to serve as that mirror to which he was irresistibly drawn. "Tony did no-

2. Navarre's statement appears in a review of *Killer* by Gabrielle Rolin, *Le monde des livres,* 18 April 1975, pp. 19–20, which bears the revealing title: "Du côté de Sodome: La chronique scandaleuse d'Yves Navarre."

thing but confront me with myself. This was the only way to delude me and destroy me" (318).

The confrontation with the self, however it is achieved, is for Navarre's homosexuals unbearable. Tony commits suicide and Killer "disappears," the presentation of this disappearance implying that Killer, too, kills himself. Violent deaths, including other suicides, are the norm among Navarre's homosexual characters, and *Killer* is as strewn with corpses as the bloodiest Elizabethan tragedy.

Just as they hate themselves and each other, so do these characters reject their sexuality. Navarre persistently terms the sex act a meaningless battle, leading nowhere. Concepts of tenderness, love, honor and happiness are treated as misleading fabrications (252), and every beloved eventually, in some manner, rejects or betrays or abandons his lover. The homosexual milieu is but "a federation of lonely persons" (253). Whenever a character mentions copulation, or describes it with a touch of campy defiance, such a concession is accompanied by cynical references to the banality of the act, along with the habitual metaphor of the struggle. Navarre never comes any closer to depicting sex as pleasure.

Michel Tournier's *Les météores* presents further instances of fundamental rejection of homosexuality. The novel develops two complementary stories, each narrated for the most part by its protagonist. Alexandre, homosexual and sanitation engineer, the "dandy of the dumps," stresses the connection between his sexual preferences and his profession, both garbage and homosexuals being rejected by society. Though his own various philosophizings show a tendency to equate homosexuality and superiority, his eventual deliberately sought death marks the internalization of society's exclusion of the homosexual. The violent death met by his lover, Daniel, also falls easily within the pattern of the obligatory tragic ending.

The story of Paul, Alexandre's nephew, provides yet another variation on the same theme. Paul seeks absolute union with his identical twin, Jean, who, for his part, rejects it. The sexual aspect of their relationship is muted, almost obscured. Predictably, the couple does not endure, though Paul ultimately believes that he has achieved a mystical conjunction by incorporating

Jean, who in reality has merely disappeared, into his own body. Although Tournier places the theme beneath multiple layers of fantasy inclining toward myth, the principal personage of *Les météores* can nonetheless be seen as basically another avatar of the narcissistic homosexual, rejected by the beloved, ultimately isolated from society, and relishing his suffering.

Le grand amour of Antoine Orezza manifests on the surface a more optimistic point of view. The character Antoine, in an unbroken interior monologue, reflects on his love of thirty years' duration for Pierre Prince, giving prominence to their developing relationship, their happiness. The book ends as Antoine, dying, achieves a quiet acceptance of all his life and his love. And yet there are somber undercurrents in his perceptions of that love and of homosexuality in general. His life has been a constant struggle against self-hatred. Thoughts of Pierre and of their happiness together elicit memories of a friend, René, who attempted aversion therapy as a means of repudiating his homosexuality. Antoine recalls the guilt resulting from his own first sexual encounters, the feeling of being condemned to "a monstrosity, a vice, homosexuality, filth, shame" (85). Triumphantly, he affirms that he and Pierre have transcended the earlier shame, but the text is replete with indications that he has not totally accepted his condition. Images of cages, prisons, and prisoners recur constantly, pointing to constraints on all apparent freedoms. He speaks of being doomed to love and be loved, and of destroying and being destroyed by the beloved. Emphasizing the rejections he has experienced, he reveals that even Pierre has betrayed him. Finally, the ultimate rejection, the complete isolation, is that of death, and Orezza chooses to have Antoine die.

Like the works of Navarre and Tournier, *Le grand amour* combines rejection of homosexuality and of self with a text which largely avoids overt descriptions of the sex act. *Le voyageur* by Tony Duvert takes the opposite approach. Here, minutely detailed accounts of various sexual practices are often the primary focus of interest. Sex is presented as a source of pleasure, not of problems, and the author and his characters assume a position of laissez-faire: "each to his own pleasure women generally or cars or sometimes pastries books animals flowers stews boys little boys big-balled kids laddies imbeciles bastards children" (173). No character ever feels the need to apologize for his homosexuality, nor is any character ever punished, either literally or symbolically, for his sexual orientation. Nature produces both the desired and the desire: "Ah, boys," a character exclaims, "if it weren't for boys, I wouldn't be a pederast" (88). Characters here do not reject their own sexuality, nor do they reject other homosexuals. Rather, they are drawn together by their common desires and pleasures and by their understanding and appreciation of these impulses in each other. Duvert's fiction, in short, displays the same stance as his nonfictional *Le bon sexe illustré* (1974), an impassioned defense of every human's right to live according to his own needs and values.

Jean Demélier's *Le rêve de Job* is equally free of traditional moralistic restrictions. René/Rémy/Job loves Gabriel/Patrick/Lari unashamedly, passionately, aware of the strength and beauty of that love. Job is "a man of integrity, upright" (363), "pure and just and innocent" (374), who remembers "that he had always been good ... and that people loved him and he loved them" (376). The author gives him no complexes about his homosexual desires, but portrays them instead as a natural part of the psychological make-up of someone representative of his era, respected by his friends, and loved by his God.

Like Duvert's characters, those of Demélier partake fully of the delights of the flesh. Acts of love are minutely articulated in ultra-lyrical descriptions which mock their own excesses while taking total advantage of them. A lushly rhapsodic exuberance characterizes the presentation of every sexual encounter. Love involves no component of jealousy. When lovers are forced to separate, they grieve; then they find love again elsewhere, for their experiences have not caused them to repress and reject this spontaneous, instinctive emotion.

It is clearly easy to separate these novels into two distinct groups on the basis of their treatment of the homosexual and of sexuality in general. *Killer, Les météores,* and *Le grand amour* maintain traditional patterns wherein homosexuality is treated as deviance, the sex act goes largely unmentioned, homosexual love leads not to fulfillment but to frustration and rejection, and the homosexual is in the end isolated from society by death or some symbolic approximation thereof. The central characters in these three books are all preponderantly narcissistic, satisfied only with total emotional possession of the beloved, even when they do not demand sexual exclusivity, and all are in some important way abandoned by the beloved. They all suffer, and, to some extent, they all cling to their suffering. Moreover, they are virtually exclusively homosexual—Paul's sexual encounter with Jean's fiancée in *Les météores* is important to him only because of its effect on his relation with Jean—with only peripheral interest in, or even active dislike for women.

The novels of Duvert and Demélier provide remarkable contrasts to those in the other group. Here, homosexuality is one of many acceptable gradations in the sexual spectrum; sex is seen as pleasure and is welcomed as such; it leads to union, not to isolation. The characters assume their homosexuality without shame or guilt, remain open to the world and capable of friendship. For Duvert's characters, sexual pleasures imagined in a homosexual context can be transposed to a heterosexual one with no diminution of intensity, and there is even at one point an idealization of woman as sex-partner (215). Demélier's character shows the same abundant enthusiasm for his heterosexual loves and couplings as for his homosexual ones.

In their relation to many of fiction's age-old aesthetic and technical traditions these five works present once again the same groupings. Since the time of the ancient Greeks, a primary purpose of fiction has been to explore alternate possible "realities." The conventions governing the forms these "realities" might take have varied enormously, but they all, in spite of occasional superficial indications to the contrary, have accepted as axiomatic the irreversibility of time, the unity and discretion of personage, and the objective truth of event. That is to say, every action leaves its indelible mark on all subsequent ones; once a change has occurred, its consequences are inevitable; the prescribed order of past, present, future is inexorably assumed, although the narrative may present this chronology in distorted or even chaotic sequence. Characters may be paradoxical or schizoid; through magic or divinity they may undergo or effect alterations of their external forms; but the reader knows that they exist as separate unified entities, ultimately definable by anyone in full possession of the necessary information. Every event, as well, is considered to occur in a single way, which may, or may not, be revealed to the reader, and which may be rightly or wrongly perceived and interpreted by those persons involved in or affected by it.

Navarre, Orezza, and Tournier fully maintain these conventions, and, in that respect, their fictions can be classified as traditional. All three have written what are essentially tales of a quest for some platonic reality, for "the truth" about someone or something which intrigues the quester. Navarre employs cinematographic flashbacks and three intertwining chronological planes to show Killer and later some unidentified interviewer in pursuit of understanding about Killer's life, his homosexuality, his friends, and his fate. Orezza's use of interior monologue makes a kaleidoscopic chronology possible, and his rapidly shifting verb tenses combined with potentially ambiguous pronouns require the reader's constant attention in this story of Antoine's effort to comprehend his homosexuality and his love for Pierre. Tournier uses a variety of narrative voices and portrays a literal quest—Paul follows Jean around the world in a vain attempt at reunion—as a way of studying the nature and the meaning of human couples in general. Each of these works is, by certain of its narrative techniques, clearly a product of the twentieth century. Yet all of them are also profoundly conventional, preserving fundamental assumptions of the mimetic tradition beneath their surface adornments: definable individuals participate in determinable events occurring in irreversible time.

Le voyageur elaborates a different concept of fiction, emphasizing above all the ludic[3] potential of the imagination and its various expressions. As in the works of Robbe-Grillet, everything which seems firmly established is subsequently called into question, shifted, demolished. All that eventually remains is a series of elusive motifs and strands of character, woven and rewoven into widely varying and mutually contradictory story lines. At no point is an event established as true, nor is the existence of such truth ever posited. Though at times characters seem to be emerging as distinct, differentiable individuals, those distinc-

3. Refers to imaginative and intellectual play.

tions eventually disappear, not because some central definable consciousness has learned new facts which negate previously held beliefs, but rather because it is never assumed that the characters exist as anything other than the fictions which they are. The chronologically progressive time of the physical world is irrelevant here, where causes do not necessarily produce effects, and where an action is just as likely to lead back to itself or to a preceding event as to a subsequent one. The technique results in a constant recognition of the fictionality of fiction, with well-nigh total freedom for fulfillment in imagination as imagination, language as language.

The comic, life-embracing attitudes which *Le voyageur* conveys result entirely from its techniques as opposed to its subjects, which represent, for their part, an unrelieved succession of horrors. But since the reality here is always textual, never referential, these examples of child-molesting, animal torture, murder, mutilation, bestiality, and sordidly pornographic sexual encounters never become threatening to the reader, never engage a sense of involvement in the actions they purportedly recount. They are always perceived instead as functions of the work's linguistic verve, its pleasure in the sheer sound of words, and its perpetually overflowing exuberance.

Le rêve de Job is in many of its technical aspects similar to Duvert's work. One is impressed by the ludic exultation in language, the technical effects which deliberately call attention to themselves, the unbounded ebullience and imagination, and the frank presentation of fiction as fiction.

Demélier's novel purposely exacts comparison with and pays homage to Beckett's *Molloy* in its plot structure. As in Beckett's work, there are two principal sections, with the name of the hero of each section evocative of the name of the other. The second section concerns the hero's assigned quest to find the missing tramp, Job, who would seem to be the hero of the first section. As in Beckett's novel, parallels between the seeker and the sought are exploited in order to suggest a confusion of identity, while at the same time their differences remain such as to confound all efforts to see them as one. Though here we can follow the story in a manner not feasible in *Le voyageur,* the events, the characters, and various moments in time nevertheless merge with and diverge from one another freely, precluding any possibility of arriving at definitions and a sequence of established "facts." The technical virtuosity of Demélier's word and language games is constantly the primary focus of interest, before which all usual norms of realistic logic are forced to give way.

There is thus a high positive correlation in these five novels between fictional form and sociopsychological content. Those works which retain traditional attitudes toward the homosexual, casting him as self-centered, self-hating, and self-destroying, rejecting and rejected by both his own kind and the rest of society, also retain the traditional mimetic approach to literature. Conversely, in those works where homosexuality is accepted as a manner of authentic self-expression, a legitimate pathway to genuine pleasure and fulfillment, fiction too is allowed to function as itself.

The correlation is clear, but what does it signify? Why is acceptance of homosexuality associated with greater fictionality, while the attempt to represent reality remains linked with rejection of the homosexual and his sexuality? These questions are perhaps too limited, for there is evidence in contemporary French literature that the same bipartite division may apply also to literature in which heterosexual relations are preponderant.

Butor's *La modification,* for example, with all its technical innovations and originality, bears the same relation to reality as do the works of Navarre, Tournier, and Orezza. And it, too, tends to gloss over the purely sexual aspects of its hero's existence. The first sexual encounter of Léon and Cécile, for example, is reduced to the coy notation, "you did what lovers do together."[4] Robbe-Grillet's *Projet pour une révolution à New York,* on the other hand, strikingly similar in multiple aspects to *Le voyageur,* revels both in its fictionality and in a basically comic exploration of numerous heterodox means to erotic pleasures. Beckett, too, with very different emphases, in eminently comic writings, exploits fiction as fiction and imposes no ordinary limits on his characters' sexuality. Molloy, for instance, thinks that Ruth, whom he buggers in his efforts to know love, is a woman, but he is not at all certain, just as he is never sure whether Lousse is

4. Michel Butor, *La Modification* (Paris: Editions de Minuit, 1957), p. 103.

male or female. His conclusion: "Don't torment yourself, Molloy, a man or a woman, what difference can it make?"[5] Such examples lead us therefore to the more general question: what is the correlation between accepted sexuality and fictionality, as opposed to repressed sexuality and "realism"?

A simplistic answer might be that in the nonfictional world sexuality is linked with responsibility in such a way as to limit self-expression. Such an argument, however, would deny the evidence of these books. Some characters of Orezza and Tournier, and most of those of Navarre and Duvert are rampantly promiscuous and deny the responsibilities usually conjoined with sexuality, while Demélier's principal character and others of Orezza and Tournier willingly assume such responsibilities. That is to say, there is no correlation between the number of sexual partners, nor the degree of responsibility assumed, and the extent to which sexuality is allowed to function as unalloyed pleasure and attainment of personal authenticity. The difference is rather one of attitudes, of the meanings attributed to and qualities associated with the individual and his sexuality.

It appears that the dynamics of these attitudes evolve not from the influence upon the author's aesthetics of his reactions to sexuality (or to homosexuality), nor, conversely, from a molding of his social attitudes effected by his artistic sense, but that both these characteristics grow out of his global approach to life and art, reflecting a basic position which may properly be described as political. Roland Barthes, noting the ideological implications of the individual's sense of privacy, furnishes an observation which supports such a conclusion. He points out that a rightist *doxa* allows for revelation of sentiment, but not of sexuality, whereas a *doxa* of the left permits open discussion of sexuality, but eschews any portrayal of sentiment.[6] The works of Orezza, Navarre, and Tournier conform to this description as it applies to the mores of conservatives, just as Duvert's novel, with virtually no trace of sentiment, provides a prime illustration for Barthes's definition of the sense of propriety found among those

5. Samuel Beckett, *Molloy* (Paris: Editions de Minuit, 1951), pp. 84–85.
6. Barthes, *Roland Barthes par Roland Barthes* (Paris: Seuil, 1975), p. 85.

of a liberal or radical persuasion. It is easy to extend the equation further and recognize the essential conservatism of the general aesthetics and psychosociological implications of *Killer, Le grand amour,* and *Les météores.* Just as evidently, *Le voyageur* allies itself, both artistically and morally, with well-defined iconoclastic goals and values, coinciding almost exactly with positions enunciated by Robbe-Grillet.

Le rêve de Job, however, defies classification in terms of Barthes's neat dichotomy. Frankly admitting all aspects of sexuality—there are examples even of joyful incest, both hetero- and homosexual—but equally open in its acceptance of sentiment, it violates the taboos of both the right and the left. The proscriptions which it rejects all subordinate individuals to a system, thus robbing them in large measure of their uniqueness. Just as *Le rêve de Job* throws off traditional novelistic restraints without subscribing to any more recently established literary dogma, it also refuses all limitations on its protagonist. René/Rémy/Job is free to be fully himself, both physically and emotionally, without recriminations and without regrets.

Barthes predicates liberty as the basis for all happiness. The description of his personal vision of Utopia, characterized by freedom of texts as well as of individuals, provides concomitantly an accurate account of the dominant features of *Le rêve de Job.* Barthes's Utopia requires that dualistic world-views be rejected, that submission to black/white, either/or systems of thought be refused. Once "sense" and "sex" have broken out of this "binary prison," they have the capacity to develop in any desired direction. The "gongoresque text" and the "happy sexuality" of this Utopia become realizable when "(polysemous) forms and (sensual) practices" enter into "a state of infinite expansion."[7] Demélier's text, by its deliberately chosen lack of control, unimpededly pursues the expression of its varied potentialities. In like manner, the central character, René/Rémy/Job, essays without inhibition or restraint multiple manifestations of himself as a person who loves and enjoys other human beings, and who, in so doing, escapes all definition in terms of some

7. Barthes, p. 137.

exclusive form of sexuality. The text is gongoresque; the sexuality is happy. And by a further noticeable conjuction of imagery, *Le rêve de Job* prefigures Barthes's notions on infinite expansion. The book closes as Job's smile, the form and the practice of his happiness, enlarges into a circle, then a sphere, and continues to expand until it merges with the infinite smile of God.

Elaine Marks

Lesbian Intertextuality

> So the first problem of mythic thought is that women must be domesticated.
> —Claude Lévi-Strauss

> Every text is absorption and transformation of a multiplicity of other texts.
> —Julia Kristeva

Women have always loved women. The investigation and quarrels about causes do not interest me here, although in other contexts they may illuminate and incite. My corpus, composed of written texts, fiction and nonfiction, many fragments, by women and men, mostly French, from Sappho through Baudelaire to Wittig (the Lesbos-Paris axis), proposes other enigmas. Through a network of anecdotes—formalized gossip that gives pleasure—and proper names—those of the protagonists who transmit and receive messages—I shall attempt to elucidate models and impose prophetic fictions.[1]

---

1. This paper was nourished by four texts: Mary Daly, *Beyond God the Father* (Boston: Beacon, 1973); Jeannette Foster, *Sex Variant Women in Literature* (Baltimore: Diana Press, 1975), originally published in 1956; Jules Michelet, *La sorcière* (Paris: Garnier-Flammarion, 1966), originally published in 1862; Edith Mora, *Sappho* (Paris: Flammarion, 1966). I discovered, after my article was completed, Bertha Harris's delightful essay "The More Profound Nationality of Their Lesbianism: Lesbian Society in Paris in the 1920's," in *Amazon Expedition: A Lesbian-Feminist Anthology,* ed. Phyllis Birkby, Bertha Harris, Jill Johnston, Esther Newton, Jane O'Wyatt (Washington, N.J.: Times Change Press, 1973), pp. 77–88.

Who's Who

Fictional characters are of two kinds. There are those who are born in the words of the text and those whose existence in a text is due to a prior existence in what it is difficult not to call "life." Most women writers and many famous and infamous women in history have become fictional characters of the second kind. Because of their double heritage they play an important role in the reader's imagination. It would be insufficient to talk about lesbianism and literature in France and mention only the better known characters.[2] Space must also be allotted for rumor about Louise Labé and Clémence de Bourges, the Duchesse de Berry and Mlle de Mouchy, Marie Antoinette and Mme de Lamballe, George Sand and Marie Dorval, Germaine de Staël and Juliette Récamier, as well as for facts about Adrienne Mounier and Sylvia Beach, Marie Laurencin and Suzanne Morand, Colette and the Marquise de Belbeuf, Lucie Delarue-Mardrus and Germaine de Castro, Natalie Clifford-Barney and a host of women including Renée Vivien, Liane de Pougy,

---

2. Martial's Bassa, Lucian's courtesans, Sapho in Brantôme's *Vie des dames galantes* (1665); Mlle Hobart in Hamilton's *Mémoires de la vie du Comte de Gramont* (1713); Mlle d'Eon, Mlle de Raucourt, Mme de Furiel, Mlle Sapho in "Apologie de la secte anandryne" (1784); the Mother Superior in Diderot's *La religieuse* (1796); Camille in Latouche's *Fragoletta* (1829); Mlle de Maupin in Gautier's *Mlle de Maupin* (1835); Margarita-Euphémia Porrabéril, Marquise de San Réal and Paquita Valdès in Balzac's *La fille aux yeux d'or* (1835); Sapho, Delphine, and Hippolyte in Baudelaire's *Les fleurs du mal* (1857); Sappho and the friends in Verlaine's *Parallèlement* (1867); the black woman in Mallarmé's "La négresse" (1866), and the two nymphs in his "L'après-midi d'un faune" (1875); Suzanne Haffner and the Marquise d'Espanet in Zola's *La curée* (1871), and Nana and Satin in his *Nana* (1879); Madeleine, Pauline in Maupassant's *La femme de Paul* (1881); Sapho in Daudet's *Sapho* (1884); Bilitis, Sappho, Mnasidika in Pierre Louÿs's *Chansons de Bilitis* (1894); Claudine, Aimée and Luce Lanthenay, Mlle Sergent, Rézi, Miss Flossie in Colette's Claudine novels (1900–1904); Mlle Vinteuil and "son amie," Albertine, Léa, Andrée, Odette, Gilberte, Mme Verdurin, Oriane de Guermantes, Rachel in Proust's *A la recherche du temps perdu* (1913–1927); Marie Bonifas in Jacques de Lacretelle's *La Bonifas* (1925); la Chevalière, Renée Vivien, Amalia X . . . , Lucienne de . . . , the Ladies of Llangollen in Colette's *Le pur et l'impur* (1932); Inès Serrano in Sartre's *Huis clos* (1944); Céline in Christiane Rochefort's *Stances à Sophie* (1963); Je, Isabelle, Hermine in Violette Leduc's *La bâtarde* (1964) and Thérèse, Isabelle in her *Thérèse et Isabelle* (1966); the *guérillères* in Monique Wittig's *Les guérillères* (1969), and J/e in her *Le corps lesbien* (1973).

Romaine Brooks, the Duchesse de Clermont-Tonnerre, Dolly Wilde.

Name-dropping in this instance is an essential preliminary activity for if Gomorrha, as Colette observed in a criticism of Proust, is not nearly as vast or as well organized as Sodom, it is nonetheless a small, cohesive world in which connections between bed and text are numerous. This is particularly true during the *belle époque* when, in the wake of an emerging feminist movement, women writers, many of whom were lesbian, appeared on the French literary scene. They came from America and England, from the demi-monde, from the bourgeoisie. A central figure in this constellation of "Sapho 1900, Sapho cent pour cent"[3] is Natalie Clifford-Barney, an American living in Paris who had great wealth, many paramours, and a prestigious salon. She was a crossroads of lesbian associations and appeared, barely fictionalized, in the texts of many of the writers of the period: as Moonbeam and Miss Flossie in Liane de Pougy's *Idylle saphique* (1901), as Miss Flossie in Colette's *Claudine s'en va* (1903), as Lorély in Renée Vivien's *Une femme m'apparut* (1904), as Geraldine O'Brookomore in Ronald Firbank's *Inclinations* (1916), as the Amazon in Rémy de Gourmont's *Lettres intimes à l'amazone* (1927), as Evangeline Musset in Djuna Barnes's *Ladies Almanack* (1928), as Valérie Seymour in Radclyffe Hall's *The Well of Loneliness* (1928), as Laurette in Lucie Delarue-Mardrus's *L'ange et le pervers* (1934). Only George Sand has been the imputed model for as many literary heroines.

The Natalie Clifford-Barney connection takes us further afield to Marie Souvestre, whose fashionable boarding schools for girls—Les Ruches at Fontainebleau and Allenswood near Wimbledon Common—have been used as referents in texts as diverse as Eleanor Roosevelt's *This is My Story* (1939), Dorothy Strachey Bussy's *Olivia* (1941), and Michael Holroyd's biography of Lytton Strachey (1968). Natalie Clifford-Barney attended Les Ruches after Marie Souvestre had left France for England, but she was already involved in the kind of *amitié passionnée* that precipitated Marie Souvestre's departure. Through an early

3. Phrase used by André Billy in his *L'époque 1900* (Paris: Editions Jules Tallandier, 1951), p. 227.

American lover, Eva Palmer, mentioned by Renée Vivien in *Une femme m'apparut* and by Colette in *Mes apprentissages* (1936), Natalie Clifford-Barney was invited to visit Bryn Mawr College. Gertrude Stein, whom she knew, but not intimately, in Paris, used the lesbian relationship between M. Carey Thomas, president of Bryn Mawr, and Mary Gwinn in one of her first novels, *Fernhurst* (1904–1905, published in 1971). Bertrand Russell also refers to the intense Bryn Mawr scene in the first volume of his autobiography (1967). In the convergence of anecdotes and proper names a paradigm emerges. From Natalie Clifford-Barney to Marie Souvestre and M. Carey Thomas, from Parisian alcoves to a woman's school or college, we are obliged to acknowledge the inevitable presence of the Sappho model.

The Sappho Model

Sapho, Sappho, Psappha, Psappho, the lesbian from Lesbos. A confusion of facts, a profusion of semantic and phonemic connotations emanate from and surround the name. The small, ugly, lewd nymphomaniac and the beautiful poetess and muse coexist in the mind of the contemporary reader. They are part of a fragmented tradition through which we can formulate the outlines of a myth intended, like so many others, to domesticate woman's sexuality as well as, in this particular case, her relation to language.

Sappho and her island Lesbos are omnipresent in literature about women loving women, whatever the gender or sexual preference of the writer and whether or not Sappho and her island are explicitly named. Through her own poetic fragments she is the unwitting initiator of three apparently distinct models which have, in fact, a common origin: the older woman who seduces beautiful young girls, usually in a school or by extension in a convent or bordello; the older woman who commits suicide because her love for a younger man is unrequited; the woman poet as disembodied muse. The first model has its origin in those poems in which Sappho, the persona, speaks about the young women—Atthis, Anactoria, Gongyla—whom she desires. In the Greek and Latin literature that came after Sappho and in many later European texts this model, with its disguised references to the mother-daughter incest taboo, was discarded, except for its pornographic, comic value, in favor of the two others more palatable to the transmitters of a patriarchal code. It was Plato who, in referring to her as the tenth muse, (in an epigram that may be apocryphal) removed Sappho from the sexual arena, thereby allowing for the greatness of her poetry. Ovid, in the fifteenth and last letter of his *Heroides,* "Sappho and Phaon," codified into one legend the double model of Sappho the poet and Sappho the woman burning with corporeal lust who, because of her desperate love for Phaon, leapt from the Leucadian cliffs into the sea. The suicide model includes such prominent progeny as Phaedra and Dido and should not be forgotten in the larger corpus of lesbian intertextuality.

Although there is no evidence in Sappho's poems to corroborate the notion that she did indeed have a school, religious or secular, for young women, the gynaeceum, ruled by the seductive or seducing teacher has become, since the eighteenth century, the preferred locus for most fictions about women loving women. The conventions of this topos are simple and limited, signifying in their constraints the marginal status of lesbians and lesbianism. In general men play secondary roles as fathers, spiritual advisers, or intrusive suitors. The younger woman, whose point of view usually dominates, is always passionate and innocent. If, as is usually the case when the author of the text is a woman, it is the younger woman who falls in love, the narrative is structured so as to insist on this love as an awakening. The older woman as object of the younger woman's desire is restrained and admirable, beautiful and cultivated. If the older woman plays the role of seducer-corrupter, as she does in texts written by men, she is intense and often overtly hysterical (although this does not prevent her from being admirable in her intensity). Whoever plays the aggressive role, the exchanges between the older and the younger woman are reminiscent of a mother-daughter relationship. The mother of the younger woman is either dead or in some explicit way inadequate. Her absence is implied in the young woman's insistent need for a good-night kiss. The gynaeceum, particularly when it is represented by a school, also controls time. Time limits are set by the school calendar whose inexorable end announces the fatal separation, which may involve a death. Temporal structures reiterate the almost universally accepted notion that a schoolgirl crush is but a phase in the emotional development of the young woman, something that will pass. The denouement in these lesbian fairy tales is often brought about by a public event during which private passions explode.

The lesbian fairy tale based on the Sappho model is written by men of letters in the eighteenth and nineteenth centuries and by women and men of letters in the twentieth. I have chosen the term fairy tale in order to accentuate the distance from an apparent, transparent "real" and to insist on structural similarities between diverse fictions: the stock characters and stock situations; the rude or blissful awakening of sleeping beauty; the lesbian as good or bad fairy who is fate. The system of relationships in lesbian fairy tales, the reiterated network of obsessions reinforce an ideological system of stereotypes based on a synthesis of religious and psychological dogma.

Some of the texts that must be included within the Sappho model, whether they are written by women or by men, whether or not the gynaeceum is the locus, present, in strikingly similar terms, an explicit apology for lesbianism: the "Apologie de la secte anandryne" in *L'espion anglais*, "Delphine et Hippolyte," *L'idylle saphique, Claudine en ménage*, passages in *Le pur et l'impur* and the *Stances à Sophie*. This apology, made by a female character, is not to be understood as authorial endorsement of women loving women; on the contrary, the intention may be ironic. But it does point to a specific mode of discourse which is a significant feature of lesbian intertextuality.

The "Apologie de la secte anandryne" contains the first and most complete formulation of this discourse. The text is composed of a speech purportedly delivered on 28 March 1778 by Mlle de Raucourt, who was in fact a celebrated actress, lesbian, and active member of the flourishing *secte des anandrynes*. Mlle de Raucourt is a narrator thrice removed in the chain of reporting, since it is Mlle Sapho who is telling her story to a male narrator who is writing it to a friend and to the reader. This combination of remote narrative distance with the use of characters for whom there are referents beyond the text is frequent in writing about lesbians. Brantôme employs similar devices in his *Vie des dames galantes* and Colette in *Le pur et l'impur*. Lesbianism often appears in literature as something about which one has heard and perhaps, because lesbianism is considered unusual, it requires the kind of validation that only real names can confer.

The speech forms part of the initiation rite during which Mlle Sapho, a novice, is presented to the other members of the sect by her mother-teacher Mme de Furiel. (The mother-daughter, teacher-pupil categories are referred to constantly, as is the notion of model. The mother-teacher incubus is a model for the daughter-pupil succubus, who will in turn become a model.) The terms of the argument are quite simple: men, although they are initially exciting, provide inadequate physical and moral satisfaction; men are responsible for woman's physical suffering both in love-making and in the pains of childbirth: "Kisses will discolor your face, caresses will wither your breasts, your belly will lose its elasticity through pregnancies, your secret charms will be ruined by childbirth."[4] Men cause women mental suffering as well because they tire quickly of their wives. Heterosexuality is presented by means of such words as "pain," "blood," "slaughter," "care," "anxiety," "torment"; man is "perfidious," "fickle," "a cheat." The most important point in the argument is not, however, the perfidy of men but the glorification of the pleasures "true, pure, long-lasting and without remorse" (170) that exist between women: "In the intimacy between women there are no frightening and painful preliminaries; everything is pleasure (*jouissance*); each day, each hour, each minute this attachment is easily renewed; it is like waves of love which follow each other unceasingly as do those of the sea" (271). This complete harmony, this constant pleasure, does not exist, according to the apology, between women and men. Delphine delivers the same message to Hippolyte, Miss Flossie to Annhine, Claudine and Rézi to each other. Colette suggests it, tentatively, in *Le pur et l'impur* and then retracts it. The possibility of this paradise of oceanic bliss can only occur in a woman's world, between "sisters" (265).

4. "Apologie de la secte anandryne," in *L'espion anglais ou correspondance secrète entre Milord All'Eye et Milord All'Ear* (London: John Adamson, 1784), Vol. 10, p. 274. The first four volumes of *L'espion anglais* were written by Mathieu François Pidanzat de Mairobert. The authorship of the last six volumes is unknown.

The "Apologie de la secte anandryne" is the one text in the corpus I have consulted that supplements this defense of lesbianism with an idyllic image of the continuity of the cult, the vision of a utopia in which "maternal tenderness" replaces the "unrestrained passion of men" (276), in which wealth is shared, in which elegance of dress and abundance of jewels are requisites of beauty and useful in proselytizing. The evangelical spirit is strong in the "Apologie de la secte anandryne." The goal of the sect is the conversion of all women, particularly aristocratic women, to lesbianism because lesbianism is the most natural, the most virtuous, and the most pleasurable way of life. This is a unique apology, an extreme and rare formulation of the Sappho model in which lesbianism has an equally glorious past, present, and future. I cannot help but wonder about the identity of the unknown author.

From Lascivious Tribade to Revolutionary Signifier

Images of the lesbian are related in any given time and place to prevalent images of women. They are influenced by the same fear, loathing, or ignorance of female sexuality apparently subsumed by male (and in their wake female) psyches under the broader category, mysteries of life and death, or universal misogyny and gynophobia. From Martial to Brantôme the lesbian character is, within the context of the male anecdote, grotesque, an exaggeratedly comic version of the Sappho model reduced to her sexual preference. She is generally referred to as a tribade, from the Greek verb *tribadein,* meaning to rub. The tribade lies on top of her partner, whom she rubs with her unusually large clitoris. The tribade is lascivious because she enjoys what she does and grotesque because she imitates a man. The tribade is a social menace because, so the rumor runs within the text, she often succeeds. The burning question thus arises: does one woman lying on top of another and rubbing constitute adultery? By means of this male obsession the tribade is assimilated into accepted patterns of heterosexuality and enters into fiction. In the texts of Martial, Lucian, and Brantôme, who incorporates and recapitulates his predecessors, the tribade is always seen at a distance; she is talked about, reported on, spied on. This distance reinforces her status as a weird, comic object. But were it not for the hyperbolic and hypothetical size of her clitoris she would be completely incomprehensible. The tribade has value as a sexual being only insofar as she participates in the worship of the phallus. The phallus is always present as prime mover in the lesbian discourse of male scriptors.

The lesbian who appears in prose texts by male writers of the eighteenth, nineteenth, and twentieth centuries may be a possessed hysteric, a charismatic evangelist, or a lascivious glutton guilty of profaning either the law of God or the natural law or both. She tries to seduce a younger woman and sometimes succeeds. She is often responsible for the death of a male figure. She is always an outlaw, a powerful challenge to one of society's most cherished principles, sexual order. The world of the text in which she appears is immediately thrown into confusion. The confusion ends with her death or disappearance, or that of her victim, or of her male antagonist. From Martial's Bassa and Lucian's Megilla, model tribades of antiquity, to the lesbians of Diderot, Balzac, Proust, and Sartre, the female homosexual incarnating the Sappho model has moved from a small corner of the canvas to a central position. The comic, lascivious tribade lives on in the demonic corrupter, but in general the imitation of the male is less pronounced than the affirmation of incomprehensible femininity.

The lesbian in lyric poetry written by men, from Pontus de Tyard's "Elégie pour une dame énamourée d'une autre dame" to Pierre Louÿs's *Chansons de Bilitis,* bears little resemblance to her prose sister. The discourse on lesbians in prose narrative tends to reproduce some culturally accepted derogatory point of view on women loving women, whereas the lyric poem tends to represent the lesbian as synonymous with a mysterious world of feminine pleasure. The prose narrative usually uses the lesbian for social or psychological censorious reporting on aberrant female behavior; the lyric poem projects through the lesbian an unattainable dream of erotic love in the absence of the censor.

A major thematic transformation takes place when women begin to write about women loving women. The experience of loving a woman is, for the narrative voice, *the* experience of awakening, the revelation of an unknown, unsuspected world which, once glimpsed, can never be ignored. It is a momentous discovery whose importance within the text and beyond was until recently obscured by the weighty screen of psychological misreadings. Women's narratives were examined for signs of deviant behavior that would reveal simplified, vulgarized Freudian categories. The lesbian had to be a pre-Oedipal polymorphous perverse child, full of rage because of an early, deprived relationship with the mother, obsessed with death, voraciously hungry for love, exorbitantly demanding and dependent. Critics reveled in images of alimentary deprivation that would prove the prevalence of the oral element in the affective life of the lesbian character. Indeed, whatever happened to the lesbian within the text, she was submerged from without by the ruling orthodoxy.

Recent feminist critics have reversed these judgments, turning condemnation of regressive behavior into exploration of uncharted modes of affectivity. Hysteria and oceanic feeling are exalted. The Minoan-Mycenean civilization that preceded the Oedipal institution of patriarchal law is glorified. What began a long time ago as the domestication of Sappho has become a concerted effort to imagine a world before the domestication of women, before the deliberate taming of her sexuality and her language. In such a world the woman who loves women and writes is the central figure in a new mythology.

Colette, the Foremother

Colette, the foremother, left God out and was accused by the morally serious and believing of frivolity. Critics, female and male, took their revenge. Silence or banter surrounded her six-year liaison with the Marquise de Belbeuf. The text which she considered to be her most important, *Le pur et l'impur,* was either ignored or treated as a bizarre excrescence. The preponderant role played by women, alone and together, in her writings, as mothers and daughters, as sisters, as friends, as lovers, received less recognition than the more obvious but fundamentally less important relationships between women and men. Colette occupies a privileged place and therefore takes up most space in a study of lesbian intertextuality. Her texts, like Brantôme's *Vie des dames galantes,* recapitulate an earlier tradition, but they also announce new departures. In 1900, for the first time since Sappho, the narrator Claudine in *Claudine à l'école* looks at another woman as an object of pleasure and without any excuses describes her pleasure. A great revolution had begun:

> She is like a cat caressing, delicate and sensitive, incredibly winning. I like to look at her pink little blond's face, her golden eyes with their curly lashes. Beautiful eyes that are always ready to smile! They oblige the young men to turn around when she goes out. Often, while we are chatting at the door of her excited little class, Mlle Sergent walks past us to go to her room, without a word, staring at us with a jealous, searching gaze. Her silence tells my new friend and me that she is furious at seeing us get on so well together.[5]

Everyone is looking at Aimée Lanthenay: Claudine, the young boys, Mlle Sergent. Voyeurism, in contrast to what transpires in male novels, is neither secret nor cerebral. It is a public activity. The originality of Claudine's voyeurism is that it is directly related to her appetites. What is less original are Claudine's insolence and impertinence, the marks of the titillated and titillating schoolgirl whose desire for Aimée and later for Rézi recalls the presence of the lesbian in many turn-of-the-century texts, a male creation, the summum of naughtiness.

From Colette's Claudine to Violette Leduc's Je and Thérèse, to Monique Wittig's J/e, female voyeurism gains in intensity as it focuses on the relation between the self and the other. At the same time the stereotypical posturing of the curious adolescent characteristic of Claudine progressively diminishes, finally disappears. The movement from Claudine to J/e is a movement from self-consciousness in culture to self-consciousness in writing, from an attempt at portraying new attitudes in an old language to an attempt at creating a language capable of speaking the unspoken in Western literature—female sexuality with woman as namer.

"Lesbian" is a word the narrator "Colette" never uses and

5. Colette, *Claudine à l'école. Oeuvres complètes* (Paris: Flammarion, 1948), Vol. 1, p. 21.

"homosexual" is reserved for men. Her female characters who are attracted to women have no labels. They do, however, fall into two major, quite traditional groups: the impudent, perverse younger woman like Claudine and perhaps Renée Vivien; the mannish woman like the Baronne de la Berche in *La fin de Chéri* (1926) or la Chevalière in *Le pur et l'impur*. The narrator's attitude toward them oscillates between a maternalistic protection—protection from the uncomprehending male, protection from the "ordinary reader" who may be smirking—and a series of mild attacks in which these women are variously seen as child-ish," "infantile," "adolescent," "crude," "promiscuous," or "de-luded." Within this spectrum female homosexuality is sancti-fied by comparisons to the mother-daughter relationship. This occurs initially and most powerfully in "Nuit blanche," a prose poem in *Les vrilles de la vigne* (1908):

> Because I know that then you will tighten your embrace and that if the rocking of your arms does not calm me, your kisses will become more tenacious, your hands more loving, and that you will give me pleasure as an aid, as a supreme exorcism which will drive out the demons of fever, of anger, of unrest.... You will give me pleasure, leaning over me, your eyes full of maternal solicitude, you who are seeking in your passionate friend, for the child you never had.[6]

All of "Colette's" empathetic attitudes toward women loving women are contained within this image and will be repeated in nonlesbian situations: in the relationships between "Colette" and "Sido," between Chéri and Léa, between all those who love passionately and exclusively. What is involved is someone younger needing protection, someone older offering a refuge and caring. The younger person receives pleasure, but the older person who gives pleasure is searching. The quest is not for the mother, the mother is always there, but for the child. The female figure who dominates in Colette's female hierarchy is the

6. Colette, "Nuit blanche" in *Les vrilles de la vigne. Oeuvres complètes* (Paris: Flammarion, 1949), Vol. 3, pp. 219–20.

mother figure, Sido crying, "Where are the children?" It is also the role of the mother who loves to preside over the sexual ritual, which without her presence is incomplete.

Le pur et l'impur restates all the forms of lesbianism and all the narrative commentary on women loving women that appear in Colette's texts from 1900 to 1932. Colette is writing with and against Marcel Proust. It is obvious that the publication of *A la recherche du temps perdu* encouraged her both to deal directly with homosexuality, female and male, and to present images of female homosexuality different from Proust's febrile Gomorrha. Within the French literary tradition *Le pur et l'impur* takes its place in the exclusive company of André Gide's *Corydon* (1924) and the overture of Proust's *Sodome et Gomorrhe* (1922) as a rare example of explicit narrative commentary on homosexuality. "Renée Vivien," one of the texts included in *Le pur et l'impur*, was published in a limited edition in 1928. The mid and late 1920's, particularly in England, were *anni mirabili* for novels by women that depict important lesbian characters or references to women loving women. It is unlikely that Colette was familiar with Virginia Woolf's *Mrs. Dalloway* (1925) or her *Orlando* (1928), or with Rosamund Lehmann's *Dusty Answer* (1927), but she did know of Radclyffe Hall's *The Well of Loneliness* (1928), and she obviously knew the screen version of Christa Winsloë's *Mädchen in Uniforme* (1931) for which she wrote the French subtitles.

Le pur et l'impur is a restless text. The narrator "Colette" struggles to maintain a deliberate and decent distance through time, texts, and translations from the variety of pseudonymous women loving women, the exotic, extinct species on which she reports: la Chevalière, Renée Vivien, Amalia X . . . , Lucienne de . . . , and the Ladies of Llangollen. "Colette" intrudes on and retreats from the text which is an organized mélange of reporting (anecdotes, portraits) and commentary (maxims and generalizations). The women who love women occupy the central parts of *Le pur et l'impur*. They are preceded by Charlotte, the woman who feigns pleasure to please her young male lover, and Don Juan who gives, according to his accounting, more than he receives, and followed by male homosexuals whose "theatrical cynicism" and "childishness" are redeemed by their capacity, which the narrator insists lesbians lack, to forget the other sex completely. The only couple in *Le pur et l'impur* to receive the narrator's benediction and admiration is the couple formed by two men. "I find it in me to see in pederasty a kind of legitimacy and to acknowledge its eternal character."[7] In the volume which "will treat sadly of pleasure" (31), this is the unique relationship which is not depicted by the narrator as an unequal exchange: one partner giving, the other receiving, in an ultimately self-destructive pattern.

Whether it be in the occasional discordance between narrative commentary and reporting, or in the shifts of tone from lyrical to ironic to lyrical, or in the sudden eruptions of moral and psychological rhetoric, the text, like the androgyne and like Renée Vivien, "wanders." The elusive text abounds in contradictions and paradoxes that reflect the narrator's variable points of view about women loving women, about what constitutes feminine/masculine behavior. Ambiguity is sustained on all levels of the text. From the mixture of real and pseudonymous anthroponyms—"Colette," Marguerite Moreno, la Chevalière—emanates a genre ambiguity (is it autobiography? is it fiction?) which mirrors the sexual ambiguity (is it female? is it male?). There is an implied equivalence between textual and sexual androgyny and travesty. The pages on la Chevalière and her group constitute an indeterminate text in which older, aristocratic women in tuxedos, wearing monocles, instruct their lower-class protégées in the ways of the respectable world. The narrator employs "these women" to insist on the sadness (her point of view), not the ridicule (but she has an eye for that too), of their impossible masculine masquerade and to reveal their ineradicable appurtenance to a woman's world. They gather together "uneasy," "haunted," in a cellar restaurant in Montmartre, seeking "a refuge, warmth and darkness" (169). There, safe temporarily from male intrusion, they indulge in an activity more subversive than love-making: they communicate with each other in woman's language. "I reveled in the admirable quickness of their half-spoken language, the exchange of threats,

7. Colette, *The Pure and the Impure*, trans. Herma Briffault, Introduction by Janet Flanner (Harmondsworth: Penguin, 1971), p. 118.

of promises, as if, once the slow-thinking male had been banished, every message from woman to woman became clear and overwhelming, restricted to a small but infallible number of signs" (69). "Slow-thinking" but dangerous, the image of the heterosexual male emerges in the guise of a retarded brute whose shadow is always present in the narrator's commentary as a reminder to her and to the reader of the certain danger that lurks outside and within "these women." The narrator's pleasure in the spectacle of women signaling together partially corrects the constant menace and the pervasive sadness that permeate the text. It is as if, near the end of the tour, the guide discovered a fragment of what it was she had been looking for initially and had been unable to locate because the site was so cluttered. When the male is removed, when the subterranean space is occupied uniquely by la Chevalière and her group (which includes the narrator-guide), the masks fall, the women temporarily, hesitantly, come out.

The transition in the text from la Chevalière to Renée Vivien is from a nonliterary to a literary milieu of the *belle époque* and from a shy discreet butch to a vulgar *femme de lettres*. The narrator quite clearly prefers, in its purity, the unwritten, "half-spoken" woman's language of la Chevalière and her group to the "cynical opinions" and the sentimental imitative poetry of Renée Vivien. The third category of women who love women is represented by Amalia X . . . and Lucienne de . . . , the fourth by the Ladies of Llangollen. It is as if the narrator were testing herself against the portraits of these women in order to determine whether or not she was a lesbian, in order to determine the limits of her understanding and her compassion. "Colette's" central obsession is with the women who imitate men (la Chevalière, Lucienne de . . . , Lady Eleanor Butler) and thereby violate what would seem to be the narrator's fantasm of an exclusively woman's world. "You see, when a woman remains a woman, she is a complete human being. She lacks nothing, even insofar as her *amie* is concerned. But if she ever gets it into her head to try to be a man, then she's grotesque. What is more ridiculous, what is sadder, than a woman pretending to be a man?" (86). This judgment, pronounced by the wise Amalia X . . ., an aging Tunisian Jewess who functions here as a second narrator, represents,

I think, the simplest but most profound of "Colette's " conclusions. The woman who imitates a man, either in love or in literature, is not an acceptable model for a woman who loves women.

Because the narrator saves them for the end, the reader assumes that the Ladies of Llangollen will be the uniquely successful couple. But the Ladies of Llangollen are set up to fall from the narrator's grace in the course of her writing about them. The pastoral tone of the introductory hymn to the Ladies' mutual love—"I want to speak with dignity, that is, with warmth, of what I call the noble season of feminine passion" (91)—is not sustained. The idyllic aura that surrounds the multiple images of togetherness, "the magic of this radiant friendship," is dissipated slowly by a change in point of view. Light mockery transforms the perfect couple into a pathetic, fragile couple. The final step is the destruction by implication and direct castigation of the original ideal image. "As usual with perfectly happy people, the younger woman neglected all means of expression and, mute, became a sweet shadow. She was no longer Sarah Ponsonby, but a part of that double person called 'we.' She even lost her name, which Lady Eleanor almost never mentioned in the diary. From then on she was called 'Beloved' and 'Better Half' and 'Delight of my heart'" (97). "Colette" interpellates Lady Eleanor Butler and accuses her of three crimes: eliminating Sarah Ponsonby's identity, behaving like a man, and creating, through her diary, a fabulous fiction. The narrator challenges "stout-hearted Eleanor's" version of the Ladies of Llangollen by imagining Sarah Ponsonby's subversive diary. The text ends with a curious reversal: a short letter written by Sarah Ponsonby after the death of Lady Eleanor Butler in which she speaks neither of her sorrow nor of her lost friend but, like Colette's mother "Sido" in *La naissance du jour* (1928), of flowers that may bloom. Although "Colette" is obliged to accept the report of the Ladies of Llangollen's fifty-year idyll, her comments betray her suspicion that it was a romantic delusion systematically sustained by Lady Eleanor Butler through her diary. But if the couple composed of women together is doomed a priori the woman alone who loves women is privileged. She has for "Colette" a *magie suggestive* that belongs to the mother-teacher-seducer exemplified by "Sido" and "Colette" herself, the signifiers of the Sappho model.

The narrator's moral and psychological conclusions which the reader distills from the totality of the text imply that "Colette" is not nearly as interested in lesbians as she is in women and the possibilities of their survival. She attempts to locate through an exploration of female sexual behavior and frequent modulations in point of view, what apparently works, what really goes on and at what price. Unlike her successors in the examination of the "dark continent" of female sexuality, Violette Leduc or Monique Wittig, Colette does not focus on love-making or the celebration of the female body. Rather she insists throughout *Le pur et l'impur* that "In no way is it passion that fosters the devotion of two women, but rather a feeling of kinship" (92), by which she means "similarities." Women who love women come together in Colette's world because they are fleeing from a painful experience with a man and are looking for a *retraite sentimentale*, "Sido's" warmth with its attendant garden and animals. Lesbianism is a *pis aller*. It is a copy of either mother-daughter or male-female love or both.

If homosexual and heterosexual coupling are unsatisfactory, if promiscuity is undesirable, then what remains is the single woman writing alone about woman's sexuality. The narrator "Colette" is almost never implicated in sexual activity, but is always, like her male predecessors, reporting on the activities of other women. When she removes the Sappho model from the schoolroom, she keeps it for herself. In Colette's ultimate expression of the Sappho model, Sappho fills her erotic needs through her creations and her readers.

The Death of God/The Birth of the Lesbian-Feminist

There is no one person in or out of fiction who represents a stronger challenge to the Judeo-Christian tradition, to patriarchy and phallocentrism than the lesbian-feminist. After the end-of-the-century wailings over the death of the ideal God, after the aesthetic retreats and constructions of the dandys in life and art, after the liberation of the male imagination through surrealist techniques, after the existentialist images of male fraternity—the band of courageous brothers facing nothingness together, or battle, and creating heroic portraits of man's dignity, man's fate, man's hope—the women began, ever so slowly, to see connections between production and reproduction, to masturbate consciously, to explore the "dark continent," and to write. The most subversive voices of the century are, and will be, in their texts. Because they are trying to displace the phallus, they propose a new pleasure and a new imagery. They propose new relationships to gender and pronouns, to the jejeune past, the hysterical present, and the luminous future. They do not intend to save the world because salvation died with God, but to create hyperbolic, sensuous fictions that illuminate possibilities for the woman as narrator and the woman as reader.

What breaks down in this new prophetic universe is the God-ruled phallologocentric system and the imaginative sensibility it exploited. As outsiders to traditional gender semiotics, innovative lesbian-feminist writers invent new forms. The established relations between the traditional female/male love story and the mythology used to transmit the story are no longer operative. The veneration of male figures and the need for their approbation disappear and with them the old categories of patriarchal solid space and past time. The elimination of the female/male opposition within the text does not, of course, eliminate feminine/masculine as biological entities or cultural signs, but the absence of the masculine figure from the text makes it possible to diminish a primary source of conflict and to reinterpret such historically male-created negative images of femininity as the Medusa, the witch, or the hysteric. The I/you opposition remains, but the other is now also familiar, familial—a sister, a friend.

The differences that we find in the textual representation of female homosexuality in Colette, in Violette Leduc, and in Monique Wittig are related significantly to the literary and social codes of the periods in which these writers began to write. There would seem to be homology between Colette and the *belle époque,* between Leduc and the flowering of French existentialism, between Wittig and the formalist-feminist movements of the late sixties and early seventies. Colette's mother figures, Leduc's young schoolgirls, and Wittig's Amazon women recall and reproduce the *monstres sacrés* of the theater world, the precocious, anguished young women who haunted the existentialist cafés, the romantic feminists and revolutionary feminists of the French women's liberation movement. The temporal distance between the narrative "I" and the other or others is also revealing: "Colette" is always looking back nostalgically to an exotic past in which women dominated the stage; Leduc as "I" struggles and desires in a present perfect; Wittig's *guérillères* and slashed "I" are installed in an eternal repetitive present which is already from the reader's point of view an apocalyptic future. Colette tells a fairly traditional story, remaining within the narrative norms established by nineteenth-century "realistic" fiction. Leduc also remains within this tradition, although she disrupts it thematically by insisting explicitly on the narrator's subjectivity, on her deepest feelings of shame and desire. Wittig, on the contrary, is working within another tradition in which the narrative conventions of plot and character have been, like the first person J/e, dismembered.

From Colette through Leduc to Wittig a sexual and textual revolution has taken place. The lesbian in literature has undergone a radical transformation from impertinent young woman, fragile couple, solitary writer, ecstatic schoolgirl, to aggressive lover and namer. The images recurrent in Colette's texts of two women seeking refuge or lying voluptuously in each other's arms and the lyrical descriptions of passionate adolescent love-making in Leduc's novels bear little resemblance to the gluttonous cannibalism of Wittig's truncated, anonymous J/e. Only the presence of the Sappho model remains constant, although the manner in which it informs the text is very different in *Le pur et l'impur* from what it is in *La bâtarde* and *Thérèse et Isabelle* or *Le corps lesbien*. In *Le pur et l'impur*, Sappho is mentioned only once in the derogatory phrase "the Sapphos met by chance" (93). In *La bâtarde* and *Thérèse et Isabelle*, Sappho is never mentioned and in *Le corps lesbien*, Sappho, the ruling muse, is invoked twenty-two times. The frequency of the name is almost as great as in the poems of Renée Vivien. But if Sappho's name is absent from *La bâtarde* and *Thérèse et Isabelle*, Sappho is inevitably present in the gynaeceum in which the protagonists spend their time seeking each other and making love. Sappho is also present in the narrator's passion for her mother, a passion which, in *La bâtarde*, has as its obsessive maternal object the grandmother and, in the later volumes of Leduc's autobiography, is focused on Simone de Beauvoir. But more importantly Sappho dominates intertextually as she does in *Le corps lesbien*, through the insistence on the physical symptoms of desire, the visceral awareness of the female body, and the endless repetitions. In Sappho's own fragments the symptomatology of love, expressed by such rhetorical devices of repetition as anaphora and anadiplosis, focuses on the exchange between psyche and soma.

Repetition underlines the obsessive nature of Sappho's, Leduc's, and Wittig's texts and reveals the writers' fantasms. But these texts go beyond idiosyncratic sexual preferences toward the creation of a new mythology in which the female body is undomesticated: "If I meet you suddenly, I can't speak—my tongue is broken; a thin flame runs under my skin; seeing nothing, hearing only my own ears drumming, I drip with sweat; trembling shakes my body and I turn paler than dry grass. At such times death isn't far from me."[8]

To undomesticate women would mean to change the relationship between nature and culture and seriously to alter the configuration of culture as we knew it. This can only be realized through the creation of images powerful enough to impress themselves on the reader's mind and to resist the pressures of misinterpretation. Sappho's texts provided the elements for a new perception of female reality, but representatives of the dominant culture fashioned from these elements the myth of romantic love, using the millenial equivalence between woman and death. Sappho is much more concrete in her poetry. She is suggesting equivalences between the physical symptoms of desire and the physical symptoms of death, not between Eros and Thanatos. The female body's initial undomestication takes place in Sappho's texts. The body and its reactions are given poetic importance. The female body and the female persona's attitudes might have become a legitimate topos for lyric poetry. But the domestication process set in almost immediately, and Sappho's texts by both conscious and unconscious misinterpretations were

8. Sappho, "He is more than a hero" in *Sappho*, trans. Mary Barnard (Berkeley and Los Angeles: University of California Press, 1958), No. 39.

incorporated into a tradition in which the independence of the female body was taboo.

There were, between Sappho and Violette Leduc, women writers who attempted to liberate women from the most obvious legal and social injustices. And although some of these writers—Christine de Pisan, Germaine de Staël, George Sand, Colette—did attack a fundamental source of woman's plight, sexual oppression, they never presented sufficiently challenging counterimages. It may well be that only a committed lesbian-feminist writer can, within our culture, succeed in transmitting cogent images of undomesticated women. In her preface to the English edition of *Le corps lesbien,* Monique Wittig situates her text among others that have lesbianism as their theme:

> a theme which cannot even be described as taboo, for it has no real existence in the history of literature. Male homosexual literature has a past, it has a present. The lesbians, for their part, are silent—just as all women are as women at all levels. When one has read the poems of Sappho, Radclyffe Hall's *Well of Loneliness,* the poems of Sylvia Plath and Anais Nin, *La bâtarde* by Violette Leduc, one has read everything. Only the women's movement has proved capable of producing lesbian texts in a context of total rupture with masculine culture, texts written by women exclusively for women, careless of male approval. *Le corps lesbien* falls into this category.[9]

Violette Leduc is the only French writer Monique Wittig acknowledges as a predecessor. It is obvious that the scenes in *La bâtarde* and in *Thérèse et Isabelle* in which young girls make love are acceptable to Wittig not merely because females are making love but because the narrator as lesbian is describing her own experience. The lesbian is no longer the object of literary discourse seen from an outside point of view. She is her own heroine:

> The hand was wandering through whispering snow-capped bushes, over the last frosts on the meadows, over the first buds as

9. Monique Wittig, *The Lesbian Body,* trans. David LeVay (New York: William Morrow, 1975), p. 9.

they swelled to fullness. The springtime that had been crying its impatience with the voice of tiny birds under my skin was now curving and swelling into flower. Isabelle, stretched out upon the darkness, was fastening my feet with ribbons, unwinding the swaddling bands of my alarm. With hands laid flat upon the mattress, I was immersed in the selfsame magic task as she. She was kissing what she had caressed and then, light as a feather duster, the hand began to flick, to brush the wrong way all that it had smoothed before. The sea monster in my entrails quivered. Isabelle was drinking at my breast, the right, the left, and I drank with her, sucking the milk of darkness when her lips had gone. The fingers were returning now, encircling and testing the warm weight of my breast. The fingers were pretending to be waifs in a storm; they were taking shelter inside me. A host of slaves, all with the face of Isabelle, fanned my brow, my hands.

She knelt up in the bed.

"Do you love me?"

I led her hand up to the precious tears of joy.[10]

The text concentrates obsessively on the actions being performed. Love-making occupies a central place in the text, although not all of the text, as in *Le corps lesbien*. But it is in large part what the text and the narrator's adventure through life are all about. These are the privileged moments, this is the paradise and the epiphany. Violette Leduc has deliberately chosen a lyrical style through which to produce the effect of joy and ecstasy. The syntax changes to accomodate longer sentences which attempt to recreate the rhythms of expectation, tension, and diffusion and to recount the gestures of both partners. Through a traditional nature code, springtime, with its flowers and its storms, invades the text associating with the pleasures of love-making the pleasures of an awakening and a renewal. It is, of course, a verbal pleasure, the moment in the writing of the narrator's greatest command over her language. The power of the word and the pleasures of the female body are intimately related. Love-making is the primary source of inspiration. It opens and defines a world whose existence had been suspected but

10. Violette Leduc, *La bâtarde*, trans. Derek Coltman, with a foreword by Simone de Beauvoir (New York: Farrar, Straus, and Giroux, 1965), p. 84.

never so explicitly stated. Within the context of lesbian intertextuality Violette Leduc is indeed the first French writer to take us
beyond the Sappho model to Sappho's own texts—the lesbian
writer writing as lesbian. But the power of this image of female
love-making is weakened in *La bâtarde* by the autobiographical
nature of Leduc's enterprise. As soon as the narrator and the
text move out of the gynaeceum into a male-dominated world,
the female body can no longer occupy the center of the stage.
Because the gynaeceum and schoolgirl love are so invested with
intertextual connotations and because Violette Leduc uses traditional nature codes for metaphoric support, *Thérèse et Isabelle* is
not nearly as original or as disturbing a text as *Le corps lesbien*:

> In this dark adored adorned gehenna say your farewells m/y very
> beautiful one m/y very strong one m/y very indomitable one m/y
> very learned one m/y very ferocious one m/y very gentle one m/y
> best beloved to what they, the women, call affection tenderness or
> gracious abandon. There is not one who is unaware of what takes
> place here, which has no name as yet. . . . not one will be able to
> bear seeing you with eyes turned up lids cut off your yellow smok-
> ing intestines spread in the hollow of your hands your tongue spat
> from your mouth long green strings of bile flowing over your
> breast, not one will be able to bear your low frenetic insistent
> laughter. The gleam of your teeth your joy your sorrow the hid-
> den life of your organs your nerves their rupture their spurting
> forth death slow decomposition stench being devoured by worms
> your open skull, all will be equally unbearable to her. . . .
> At this point I invoke your help m/y incomparable Sappho, give
> m/e by thousands the fingers that allay the wounds, give m/e the
> lips the tongue the saliva which draw one into the slow sweet
> poisoned country from which one cannot return. . . .
> I discover that your skin can be lifted layer by layer, I pull, it
> lifts off, it coils above your knees, I pull starting at the labia. . . . [11]

In *Le corps lesbien* Monique Wittig has created, through the
incessant use of hyperbole and a refusal to employ traditional
body codes, images sufficiently blatant to withstand reabsorption
into male literary culture. Wittig has taken Sappho out of the
gynaeceum in which she had been confined for so long. She has

11. Wittig, pp. 15, 16, 17.

brought her back to Lesbos and placed her among the Amazons. A recognizable social context, itself a purveyor of labels, has been replaced in *Le corps lesbien* by a stylized decor composed of conglomerate elements of the Sappho and Amazon legends: islands, a beach, the sea, the color violet, strong female bodies, uniquely female names. This hymn to the lesbian body is also a hymn to the body from Lesbos who is not only lover, writer, muse, but potent goddess, the central figure of a new mythology. There would seem to be little doubt that for Monique Wittig, who has the passion of the true believer, lesbianism is a cause, the only conceivable rallying point for the elaboration of a woman's culture. As an ideology on which to impose a fiction, the possibilities as well as the risks of lesbianism are enormous. Monique Wittig has chosen, in this text, to use lesbianism as a means of destroying the accepted male love discourse as well as the accepted male literary stereotypes about the female body. The destruction begins with the "farewells" of the first sentence and continues through reiterated parodies of sacred literary texts to the torturing, beating, flaying, peeling, devouring, vomiting, and caressing of female flesh. The physical exchange between J/e and Tu is reminiscent at times of a *pas de deux,* at times of a boxing match, at times of a surgical operation. But destruction of one order of language and sensibility implies creation of a new order. The J/e of *Le corps lesbien* is the most powerful lesbian in literature because as a lesbian-feminist she reexamines and redesigns the universe. Starting with the female body she recreates through anecdote and proper names a new aqueous female space and a new female time in which the past is abolished. She is, in fact, the only true anti-Christ, the willful assassin of Christian love.

Provocation exists at every level of the text: in the monotony of the lists, in the female endings attached to masculine proper nouns, in the typography, and in the verbal violence. J/e names the hitherto unnamed. The desperate desire for impossible union is described through the trajectories traced by fingers, hands, tongue outside and inside the body. The female body, whose every part is enumerated, destroyed, and reassembled is the alpha and omega of Wittig's fiction. In the beginning is the body and at the end; an indestructible body, singular in the text, but signifying the potentiality of all female bodies.

No one since Sappho herself has made a greater contribution to lesbian intertextuality than Monique Wittig. Not only has she restructured elements of the Sappho model, eliminating the enclosed spaces of school or convent, cellar restaurant or alcove, but she has transformed the image of Sappho by associating Sappho's verbal power with the physical power of the Amazons. Wittig has abandoned any attempt to insert Sappho into male culture. *Le corps lesbien* is a textual and cultural gamble. It is a courageous aspiration toward the creation of a linguistic behavior that would, by its very existence, prepare the way for the undomestication of women. Whatever the ultimate fate of the book and the revolution it solicits, it does herald the second coming of Sappho.

Because the corpus of texts that contain the Sappho model is small, any major alteration in the angle of vision transforms the entire body, illuminating forgotten fragments, suggesting new correspondences. The poems and stories of Renée Vivien, for example, begin to emerge from almost complete oblivion under the new lighting. Instead of dismissing them as poor imitations of the Baudelairean lyric or as examples of the inferior "feminine" writing of the *belle époque,* we can now see them as interesting attempts by a lesbian to write as a lesbian about lesbianism. As our awareness of the Sappho model grows, a writer such as Renée Vivien takes her place within a canon that has been until this century an exclusively male creation. Perhaps the most tenacious and pernicious element in this creation, reiterated by almost every writer, female and male, with the exception of Monique Wittig, is that lesbianism implies a nostalgic regression to the mother-daughter couple and is therefore not viable. A text such as *Le corps lesbien* is not concerned with psychological causality. Lesbian intertextuality will never be the same.

Notes on the Editors
and Contributors

George Stambolian teaches French and comparative literature at Wellesley College. He has written *Marcel Proust and the Creative Encounter* and articles on modern French literature and American drama, and is the editor of *Twentieth Century French Fiction: Essays for Germaine Brée.*

Elaine Marks is director of the Women's Studies Research Center at the University of Wisconsin (Madison). She is the author of *Colette, Simone de Beauvoir: Encounters with Death,* and articles on autobiography, women writers, Proust, Sartre, and Cioran.

Jean-Paul Aron is a historical anthropologist living in Paris. He is the author of *Essais d'épistémologie biologique* and *Le mangeur du XIXe siècle* and a co-author of *Anthropologie du conscrit français.* He has also written novels, *La retenue* and *Point mort,* and a collection of plays, *Théâtre.* He is co-author with Roger Kempf of *Le pénis et la démoralisation de l'Occident.*

Cécile Arsène teaches French literature and is active in teacher training at the University of Paris.

George H. Bauer teaches French literature at the University of Southern California. He is the author of *Sartre and the Artist* and several articles on modern French writers and is an editor of the Pléiade edition of Sartre's *Romans*.

Eric Bentley taught dramatic literature at Columbia University for many years. He is presently visiting professor at the State University of New York (Buffalo). His critical works include *A Century of Hero Worship, The Playwright as Thinker, Bernard Shaw, In Search of Theatre, The Dramatic Event, What is Theatre?, The Life of the Drama, The Theatre of Commitment,* and *Theatre of War.* As a playwright he has written *Orpheus in the Underworld, A Time to Die and a Time to Live, The Red, White, and Black, Are You Now or Have You Ever Been?, The Recantation of Galileo Galilei, Expletive Deleted, From the Memoirs of Pontius Pilate, Posing as a Sodomite,* and *Lord Alfred's Lover.* He is the author of numerous articles and editor of several anthologies on the theater, and has edited and translated the plays of Brecht, Pirandello, and Wolf Biermann. He has also recorded seven albums of songs and texts, primarily by Brecht.

Frank Paul Bowman is a member of the Department of Romance Languages at the University of Pennsylvania. He is the author of *Prosper Mérimée: Heroism, Pessimism, Irony* and *Montaigne: "Essais"* as well as *Eliphas Lévi, visionnaire romantique* and *Le Christ romantique,* and has written numerous articles on French romanticism, autobiography, and the Renaissance.

Germaine Brée is Kenan Professor of French at Wake Forest University. Author of *Du temps perdu au temps retrouvé: introduction à l'oeuvre de Marcel Proust, André Gide, l'insaisissable Protée, Camus, Albert Camus, The World of Marcel Proust, Camus and Sartre: Crisis and Commitment, Women Writers in France: Variations on a Theme, Littérature française: le XXe siècle II, 1920–1970,* and co-author of *An Age of Fiction: The French Novel from Gide to Camus,* she has written articles on all aspects of modern French literature and has edited several texts and anthologies.

Robert Champigny, Research Professor in French at Indiana University, is the author of *Portrait of a Symbolist Hero, Stages on Sartre's*

Way, Sur un héros païen, Le genre poétique, Le genre dramatique, Pour une esthétique de l'essai, Ontologie du narratif, Humanisme et racisme humain, and *Le jeu philosophique,* as well as numerous articles on genres and twentieth-century writers. He has written five volumes of poetry: *Monde; Horizon; La mission, la demeure, la roue; Les passes;* and *L'analyse.*

Hélène Cixous teaches English literature at the University of Paris (Vincennes). Her novels and "fictions" include *Le prénom de Dieu, Dedans, Le troisième corps, Les commencements, Un vrai jardin, Neutre, Tombe, Portrait du soleil, Souffles, Partie, La, Angst,* and *Préparatifs de noces au delà de l'abîme.* She has also written plays, *La pupille, Le paradire, Portrait de Dora,* and critical studies, *L'exil de Joyce ou l'art du remplacement, Prénoms de personne, Un K. incompréhensible,* and *La jeune née* (with Catherine Clément).

Isabelle de Courtivron teaches French at the Massachusetts Institute of Technology. She is co-editor with Elaine Marks of the forthcoming anthology, *New French Feminisms.*

Serge Doubrovsky teaches French literature at New York University. He is the author of *Corneille et la dialectique du héros, Pourquoi la nouvelle critique: critique et objectivité,* and *La place de la madeleine: écriture et fantasme chez Proust.* He has also written a collection of short stories, *Le jour S,* two novels, *La dispersion* and *Fils,* and several essays on classical and modern French literature.

Wallace Fowlie is James B. Duke Professor emeritus of French at Duke University. His books of criticism include *A Reading of Proust, Stendhal, Rimbaud: A Critical Study, André Gide: His Life and Art, Mallarmé, Age of Surrealism, Love in Literature, Paul Claudel,* and *Letters of Henry Miller and Wallace Fowlie.* He has translated works by Rimbaud, Saint-John Perse, Molière, and Claudel. His most recent book, *Journal of Rehearsals: A Memoir,* contains an account of his first meeting with Gide.

René Galand is a member of the Department of French at Wellesley College. He is the author of *L'âme celtique de Renan, Baudelaire:*

poétiques et poésie, and *Saint-John Perse,* and the co-author of *Baudelaire as a Love-Poet and Other Essays.* In addition to his articles on nineteenth- and twentieth-century French literature, he has written three collections of poems and several short stories in his native Breton language.

Félix Guattari is a psychiatrist who has practiced at the unorthodox La Borde clinic. He is the author of *Psychanalyse et transversalité* and *La révolution moléculaire,* and co-author with the philosopher Gilles Deleuze of *Capitalisme et schizophrénie: l'anti-Oedipe, Kafka: pour une littérature mineure,* and *Rhizome.*

Richard Howard's six books of poems are *Quantities, The Damages, Untitled Subjects* (Pulitzer Prize, 1970), *Findings, Two-Part Inventions,* and *Fellow-Feelings.* He has also translated over 150 works from the French, including works by Gide, Giraudoux, Breton, Barthes, Robbe-Grillet, Butor, Gracq, Cocteau, and Camus, and has written two volumes of criticism, *Alone with America* and *Preferences.*

Roger Kempf holds the Chair of French Language and Literature at the École Polytechnique Fédérale in Zurich. He has written *Diderot et le roman, ou le démon de la présence, Sur le corps romanesque, Moeurs: ethnologie et fiction, Dandies: Baudelaire et Cie.* (Grand Prix de la Critique Littéraire, 1977), and several articles on eighteenth- and nineteenth-century French literature and culture. He is co-author with Jean-Paul Aron of *Le pénis et la démoralisation de l'Occident.*

Hélène Klibbe chairs the French Department at Montclair College. She has written articles on contemporary French literature.

Serge Leclaire, a former student and colleague of Jacques Lacan, is founder of the Department of Psychoanalysis at the University of Paris (Vincennes) and a practicing psychoanalyst. He is the author of *Psychanalyser, Démasquer le réel, On tue un enfant,* and numerous articles on questions of psychoanalysis.

J. E. Rivers teaches English and comparative literature at the University of Colorado. He has written articles on Proust, Aristophanes, Theocritus, André Chénier, and troubadour poetry, and has recently completed a book on sexuality and homosexuality in Proust.

Alain Robbe-Grillet, the leading practitioner of the "new novel" in France, has written *Les gommes, Le voyeur, La jalousie, Dans le labyrinthe, La maison de rendez-vous, Projet pour une révolution à New York,* and *Topologie d'une cité fantôme.* His films include *L'année dernière à Marienbad* (with Alain Resnais), *L'immortelle, L'homme qui ment, Trans-Europ-Express, L'Eden et après, Le jeu avec le feu,* and *Glissements progressifs du plaisir.* His early theoretical essays are published in *Pour un nouveau roman.*

Christiane Rochefort's novels include *Le repos du guerrier, Les petits enfants du siècle, Les stances à Sophie, Une rose pour Morrison, Printemps au parking, Archaos ou le jardin étincelant,* and *Encore heureux qu'on va vers l'été.* She is the author of two essays, *C'est bizarre l'écriture* and *Les enfants d'abord.*

Paul Schmidt teaches Slavic literature at the University of Texas (Austin). He is the author-translator of *Arthur Rimbaud: Complete Works in Translation* and has written articles on Russian and American film and film criticism and on the theater of V. E. Meyerhold.

Stephen Smith teaches French at Central Connecticut State College. He has written articles on Molière, Renaissance architecture, and Le Clézio.

Jacob Stockinger has recently completed his doctoral thesis on Violette Leduc at the University of Wisconsin (Madison) and is a contributing editor of the *San Francisco Review of Books.* He has written several articles on homosexuality and literary criticism.

Gerald H. Storzer teaches French at Brooklyn College. He is the co-author of *Dictionary of Modern French Idioms* and has written articles on Camus, Chateaubriand, Gide, and the contemporary African novel.

Monique Wittig's novels and "fictions" include *L'Opoponax, Les guéril-lères, Le corps lesbien,* and *Brouillon pour un dictionnaire des amantes.* She is a contributor to the journal *Questions féministes.*

Index

Homosexualities and
French Literature

Designed by G. T. Whipple, Jr.
Composed by The Composing Room of Michigan, Inc.
in 10 point VIP Baskerville, 2 points leaded,
with display lines in Optima.
Printed offset by Thomson-Shore, Inc.
on Warren's Number 66 text, 50 pound basis.
Bound by John H. Dekker & Sons, Inc.
in Joanna book cloth
and stamped in All Purpose foil.

Library of Congress Cataloging in Publication Data
(For library cataloging purposes only)

Main entry under title:
Homosexualities and French literature.

    Includes index.
      1. French literature—History and criticism—
Addresses, essays, lectures. 2. Homosexuality in
literature—Addresses, essays, lectures. 3. Homo-
sexuality and literature—Addresses, essays, lectures.
I. Stambolian, George. II. Marks, Elaine.
PQ145.1.H66H6   840'.9'353   78-25659
ISBN 0-8014-1186-6

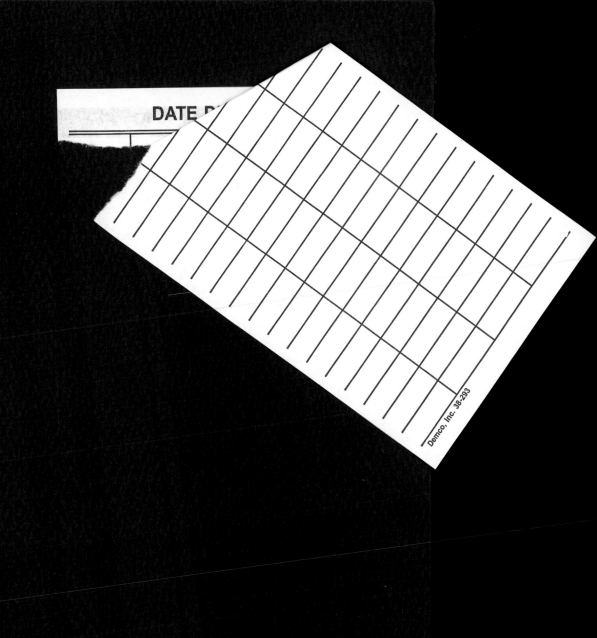

DATE D